THE CHRISTIAN FAITH

SECOND EDITION

THE CHRISTIAN FAITH

Theodore J. Hopkins
Robert Kolb

A Lutheran Exposition

SECOND EDITION

CONCORDIA PUBLISHING HOUSE • SAINT LOUIS

Published by Concordia Publishing House
3558 S. Jefferson Ave., St. Louis, MO 63118-3968
1-800-325-3040 • cph.org

Manufactured in the United States of America

Library of Congress Cataloging-in-Publication Data

Names: Hopkins, Theodore J., author. | Kolb, Robert, author.
Title: The Christian faith : a Luther exposition / Theodore J. Hopkins and Robert Kolb.
Description: Second edition. | St. Louis, MO : Concordia Publishing House, [2024] | Revised edition of: Christian faith / Robert Kolb. St. Louis, MO : Concordia Pub. House, [1993]. | Summary: "This second edition of The Christian Faith presents the fundamental topics of biblical teaching according to the Lutheran Confessions, along with the insights of Luther, his contemporaries, and their successors down through five centuries. Students, church workers, and adults interested in Lutheran theology will find a clear and helpful discussion of the wide range of approaches to the content of Scripture and the challenges of twenty-first-century life in local and global contexts"-- Provided by publisher.
Identifiers: LCCN 2024003071 (print) | LCCN 2024003072 (ebook) | ISBN 9780758677358 (paperback) | ISBN 9780758677365 (ebook)
Subjects: LCSH: Lutheran Church--Doctrines.
Classification: LCC BX8065.2 .K584 2024 (print) | LCC BX8065.2 (ebook) | DDC 230/.41--dc23/eng/20240513
LC record available at https://lccn.loc.gov/2024003071
LC ebook record available at https://lccn.loc.gov/2024003072

---

2 3 4 5 6 7 8 9 10 33 32 31 30 29 28 27 26 25

CONTENTS

PREFACE

"Do not be alarmed. You seek Jesus of Nazareth, who was crucified. He has risen; He is not here. See the place where they laid Him. But go, tell ..." (Mark 16:6–7). Christian theology begins right at this place: Jesus of Nazareth, the Son of God, who was killed upon a cross, is risen from the dead. Like the women who witnessed the empty tomb and heard the good news, Christians become witnesses to the risen Savior through hearing the Gospel message of what Jesus has done for us and our salvation and becoming part of the story by Baptism into Christ's death and resurrection. By the preaching of repentance and forgiveness of sins (Luke 24:47), sinners become believers, God's adopted children, called to "go, tell" the message of what Jesus has done for the world.

The message of the Gospel, the good news of Jesus, is at the heart of Lutheran theology. Lutheran theology insists that God justifies—declares and makes right with Him—sinners in Christ without any merit or worthiness in them. This Gospel message is received by faith as the Holy Spirit reveals who God is, what God has done for us, and who we are as God's creatures. God, therefore, is the main actor of the Bible, from beginning to end. God creates; God promises; God delivers; God humbles; God restores; God sends; God dies; God rises; God fulfills; God forgives; God justifies; God liberates for living truly human lives; and God will make all things new. Over and over again in the Scriptures, human beings stand in need, like the man in Jesus' parable, fallen in the ditch, beaten and half dead, completely helpless (Luke 10:29–37). And Jesus comes to such helpless creatures and makes them His own by His initiative and according to His mercy. "You did not choose Me, but I chose you" (John 15:16). Lutheran theology confesses that human beings are fundamentally receivers, dependent upon God for everything.

What is true about all people as sinful, broken creatures dependent upon God's creative and re-creative work is also true of theologians. Lutheran theology insists on humbly receiving from God not only salvation but also our knowledge of Him. God speaks, and Christians listen. When Lutheran theology is functioning properly, it is not only a set of doctrinal topics or teachings from the Scriptures, but it also embodies humility, listening to God and His Word, and speaking that which God says sensitively to those whom God has given us as hearers of His Word. Therefore, believers need to listen first so that they can speak God's Word properly, distinguishing between Law and Gospel in the proclamation of repentance and forgiveness of sins. Theology, then, begins with receiving: Christians first listen to God in the Scriptures and second to the neighbor so that they "go, tell" in faithfulness to God and in a way that can be heard by others.

Said this way, Christianity is simple: hear the Gospel of Jesus, believe it by the Spirit, and confess the same Gospel before God and to others. At the same time, the prior sentence is deceptively complex. To whom should one listen? What does it mean to believe? What should one believe? Most important, what is this Gospel and who is this Jesus? **Doctrinal** (also called **systematic**) **theology** seeks to understand the Bible, the history of the church, and the modern world in order that the same Gospel message proclaimed by the angel at the empty tomb might be proclaimed again for people today.

In view of this, doctrinal theology—the organized study of God's revelation in Christ testified to in Holy Scripture (and thus this book)—is necessary in every generation for three reasons. First, doctrinal theology functions in a regulative fashion to show the limits and possibilities of Christian speech. In other words, doctrinal theology names the boundaries of Christian language, showing the potholes and pitfalls one must avoid in order to speak the Gospel with the prophets and apostles. In each generation, the boundaries are tested anew with new language and new thought forms, and doctrinal theology must test those formulations. Using the history of the church and its creeds and confessions as guides, doctrinal theology articulates speech that is faithful to God's revelation in Christ within the language and thought forms of contemporary people. Second, each generation has its own barriers that prevent ears from being open to hear God's Word. Although doctrinal theology dare not be reduced to this apologetic function, theologians must formulate Christian doctrine in such a way that contemporary people are confronted by God's Law and barriers are removed so that the Gospel may be heard. The goal is not to avoid scandal altogether, but to make sure the scandal (derived from the Greek word for "stumbling block") is in the right place: Jesus, and not theological rhetoric or church tradition. As St. Paul writes: "We preach Christ crucified, a stumbling block to Jews and folly to Gentiles, but to those who are called, both Jews and Greeks, Christ the power of God and the wisdom of God" (1 Corinthians 1:23–24). Third, doctrinal theology, especially emphasized in the Lutheran tradition, is intended to lead Christians to confess and proclaim the same Gospel, the same old, old story, in the contemporary world. Theology has its proper end not merely in right ideas, true distinctions, or accurate concepts but in faithful speech, words that proclaim the good news of Christ so that sinners are led to confess that Jesus is Lord, to the glory of God the Father (Philippians 2:11; cf. Romans 10:9). As a practical discipline that aims toward confession of faith, theology cannot be satisfied with articulating universal truth in and of itself, but must continue to formulate the Word of God to point each new generation to the depth of their depravity and the glory of the Savior born a babe in Bethlehem.

As the title names, this book is a "Lutheran exposition" of the Christian faith. In North America where denominations and nondenominations are as ubiquitous as sand on a seashore, the name "Lutheran" can be easily misunderstood as a mere denominational marker, which would simply distinguish this text from a Roman Catholic or Reformed or general Protestant interpretation of the Christian faith. Although we will be making scriptural arguments for a Lutheran understanding of Christian doctrine, "Lutheran" does not primarily name a denomination or institution. "Lutheran" instead designates a confession of faith. In fact, Luther and his fellow Lutheran reformers never believed they were confessing anything other than the faith of the whole church: the faith preached by the prophets and confirmed by the apostles, centered in Jesus Christ. As such, the Lutheran tradition is both **catholic** and **evangelical**, both universal in its scope in time and space and centered on the Gospel (the *evangel*) of Jesus. The Lutheran tradition is catholic because Lutheranism stands in the apostolic tradition of the church, confessing the truth of God's Word proclaimed by the prophets of the Old Testament and taught by the apostles in the New Testament. As the 1530 Augsburg Confession—which is the most authoritative document of the sixteenth-century Lutheran Confessions—makes clear, Philip Melanchthon and Luther never expressed Lutheran doctrine as something other than the faith of the church catholic, expressed by prophets, apostles, and many church fathers. At the same time, to be Lutheran is to be evangelical because the center of the catholic tradition is the Gospel of Jesus. The Gospel of unmerited and undeserved forgiveness for sinners has come in the holy history of the humiliation of the Son of God sent by the Father in the power of the Spirit. The forgiveness of sins in Jesus' name is not a secondary aspect of nor a tertiary conclusion from Christianity, but its center. For Lutherans, no confession of faith is properly catholic unless it is fully evangelical, wholly Gospel-centered in the cross and resurrection of Jesus Christ.

This new edition of *The Christian Faith: A Lutheran Exposition* is hardly a full rewrite, but neither is it just a new wineskin for old wine, a new book cover for an old book. To be clear, the skeleton of the first edition remains.

Nearly a decade ago, Hopkins began a search for the best theology text for undergraduate students. After searching through dozens of options, Hopkins found no texts that could stand up to *The Christian Faith*. Kolb's first edition accurately and concisely teaches deep theological truths while also shaping readers to divide Law and Gospel and embody the proclamation of God's Word themselves. Hence, Kolb and Hopkins started with the first edition in order to keep the same combination of content and disposition that made the first edition so valuable for more than a generation of students.

At the same time, thirty years have passed since the first edition was published, and new challenges have arisen that need to be addressed. Four things in particular necessitate this new edition. First, "Christendom" is coming to an end, and the church does not hold the same position of authority in society as it once did. In this new situation, the church's mission must be considered not as a mere topic of theology but as a task that permeates all of theology. In addition, the attitudes and beliefs of the average Christian and the average American are not what they were thirty years ago. Christ Jesus remains the same, as does the text of the Bible, but North Americans do not. As culture and people change, distinguishing between Law and Gospel in the presentation of Christian doctrine demands a different approach in some topics. Second, new literature and emphases in Christian theology in the last thirty years need to be addressed. While an introduction to Christian doctrine is not the place to have a comprehensive bibliography on every topic, updated footnotes with new sources will best serve students for the next generation who want to learn more about a topic or are tasked to write research papers for class. Third, the original text needed improvement on certain aspects of readability. The new text includes key terms in **boldface** to help both instructors and students. It also more clearly defines when Lutheran theology is distinct from that of other Christian groups. Finally, most obviously, Hopkins has been added to the title page to shape the text for a new generation of students and add his own insights into contemporary systematic theology. Since Hopkins teaches undergraduate students and Kolb teaches seminarians—and both of us regularly teach and interact with laypeople—we are well suited to be sensitive to different levels of readers, both the novice theologian and the maturing one. In addition, Kolb's own thinking has matured through extensive research in the works of Lutheran theologians of the sixteenth and seventeenth centuries, and the book intends to better represent Kolb's new insights into Luther and Lutheranism.

The Christian Faith: A Lutheran Exposition has in mind three primary audiences. First, students studying for a church work vocation in Lutheran churches will find our book helpful for shaping them to be teachers and witnesses to Jesus and His Gospel in their future ministry. The book will prepare students for ministry both by addressing the perennial questions of the Christian faith—for example, how can Jesus be true God?—and guiding students to navigate questions asked in contemporary culture—for example, how can a good God allow evil?—using biblical and theological resources in the Lutheran tradition. Second, our book is useful for newly catechized Christians who want to understand Lutheran doctrine and be equipped for teaching their families the Bible and the Christian faith and for being witnesses to Christ in their homes, neighborhoods, and vocations. To help these readers in particular, we try to keep additional academic resources in footnotes for the interested readers while not bogging down the conversation by too many technical points. Third, while Lutherans will more naturally be drawn to read such a book, other Christians who believe in the truth of the Bible and the importance of understanding that truth to teach and proclaim it will find great value and resources in this text. We will be unapologetically Lutheran; we do so not to denigrate other Christians and their views but to proclaim clearly and faithfully the Gospel of Jesus to the world today and to bring some clarity to conversations between Lutherans and Christians of other confessions.

Readers can expect to be led into the Bible above all else since Lutheran theology is committed to be an exposition, an interpretation, of the biblical text understood through the Gospel of Jesus Christ. Our book will have done its task if readers are more equipped to understand and engage in the Bible and see Jesus throughout all of Scripture. Readers can also expect to understand the basic questions and answers of Western Christianity, Protestantism, and Lutheranism. The central Lutheran questions of justification and the comfort of the Gospel will take center stage, such as in election and the Sacraments, but readers will also become better acquainted with the conversation of the Western Church, especially as it has developed in Protestantism. Throughout the five hundred years of Lutheran history, Lutherans have striven to be in conversation with other Christians. Sometimes the conversation was filled with critique; for instance, the Jesuit Robert Bellarmine set the agenda on many topics for the seventeenth-century Lutheran theologian Johann Gerhard, one of the foremost representatives of Lutheran theology in the period labeled "Orthodoxy." At the same time, Gerhard did not hesitate to incorporate insights into his positive presentation of biblical teaching that he found in, for example, at least one English Puritan writer. As in Gerhard, this volume, too, will include both criticism of and constructive use of Western theology in order to proclaim the message of Christ in our day in consonance with the Scriptures and the Lutheran Confessions.

Before we begin, four quick notes on methodology are necessary to help the reader. First, our method of exploring key biblical topics—the *loci* method—stems from the first Protestant/Lutheran text in doctrinal theology: Philip Melanchthon's 1521 *Loci Communes*. As in the 1521 *Loci*, we use the major themes of Scripture to drive readers back into the Bible and into church history to better understand both the center of the faith and the pitfalls that must be avoided. Second, the book includes key terms in **boldface** throughout the text. These are terms which students should know in order to understand the basic conversation of Christian and Lutheran theology. Third, each chapter begins with the central point of the chapter, to which each other point relates in some way. Theology is not like a historical time line in which each event successively follows the other, but more like a body in which all parts are interrelated and interconnected. As such, the introduction section ought to be understood as setting the stage and opening the discussion, and the rest of the chapter fits into that main point. Finally, practical matters are spread throughout the book rather than segmented into special sections. Since all of theology is intended to be proclaimed to the glory of God and the strengthening of the faith of God's people, practical concerns and issues will be regularly threaded throughout the book, shaping the reader to speak God's truth in a way that humbles the exalted and lifts up the lowly.

We pray that this book will lead readers not only to understand the Christian faith but also boldly to become witnesses themselves who teach the Bible to their families and their neighbors and "go, tell" to the world the Gospel of Christ crucified and risen. This is the task of the church until theology finds its end when Jesus returns and all people bow before Him and proclaim Him as Lord.

Theodore J. Hopkins and Robert Kolb
Lent 2024

CHAPTER 1
THE WORD OF GOD AND THE TASK OF THEOLOGY

IN the beginning was the Word" (John 1:1). The Scriptures begin not with a cosmic explosion, a battle, or an idea but a voice, the living voice of a person: "And God said, 'Let there be . . . ,'" and all that exists came into being, by the power of God's Word (Genesis 1:3, 6, 9, 11, 14, 20, 24). The Word of God is the invigorating, creative, and life-giving heart of reality itself. Theology's first task is, accordingly, to listen, to hear God speak, and only then to move to the second task, to teach and proclaim God's Word according to His command and promise.

The significance of God's voice resounding through the primordial void to bring all things into being is easy to overlook, especially in our technological age. We are saturated with images and videos that fill our minds and capture our imaginations. We communicate with pictures as often as words. Compared with images, words appear to have little power; they seem flimsy and forgettable, vanishing into vapor as soon as they are spoken. Hence, the cliché: a picture is worth a thousand words. Even in everyday experience, however, words are far more important than most of us think. The weightiest moments of life involve verbal promises, vows, and commitments. On the wedding day, a wife and husband pledge to stay true to each other and to God's design for marriage "through richer and poorer, in sickness and in health." Parents declare their love and care for their children: "I love you. I'm proud of you." A new confirmand swears fidelity to the Lord Jesus even to death. A new church worker vows to uphold God's Word and live according to it. These crucial events necessitate and demand words. The verbal components of these actions are not ornaments that adorn nor mere information that adds to the events. The words are the whole point in these most meaningful moments and relationships of life. Without words, insecurity reigns.

If human words are so meaningful, how much more significant is God's Word that "gives life to the dead and calls into existence the things that do not exist" (Romans 4:17)! God's Word does not primarily describe reality. It creates reality, bringing all things into being by the power of His voice, and re-creates reality, forming faith in those dead in their sins and enlivening dry bones with His life-giving Spirit (Ezekiel 37:1–14). When the first human creatures doubted the word of the Lord and fled from His presence, He went down into the Garden of Eden to call them back to Himself (Genesis 3:9). To reclaim and restore all the sons and daughters of the first doubters, God has placed His power in human language. His Gospel of Christ crucified and risen is the power He uses to bring people to salvation (Romans 1:16). God's good news restores fallen human creatures to that relationship within His grace and favor for which He designed them in Eden. This message of forgiveness and new life restores these sinful creatures to a full and perfect relationship with Him. That relationship of righteousness is ours because we are remade to grasp its word of promise in faith (Romans 1:17).

This chapter is what is traditionally called a **prolegomena**, which literally refers to the things said ahead of time. It is an introduction that sets the stage for the teachings of the Christian faith. The chapter will outline the task and conceptual framework of Lutheran theology, clearing the way for the formal treatment of theological topics in the chapters to come. The theological distinctions explored here form a skeletal structure for the rest of the book. This chapter, therefore, permeates the rest of the book, and the rest of the book permeates this first chapter. Later topics, such as the doctrine of God, Christology, and justification, must be discussed already even though they will be presented formally later. The reader should expect to see a skeletal structure of Lutheran theology forming in this chapter—for instance, the story of Christ as the backbone, the distinction between Law and Gospel as the marrow, the two kinds of righteousness as the rib cage, and the theology of the cross as the skull and neck—but most of the body will remain empty at this point in the book. Later chapters delve into each theological topic while keeping in mind the theological task and framework described in this chapter.

What Makes Faith *Christian*: The Gospel in a Religious World

Both Kolb and Hopkins grew up in twentieth-century North America, a world in which the adjective *Christian* could be assumed. Most people went to church on Sunday because that's what people did. The Bible was part of the basic grammar of society; just about everyone knew the characters and stories of the Bible even if they did not go to church. Being an American or a Canadian and being Christian were nearly synonymous. For many twenty-first-century readers of this book, however, the modifier *Christian* may feel weird and strange in the culture. Although this sense is relatively new in

North America, it was true for most Christians in the first three centuries after Christ and has remained true for many Christians around the globe. St. Paul, for example, entreated the first-century Philippian Christians not to follow the ways of the world but to "keep your eyes on those who walk according to the example you have in us," following the ways of God, since "our citizenship is in heaven" (Philippians 3:17, 20). Similarly, Jesus refers to His disciples as in the world but not of the world (John 17:11–18). According to Scripture, Christians may not always fit into the ways of the culture even as we are fellow creatures called to speak to the culture in truth and love.

What makes Christianity true is not its power or influence in the culture, but its origin and goal in God and His Word. In other words, the *Christian* faith does not stem from political power, Western philosophy, or religious feelings, but from the Father who sent His Son, the Word, by the power of the Spirit into the world to become flesh and dwell among us (John 1:14). The Christian faith, therefore, is not a human invention but had to be revealed by God (Matthew 16:17). Christianity has many human traditions and components, but the center of the Christian faith is not human rituals, traditions, or communities, but a crucified Nazarene, scorned by all, yet raised bodily from the dead three days after His burial. The distinctive adjective *Christian* reminds us that the Christian faith has its center in this true story of the Son of God who suffered under Pontius Pilate, was crucified, died, buried, and raised from the dead on the third day to reign as King of all creation.

The common perception of Christianity, including among many Christians, is that the Christian faith is a system of beliefs and rules for people to follow. In this understanding, what makes one a Christian is holding the right beliefs and doing the right deeds. What makes faith Christian, then, is not the Gospel—God's good news of forgiveness of sins secured for sinners in Jesus' death and resurrection—but the Law, that is, human creatures following Christian rules. In this faulty understanding, the work of God as Creator and Savior becomes secondary to legal requirements and human traditions in which the Law trumps the Gospel, and we begin to imagine that human beings are the center of the faith rather than Jesus.

Another danger lies close at hand when we imagine that Christianity is fundamentally about holding the right beliefs and doing the right deeds. Such thinking engenders **self-justification**, where we are convinced that we are justified because we believe the right things or have lived the right way. St. Paul writes: "None is righteous, no, not one" (Romans 3:10) and "God has consigned all to disobedience, that He may have mercy on all" (Romans 11:32), but we convince ourselves that we are righteous because we are insiders, members of the right group. As a result of our self-justifying attitude, we look down on others who are not like us. We have climbed the ladder of religious success, and we can safely look down and judge those below us as unrighteous and ungodly.[1]

Jesus' parable of the Pharisee and the tax collector was designed to point out this almost natural, *religious* sin (Luke 18:9–14).[2] In the parable, a Pharisee—a religious leader in first-century Judaism—entered the temple courts with a tax collector. The Pharisee had kept all the rules; he held a position of authority and status; he was the role model. According to human standards, the Pharisee was blameless. The tax collector, on the other hand, was an obvious sinner. He was in league with the enemy, Rome, by collecting money on its behalf, exploiting his fellow Jews. The tax collector had the stench of a thief, a traitor, and a Gentile. Everyone who heard Jesus' parable expected the Pharisee to be right with God and the tax collector to be the outcast.

Jesus, though, showed how differently God sees the world, and how different the Gospel is from sinful, human thinking. Jesus pointed out the different attitudes of both men, shown forth in their prayers and their posture. The Pharisee differentiated himself from the crowd, standing by himself, aloof from everyone, and his prayer expressed his holy, justified status in his own eyes: "God, I thank You that I am not like other men" (Luke 18:11). The tax collector, however, stood far off from the crowd, refusing even to look up to the place of God's presence. Instead, he kept his eyes down and prayed for mercy: "God, be merciful to me, a sinner" (Luke 18:13). According to all outward appearances, the Pharisee was the holy one, and the tax collector was a pure sinner. Yet Jesus declared that the tax collector was the one right before God, not the Pharisee.

The point of the parable is not to create a new three-step formula—be humble, admit you are a sinner, and pray for mercy—that makes one right before God. The point of the parable is first to illumine how we blind ourselves from seeing our need for God's mercy, even using religion to do so. Religion can become a matter of control, trying to place eternal fate in our own hands rather than trusting in God's grace. In fact, we are just as capable of refusing God's mercy by following the rules in order to remain in control as we are of rejecting God by our disobedience. Second and more important, Jesus wants to startle us into recognizing that God alone is the one who justifies. No one can compel God to do something; God is not in debt to humans; nor can God be swayed by human beings. Thus a right relationship with God is not in human hands. All people need God's mercy and grace, and we are entirely at His disposal. We dare not think that if we change our

---

1 Timothy Keller, *The Reason for God* (New York: Penguin, 2018), 56–61 and 184–86.

2 Luther, in the Smalcald Articles III VIII 5, refers to the devil as leading Adam and Eve not into irreligious but religious sin: enthusiasm.

outward behavior to be more like the tax collector than the Pharisee, then God would save us. Instead, we need to die to our captivity to the way of the Law (cf. Romans 6); we need to give up control over our eternal fate and rely completely on the mercy of God shown forth in the Gospel.

In the Gospel "the righteousness of God is revealed" (Romans 1:17). The Gospel displaces humanity from the center of the story in favor of God's grace. The Gospel is the forgiveness of sins that God promises to sinners through the death and resurrection of Jesus Christ, delivered by the Spirit in preaching, the Sacraments, Christian conversation, and Scripture. The Father sent the Son in the power of the Spirit, and Jesus willingly came "under the law" and took "the form of a servant" to take humanity's place under the power of sin and death (Galatians 4:4; Philippians 2:7). Without human consent, desire, or permission, Jesus took on our humanity and defeated the enemies of God from the inside of our history and humanity, becoming the Savior of all through Calvary's cross and the empty tomb. The Gospel is this good news of what God in Christ has done for the world. The Gospel is the message that God has accomplished everything in His Son and by His Spirit to save humanity from its captivity to sin, death, and the devil. St. Paul thus writes: "It is God who justifies" (Romans 8:33). Jesus declares, "I give [My sheep] eternal life, and they will never perish, and no one will snatch them out of My hand" (John 10:28). In the Christian faith, a right relationship with God is not earned, merited, or deserved. Instead, it is given as a gift, for Jesus' sake.

This Gospel is good news for sinners, for the ungodly, for the grieving and the dying, for victims of injustice, for the persecuted, and even for victimizers. "While we were still weak, at the right time Christ died for the ungodly" (Romans 5:6). Jesus declares, "I came not to call the righteous, but sinners" (Mark 2:17). The sinful tax collector "went down to his house justified, rather than the other" (Luke 18:14). The Gospel does not demand or require, but simply gives the mercy of God in Jesus Christ. The *Christian* faith is not based on human rules or human-created beliefs. "All this is from God, who through Christ reconciled us to Himself and gave us the ministry of reconciliation" (2 Corinthians 5:18).

We Live by Faith

The second key word of our title—*Faith*—also holds great significance. We use the word **faith** in two different senses. Faith can refer to the object of our trust, what we believe in. Faith also refers to the act of believing, of trusting, of placing our confidence in and depending on someone or something. In the second sense, faith is the core of our being; it is our basic grasp on reality. If faith is misplaced, then all of life is skewed. If faith is misdirected toward one of God's creatures, rather than directed toward the Creator Himself, then life goes sour and spoils.

Faith—in the sense of the trust that provides the core orientation for our lives—is among the most important words in the human language. In the twentieth century, the Harvard psychologist Erik Erikson affirmed what the biblical writers told God's people centuries ago. He devised an eight-stage basis for analyzing human development, the course of human life. The first and fundamental stage of human existence, in the years between birth and age 2, revolves around trust or faith. This fundamental orientation, according to Erikson, largely determines the way in which individuals view the world, relate to others, and experience life's challenges. Learning to trust, or mistrust, frees or binds us at all subsequent stages of our development. Learning to trust, or mistrust, the world around us determines much of our personality and the course of our life, Erikson insists.[3]

We trust our mother first, and then our father, Erikson observes, because we are first of all children, infants, dependent creatures. When we are born into this world, we are at the mercy of those around us. They become objects on which we depend. How they perform as objects of our dependence determines how we view ourselves—and everyone and everything around us.

From those whom we trust we gain a sense of **identity**, **security**, and **meaning**. Without a sense of who we are, without a sense that we are safe and will continue to exist, without a sense that our lives have purpose and worth, we die. People wither when they have little or no sense of identity, security, and meaning. Being uncertain about these things takes a tremendous physiological toll—to say nothing of the psychological damage such uncertainty inflicts upon us. We cannot survive without a sense of our ultimate identity, security, and meaning.

We Find Identity, Security, and Meaning in Our God(s)

In his explanation of the First Commandment in the Large Catechism, Luther defines the word *g-o-d* in terms of trust: "A 'god' is the term for that to which we are to look for all good and in which we are to find refuge in all need. Therefore, to have a god is nothing else than to trust and believe in that one with your whole heart. … For these two belong together, faith and God. Anything on which your heart relies and depends, I say, that is really your God."[4] According to Luther, everyone has a **god**, for everyone depends ultimately on someone or something—or several persons and things—for identity, security, and meaning. False gods abound. The Protestant reformer

3 Erik Erikson, *Childhood and Society* (New York: Norton, 1950); and *The Life Cycle Completed* (New York: Norton, 1982).

4 Large Catechism I 2–3.

John Calvin famously called the human heart a perpetual idol factory because of the human need to devise gods out of created things.[5] Trusting **idols**, false gods, is the root of all disruption in human life, that is, of all sin, and no one can exist for long without a god or two.

God has so structured human life that we find *secondary* levels of identity, security, and meaning in family members, friends, work, our accomplishments in the community, and congregational service. Behind such secondary sources of identity, security, and meaning, however, lies what ultimately gives us our "name," our sense of who we are. Behind these secondary sources of security and meaning lies what ultimately gives us haven from life's storms and affirms that our personalities, roles, and actions are ultimately worthwhile. That primary source of identity, security, and meaning is one's god.

We can easily pervert what God has given us as secondary sources of identity, security, and meaning into gods. Spouses are wonderful gifts of God. After many years of marriage, husbands and wives have interdependent identities. Both husband and wife are who they are because of the other. Such interdependence is part of God's design for marriage! At the same time, however, spouses can become idolaters in their marriage. A husband can regard his wife as the ultimate source of identity. When this happens, both spouses are imprisoned. The wife becomes imprisoned in a false set of expectations for her, expectations she cannot possibly meet. She may be the best wife in the world, but as a god she has her inadequacies. And the husband imprisons himself in his dependence on her to meet impossible expectations. The husband inflicts suffering on both when he worships her instead of cherishing her as a gift of God.

An occupation may become an idol in a similar fashion. Jobs are gifts of God, avenues of service to other people and to the whole of creation. We rightly receive some sense of identity from them. At a party, when we meet someone, we often identify ourselves by our occupation and place of employment. Work, however, may warp into an idol. When we strive endlessly for promotions, raises, and praise from the bigwigs, a job has become a god. When we cannot feel secure apart from a higher salary, or we have no sense of worth outside of our job, we risk turning God's good gift into an idol.

Because of sin, we are always in danger of turning our secondary identities—such as God's gifts of family, friends, money, possessions, nation, culture, talents, and skills—into our ultimate identity. The whole Christian

5 John Calvin, *Institutes of Christian Religion*, trans. Henry Beveridge (n.p., 1845), 97, book 1, ch. 11: "The human mind is, so to speak, a perpetual forge of idols." See https://ccel.org/ccel/calvin/institutes/institutes.iii.xii.html.

life is thus one of repentance, turning away from our unbelief and idolatry to trust in the promise of the living God.

The Faith as Object of Faith

The trust that is at the core of our being does not exist by itself. It always rests on something or someone, our gods. In popular culture, faith is treated as if it is the object of itself: "You just have to believe"; "Have faith in faith." Objectless faith, however, does not exist. When faith is treated as object-free, such faith is generally a disguised form of self-confidence, faith in oneself. Until the true God breaks through deaf ears by His Word and implants in sinful hearts faith that grasps hold of Him through His promise, we cannot help but make idols into the objects of our faith. To control the idols and gain rewards from them, human beings create systems that offer identity, security, and meaning from our gods. These religious systems of establishing our ultimate sense of identity, security, and meaning differ from idolater to idolater, but all of them are expressions of trust in objects of faith. Idols seem to allow human beings to remain in control, achieving success by holding the right beliefs and living according to the right morals, dictated by our gods. Human beings put faith in these systems that ground our ultimate identity, security, and meaning, and these systems are called faith systems or belief systems. They can be called "the faith" in the sense of what we believe in.

Christian Faith Takes Form in God's Word and Our Words

For Christians, faith rests upon the person of our God, who has revealed Himself in Jesus of Nazareth. Our faith rests upon who He is and upon what He has said to us. We have the revelation of His identity, what He has done, and His message for us in the Holy Scriptures. He has established our identities anew by planting His mark, the cross, on our heads and on our hearts. He gives this new existence reality as He sustains us with His word of promise, giving our lives purpose and certainty of His grace. He is the only source of our ultimate identity, security, and meaning.

Through God's Word, we are people of faith; we are believers. The term **believer** reminds us that we are dependent upon the object of faith, the God in whom we believe. Some people distinguish believers from disciples. A *disciple* is "one who follows Christ and learns from Him." In their biblical sense, both words can be used interchangeably: believers are disciples, and disciples are believers. Some contemporary Christians, however, try to distinguish those who excel at the performance of certain good works, following Jesus with their actions (disciples), from those who are just church members, who "merely" trust in Jesus as Savior (believers). This is not a biblical distinction. What we do as Christians is always secondary to, and a result of, who we are as children of God. Our actions flow from our trust in Jesus Christ. To establish Christian identity upon what we do, rather than upon what God has done for us, always ends in idolatry. We are first believers even as we follow Christ in our actions. There is nothing wrong with the term *disciple*, but disciples are first and foremost believers.

Believers are children of God. Children do not create the objects of their faith. As earthly children, our mothers were there—simply there—to be objects of faith. Our fathers picked us up so that we could learn to feel safe in their arms. Faith cannot exist unless its object elicits it. Thus faith is not a good work over which we can exercise control. Faith is a gift from its object. It is also important to note that this trust is more than mere beliefs (as if there could be an indifferent acknowledgment of the God who loves us to death upon a cross). Trust is more than intellectual assent to beliefs or ideas. This trust grasps all of life; it permeates the entire person and shapes all decision-making for daily living. This trust brings us to confess our faith, to speak back to God and before the world what He has given to us in His Word. In this sense, theology is nothing more than speaking after God's Word,[6] learning to "speak like an apostle," as Luther said.[7]

God creates trust in human hearts and brings us to confess our faith by talking to us, like how our earthly parents shape our lives through their words. He speaks to us. He gives us His Word, a word of promise, and we respond with trust. We trust in Him first because we hear Him. He teaches us who He is, who we are, and the character of His world.

Doctrine: Its Content and Its Conveying

Teaching, like faith, is a word with two meanings. It is both the object, or content, that is taught, and it is the action of teaching. When professors speak of their "teaching," they may be referring to what they want you to learn, or they may be referring to the way in which they convey what they want you to learn. As a matter of fact, you cannot have one without the other. Content and the conveying of content are inseparable. Good content will not be learned if it is poorly conveyed. The most skillful, charismatic conveying of wrong content only does harm.

The Latin word for "teaching" is *doctrina*. From this comes the word **doctrine**. Christian doctrine is simply the teaching of the Word of God. According to Luther and Philip Melanchthon, his colleague at the University

---

6 The twentieth-century Protestant theologian Karl Barth famously called theology *nachdenken*, a German word that means "thinking-after" God's Word, but for Lutheran theology it is better called *nachsprechen*, "speaking-after" God's Word.

7 Robert Kolb, *Martin Luther: Confessor of the Faith* (Oxford: University Press, 2009), 43.

of Wittenberg in the early sixteenth century, *doctrina* was a "verbal noun." In other words, pure doctrine or true doctrine is not only the correct content of the Scripture, but it is also that content conveyed effectively into the lives of the hearers of God's Word.[8]

C. F. W. Walther, the first president of The Lutheran Church—Missouri Synod, said it this way in his theses on Law and Gospel: "If you wish to be an orthodox teacher, you must present all the articles of faith in accordance with Scripture, yet [you] must also correctly distinguish Law and Gospel."[9] Walther was saying that it is not enough to repeat biblical truths accurately. They must also be applied to the specific situation, the specific needs, of hearers. Two errors must be avoided. On the one hand, many immature students of theology think that speaking the truth is all that matters, and they employ the truth as a sledgehammer without concern for the hearers. On the other hand, contemporary culture is so concerned with everyone living their own truth that God's truth can be sidelined. Proper biblical teaching avoids both errors by "speaking the truth in love" (Ephesians 4:15), confessing the truth of God's Word over the long haul and doing so with sensitivity to how it will be heard. Biblical teaching thus bridges the gap between God's Word and the sinner who needs to hear it. This teaching aims not at mastery of information but at forming a relationship. This teaching of the biblical message introduces two people to each other: our God and a human creature.

As a matter of fact, one of the Latin words for priest, *pontifex*, comes from two words that mean "bridge builder." The priests of God, all believers, are called to be teachers of God's Word. They build the bridge between God, as He speaks His Word in Scripture, and the lives of those around them. God's priests connect those around them to God and to God's people.

For sixteenth-century Lutherans, **doctrine** was used generally in the singular. They seldom spoke of doctrines in the plural. There is one biblical teaching; the content of the Scripture is a unit. These Lutherans recognized, however, that human creatures ask a variety of questions regarding the things of God. As believers formulate answers to these individual questions, they are using parts of the one doctrine, or teaching, of God in the Scriptures. We label these individual answers **doctrines**. Luther and his contemporaries had two terms for what we call doctrines, in the plural. In writing confessions, such as the 1530 Augsburg Confession, the principal confession of the Lutheran Church, these Lutherans divided biblical teaching into "articles of

---

8 Peter Fraenkel, "Revelation and Tradition: Notes on Some Aspects of Doctrinal Continuity in the Theology of Philip Melanchthon," *Studia Theologica* 13 (1959): 97–133.

9 C. F. W. Walther, *Law and Gospel*, trans. Christian C. Tiews, ed. Charles P. Schaum (St. Louis: Concordia, 2010), Thesis II, 26.

faith"; in writing textbooks on Christian teaching, they divided the doctrine of the Scripture into "topics," often referred to by the Latin *loci*. The number of topics or articles of faith varied from time to time, depending on what questions society raised for the church to answer. Certain topics are always going to be treated by believers as they teach the faith to others. Other topics may be given greater or lesser emphasis depending on the situation. For example, sixteenth-century Lutherans did not treat the topic of Scripture comprehensively in their confessions because people in their Christian world agreed to a large extent on the nature of the Scriptures. They gave extensive attention to the topic of how sinners become righteous in God's sight because there was substantial disagreement on that topic.

Some theologians emphasize the distinction between **proclamation**, or *kerygma* in Greek, and **teaching**, or *didache* in Greek. Proclamation confronts people with the Word of God and is aimed at inviting and drawing them into trusting God. It is God's direct address to His people: "I am your God. You are My people." Teaching follows with a broader understanding of what God says in His Word. Teaching is third-person discourse: it describes God and us. The distinction ensures that God's Word is recognized as the living voice of God by which His Spirit is at work to confront sinners and forgive their sins in Jesus. God's Word can never be understood as mere information, even true information, because God's Word is effective in forming a relationship with His creatures. Despite the importance of the distinction, however, it is impossible to draw precisely. Proclamation involves teaching, and teaching the Word of God can never be simply dry study and description of some object. Teaching the Word of God always grabs our hearts because God is at work in His Word. Teaching confronts, invites, and draws us into trusting this Word from our God.

The church formalizes the teaching or doctrine of Scripture in **dogmas**. Often, dogmas were formulated because of specific challenges to the biblical truth raised by those inside or outside the church. Those who raise such challenges inside the church are called heretics, those who cause divisions among God's people. **Heresy**, a false teaching ruled out by church dogma, often begins as a well-intentioned attempt to bridge the gap between the biblical message and the culture. Such attempts become truly heretical when the message of the biblical writers is abandoned in favor of incorporating the deceptions of this world into the church's speech. Believers are always faced with the temptation to make sense of the Scriptures within cultural frameworks. We must be careful to let God's Word shape the culture rather than the other way around, even as we seek to be bridges within the culture. This natural tension means that the whole life of the teacher of the church must be a life of reexamination and repentance.

The Body of Doctrine: How Biblical Teaching Fits Together

Some people define biblical teaching as a series of topics. Understood like pearls on a string, all topics are roughly of equal importance. If doctrine is conceived in this way, losing any single pearl has the same effect on the whole of biblical teaching as losing any other pearl. Some people would argue that you dare not lose any pearl if you are to be dressed suitably for the Host of the heavenly banquet. According to them, the loss of any teaching destroys the whole of biblical doctrine. Others would say that as long as you hold the bare minimum of biblical teaching, at least a pearl or two left on the string, you are ready to be received at His table.

Another way to view biblical teaching is a wheel, with a hub, spokes, and a rim. This view recognizes the interconnections of Christian doctrine: wheels cannot exist without hub, rim, and at least some spokes. In this view, the hub and rim are necessary, but many of the spokes are extraneous. While some spokes are necessary, others may be broken without immobilizing the wheel.

Neither the string of pearls nor the wheel metaphor adequately describes the nature of biblical teaching. Instead, we should understand the doctrine of Holy Scripture as a human body. The body of doctrine cannot exist if Christ, the Head, is decapitated. It dies without the heart of our understanding of how we become right with God pumping away—although the heart, the doctrine of justification, may be diseased and still pump, at least for a time. This was evident in the medieval church, when preachers put a high but false premium on good works and still pointed people to Christ's saving blood. We see this in contemporary Christians who emphasize the contribution of an individual's personal decision in coming to Christ while also cultivating trust in God's grace. If an arm—the doctrine of Baptism, for example—is severed, the body may be able to survive. It may, however, hemorrhage and die. If the leg of the doctrine of the church becomes paralyzed, the body may survive, but it will be crippled at best, and it may fall down in a heap and crack the head too.

By conceptualizing biblical teaching as a body, the common question "How much doctrine must be pure if one is to remain a Christian?" is exposed as a wrong kind of question. We should not be focused on what we must get right and what we can get wrong, but on understanding God's Word in its totality and conveying it faithfully to others. Teaching the Christian faith involves making connections among the individual topics, God's whole revelation of the Gospel of Jesus (doctrine in the singular), and the situations of the hearers. Doctrinal error can thus occur on any one of these three levels: understanding the individual topic according to the Scriptures, the place of the topic within the whole of Scripture, and properly distinguishing between Law and Gospel for the hearers. Each teaching, then, must be conveyed faithfully according to the truth of the topic, the truth of the revelation of God in Jesus, and the reality of the listeners. When an individual topic is understood in error, such errors are dangerous to faith, but it does not always break the relationship with our Lord. Understanding Christian doctrine faithfully according to the Bible is essential, but God's relationship established with us goes far beyond an accurate articulation of each topic.

Americans are accused often of pragmatism—not being interested in what is true but only in "what works." Relativism regarding great truths is said to govern human thinking in our culture. This may seem to be true, but in fact people are indifferent to what is true and false only in those areas of life that do not seem important to them. When it comes to what matters most, everyone wants to know the truth. Relativism in religion only makes sense when people do not believe religion is central to reality. From the standpoint of the Christian faith, the most important truth of all is centered on the God who created all things, became incarnate in His Son, Jesus, was killed on a cross, and rose from the dead. The reality of God creates the truth of the world that we are creatures captive to sin and in need of salvation.

Even Americans know the importance of truth in some areas of life. For instance, who is comfortable with relativism when it comes to fixing the car? Would anyone say "You do you" or "Live your truth" to a mechanic changing a car's spark plugs? Even cynicism about truth in social and political life has not dampened the need for one to be in the truth. This is obvious when it comes to relationships. Who is comfortable with uncertainty in whether our parents love us? What person is comfortable with ambiguity about how a close friend feels about him? What wife can sleep soundly when she wonders whether her husband is still committed to her? When we form a relationship with another person, we want to know the truth about that person.

The biblical message does not primarily give information, though it is full of true information. The biblical message creates a relationship between God and those who hear the Word. That relationship depends on expressing God's love in our teaching. We must always be concerned that our teaching accurately reflects what the Bible says, for therein lies God's word of love for those around us. In teaching His Word faithfully, we will serve as faithful instruments in establishing the relationship of the loving Creator and the dependent creature captive to sin who needs to know God's love and forgiveness. But this accuracy is never an end in itself. It is God's means of forming a relationship with His children.

Presenting the Biblical Message: The Habits of Lutheran Theology

No matter how much a person may try to read the Bible as a blank slate, with no presuppositions or assumptions, it is neither possible nor desirous to do so. We always understand God's Word and His world through the lens of the culture in which we live. At the same time, we must always strive to discipline our perceptions of reality by Holy Scripture. In the Scriptures alone we receive the bedrock of our view of reality. Whatever practices and beliefs culture may bestow on us that frame how we see the world, beneath these cultural perspectives must lie the mind of Christ. Within different cultural contexts, Christians may have to answer different questions or address different topics with sensitivity to the culture, while always conforming our thinking and speaking to the Word of God. God's Word alone sets in place the fundamental relationships that comprise our sense of reality, that is, our views of the relationship between the human creature and God, and the relationships among human creatures themselves.

Although many speak of a worldview that functions as a set of presuppositions for understanding the biblical text and teaching it to others, the presuppositions of Lutheran theology operate more like a set of habits. These habits are a combination of beliefs and practices. They are practices in which beliefs are embedded, and they are beliefs in which practices are embedded. To be clear, the point in calling them habits of mind is to emphasize that these presuppositions of Lutheran theology are not merely ideas to be thought, but *practices to use* when one reads the Bible, teaches the faith, and proclaims the Gospel. In other words, these habits of a Lutheran mind express how Lutherans read Scripture, understand the world, and articulate the Bible's message. They are the presuppositions and practices *with* which to think, not merely thoughts *that* we think.[10] These habits are essential to grasping how to approach God's Word and teach it faithfully to others according to the wisdom of the Lutheran tradition.

Learning these habits is the hardest part of understanding Lutheran theology. After all, a book presents ideas and concepts, but these habits are solidified by experience. We learn the distinction of Law and Gospel best when encountered by despair that was hiding under bravado, and we see what the Law does when it strikes the despairing and what comfort forgiveness of sins brings to the sorrowful and the guilty. We grasp the importance of the two ages when faced with the conundrum of evil persistent in this redeemed world, and we recognize how the response to the problem of evil is solved only by the return of Jesus Christ. We become theologians of the

10 This phrasing is influenced by Joel Okamoto.

cross when we are encountered by God's Word that points us to the shameful cross which is our salvation that reveals the Father's heart in His Son's death and resurrection. In these experiences, the Spirit forms in us the mind of Christ, as God's Word shapes us in the crucible of experience, so that we hear and speak His Word faithfully.[11]

God Is the Creator and Human Beings Are Creatures

For Lutheran theology, understanding God as Creator and human beings as creatures is not merely an important concept but a habit of mind that must pervade all aspects of theology. God created all things, and human beings are fundamentally creatures made for conversation and community with Him and with others. Many people across the globe believe in divine creation, but contemporary Western culture has cultivated numerous instincts that deny this belief. The most obvious tension with biblical teaching is scientific or philosophical naturalism, which claims that all reality is empirical and measurable, open to scientific study by human beings. Such a belief, discussed more thoroughly in chapter 3, denies the existence of anything supernatural and cannot be squared with Christian doctrine. More insidious in the Christian Church is the way that Western culture denies that human beings are creatures, totally dependent on God and made for discourse with the Creator. Westerners instinctively believe that freedom is their most important right, and that freedom means we are in charge of our own lives and can be whatever we want to be. The Bible, however, insists that freedom is being in right relationship with God and being who and what God wants us to be. Freedom is a gift, not a right, and we have lost this gift in its most significant dimensions through our sinfulness. Believers must allow our belief that we are creatures, made for relationship with the Creator, to infuse how we understand ourselves and teach Christian doctrine.

Since God created all things, both seen and unseen, Lutheran theology also confesses that the spiritual is not superior to the material but that the Creator has made both visible and invisible aspects of His creation good. In fact, God works through the material things of His creation—words and water, bread and wine, human creatures—to deliver His promises and care for His world. God even became incarnate in His Son to enter into this creation and walk among us to become our Savior. The material creation must be good in God's eyes if the Son of God took on a human body to restore the broken creation to Himself by His cross and empty tomb.

---

11 Luther, *Table Talk*, AE 54:7, no. 46: "Experience alone makes the theologian."

The Cosmos Exists in Two Ages

Most people organize the world spatially: heaven and earth, sinners and righteous. These realms often act as completely different spheres that do not intermix. The Bible, however, does not differentiate spatially as often as temporally, in terms of ages rather than realms. Paul says, for example, "In this hope we were saved" (Romans 8:24). The grammar is instructive: we *were* saved, past tense, Paul writes, yet we were saved *in hope*, future tense.[12] Paul's sentence—and Paul's entire teaching—will not be properly understood unless we recognize the two ages that cut through the entire cosmos and through every individual. Believers are saved now, yet we wait for God's final salvation in hope. We are righteous now, yet we wait for our sinful nature to be drowned eternally. We are children of God now, yet our full formation into Christ is not yet complete (1 John 3:2).

The essential teaching that structures Lutheran theology is the distinction between two ages, the eon of sin and death, with Satan as its tyrant, and the era of God's total, visible reign, with Jesus as its King. The current, dying age is what the Scriptures variously refer to as "the present evil age" (Galatians 1:4), "this present darkness" (Ephesians 6:12), and the time of creation's "groaning" in anticipation of its salvation (Romans 8:20–22). When Adam and Eve rebelled against their Creator, they corrupted God's good world and made all things fall apart. This brokenness included not only the human relationship with God—which became one of distrust, enmity, and strife—and human relationships with one another but also the entire nonhuman creation, which fell into disarray, disease, and death. God's creation remains good as creation, but a systemic cancer has infected it, contaminating every nook and cranny. This cancer, this sinfulness, is at the heart of the present evil age, along with its despot, Satan, and its instrument, death. God is Lord of all, even Satan, but the creation is in captivity to sin, the grave, and the power of the devil, and it waits with "eager longing" for the day of the Lord (Romans 8:19), when all knees will bow to the Lord Jesus (Philippians 2:10) and God's kingdom of peace and justice will reign visibly over all.

Central to the recognition of the present evil age is the understanding that human creatures have rebelled against God and abandoned their relationship of trust in Him. As a result of this rebellion, evil pervades *all* of human life, down to the heart and the soul (Genesis 6:5; Matthew 15:19). In a sense, original sin is the one biblical teaching that is empirically verifiable, as the twentieth-century American theologian Reinhold Niebuhr famously

---

12 Jeffrey A. Gibbs, "Regaining Biblical Hope: Restoring the Prominence of the Parousia," *Concordia Journal* 27 (October 2001): 310–22.

quipped,[13] but many Westerners are extremely optimistic about human potential. Many believe that people are basically good. What people need is not a wholesale re-creation, in this view, but a little education or help with mental health, and these small fixes will clear up a lot of bad action. On the contrary, biblical teaching recognizes that people's hearts and attitudes are perverted by our sinfulness, even when our outer actions look quite good.

The teaching of the two ages presumes not only the current sinfulness of the world but also the advent of the new age of God's reign in Jesus' life, death, and resurrection. In Jesus Christ, God has inaugurated a new age, His own rule of **shalom**—a Hebrew word meaning "wholeness and harmony, justice and peace"—amid the tyrants of this present darkness. In the midst of the old era of sin, Jesus Christ has established a new age, the eternal eon of God's reign. Although the old age permeates the hearts of all, including Christians, Jesus has promised to make all things *new* (Revelation 21:5; Isaiah 43:19; 65:17). Jesus' power, parables, preaching, and above all His crucifixion and resurrection testified to this kingdom of God come in Him. This new age of eternal life in the Spirit is given to Christ's people by His means of grace that make us children of God. Thus Christians live simultaneously in two ages, sinners and righteous at the same time, dying yet we live, and captive to the flesh yet forgiven and free in the Spirit. The two ages run right through the heart of every person and through the cosmos itself. This new age is here **now**, but it is **not yet** fully here. Biblical hope is that the new age inaugurated by Jesus and present in the Spirit will become the only age, purifying the entire cosmos, visible and invisible, by God's glory permeating all things, just as it filled the tabernacle in the days of Moses.

Through this teaching of the two ages, Lutheran theology inculcates a habit of taking seriously the enormity of evil while also boldly believing in the Savior from all evil. We can confess our sins boldly because we know the forgiveness promised and given to us in Jesus (1 John 1:9). We do not have to hide from the threat of evil outside or pretend that there is no evil inside, for we know that Christ has conquered evil and has promised to return to His world to complete His victory. Therefore, we can confront the evils of this present age, including the evil inside of us, without fear. Our Lord has already achieved the victory! We can even confront the problem of evil itself, the perplexing question of why evil exists in God's world, although we know a logical answer will elude us.

---

13 Niebuhr is actually quoting the "London Times Literary Supplement." See Reinhold Niebuhr, *Man's Nature and His Communities: Essays on the Dynamics and Enigmas of Man's Personal and Social Existence* (New York: Scribner, 1965; repr., Eugene, OR: Wipf & Stock, 2012), 24.

Law and Gospel

The confession that the Creator is a God of conversation and community leads to a set of interrelated, governing principles that stand at the heart of Lutheran theology: the distinction between the Law and the Gospel, the two kinds of righteousness, and the two dimensions of human life. The distinction between Law and Gospel recognizes that God does not intend to do one thing by His Word but two.[14] In other words, to accomplish God's ultimate end of making sinners His own children, God speaks two distinct words that function in different ways. We must learn the habit of reading the Bible with God's distinct intentions in mind and distinguishing between these two words when we teach the faith to others.

On the one hand, God's **Law** puts the burden on the human creature. Everything that calls for human action is Law. The Law is God's design for human life and is in itself good, directing human creatures to follow God's pattern for a creaturely life well lived. In our sinfulness, however, we have brought the burden of the Law upon ourselves with crushing force. We feel the force of God's Law as our adversary and enemy because we are captive to sin and thus under the Law's accusation. "The law brings wrath" (Romans 4:15), but God's wrath is aimed toward His Gospel as the Spirit of God uses the Law to cause sinners to recognize our bondage to selfishness, idolatry, and false belief and to open us to the need for God's saving mercy.

On the other hand, God's **Gospel** grants His saving mercy in Jesus Christ. The Gospel demands nothing at all from humanity but puts the burden entirely on Christ. In the Gospel, God promises, gives, and offers everything, even His own life in Jesus, that sinful humanity might be children of God, rescued from sin, death, and the devil, and made heirs of the treasures of heaven through Christ. In one sense, the Gospel is God's expression of love for His creatures in every way in which He shows Himself to be our good and gracious God, our loving Father, our Savior, and our protecting and providing Lord. Above all, and in its most important sense, however, the Gospel is God's love in Jesus, in His self-sacrifice for us on the cross and in His gift of life through His own resurrection. The Gospel is good *news* because Jesus has already initiated the new creation of His righteous people (2 Corinthians 5:17); He has accomplished this saving work for all people, and He offers forgiveness of sins through the Word, proclaimed and taught. The Spirit turns sinners to believe this Word and receive everything that it promises: forgiveness, life, and salvation, the very kingdom of God.

---

14 Classic expositions of this distinction include Walther, *Law and Gospel*, and in narrative form, Bo Giertz, *The Hammer of God*, trans. Clifford Ansgar Nelson (Minneapolis: Augsburg, 1973).

This distinction of Law and Gospel guides our thinking as we use and teach all the topics that are discussed in subsequent chapters of this book. This is necessary not only because the Bible is rightly divided into Law and Gospel but also because the distinction between these two words is necessary to apply in the lives of those who hear God's Word. To apply this insight practically, it is essential that Christians do not merely speak the truth but learn the situations of the hearers. Whenever someone asks a significant question about God or human life, Kolb has long taught his students to ask another question in response: "Why do you want to know?" The point is not to be coy or evasive, but to recognize the real motivation behind a person's question. Until we know someone's reason for asking a question, we may give an answer that is technically correct but inappropriate and false for the situation in which the questioner is living. We must distinguish whether the question arises out of a false confidence in false gods or out of discouragement and despair over false gods. We must tune in to the specific needs the question expresses. For example, "Am I an elect child of God?" must elicit the Gospel's promise for the despairing. A technically correct answer distinguishing foreknowledge and election would be in reality false to one in doubt concerning her salvation, if it does not give God's promise: "You are baptized! God has chosen you to be His own in Jesus." To someone who is seeking a license to sin, however, the same Gospel promise may be true but not helpful. Secure sinners cannot understand the Gospel and need to hear God's convicting Law. The conversation should not merely offer a Gospel answer to the question as it stands but call the person to repentance. Therefore, the proper distinction of Law and Gospel involves more than the repetition of Bible passages; it involves death and life.

Two Kinds of Righteousness and Two Dimensions of Human Life

Two closely related presuppositions of Lutheran theology are the distinction between two kinds of righteousness, passive and active, and the two dimensions of human life, vertical and horizontal.[15] Luther emphasized that what makes life right, whole, or good in relationship with God is not the same as what makes life right, whole, and good in relationship to other people or in other arenas of life. In fact, God is at work in different ways in relationship

15 On the two kinds of righteousness, see Luther, *Lectures on Galatians* (1531), AE 26:4–12; *Two Kinds of Righteousness* (1519), AE 31:293–306. On the two dimensions of human life, see F. Edward Cranz, *An Essay on the Development of Luther's Thought on Justice, Law, and Society* (1959; repr., Mifflintown, PA: Sigler Press, 1998); Gustaf Wingren, *Luther on Vocation*, trans. Carl C. Rasmussen (Philadelphia: Muhlenberg, 1957); and George W. Forell, *Faith Active in Love: An Investigation of the Principles Underlying Luther's Social Ethics* (Minneapolis: Augsburg, 1954).

to Himself compared to our relationships with other human creatures. In the **vertical relationship** with God, the Holy Spirit works through the Word to convict sinners by the Law and bring them to faith by the Gospel. God's love for His creatures is delivered through the proclamation of the Gospel that brings us to love God with our whole heart, soul, and mind and to be formed for our horizontal relationships of loving our neighbors as ourselves (Matthew 22:37–40). In the **horizontal relationships** with other creatures, God is at work in a different way and for a different goal through the Law. God works in this realm not only by divine Law but natural and civil law to order human relationships to be peaceful and good so that we can live out God's design of service for our fellow human creatures.

More important for understanding Lutheran doctrine, especially justification, is the distinction between two kinds of righteousness. Our relationship to God is a relationship that originates in His love for us, His creatures. We never move beyond being God's children, always dependent on Him, always recipients of His love, always moved by His gracious Word to trust in His promises. In this relationship, we are right, or righteous, before God not because we do anything but because God acts for us and in us. Hence, Luther called this kind of righteousness "passive righteousness." We are passive as God is active to save, speaking His Word that shatters our sinful deafness. In this **passive righteousness**, we are saved—placed into a right relationship with God as His children—not because we did anything, are doing anything, or will do anything. Our being right with God consists only and always in what Christ has done for us. He is our righteousness. He is all that is right about us (1 Corinthians 1:30). We are justified, then, as we are brought to trust in Christ by God's loving kindness, His grace, alone. In the words of Paul: "For by grace you have been saved through faith. And this is not your own doing; it is the gift of God, not a result of works, so that no one may boast" (Ephesians 2:8–9). This salvation is a gift that cannot be earned but only received by faith. Believers must learn the habit of giving all glory to God and refusing to boast, because God is the one who justifies.

The other kind of righteousness is called **active righteousness**, which flows from our passive righteousness. God's Spirit dwells in the heart by faith—passive righteousness—and the Holy Spirit leads God's people to respond accordingly: to pray boldly and confidently, to give thanks always to our God, and to serve our neighbors in love and joy. We love God and others because He loved us and has generated love in us by His Spirit (1 John 4:7–12). Even when we are acting, God is working through us to follow His will and serve in His ways. In active righteousness, our actions are always responses to His love, which elicits our love toward Him and our loving service toward our neighbor. This active righteousness, a life spent profitably according to God's will, occurs not because we do the work on our own but because we act on the basis of the righteousness God bestows on us as His children. Those enthralled with the ways of the evil age, as we all are on our own, cannot do good work, either in response to God or in response to the needs of other human creatures, in a God-pleasing way apart from the power of the Gospel.

The Latin and German terms usually translated "two kinds of righteousness" can also be rendered "twofold righteousness." The former emphasizes the contrast of God's activity and the result of God's activity in the believer's life. The latter accentuates the fact that there is just one person who is this righteous believer so that the two kinds of righteousness go together like horse and carriage: you do not have one without the other. Passive righteousness always flows into active righteousness as the fruit of the Spirit is produced by God's Spirit who dwells within believers by the promise.

There is also a third kind of righteousness, less significant theologically, that Luther and the Lutheran Confessions call "civil righteousness," which deals exclusively with our horizontal relationships with other human creatures. These relationships are many and various, but all of them demand proper performance. Adults are required to function as adults, to follow the law, and to perform their responsibilities well. For example, as a professor, Hopkins requires that his students read the textbook, turn in their assignments, and articulate biblical teaching accurately. These are the standards that he uses to determine "righteousness," grades, in his classroom. This kind of righteousness is called **civil righteousness** because civil society, like a classroom, operates according to human performance, determined by appropriate rules and responsibilities. Those outside the Christian faith can conform to the outward requirements of God's Law just as well as Christians can, even though they act out of motivations other than God-pleasing trust. This means, among other things, that Christians can work with those outside the faith to seek the welfare of civil society (cf. Jeremiah 29:5–7). Believers recognize in this sphere of life that perfect can be the enemy of good and are willing to accept less-than-perfect, but not ungodly, solutions to problems of this life. In horizontal relationships, God has given us responsibilities to meet the needs of others and show His love to those around us. Here our righteousness consists in what we do for others, according to God's design for His human creatures.

The Theology of the Cross

The final habit of Lutheran theology to be described in this book is a collection of biblical observations about God and human creatures that shape how Christians understand God's Word, themselves, and reality. Luther labeled this way of doing theology "the theology of the cross."[16]

God Hidden and God Revealed (in Hiddenness). The first of the five points of the theology of the cross considers our teaching about God. Luther distinguished "the hidden God" from "the revealed God." Luther recognized how often people try to know God from nature, emotion, conscience, and philosophy—in short, from human abilities—rather than by attending to God's Word. God is hidden in that God lies beyond human grasp, beyond human knowing; the true God is concealed from human abilities. Thus if we try to describe God through human methods, we succeed only in presenting God according to human imagination. Such a depiction of God must be, in the words of the nineteenth-century German philosopher Ludwig Feuerbach, "God created in the image of man."[17] A picture of the **hidden God**, fashioned by human speculation, usually presents a God of glory, power, and might. This is the opposite of the God whom we see on the cross. God is hidden behind His own cloud of glory, and we cannot penetrate that cloud to see what He is really like. Our depiction of God, apart from His revelation, is largely a reflection of human feelings and fears.

Parental images and the experiences behind them may shape our imaginations of the divine. In past eras the experience of parents as angry, even vengeful, dictated the feelings of many toward God. Today we more often encounter those who believe that God is uninterested in them, a neglectful God, perhaps even abusive. Others have created a divine butler, at our beck and call when we need Him, but who largely stays out of our way and lets us do what we want. These idolatrous notions of God encourage some to strive to please the divine with their behavior, others to be mired in resentment and rejection, and still others to condone destructive tendencies and self-centeredness in the name of love while condemning all who might speak out. These divine projections may seem harmless, but in reality standards are created that we cannot meet. As Paul writes: "For in passing judgment on another you condemn yourself, because you, the judge, practice the very same things" (Romans 2:1).

The heart of this natural religion, sometimes labeled as **natural theology**, is control. Just like traditional, animistic religions that place divine power within created objects rather than in the Creator, sin-ridden human

---

16 Luther, *Heidelberg Disputation* (1518), AE 31:35–70. See also Gerhard Forde, *On Being a Theologian of the Cross: Reflections on Luther's Heidelberg Disputation, 1518* (Grand Rapids: Eerdmans, 1997), who emphasizes the theology of the cross as creating a certain kind of person, one who exhibits a particular character or habits, to use the language of this chapter.

17 Ludwig Feuerbach, *Das Wesen des Christentums* (1841); *The Essence of Christianity*, trans. George Eliot (New York: Harper, 1957), 13–14, 22–43, 108.

minds seek to control their gods with their rituals, accomplishments, and performance. The ideas about God that occur to us "naturally," as sinners, deny Him His rightful place in our lives. We create gods that we can grasp with our powers and control with our actions. God, however, hides Himself to remain outside of our control so that He can grasp us with His surprise confrontation in the last place we would ever expect.

The **revealed God** is God as He presents Himself to us, as Luther liked to say, in crib, cross, and the crypt He left behind. The revealed God is the God who speaks to us, as the Word made flesh and in His inspired Scriptures. The revealed God is the God whose power is made perfect in weakness (2 Corinthians 12:9), both ours and His. God's weakness in the cross of Christ is stronger than all human might and power. God's foolishness in the cross of Christ is wiser than all human wisdom (1 Corinthians 1:18–2:9). The last place human power and wisdom would look for God is in a manger, in diapers, or on a cross, on the way to the tomb. But it is precisely there that our God reveals what He is really like. He reveals His unconditional and absolute love for fallen sinners in a man crucified and buried in a tomb.

Lutheran theology asserts that God is rightly known only as the revealed God, in the Scriptures, in the Word made flesh, in human language about this incarnate Word as it is preached and proclaimed, in sacramental forms at God's font and God's feast. Other descriptions of God tell us more about ourselves than about Him. Luther insisted: "God does not want to deal with us human beings except by means of his external Word and sacrament. Everything that boasts of being from the Spirit apart from such a Word and sacrament is of the devil."[18]

God, therefore, is outside human control. He addresses us. He calls us. He invites us and draws us into His family. We can only respond. He came to ask Adam: "Where are you?" (Genesis 3:9). He has determined our rightful place. He declares what constitutes our righteousness. Some view "excessive" exaltation of God as a threat to our humanity. Recognizing God's place "above" us, as our Creator, however, does not deny our humanity. The revealed God shows us also what it means to be free as human creatures, to be as God designed us to be (Colossians 1:13–23). Therefore, Lutherans recognize throughout their interpretation of God's Word that we have access to God and His character only through His revelation of Himself.

The Epistemology of Faith. The second point of the theology of the cross focuses on how we know this foolish and weak God. The Jews demanded signs, Paul reported. They wanted empirical proof. The Greeks demanded wisdom. They wanted a logical explanation (1 Corinthians 1:18–2:16). Both Jews and Greeks wanted to know God on the basis of a process that human

18 Smalcald Articles III VIII 10.

creatures control. They wanted to pin God down on their own terms. "Prove it" is still a common response to the Christian message. People want empirical data; people want logical proof.

Our understanding of how God's Word functions depends in part on our understanding of how human learning functions. Epistemology is the study of how human creatures learn and know. God has provided us with several methods of learning, each appropriate for gaining knowledge in various areas of human life. While all these ways are valuable in their spheres, we must be careful to recognize how knowledge of God differs from other kinds of knowledge because these methods can be used sinfully.

Empirical learning and knowing. By and large, people in contemporary Western culture believe that the most valuable approach to gaining information lies in the empirical or experimental method, the scientific method of learning. This method relies first on the human senses to evaluate data on the basis of scientific experimentation. The method presumes that knowledge can be proven by repeated testing. It claims an objectivity to its findings because they can be submitted to trial by others. Fellow scientists can repeat the experiment to determine whether the original judgments were correct. Objects that cannot be subjected to repeated experimentation lie outside the command of this approach to human knowledge.

Empirical epistemology puts human creatures in control of the process of gaining knowledge and thus in control of the knowledge gained from experiments. In one sense, good empirical research forces a scientist to submit herself to the data; the reality of the data can surprise the scientist, contradicting the initial hypothesis. In a deeper sense, however, the individual scientist remains in control, and certain results are ruled out by the presuppositions brought to the experiment. The scientist frames the rules for conducting the experiment. The scientist performs the experiment and interprets its results. The scientist determines what truth it tells.

People have always used experiments to gain knowledge, but the much-vaunted authority of the experimental method dates back to the scientific revolution of the seventeenth century. This methodology has produced wonderful advances in arenas such as medicine and technology. This method of learning has enhanced the human ability to solve problems in the earthly realm and to extend many of God's temporal blessings for great portions of the world's population. Although it is limited to a certain sphere of life, empirical testing is an essential way to learn about God's creation. Believers should recognize the blessings God has given His world through scientific research.

At the same time, many think that experimental testing offers the only path to reliable knowledge. They fail to recognize that the presuppositions of the researcher, the reliability of the instruments used in the experiment, and a host of external conditions influence the results of the experiment. Something akin to religious faith enters into this approach to knowledge, at least at the level of presupposition. For instance, many today trust that every problem can be solved through technology; they presume that the major challenges of the world are not moral, spiritual, or relational but scientific problems in need of technological solutions. In so doing, they neglect both the great destruction that technological advances have wrought in sinful human hands, such as deadly wars and genocides, and the importance of the relational and moral character of the world, which is not easily investigated by empirical research.

It must not be forgotten that those who pursue knowledge produced by empirical investigation do not view it as "fact" but as working theory. Therefore, for the empiricist, the status of theory is not at all inferior to the status of fact. This appraisal of knowledge in the horizontal realm is a healthy view. It can reflect the presumption that through God's gift of empirical testing human creatures never attain full mastery of God's creation, full knowledge of how everything works.

Learning and knowing through reason. The second method of learning and knowing relies on human cognition and cogitation to gain the truth. Information and insight are acquired through human reasoning, expressed in formal logic, such as syllogisms, or in the form of everyday common sense. Philosophers have disagreed on whether the basic principles of logical thinking arise out of the human mind naturally, or whether they are grasped through human experience. In either case, the presumption of this approach to human knowledge asserts that human powers of reasoning can understand the self and the world around us. Human logic can master the data that bombards us from nature and human experience.

Much of Western culture has relied on the grand thoughts of philosophers and the common thoughts of everyone to solve problems and push back frontiers of knowledge. Without rational knowledge, life in the horizontal realm could not function. Human creatures enjoy this good gift of God and profit from its proper use. Within Western culture, however, different systems of logic have developed, and they do not all lead to the same results. Between cultures gaps in logic open up. Not only do we lack agreement on the basic principles of logic, but we find that using the same principles can still result in different conclusions. Presumption, presupposition, and predisposition all shape the way we use our minds and the conclusions we reach.

Aesthetic learning and knowing. A third kind of knowledge gives human creatures access to the appreciation and enjoyment of the beauty of God's creation. Human reasoning and human emotion combine with sense perception to enrich our lives with the glories of color, shape, and form; of melody, harmony, and rhythm; of sights and sounds; of tastes, smells, and textures. Most people would agree that beauty is not merely a matter of individual taste. Most also acknowledge that their own concept of beauty and their appreciation of its blessings differ from the tastes of others in their own culture and certainly from the tastes of other cultures. This form of knowledge does not demand the same kind of reliability that the empirical and rational approaches to learning require. At the same time few would dismiss the deep significance this kind of knowledge has for daily life and the appreciation of our humanity and God's creation. Nonetheless, the raggedness of human knowing becomes apparent also in aesthetic knowledge.

Learning and knowing from authority. The fourth form of learning conveys information and insight through the voice of an authority. Most human learning and knowing takes place through this method. Few human creatures have had time to learn experimentally or to analyze rationally all that they need to know. We hope that voices of authority have the truth, and we listen for the ring of truth in their words. We review the conclusions of those voices of authority against the test of our own presuppositions. We nonetheless make a leap of faith to embrace the judgments of those who fix our appliances, manufacture and advertise a host of products for daily use, and plan our political and social policies. Far less often than we care to admit to ourselves do we pause for testing or rational evaluation.

God has so fashioned His human creatures that we can learn a great deal through empirical testing, reason and logic, and aesthetic experience. But we often depend on the voices of authority for the information we need. In the horizontal realm each of these four ways of learning can be helpful and appropriate, in specific situations. In the vertical realm, however, the first three cannot lead us to truth. They always leave the human knower in control. When the epistemologies of human experiment, human rationality, or human aesthetic judgments try to define the origins and bounds of reality, they have gone beyond the limits of their competence. They go astray when they attempt to answer a different kind of question from the questions for which they were designed. Information about God must be learned through another means. It must be heard from the voice of authority, the voice of God Himself.

The common definition of the word **theology** as "study of God" can confuse us into misunderstanding this. While theology seeks to understand God and God's world from His Word, theology cannot study Him in the same way that scientists study rocks. God is not available to human knowledge or control as if we could put God under a microscope. Knowing God and understanding His Word require us to "let God be God," to place ourselves under the authority of God's Word, hear it in humility, and echo it faithfully to others.[19]

The theology of the cross teaches that neither the human eye nor the human mind controls our access to God. He controls that access, and He creates that access through His Word. He speaks, and the human ear listens. The human heart responds to His Word in faith. "I believe that I cannot by my own reason or strength believe in Jesus Christ, my Lord, or come to Him."[20] God must step out of hiding. He must take the initiative. And He does so with a promise. By its nature a promise invites faith. The theology of the cross confesses that we know God not through empirical proofs or logical reasoning, but only through faith. The faith the revealed God elicits from us through His Word relies on God's foolish and weak approach to us in the suffering and death of His Son.

Faith is not objective, dispassionate knowledge—the kind of knowledge the Enlightenment of the eighteenth century invented to assure objective, dispassionate human control. Faith is active; it is engaged with its object. It is knowledge that unites the one who trusts with its object. It is knowledge "in the biblical sense" (the euphemism for the intimate knowledge of husband and wife). Faith embraces its object as a bride embraces her bridegroom. Faith rests in God's promise, which contradicts our attempts to hang on to life. Thus this knowledge carries us out of the realms in which we retain control over our own destinies. Faith alone gives access to God.

The faith of the believer does not rest upon anything else but Jesus. Neither signs of blessing nor signs of suffering will be taken as proof that the believer's relationship with God is working or failing. Christians who point to their blessings as signs that God must love them are relying on a false basis for faith—just as much as are those who trust that God has to love them because they are suffering so much. Reliance upon faltering feelings can betray us—we do not know God through them even if we may feel good when we know God—but God's promises to us never fail us. Confidence in God's faithfulness to us will not rest in the good works we produce; God is faithful when we are not (2 Timothy 2:13). Even the existence of our faith cannot be turned into a basis for our faith. When faith weakens, God remains strong in His love for us. Faith rests on Christ alone. Faith rests on His promise to be our Lord.

Dying to Death, or Crucified with Christ. The third point of the theology of the cross focuses on what God did on the cross (1 Corinthians 2:2).

19 Compare Philip S. Watson, *Let God Be God! An Interpretation of the Theology of Martin Luther* (1947; repr., Eugene, OR: Wipf & Stock, 2000).

20 Small Catechism II 6 (*LSCE*, 17).

There God atoned for sin and swallowed death. There, in His own impotence and foolishness, He succeeded at the task of setting aside all that keeps us from Him. There He succeeded at re-creating us to be children of the heavenly Father, remade in God's own image. Luther called what happened on the cross "the joyous exchange." Life is restored to sinful human creatures, dead in trespasses and guilt, only because God has exchanged human sinfulness for Christ's righteousness. We live because Jesus died with our sins on His back and buried them in His tomb, the only place in the universe where our heavenly Father no longer looks. We live because Jesus shares with us His own eternal life.

In Him, wrong is made right, and death is left behind for life, through God's peculiar way of doing things. The theology of the cross presupposes that the cross, death, is the path to life. The final result of this joyous exchange is that we who were buried and raised with Christ in Baptism (Romans 6:3–11; Colossians 2:11–15) are joint heirs with Him, even as we suffer with Him and will share glory with Him (Romans 8:17).

Thus the theology of the cross spells the death of all human pretension to merit and success before God. It announces the death of human control over our destiny. The theology of the cross announces the death of sinners to sin and their resurrection to new life in Christ. It announces the death of death itself. This announcement liberates human creatures from the threat of death and thus bestows upon them genuine human freedom. Once sinners have seen the cross, there can be no more wallowing in guilt. Freedom is bestowed on us through God's own death, as the Second Person of the Trinity went to the cross to save sinners, to restore their humanity through faith in Him.

The Church Suffers. Fourth, the theology of the cross explained for Luther why the church and its individual members suffer persecution and temptations of various kinds. Servants are not better than their masters (John 15:20; cf. John 1:16), so that believers should expect to suffer in similar ways to how Christ suffered. After all, God wages His warfare against Satan on the battlefield of the church's life. His victory is certain, but His method has not changed since Calvary. In weakness and foolishness believers stand against the old evil foe. They stand against the devil on the certainty of words, promised in human voices, water, bread, and wine. These weak ways are yet God's way of combating the forces of the evil age. Believers stand certain that the Lord will deliver them from evil even though they do not understand how the Holy Spirit is using them in the impotence and imprudence they experience in the battle. Their voices seem far too feeble, and their lives far too broken. Yet they are God's chosen instruments to carry the message of

His Gospel. Believers simply witness in confidence that the ultimate victory has already been assured by Jesus' life, death, and resurrection.

Discipleship under the Cross. Fifth, the theology of the cross confesses that the life of the believer, the life of discipleship—learning from and following after Christ—is a life under the cross of the neighbor's need (Matthew 16:24–26). Within the span of life, believers encounter and take up plenty of crosses, of family, friends, and colleagues, and lay plenty of crosses at the feet of fellow believers. Hence Paul urges Christians to "bear one another's burdens, and so fulfill the law of Christ" (Galatians 6:2). Our crosses do not save ourselves or save others. Instead, they convey the love of Christ to others in a sinful world of suffering. As we take up our crosses and follow our Lord, we are living as life must be lived if the good and gracious will of our heavenly Father is to be done in this age of sin and suffering. Neither blessing nor cross determines whether we are in God's favor. Only His Word determines that. We should not be surprised when our faith leads us into suffering for the sake of the neighbor. That is often the means the God of the cross uses to battle evil.

Life under the cross crucifies the habits of hell. The strong pruning hook of the Law combines with the believers' confidence in Christ's deadly death, and these believers find they have no need to use their hellish habits to defend themselves. Life under the cross gives rise to the habits of heaven. Faith perceives how God succeeds, in His own self-sacrifice and self-surrender, in His submission to human needs, His suffering, and His willing service. Faith, then, follows in Christ's way.

Lutheran theology is eminently practical. It takes shape in daily life, where it gives form to believers' attitudes and actions in the mundane course of everyday existence. It centers around the God of conversation and community who speaks the creative Word that brought all things into being and that breaks through sinful, unhearing ears to create faith in fallen human creatures. Lutheran theology shapes us to first hear this Word of God and come to know God in Christ through the revealed Word. As the theology of the cross describes, we understand who God is in the cross; we learn how we relate to Him in faith; we see how He has conquered sin, death, and the devil by His death; we gladly witness to and take part in the weak ways of Christ in the battle against evil; and we serve our neighbors under the cross.

This chapter's habits of Lutheran theology provide a kind of "grammar of faith" that shapes all the topics discussed in this book. These habits recur through each topic, often explicitly but sometimes implicitly. On the implicit level, the scope of God's story of creation, fall, and Christ's inauguration of the saving reign of God pervades every topic, but will often remain under the surface. On the explicit level, when we treat the doctrine of God, for example, we seek to listen to God's disclosure of Himself to know His nature rather than making conclusions based on nature or reason.

What makes a theologian is not merely asserting the right doctrines but being shaped by Holy Scripture to pray boldly to the Father and to search the Scriptures diligently to know Christ—what Luther called *oratio, meditatio, tentatio* (prayer, meditation, and the agonizing struggle).[21] Lutherans have thus cultivated certain habits of mind that come from Holy Scripture in order to proclaim the cross of Jesus Christ as the salvation of sinners and to teach the Scriptures faithfully in all topics.

---

21 *Preface to the German Writings* (1539), AE 34:285–87.

CHAPTER 2
GOD

FROM the inner workings of the smallest atoms to the structures of galaxies, the Scriptures testify that all things witness to God's handiwork and proclaim His glory (Psalm 19:1–2). When one has eyes to see and ears to hear, traces of the Creator can be recognized throughout the creation. For Christian theology, however, this natural revelation cannot structure our knowledge of God. In sin, human beings do not gladly receive God's gifts *as gift*, nor do we know God rightly in creation. Instead, we construct our own ways to God, turning created things into idols. No matter how much natural revelation may testify to the true God, we are unable to see God's handiwork apart from the Holy Spirit; God remains hidden apart from where He wants to reveal Himself to us. After all, we cannot think our way to God, nor calculate what divinity is really like. We need God to come to us, and reveal Himself to us, starting the conversation with His creatures, giving us Himself by His Word.

The God Christians worship is not a generic creator deity nor an abstract unity of attributes that can be apprehended with logic and reason. He is Yahweh, who has revealed Himself in conversation with His people. The God Christians worship is the God who called Abram out of Ur to the land of Canaan; who remembered His promises to Abraham, Isaac, and Jacob in saving Abraham's descendants, Israel, from slavery in Egypt, and who raised His Son, Jesus, from the dead on the third day by the Spirit. The sun, moon, stars, and galaxies testify to this God, but we cannot know His name, His identity, or His Gospel through them. Christians come to see God in the much smaller things by which He has chosen to reveal Himself: a conversation with a believer, the water of Baptism, a sermon from a pastor, the pages of Scripture, Christian conversation focused on Christ, and in the bread and wine of His Supper. As God discloses Himself in His Word, we come to know Him as He is—the Father who sent His Son in the Spirit to bring rebellious human creatures back into fellowship with Himself.

Natural Revelation, or Glimpses of the Hidden God

God has left traces of His existence strewn all over creation. Even those whose sin has deafened them to His call still catch fleeting glimpses as they hurl themselves headlong from His presence. Sinners often abstract some nugget of truth from these glimpses. We construct a picture of God from the hints we sense in the creation around us. These pictures reflect more of ourselves than of God, as the theology of the cross reminds us.

Theologians label the traces and hints of God that fallen human creatures use to paint their own pictures of God **natural** or **general revelation**. For Christians, who have come to know God in the word of the cross, natural revelation can remind us that Christianity is not irrational or mythical. The story of the Scriptures makes sense of the world that we experience, and the world that we experience is none other than the world created and redeemed by Jesus Christ. At the same time, however, natural revelation offers only partial pictures of the Creator's character. When these pictures are not subordinated to the special revelation of God's Word, they quickly become idols. In sin, we project and construct the entirety of God from some small sense of Him that fits our preferences. Therefore, the impressions of God that arise from natural revelation resemble the pictures of an elephant sketched by blindfolded people who each have hold of a different section of elephantine anatomy. At best these impressions are inadequate. At worst they deceive in a demonic way, for they set the sinners off in wrong directions as they seek the hidden God apart from His Word.

Nature

God has left vestiges of Himself in at least five places. Nature is the first. Paul pointed out that God has left the mark of His invisible nature, His eternal power and deity, in the things He has made (Romans 1:20). God has left a witness to Himself in the goodness with which He satisfies hearts with food and gladness, through rain and fruitful seasons (Acts 14:17). The argument that there must be a God because of the existence of creation is called the **cosmological argument**. The basic contention runs this way: Everything in human experience has a maker. The computer was constructed by an engineer; humans by other humans. Nothing gives rise to itself. What created the cosmos? That Creator is called God.

A related argument, also based on nature, is the **teleological argument** for design and thus for a designer, God. It contends that the *telos*—the Greek word for "goal," "purpose," and "end"—of nature proves that there must be a designer of it all. The creation functions smoothly as a unit with disparate pieces working together. For a simple example, consider the interrelations of monarch butterflies and milkweed. Monarch caterpillars only eat milkweed so that without milkweed, there cannot be monarch butterflies. On a larger scale, the universe cannot exist at all without the natural physical constants—such as the speed of light, the strength of gravity, the strength of the electromagnetic force, and many others—being within specific narrow ranges. That all these physical constants seem to be tuned perfectly to existence and life on earth is suggestive of a designer who ordered and planned the universe. To the eye of faith, God's glory and presence are reflected in the creation as a whole, as well as in the construction of the human creature (e.g., Isaiah 40:12, 21–26; Job 9:4–12; Psalm 139:13–16).

Today, in Western culture, many reject such reasoning. Although nature shows glimpses of its design for people of faith, explanations have developed for nature's existence and order that do not need any gods. We tend to think that these modern atheistic arguments are novel, but godless explanations for an eternally self-recycling universe have existed since at least the ancient Greeks. Still, some of the most difficult points of tension between Christian faith and contemporary culture arise in this scientific arena, and Christians should not simply dismiss scientific questioning as atheistic. Many people will need patient and winsome ministry so that they do not remain in the tangles of scientific explanation but rather hear the good news of the Gospel. After all, nature cannot prove God's existence, but neither can nature disprove God's existence. Christians must be prepared not to "prove" the truth of natural revelation with arguments forged on scientific presuppositions but to be witnesses to the Creator, who made Himself known in Jesus, crucified, raised from the dead on the third day in the Spirit, and present in the Word proclaimed in the church.

History

Some argue that God can be seen as He guides and directs human history. According to the **argument from history**, the triumph of good and the punishment of evil in the annals of nations demonstrate that some divine person or force must be channeling human activity. This is easier to defend when the enemies are losing. Although the triumph of Christianity in the Western world—the rise of Christendom—made this argument appealing for some, this glimpse of God, or of God's work, has severe limitations. God is indeed Lord of human history, just as He is Lord of nature, but from any individual's perspective human evil or human aspiration is easily confused with God. If we did not have God's revelation of Himself, even the history of God's people would not be a clear sign of God's presence or goodness. God's lordship of history can only be seen from the end of the story and must be believed now in hope.

Many people could conclude from history that if God is in charge, He has a mean streak. In the prior century we have probably witnessed no increase in human villainy and turpitude; it only seems so because human hatred and meanness have harnessed advanced technology to carry out their evil designs. Nevertheless, survivors of Nazi death camps, Cambodian killing fields, and Rwandan Interahamwe; of Dresden, Hiroshima, and Baghdad; of civil wars, apartheid, and terrorism might well conclude that no God worthy of the name had been minding their store.

Conscience

Within the human creature lurks a longing for divine company. Paul pointed out that Gentiles, who knew nothing of Moses' Law, still lived to a large extent according to God's plan for human life (Romans 2:14). It is notable that many different religions agree on the golden rule: do to others as you would have them do to you. Conscience, the universal sense of right and wrong, points inevitably to the One who designed right and wrong for human creatures, the **argument from conscience** runs.

Anthropologists have produced something of a counterargument. They suggest that there are only two universal taboos, incest and cannibalism of kin; no universal definitions of right and wrong exist. The argument from conscience, however, does not function apart from human moral reasoning. In other words, just because some people do not live according to the typical moral code does not invalidate the argument. When human beings live together, they realize over time that certain standards need to be followed: these standards point toward the design of the Creator. Hence, a large part of the moral code of any culture is operative in most other cultures. Even if there were only two universal taboos, the extensive overlap of agreement among cultures on how human creatures should behave remains suggestive. To be sure, to those who do not want to believe that God has shaped right and wrong for His creatures, any agreement on morality indicates no more than a commonality of human experience. Believers, however, recognize that God has given them their sense of right and wrong for good human living while others may reject the argument that conscience or morality points toward the existence of God.

Furthermore, when conscience speaks, it tells us that we are guilty or that we are morally superior to others. Our consciences make us feel guilt or pride. In guilt, the "god" that conscience abstracts is an angry god, who reaffirms our own anger with ourselves at failing to achieve good performance. In pride, the only god is the self as we stand confidently in our own actions, believing that we are better than everyone else. Conscience contains hints of God's design, but these hints hardly serve as the basis for a friendly conversation.

Reason: The Ontological Argument

"But is it not simply *reasonable* to believe in God?" Different systems of reasoning have constructed different logical arguments for the existence of some kind of greater being. In recent centuries, some mathematicians have even used mathematical logic to prove God's existence. Classically, the **ontological argument**—the logical argument from existence itself—suggests that it is only common sense that there is someone or something greater than which nothing else is. That "greater than all else" must be God. More down-to-earth, daily experience demonstrates that one thing is greater than other things. At the top of such a pyramid must sit God.

This argument will not convince many. For one thing, the argument must be true, which is its greatest weakness. Reality is always more complicated than the rules by which we try to understand it. The argument may be logical and coherent, but it does not prove that reality works according to its rules. This argument's greatest strength is to suggest that belief in God is not nonsense, as many contemporary people think. It is reasonable to believe in some kind of god even though unassisted reason—believers will readily concede—cannot give us a glimpse of the true God of the Gospel.

Emotion: Encountering the Numinous

Finally, human emotion, it can be argued, betrays some sense of the divine. Early in the twentieth century the German theologian Rudolf Otto posited the sense of the "numinous" within the human creature. All people, he argued, have a nonrational and amoral conviction that someone or something greater than the merely human is out there, influencing their lives. This conviction forms the foundation of the human sense of the divine. Human creatures are "naturally" fascinated with the awe-inspiring powers that exercise control over their lives and "naturally" abase themselves before these powers, according to Otto.[1]

Otto's conviction seems to hold in contemporary Western society. Although traditional belief in God has waned, all kinds of other religious beliefs have increased, and interest in the supernatural is just as high as ever.[2] In fact, recent data on religion has shown *more* North Americans

1 Rudolf Otto, *The Idea of the Holy: An Inquiry into the Non-Rational Factor in the Idea of the Divine and Its Relation to the Rational*, trans. John W. Harvey (1917; repr., New York: Oxford University Press, 1958).

2 Graham Ward, *The Politics of Discipleship: Becoming Postmaterial Citizens* (Grand Rapids: Baker Academic, 2009), 139–46.

believe in an afterlife than fifty years earlier even though fewer believe in God.[3] Human beings do seem to have a hunger for eternity, for beauty, for truth, for justice, and for God. Some argue that this hunger itself is evidence for the reality of these things, just as literal hunger for food is evidence that food exists.[4]

These feelings may point toward God, but they have been conscripted in service of idolatry and sin. Human fears and human hopes have shaped alternative pictures of the numinous. Human fears imagine a strong judge who makes a list of good and bad behavior. For most of human history hope has fashioned a powerful god who can save. Recently, however, some contemporary thinkers have tried to abstract a suffering god, a simulacrum of Christ on the cross, who joins vulnerable humankind in its suffering. God's omnipotence is sacrificed, in such a picture, to solve the problem of evil by placing God squarely and solely with His suffering people. This abstract sufferer reveals something of the hidden God but discounts what most humans, and all believers, have known about God: only an omnipotent God is worthy of the name.

The gods of human imagination and construction all break down. They reveal themselves sooner or later as idols created in the image of humanity that, at best, reflect only a small part of the reality of God in Christ. Arguments from natural revelation may help to show that Christianity makes sense in the world of experience, but they cannot be the basis for how we know the God of Jesus. We cannot allow our ideas or feelings of what God "must" be like to prevent us from listening to His Word and knowing Him in the cross.

Believers take pleasure in knowing that God reveals Himself in the majestic display of color in a sunset and a sun-illuminated canyon wall. They will acknowledge signs of His wrath and His mercy in the unfolding of human history. They will notice the effect of His creative hand in the operation of their own conscience, reason, and emotions. But they will also concede the severe limitations of making an argument on such bases to those who stand outside the faith. When unbelievers can be moved in the direction of knowing the true God or Christians can be encouraged in their faith through such arguments, believers will employ them. In general, however, they will cut the "small talk," talk of a God too small when captured in the limited descriptions of natural or general revelation. They will turn instead to God as He speaks with fallen humankind. This God says "I love you" from a cross, and "I have life for you" from the mouth of a tomb.

---

3 Mark Chaves, *American Religion*, 2nd. ed. (Princeton, NJ: Princeton University Press, 2017), 36–37.

4 Timothy Keller, *The Reason for God* (New York: Penguin, 2008), 139.

Specific/Special Revelation: Listening to the Revealed God

The Word of God became flesh (John 1:14) so that He might tell us directly: "I have come that [you] may have life, and have it abundantly" (John 10:10). This voice cuts through the abstractions of the constructed gods, fashioned in our own image out of the raw material of human premonitions and suspicions. From the cross this voice calls human creatures to die under God's wrath (Galatians 6:14); from the mouth of the tomb this voice breathes the forgiveness of sins upon fallen human creatures and raises them up once again to life (John 20:22–23). Only through Jesus of Nazareth, crucified by His own people and raised by God from the dead, can salvation for sinners be found (Acts 4:10–12). We must be drawn to the Word of the Lord and listen to His voice so that we can know God as He is and find the peace and joy for which God designed us in Eden.

God's Mighty Acts and Their Interpretation

The handiwork of God's creation speaks only in muffled tones to sin-deafened ears, but God has spoken the Word to cut through our deafness and give Himself to us. While human beings have used many forms of discourse to describe reality, from philosophy to poetry, from metaphysics to fiction, God chose human history as the medium for His self-revelation. He intervenes in human history, in mighty acts of judgment and liberation. The Creator of all has made Himself a part of the history of creation in order to save His creatures from the power of sin, death, and the devil. God chose Abraham from all the people on earth to be His own, to travel to the promised land, and through him God would bless the entire earth. Abraham's descendants witnessed in the exodus God's judgment upon Egypt and His mercy toward the downtrodden and enslaved. Israel perceived His judgment upon them in the exile and His mercy toward them in the return. God's people acknowledged God's intervention to save humankind in the incarnation of His own Son, where God entered personally and directly into human history to save the creation, making Himself known in the wisdom of the cross.

Apart from God's Word and the movement of God's Spirit, these interventions in human history would be subject to the whims of human speculation. Some may have thought that the exile and return of Israel were merely coincidences—lucky circumstances—but God's Spirit moved the prophets to speak God's promise ahead of time that manifested God's intentions in the midst of the ambiguity of human history (2 Peter 1:21). In the New Testament, Jesus Himself indicated the meaning of His miracles, parables, death, and resurrection and directed the apostles to proclaim Him and His teaching for repentance and forgiveness of sins for all people (Luke 24:45–47). In Acts, Jesus sent His Spirit upon the church in order that they would be His interpreters to the world, proclaiming God's Word that reveals who we are before God and who God is for us, the true reality of all things. God likes to communicate with His creatures not through wind, earthquake, or fire, but in human language, in a still, small voice (1 Kings 19:11–13).

God's Talk and Its Written Form

God used the many and varied voices of the prophets to convey His message to His people (Hebrews 1:1), and He spoke the final, complete Word through His Son (Hebrews 1:1–2). His Word, His message for us, came in human flesh, as Jesus of Nazareth, who claimed all authority in heaven and earth because He is the author of life and the author of new life (Matthew 28:18). Human language lies at the heart of our existence. It marks us as the creatures we are, distinct in our own persons and cultures by the way we talk, yet able to communicate across linguistic lines as we learn one another's languages. Human creatures may, indeed, have feelings too deep for words. They may enjoy music and the arts without being able to express verbally what they feel. But we talk, even to ourselves. As we think, we usually organize life verbally, in propositions with subjects and verbs, implied if not stated, and certainly we cannot relate our precise thoughts to others without words. The full enjoyment of our humanity depends on verbalization. God knew that. He designed human creatures that way. Hence, God not only acted out His love in human history, but He also explained His actions through the prophets. More than that, He spoke His love directly to His people through the prophets' mouths. These prophetic voices have been made "more fully confirmed" in the record of the Holy Scripture. This prophetic word enlightens human hearts and brings the dawning of the day to lives that lay in darkness (2 Peter 1:19–21) until the true Light of the World made flesh enlightened humankind (John 1:9). This Word, Jesus Christ, represents the culmination of all God's talk (Hebrews 1:1–2). The nature and function of the Scriptures, as they give witness to God's redeeming work in history and address us with His saving love (2 Timothy 3:15–16), will be discussed in a later chapter.

God's revelation of Himself—in human flesh and in the inspired Scriptures—addresses us directly. God does not merely talk about Himself, giving us information about His character and work. God's address focuses on the relationship between Himself and His human creatures who have rebelled against Him. God thus confronts us, speaking to us in first-person, primary discourse, in order to draw us into relationship with Him by faith. God promises: "You are My child." He proclaims: "I am your God." He gushes: "I forgive you all your sins. I love you." In His voice, conveyed in the incarnate person of God, Jesus of Nazareth, in the pages of the Bible, and in the preaching and sharing of Christians with one another, such statements verbalize God's presence and power among us, according to His promise (Matthew 18:20; 28:18–20; Acts 1:8; Romans 10:8–10, 17). In the words of His Gospel He has placed the power to save (Romans 1:16).

At the same time, we must be careful not to think of God's Gospel address as purely emotional, lacking content. To be sure, God's direct address usually creates an emotional response in those who are convicted of their sin and are freed from guilt and shame through Jesus' death on the cross. But the Gospel is more than a word that comforts. Faith involves both the emotional embrace of God's promise as well as its content, expressed in propositions, in subjects and verbs. In fact, God's promise and His commands cannot be conveyed apart from propositions, propositions that introduce the person of Jesus Christ to others, tell the story of what Jesus has done, express His love for His people, and inform us of the Spirit-filled life in the Gospel. These propositions include biblical content that we are responsible to know and teach faithfully, but they are not *mere* propositions. They are human words with God's power in them. They do His work. They accomplish His purposes (Isaiah 55:11).

These human words are not magical code or mystical nonsense that must be deciphered into God's Word. They are just plain, ordinary human language, as Jesus of Nazareth was a plain, ordinary human creature. These easily apprehensible words, however, cannot be known and trusted as God's own word of command and promise without the gift of the Holy Spirit. Although the meaning of the words can be ascertained by all, the words cannot be accepted as God's voice and address without the Spirit's gift of trust. The apostle Thomas confessed that the crucified man in front of him had risen from the dead and was indeed "my Lord and my God" (John 20:28). The words are clear and easy to understand in themselves. The account makes no sense, however, unless our minds have been given the gift of grasping God's gracious intervention in human history as Jesus of Nazareth. These words are absurd until the Spirit puts us in the place of Thomas, where we make the same confession of who Jesus is and what He has done without seeing the nail marks. This lack of comprehension may be partly a human problem—creatures will never be able to get their minds completely around their Creator—but it is far more a problem of sin. Sinners resist an unpredictable God whom we cannot control, and we refuse the free goodness of God who intends to rescue us from our sin and restore us to His family.

God Addresses His Children

God's message for human creatures comes in the forms of Law and Gospel. His design for human life takes shape in commands. His gift of new life for human creatures is conveyed through His promise to be our God, His promise to regard and keep us as His children. Even those who have not been given the gift of faith can make rather accurate guesses about His design for human life. The Law speaks to fallen sinners through any number of human experiences—what was called general revelation above. But God gives access to the Gospel, to His fatherly and gracious intention for fallen sinners, only through His intended messengers: in the specific revelation of His incarnate Son, Jesus Christ; in the inspired words of the prophets and apostles—collected in Holy Scripture—as they give testimony to God's love in Christ; and in the words Christians use to convey this proclamation of His love to others by the Spirit.

The form of His specific revelation comes in an authoritative word of pronouncement. As noted in the prior chapter's discussion of epistemology, God has given His human creatures several ways to learn how human life and the world operate on the horizontal plane. Contemporary Westerners prefer knowledge that comes through experiment, logic, or aesthetic appreciation, all of which stand under human control. Authoritative knowledge, however, remains outside of the learner's control. When we learn from the voice of authority, there is no test but trust. If we acknowledge our status as creatures, then we must learn of the Creator from His voice, on the basis of His authority. Sinners prefer to do experiments or evaluate signs; they prefer to analyze rationally or evaluate wisdom. God speaks and elicits trust. Sinners regard His speaking as foolishness and weakness, but that is the form His authoritative voice takes as it conveys His power and wisdom to us (1 Corinthians 1:18–2:16). Such is the epistemology of faith.

God's specific revelation of Himself comes in personal and propositional forms. He speaks to us on a human level, through human creatures and in the human language we understand and use for sustaining daily existence. He speaks nonetheless of our sin and His grace, a subject higher than our ability to comprehend it. He tells us what we need to know—though not all that we would like to know—about Himself. He speaks to save.

God Has a Name and a History

God spoke to Moses and identified Himself: "I AM WHO I AM" (Exodus 3:14). Interpreters of this name have proposed various explanations of what it means. We may be able to see in it hints of God's eternality and the enigma of God's nature in distinction from human creatures who were not, were, are, and will be, whereas God simply is. Above all, though, the divine name remains a mystery, a sign of His grace, giving us a name to speak, but unable to figure Him out on its basis.

The ancient Jews modestly refused to let this holy name—Yahweh, as they would have spoken it if they had done so—pass through unclean lips. They simply said "the Lord" when they read His name in Scripture. North Americans want to be on a first-name basis with everyone; they have begun to call God, for the first time in the history of the church, "Yahweh." He also goes by the name "Jesus, the Christ." Unlike Yahweh, this name is quite clear. It tells us that God has come in human flesh as the promised Messiah, the anointed Rescuer and King of Israel. In human history, God claimed a name by which we could speak to Him and about Him. God claimed a name among us so that we could know Him not as an idea but as a person with a history on earth.

Hence, when God spoke to Moses at the bush, He not only gave Moses the divine name, Yahweh, He also named Himself in terms of His promises and personal relationships with His people. He is the God of Abraham, Isaac, and Jacob (Exodus 3:6). We often talk about God in terms of His attributes or His character—as, for example, the all-powerful one who is present everywhere—but God names Himself in terms of His history and His promises. God identifies Himself as the one who called Abraham, who promised to be his God and bless all people of the world through him. God identifies Himself as the one who committed to the deceiver, to Jacob, and to his descendants. God identifies Himself to us as the one come in Jesus, promised to deliver all from sin, death, and the devil through the cross and empty tomb of the Messiah. This history is not accidental or incidental to God's identity, but it is God's history among humanity by which He has identified Himself.

Some modern people want to believe that the ultimate power of the universe is not personal but rather a generic, divine force. This denial of the personhood of God may spring from human discouragement with their own persons. If I have made a wreck of my own person and my own personal relationships, I will hope for something more in my deliverer than a *mere* person. Others believe that to ascribe personhood to God is to belittle Him. God must be bigger than mere personhood. Ascribing Him personhood is anthropomorphizing Him: reducing Him to human form.

Others shy away from acknowledging God's personhood, however, because they properly recognize that the personal is superior to the impersonal. They want to contend with a divine force rather than a divine person because they sense that impersonality may even the odds between the human and the divine. Encapsulating the divine in the form of a force may tame its power. Interestingly, even when we do so, we are tempted to personalize this force, as in the Star Wars movies—"May the Force be with you." Nature may replace God but in so doing becomes our mother. Perhaps we strive against the depersonalization of God because we suspect that depersonalizing Him depersonalizes us. Reducing Him from person to force reduces us.

Of course, God "reduced" Himself to human form in the person of Jesus of Nazareth. He is the original anthropomorphizer. It is not because we cast Him in our own image that we think of Him as a person. We are only persons because God is a person. His person existed before our persons could be conceived, and we are persons because He made us in His image (Genesis 1:27; Colossians 3:10).

Thus He is the person who is, always. He is the first and the last. Before and beside Him there is no other God, no other origin and originator of all (Isaiah 44:6; 45:5). He graciously entered into the fallen world to be the God of Israel and save sinners through His eternally begotten Son, Jesus of Nazareth, and by His Spirit who proceeds from the Father and the Son. He not only deserves ultimate trust as Designer and Creator of human life (Genesis 1:27–2:25), but He also creates that trust in us, giving Himself to us in the material world of history and giving us a word of promise to grasp in faith. He is the only reliable source of ultimate identity, security, and meaning for human creatures. He is God.

The Attributes of God

When Christians think about God, the first things that come to mind are often divine attributes, characteristics of what God is like. God, for instance, is free and sovereign, gracious and loving. Such descriptions certainly flow from the biblical account of God and His history with His creation. We must be careful, however, not to allow our understanding of God's attributes to determine who God is, but recognize the attributes as descriptions of what God is like on the basis of His revelation of Himself. In other words, we should not allow our human understanding of certain attributes to dictate what God "must" be like. Instead, we should see the attributes of God as descriptions God has said about Himself in the Word made flesh and the testimony of the prophets and apostles in Holy Scripture.

The seventeenth-century Lutheran theologian Johann Andreas Quenstedt listed the attributes of God: perfection, majesty, blessedness, unity, simplicity; He is spirit, invisible, faithful, good, independent of all else, eternal, immeasurable, omnipresent, immutable, and unable to be grasped by His creatures. He possesses life, immortality, the ultimate intellect, all knowledge and wisdom. He embodies will, freedom, kindness, love, grace, mercy, patience, holiness, righteousness, power, and truth.[5] Quenstedt and his contemporaries divided their lists of God's attributes into categories: those that describe God in terms not applicable to humans (eternal, infinite) and those that apply to humans in a lesser way (good, wise); those that speak of God in Himself (eternal) and those that speak of Him in relationship to His human creatures (gracious); those that describe Him positively (good) and those that describe Him negatively (immeasurable). Both the philosophical tradition of the West and the Scriptures had provided material for such lists and classifications.

The biblical writers described God largely in terms of His encounters with human creatures and often through titles that embraced certain characteristics. In the Old Testament, God is frequently described as the King of His people, and royal characteristics are ascribed to Him. God the King rules with power and glory forever; this King is praised for being faithful and gracious, for preserving and providing for His people and for hearing their cries (Psalm 145:11–20; cf. Psalms 93, 96, 97, 99). This King functions as Judge, Ruler, and Savior (Isaiah 33:22). He dwells in the midst of His people and replaces their fears and weaknesses with gladness and joy as He renews them in His love, as He removes disaster from them, brings them home, and restores their fortunes (Zephaniah 3:15–20). God the King subdues other peoples and chooses His own people for Himself (Psalm 47).

In the New Testament, God is still acknowledged as King in ascriptions of praise (1 Timothy 1:17; 6:15; Revelation 15:3). His rule is frequently expressed in terms of His reign and kingdom (Matthew 6:33). But Christ directs prayer to God not as King but as "Father" (Matthew 6:9; Luke 11:2). Paul came before God in prayer with the intimate cry, "*Abba*, Father" (Romans 8:15; Galatians 4:6). Paul began most of his letters with acknowledgment of God as Father (Romans 1:7; 1 Corinthians 1:3; 2 Corinthians 1:2; Galatians 1:3; Ephesians 1:2; Philippians 1:2; Colossians 1:2; 1 Thessalonians 1:1; 2 Thessalonians 1:2; 1 Timothy 1:2; 2 Timothy 1:2; Titus 1:4). Peter also called God "Father" (1 Peter 1:17). God the Father is glorious (Ephesians 1:17) and worthy of thanksgiving (Ephesians 5:20). This Father has chosen and predestined His people to be His own family (Ephesians 1:3–6; 1 Peter 1:2) and stands as their judge (1 Peter 1:17). This Father has qualified His people to share in the inheritance of the saints, has delivered them from the kingdom of darkness and transferred them into His own Son's kingdom (Colossians 1:12–14). This Father embraces His children, loving them and giving them eternal encouragement and good hope through His grace (2 Thessalonians 2:16–17).

5 Johann Andreas Quenstedt, *Theologia Didactico-Polemica* (Wittenberg, 1685), 1:284–85.

Where God has chosen to be known above all is in His Son, Jesus Christ. Jesus says, "Whoever has seen Me has seen the Father" (John 14:9). Paul adds that Jesus "is the image of the invisible God" (Colossians 1:15). The author of Hebrews proclaims that the Son of God "is the radiance of the glory of God and the exact imprint of His nature" (Hebrews 1:3). Hence, the Bible does not normally call God "Father" because human beings are His creatures, *but* because they have been brought into fellowship with the Son. Jesus makes us His own sisters and brothers and thus children of the heavenly Father, who know God as true King and loving Father through Calvary's cross and the empty tomb. Through the cross, God's omnipotent rule is revealed in the weakness of death, and His holiness is revealed in shame—all for the sake of reconciling sinners to Himself by His Son. Only in Christ, the wisdom and power of God (1 Corinthians 1:24), do we know God and His attributes aright.

The Trinity

As God has made Himself known through the prophets and apostles, God shows Himself to be one (Deuteronomy 6:4), yet never alone. In other words, the Scriptures reveal God to be more complex than one singular person. Already in the Old Testament, hints of divine complexity permeate the patriarchal history, the Prophets, and the Psalms. For instance, the Angel of the Lord—an essential and pervasive figure in the Old Testament—speaks about God, yet also speaks *for* God, suggesting that this messenger is both distinct from God and one with God (e.g., Genesis 22:11–12, 15–18). Other figures such as the Spirit, Wisdom, and the Son of Man also point toward this divine complexity. In the New Testament, three figures stand out as divine who are united in substance, identity, and the story of redemption: the Father, the Son, and the Holy Spirit. Jesus calls Himself one with the Father as the beloved Son (John 10:30), yet also prays to the Father and invites His disciples to pray to the same Father in the Spirit (Luke 11:1–13). The Spirit, too, has the same divine characteristics as the Father and the Son while also being distinct from the Father and the Son. Human minds may be unable to grasp fully this mystery of one God who is three distinct persons, but we must learn to confess with Holy Scriptures that the three distinct persons of the Father, Son, and Holy Spirit constitute the one God.

The Christian dogma of the **Trinity** comes from this biblical testimony. The term *Trinity* cannot be found in the Bible even though the triune revelation of God is apparent in Holy Scripture. The term expresses the biblical reality that the three (tri-) are truly unified (-nity): the Father sent His only-begotten Son in the Spirit who binds them together in love so that by the Son's death and resurrection the Spirit might bring the fallen creation to praise the Father through the Son in the Spirit. These three are the one God.

On the one hand, the basic formulation of the Trinity is expressed quite simply: God is three distinct persons in unity. Otherwise stated, the Father, Son, and Holy Spirit are equally divine persons who constitute the one God. On the other hand, a unity of three does not follow mathematical logic but is an ineffable and incomprehensible mystery. We are used to a linear rationality where one plus one equals two, but the logic of the Trinity is different: relational and even circular, a matter of special revelation. Each divine person is not without the others as each *is* in relation to one another. The Spirit is the Spirit of the Father and the Son, working to bring the fallen creation to believe in the Son and give praise to the Father. The Son is the Son of the Father whose life in the Spirit testifies to the almighty Father as He unites sinners to Himself through the same Spirit that abides in Him. The Father is the Father of the Son who sends out both Son and Spirit to incorporate even the fallen creation into this divine dance of love. The three are one not only in characteristics—attributes—but in the story of creation and redemption, in the divine history by which God creates all things in love and seeks to bring all things into His love by the Son in the Spirit to the praise of the Father in the life of the age to come.

The New Testament Confession of Jesus Christ

This dogma of the Trinity may not be easy to understand, but it reflects the earliest conviction of Christ's followers that Jesus claimed to be God, one with the almighty Father. It reflects the apostolic assertion that the Holy Spirit is also God, which will be addressed in a later section. The New Testament in particular witnesses to the reality that the Son and the Spirit are one God with the Father.

Among the earliest of Christian confessions was the simple formulation "Jesus is Lord" (1 Corinthians 12:3).[6] That confession went to the heart of the matter. It affirmed the lordship of Jesus not only over against Caesar of the Romans—who claimed to be lord and among the gods—but also as inseparable in identity with Yahweh, the Lord. God Himself proclaimed through the prophet Isaiah: "Thus says the Lord, the King of Israel and His Redeemer, the Lord of hosts: 'I am the first and I am the last; besides Me there is no god'" (Isaiah 44:6). In this light, the New Testament links Yahweh's identity to Jesus of Nazareth, confessing Him to be God come in

6 J. N. D. Kelly, *Early Christian Creeds* (New York: McKay, 1960).

human flesh.[7] When Thomas confessed the resurrected Jesus to be "my Lord and my God," he was confessing Jesus to be one with the God revealed by the prophets, Yahweh, who saved Israel from slavery in Egypt and now was doing a new thing in the crucified and resurrected Christ (John 20:28).

The apostle Paul—in one of the earliest writings of the New Testament—expressed the same conviction in his letter to the church at Philippi. According to Paul, because of Christ's humiliation to death upon the cross, "God has highly exalted Him and bestowed on Him the name that is above every name" (Philippians 2:9). The name in question is not Jesus, the personal name of the Messiah, but the sacred name of God, the tetragrammaton, YHWH.[8] In sharing the name of God, Jesus shares the glory of God, the worship of God, and must be Himself true God. Paul continued in Philippians to say that on the Last Day every human being will worship Jesus and every person recognize Him as true Lord of the earth: "At the name of Jesus every knee should bow, in heaven and on earth and under the earth, and every tongue confess that Jesus Christ is Lord, to the glory of God the Father" (Philippians 2:10–11). In this way, Paul shows that Jesus deserves worship in the way that only God does; Jesus is the true Lord of the world, deserving of praise that gives glory to His Father. Particularly striking is that Paul's confession of Jesus echoes the words of the prophet Isaiah, spoken by God Himself: "To Me every knee shall bow, every tongue shall swear allegiance" (Isaiah 45:23).[9] Only one conclusion holds together Paul's logic: Jesus is not a mere man or even a lesser divine being but is true God with the Father.

John the evangelist also professed that the same Jesus is God come in the flesh. "In the beginning was the Word, and the Word was with God, and the Word was God" (John 1:1). John emphasizes that the same Word, who is one with the Father, became a true human being: "And the Word became flesh and dwelt among us, and we have seen His glory, glory as of the only Son from the Father, full of grace and truth" (John 1:14). The middle of John's Gospel includes Jesus' claim that "I and the Father are one" (John 10:30) and the many "I am" statements from Jesus' own lips, which echo the Greek of the divine name. At the end of the Gospel, the confession of Jesus as true God comes to the fore again as Thomas confesses Jesus to be "my Lord and my God," and Jesus blesses us who do not see what

---

7 Luke's Gospel links Jesus' identity with Yahweh's, especially in Luke's use of the title "Lord." See C. Kavin Rowe, *Early Narrative Christology: The Lord in the Gospel of Luke* (Berlin: de Gruyter, 2006).

8 Richard Bauckham, *God Crucified: Monotheism and Christology in the New Testament* (Grand Rapids: Eerdmans, 1998), 34.

9 Bauckham, *God Crucified*, 52.

Thomas saw and yet believe the same (John 20:28–29). To be clear, it is not that Jesus is the same person as the Father—the distinction of the persons also comes out in Holy Scripture since the Word become flesh is *both* God and *with* God (John 1:1)—but that Jesus is one of the Trinity, come into the flesh, true God with the Father and the Spirit, distinct in personhood while unified in substance.

In addition to these specific passages that speak of Jesus' identity with the Father, we also need to recognize that the Bible shows Jesus doing work that only God can do, having characteristics that only God can have, and deserving of honor that only God deserves. Jesus creates (John 1:3; 1 Corinthians 8:6; Hebrews 1:2–3), saves (Romans 3:24–25; 5:6–11, 17; 1 Peter 2:24), judges (Matthew 26:64; Acts 17:31; Revelation 22:12), and reveals the Father's heart (John 1:18; 14:7; Colossians 1:15; Hebrews 1:3). Jesus is eternal (John 8:58), omniscient (John 16:30), omnipotent (Matthew 28:18), and omnipresent (Matthew 18:20; 28:20). Jesus receives human worship, prayer, and praise (Matthew 2:11; 14:33; 28:17; John 9:38; Philippians 2:10; Revelation 5:8–14).[10] Jesus calls Himself the "Son of Man," identifying Himself with Daniel's vision of "one like a son of man," who has divine attributes and is coming to judge all things (Daniel 7:13–14; Matthew 26:63–65).[11] The Scriptures not only have specific passages that assert Jesus' true divinity, but the overall scope and story of the Bible point in the same direction: the eternally begotten Son of God became flesh through the Spirit to bring the fallen creation back to the Father through the cross and empty tomb.

The Heretical Counterclaims

The claim that Jesus is one God with the Father was a little difficult for many to believe. In fact, it was impossible to believe apart from the Holy Spirit's gift of faith (1 Corinthians 12:3). It is little wonder that Jews in particular, who confessed that God was completely distinct from His creatures and was one single Lord (Deuteronomy 6:4), found it difficult to accept Jesus' claim to be the Son of Man, and thus one identity with the Lord God. In the succeeding three centuries, people who wanted to follow Jesus but who also felt compelled to make sense of His claim to be God formulated a number of heretical solutions, trying to find logical ways to get out of the Bible's assertion that God has come into the flesh in Jesus of Nazareth.

Modalistic Monarchianism. One heretical solution was provided by the modalistic monarchians, who taught that the one ruler (Greek: *monarch*) or God appeared in three different modes, as Father, Son, and

10 See Larry W. Hurtado, *How on Earth Did Jesus Become a God? Historical Questions about Earliest Devotion to Jesus* (Grand Rapids: Eerdmans, 2005).

11 For the significance of "Son of Man" as a divine title, see chapter 8.

Holy Spirit, but did not consist of three distinct persons. **Modalism**, as it is commonly called, recognizes the true divinity of each person but denies real distinctions among the persons. For modalistic monarchians, the actor or person behind the Father, the Son, and the Holy Spirit is always the same—God—just with a different appearance during different times and places. Modalistic monarchianism was also called **patripassianism**, which literally means "the Father suffers." Modalism can be so called because if the Son is the same person as the Father, the Father suffered on the cross but in the mode of the Son.[12] Modalism remains a common misunderstanding of the Trinity among lay Christians who have learned to focus on the unity of God without recognizing the distinctions among the divine persons.

Dynamic Monarchianism. Another heretical solution was proposed by an ancient group known as the Ebionites, who taught a version of dynamic monarchianism, commonly known as **adoptionism**. In dynamic monarchianism, the Father is the lone divine monarch who chooses, adopts, a good man to be His son by placing a power—*dynamis* in Greek—in him. It is as if God looked down from heaven and saw how good of a man Jesus was, and because of his moral and spiritual superiority, God sent His spirit upon Jesus at his Baptism (or at the resurrection or ascension), placing a special power upon him and calling Jesus His son. In this heresy, the son is not eternally God like the Father, but a creature who was made to be God's son by virtue of his excellence. Although the ancient church rejected this view as heresy, it has recurred from time to time among Gnostics, Unitarians, and other sectarian Christian groups.[13]

Subordinationism. In the ancient world, the heresy of subordinationism stood out as a pernicious heresy regarding the Trinity. It was named subordinationism because the Son of God was believed to be subordinate to, or less than, the Father, not equal in identity or attributes. A theologian from Alexandria, Arius (ca. 250–336), taught subordinationism—often designated **Arianism** because Arius was a chief advocate—in trying to defend the unity of God. In order to protect God from the mutable and sinful world, Arius focused on Jesus as the Word of God through whom all things came into being. He fit the term *Word* from John 1 into the framework of contemporary Neoplatonic thought, claiming that the Son of God was the first creature of God, through whom God created everything else, and thus of a different substance or essence than God. For Arius, the Son is not eternal

---

12 J. N. D. Kelly, *Early Christian Doctrines* (New York: Harper & Row, 1960), 119–23; Jaroslav Pelikan, *The Emergence of the Catholic Tradition (100–600)*, vol. 1 of *The Christian Tradition: A History of the Development of Doctrine* (Chicago: University of Chicago Press, 1971), 176–82.

13 For more detail on adoptionism, see chapter 8.

or immutable as the Father is. Rather, the Son stemmed from God's will or choice at a particular moment, and there had been "a time when he was not." According to Arius, the Son of God is more divine than other creatures, but He is not equal to God the Father. He was a being not so completely perfect as God Himself.[14]

"Of One Substance with the Father": The Unity of Persons in the Nicene Creed

Arius's teaching encountered much opposition within Alexandria, Egypt, and throughout the Christian Church in the fourth century. The most notable of Arius's opponents was a fellow pastor in Alexandria who later became bishop of the city: Athanasius (ca. 293–373). After their argument over the status of the Son of God blew up to encompass church leaders throughout the Roman world, an ecumenical—whole church—council was called at Nicaea in 325. The Nicene Creed began there, although the Nicene Creed as it is confessed in Christian churches today was further developed at the Council of Constantinople in 381. The original Nicene Creed sought to reject Arius above all,[15] but Athanasius, Basil the Great, and Gregory of Nyssa, among others, confessed the creed as a true exhibition of Holy Scripture. In other words, the Nicene Creed, these theologians insisted, confessed the biblical teaching that Jesus Christ is God in human flesh. It may have done so in terms current in the theological debates of the time, influenced as they were by contemporary philosophical presuppositions, but Nicene theology intended to speak scriptural truth in the Roman Empire of the fourth century.[16]

Against Arius's belief that the Son was subordinate to the Father, the Nicene Creed confessed that the Son of God is "God of God, light of light, very God of very God." The Son was not made or created but "begotten of His Father before all worlds," using John's enigmatic description of Jesus as "only begotten" (John 1:14; 3:16 KJV). The point was not that the Son was begotten—fathered—like other human beings are, but the Son is *eternally* begotten, forever the Son of the Father. Thus there was no time when the Son was not the Son of the Father, and the Father was not the Father of the Son. The Father and Son are inseparable and united in identity, just as they

14 Kelly, *Early Christian Doctrines*, 223–51; Pelikan, *Emergence of the Catholic Tradition*, 191–200. Compare Oskar Skarsaune, *Incarnation: Myth or Fact*, trans. Trygve R. Skarsten (St. Louis: Concordia, 1991), 98–101. For a longer explanation of subordinationism, see chapter 8.

15 Lewis Ayres, *Nicaea and Its Legacy: An Approach to Fourth-Century Trinitarian Theology* (Oxford: Oxford University Press, 2004), 99.

16 Ayres, *Nicaea and Its Legacy*, 39.

are one in substance or essential characteristics. In fact, the most important formulation of the Nicene Creed speaks to exactly this complete unity of substance. The creed states that the Son is "of one [the same] substance" [Greek: *homoousious*] with the Father. The Son is not less than, unlike, or even merely similar to the Father in essence, but the Father and the Son share the same substance (also with the Spirit). In less formal terms, there is no difference between Father and Son with regard to their divinity. What the Father is, so the Son is (and so the Spirit is), as the Athanasian Creed maintains. What the Father does, so the Son does (and so the Spirit does), as encapsulated in the ancient maxim *opera Trinitatis ad extra indivisa sunt*—the works of the Trinity to the outside are indivisible. The Nicene Creed affirmed in the language appropriate to its time what the prophets and the apostles confessed about the Christ: He is God.[17] In so doing, the Nicene Creed enables reading the Bible to see its truth. What Jesus does in His incarnation, ministry, cross, and resurrection is no mere human work, but it is the work of the Creator to save His sinful creatures in the throes of death and the devil.

Although disputes over the divinity of the Holy Spirit were less prominent, the church had to defend the biblical teaching in this regard as well. Jesus Himself had affirmed that the Holy Spirit is true God by warning against blaspheming the Spirit (Matthew 12:31), and Peter equated the Holy Spirit with God in a similar admonition to Ananias (Acts 5:4). Moreover, the Holy Spirit does what God does: re-creates, regenerates, and renews the people of God as the Spirit brings them into new life (Titus 3:5). The Spirit may not come to the fore as often as Jesus does in Holy Scripture, but when the Spirit is revealed, God's attributes and God's work are clear in the Spirit. Accordingly, both Christ and Paul affirm the equality of the Spirit with the Father and the Son (Matthew 28:19; 2 Corinthians 13:14).

The teaching of the church on the Trinity was summarized in a litany that assumed the status of a creed. Named for St. Athanasius, whose teaching lay at its heart, it reflects some later doctrinal developments regarding both the Trinity and Christology. Probably written in the fifth century, the Athanasian Creed confesses that God is one God, with three persons; the Godhead is not divided, and the persons are not to be confused with one another. All three persons are uncreated, incomprehensible, eternal, and almighty, yet there are not three uncreated, incomprehensible, eternal, and almighty gods but only one. All three are God and Lord, but there are not three Lords or three Gods but only one.

---

17 Kelly, *Early Christian Doctrines*, 252–69; Pelikan, *Emergence of the Catholic Tradition*, 211–24. Compare Skarsaune, *Incarnation*, 98–111.

The Trinity Is Three Distinct Persons

The Father is God, the Son is God, and the Spirit is God, but these three are one God. Although the three are one in **substance**, as the ecumenical creeds confess, the three are distinct in **person**. The divine identity unfolds itself in the relations of these three persons, who constitute the one God. This is an unfathomable mystery for human reasoning. The church has described the distinctions of one person of the Godhead from another by using biblical terms to point to these distinctions even though we are unable to analyze the inner relationships of the Godhead directly. The church seized upon John's designation of Christ as "the only begotten Son" (John 3:16, 18 KJV) and upon Christ's description of the Holy Spirit as one who "proceeds from the Father" (John 15:26) to point to the inner distinctions within the Trinity. Although the latter context refers to God's mission during which the Father sends the Spirit on His people for ministry to the world—and not to the inner workings of the Godhead directly—these biblical terms are useful for affirming the distinctions of the persons while confessing their unity in the Godhead. The Father is neither begotten nor proceeding; the Son is begotten but not proceeding; the Spirit is not begotten but proceeding.

The eternal God is neither an all-powerful monad nor three independent personalities, but three distinct persons deeply intertwined in love. The Father loves the Son eternally and freely in the Spirit. The Son loves the Father in return in the same Spirit who binds them in this unity. This is what we see in the story of Scripture as the Father sends His beloved Son in the Spirit, and the Spirit moves through the Son to enact God's own reign on earth as it is in heaven to the glory of the Father. After the resurrection, the Son with the Father sends the Spirit onto the church so that God's mission of salvation goes out to the world. Through the proclamation of repentance and forgiveness, the Spirit graciously draws that which is not God into the love of God, drawing the creation that had rebelled against its Creator and Lord into the divine life as sinners receive the promise of everlasting life through the Spirit by faith in the Son to the glory of God the Father.

While the words "unbegotten" and "not proceeding," "begotten," and "proceeding" signify the distinctions among the Father, Son, and Spirit with regard to their relationships, just as central to biblical logic are the distinctions of the persons in terms of the mission of God, the story of salvation. In Holy Scripture, the Father is the sender who is never sent. The Father sends out His Son and His Spirit for the salvation of the world, but He Himself is never sent. The Son is sent by the Father through the power of the Spirit to become a human being in the incarnation. Neither the Spirit nor the

Father are incarnate but only the Son. The Spirit alone was borne by the Son, anointing Jesus in His Baptism to begin His ministry as the Christ of God (Mark 1:10), driving Him to the wilderness to be tempted (Mark 1:12), and raising Him from the dead (Romans 1:4). The Spirit, too, was sent upon the church by Jesus and His Father to bring repentance and forgiveness of sins to the world (John 20:22–23). Although the entire Trinity participates in the work of each person—the three do not act independently but interdependently in love—each person also has a distinct role as part of God's mission of salvation.

In the story of salvation, then, the Father is the sender, the Son becomes a human being to suffer and die for the sins of the world, and the Spirit alights on the Son, propels Him to mission, and is sent by the Son and the Father on the church. Through the work of the Son and Spirit, the sinful creation is brought into the bosom of the almighty Father. This account can be summarized as the *a pater, ad patrem*—from the Father, to the Father—emphasizing the trinitarian mission that begins with the Father, is enacted through the Son and the Spirit, and is finished when all things are given over to the Father to His glory (1 Corinthians 15:24–28). In this story, there is only one God who does the one work of salvation by the three distinct persons of the Father, Son, and Holy Spirit.

Although each person has a unique role in the mission of God, the three can only be distinguished from one another in their work in these specific instances. What one person of God does, the whole Trinity does, according to the Bible. Although we often speak as if the Father creates, the Son saves, and the Spirit sanctifies (makes holy), that is not strictly true. The Bible does *often* speak that way, but not exclusively, which has given rise to a doctrine known as **attribution**. Because the Father is generally spoken of as Creator in the Bible, we attribute creation to the Father. At the same time, the Son creates (John 1:3; 1 Corinthians 8:6; Colossians 1:16; Hebrews 1:2) and the Spirit creates (Genesis 1:2; 2:7; Psalm 33:6). We attribute salvation to the Son, but the Father saves (John 3:16; Romans 3:26; Ephesians 1:4–6; Titus 3:4–7) and the Spirit saves (John 3:5; 16:8–11; Galatians 4:6–7; Titus 3:4–7). By attribution, we speak of the Spirit dwelling in Christians by faith for the purpose of sanctification, but the Bible asserts that the whole Trinity abides in Christians by faith (John 14:23–26; Romans 8:9–11; 1 Corinthians 6:19–20; 2 Corinthians 13:5; Ephesians 3:16–19). Despite the fact that each divine person has a distinct role in the mission of God, their work is also indistinguishable as the whole Godhead creates, saves, and sustains the people of God by faith until the resurrection of the dead and the life of the age to come.

THE FILIOQUE: THE SPIRIT PROCEEDS FROM THE FATHER *AND THE SON*

Although the Nicene Creed is the one truly ecumenical creed, confessed throughout the world, Christians of the Eastern Orthodox confession have criticized the Western catholic tradition for asserting that the Holy Spirit proceeds from the Son as well as from the Father. The center of this debate is the Latin term *filioque*, which literally means "and the Son." The idea of the double procession of the Spirit has been part of Western Christianity since the fourth and fifth centuries through the influence of St. Augustine. It was widespread enough that it was referenced at the third council of Toledo in 589, even though it may not have been added to the Nicene Creed until the time of Charlemagne in the eighth century.[18] Eastern Orthodox Christians criticize Western Christians on this point because John 15:26 mentions only the Spirit proceeding from the Father, and the unity of the Trinity is threatened if the Son is understood as equally the origin of the Spirit with the Father.[19] (The more germane reason, however, may be the fact that the Western Church adopted this word without consultation or discussion with the East.) To be fair, the Western Church was responding to the ongoing influence of Arianism, as some used the notion that the Spirit proceeds only from the Father to allege the Father's superiority over the Son. Against this, the Western Church affirmed the full divinity of Christ by adding the *filioque* to the Nicene Creed. Since the term in the creed refers to the relationships among the three persons of the Trinity—and is only borrowed for this purpose from John 15:26—it may properly be used in this way.[20] After all, the confession that the Spirit proceeds also from the Son asserts the full interrelations of the three who are one and stresses the complete equality of each divine person within the Godhead.

It has been said that the formulation of the dogma of the Trinity reduced the biblical message to Greek philosophical categories and abstracted its living vitality into foreign forms of thought. This is not so. Instead, in formulating trinitarian language, Athanasius, Gregory of Nyssa, and the pro-Nicene theologians built a bridge from the biblical message into the thought

18 Charles P. Arand, Robert Kolb, and James A. Nestingen, *The Lutheran Confessions: History and Theology of the Book of Concord* (Minneapolis: Fortress, 2012), 35.

19 See David Bentley Hart, "The Myth of Schism," in *The Hidden and the Manifest: Essays in Theology and Metaphysics* (Grand Rapids: Eerdmans, 2017).

20 Kelly, *Early Christian Creeds*, 358-67; Pelikan, *Emergence of the Catholic Tradition*, 212, 293; Jaroslav Pelikan, *The Spirit of Eastern Christendom (600–1700)*, vol. 2 of *The Christian Tradition: A History of the Development of Doctrine* (Chicago: University of Chicago Press, 1974), 183–98.

world of their own day, effectively combating attempts to subvert the biblical message into cultural forms that misrepresented it.

The truth of the Holy Trinity that they confessed is just as essential for us today. Whether we encounter denials of the fundamental teaching of Scripture in mainline Christianity or in sects such as the Jehovah's Witnesses, we must confront them with the plain argument of Holy Scripture. Jesus and His earliest followers claimed Him to be God in human flesh. Every biblical expression of this confession that Jesus is God should be marshaled to combat such rejections of the heart of God's revelation of His love for fallen sinners. Even the earliest written texts of the New Testament—the epistles of the fiercely monotheistic Jew, Paul—speak powerfully to the confession that Jesus the Christ is God and Lord with the Father.[21] The New Testament may not have a developed doctrine of the Trinity, but the unity and distinctions of Father, Son, and Spirit are apparent in its pages.

We dare never forget that human wisdom cannot pierce the mystery of God's internal makeup or working. We can only confess the wonder of His being and the beauty of His work for us. At the same time, we must be bold to confess the reality of what God has said about Himself. Our God is one Lord and three persons, distinct within the Godhead but eternally inseparable. Only when we confess the Trinity can we see the depth of the good news of the Gospel: Jesus is God come down to save in human flesh, giving His own body to death on the cross that sinners might not die eternally but receive the Holy Spirit, also true God, as a seal of eternal life to the glory of God the Father.

---

21 See Bauckham, *God Crucified*.

CHAPTER 3
THE CREATOR AND HIS CREATION

IN the beginning, God *created* …" (Genesis 1:1). Creation is not a secondary aspect of God's work, nor is it merely one activity among many that characterize divinity. Creation identifies who God is and how God relates to everything else. God is Creator, Progenitor, and Father. He cares about us, and He loves us. He protects us and provides for us. He is the ultimate source of our identity, security, and meaning. God, then, is the very center of our lives, and it is impossible to marginalize Him. He is either there, where He belongs, or He is absent, thrown out of our lives. As Creator, God establishes His authority over what He has made, making Himself not only the originator of all that is but also the giver of life, health, and purpose, who sustains all things from beginning to end. In short, the Creator determines the creatures, making us dependent receivers who rely completely on our generous and gracious God.

Although the doctrine of creation brings to mind the original creation at the beginning, we first encounter the Creator not as the one who brought forth the universe but as the gracious giver of all things. We simply recognize ourselves as alive, breathing, hearing, feeling, talking, being loved, and loving. We did not bring ourselves into the world. We did not create our bodies or souls, or form the relationships that make life worth living. We were given everything from the outside, as gifts. Hence, Luther confesses the meaning of the First Article of the Apostles' Creed with reference not to the origin of the world but to God's continuous giving of identity, security, and meaning to *me*:

> I believe that God has made me together with all creatures; that He has given me my body and soul, eyes, ears, and all my members, my reason and all my senses, and still takes care of them. He also gives me clothing and shoes, food and drink, house and home, spouse and children, land, animals, and all I have. He richly and daily provides me with all that I need to support this body and life. He defends me against all danger and guards and protects me in the face of all evil. All this He does only out of fatherly,

> divine goodness and mercy, without any merit or worthiness in me. For all this it is my duty to thank and praise, serve and obey Him.[1]

According to the doctrine of creation, Christians not only confess God as maker but also learn to trust in Him as giver, depending on Him for all things.

Chapter 4 will focus on who we are as human creatures and what that means for our identities and lives of faith. This chapter focuses on who God is as the Creator and the structure of the creation that God brought into being. It is easy to overlook the significance of God's creative work, but the Scriptures continually point to God not only as Savior but as Creator who is over all and through all and in all.

In the Beginning, God

"In the beginning, God ..." (Genesis 1:1): so begins Holy Scripture in its canonical order. John's Gospel reveals to us the same reality of God who stands "before" the beginning: "In the beginning was the Word, and the Word was with God, and the Word was God" (John 1:1). When there was no when, God spoke and time began. When there was no space or form or thing, God's Word made the heavens and the earth. When there was not yet darkness, God brought forth light by the power of His voice.

In our contemporary age, we cannot help but think of creation—Genesis 1 and 2—in scientific terms. From elementary school, science classes teach the wonders of nature: the diversity of life in all its forms, the 200 billion galaxies in the universe, the 200 billion trillion stars, and the presumed billions of planets. Genesis 1, though, hardly speaks to these matters, and certainly not in the same way or with the same detail as modern science. Many people, both Christian and non-Christian, want Scripture to speak to scientific concerns and issues that contemporary people have. We think scientifically about the world, and we want to match scientific processes and accounts of the origins of creation with the order in Genesis. On the one hand, conservative Christians want to prove the scientific truth of the Genesis account. In using current scientific standards for determining the truth, they surrender the battlefield just as the battle begins. The so-called new atheists, on the other hand, want to disprove the Scriptures by showing how Genesis 1 does not correspond to the hypotheses of modern science. Although conservative Christians and new atheists disagree completely in their beliefs, both think that Genesis 1 can find meaning only in its correspondence to currently held scientific theories.

1 Small Catechism II 1 (translation adjusted).

The Bible, however, is largely uninterested in a contemporary, scientific account of the universe. The Scriptures do tell us what is real—they are not metaphoric or symbolic—but they do not testify to God or the world in a scientific way. The Word witnesses to the wonder of many and various creatures and the wise order instituted by the Creator.[2] In this way, the Bible reveals the reality of God and ourselves, the Creator and the creatures, revealing the good news of our Creator and His design for creaturely life. The Scriptures speak beyond the contemporary, narrow emphasis on scientific explanation and material causality to testify to God as the Creator, Giver, and Provider of all things without any merit or worthiness in us. We do well to listen to Scripture speak on its own terms rather than transforming it into a scientific tongue.

Central to a theological understanding of the Creator is that God created all things out of nothing. Although Genesis 1 and John 1 do not state this doctrine directly, God's creation from nothing is implied. "In the beginning, God ..." not only confesses that God created the heavens and the earth, all that is, but also that there was a beginning, to which we cannot return. No matter how advanced we become technologically, we are unable to look back and see what is prior to the beginning. In fact, whatever we see through our scientific instruments is severely limited. We can only view the universe through our limited perspective, limited both by the particularities of being human creatures on the third rock from the sun and by the fact that we live at the beginning of the third millennium after the Christ. No matter how hard we may try to see the earliest light from the universe, we cannot get to the beginning or beyond it. The limit has been reached. None of us is the Creator. We were simply born into a relationship with Him. This Creator, Scripture confesses, is the one who precedes the beginning and thus transcends us and all creation. We exist only because the Creator exists, and He made us and all things. This reality of God as the one who transcends His creatures reminds us that the universe exists at His good pleasure and because of His love. The universe *is* because the Creator made it.

God Created All Out of Nothing

The Bible confesses that the triune God—Father, Son, and Holy Spirit—existed "before" the beginning, and everything came into being by the breath and word of God's mouth (Psalm 33:6). The apostle Paul proclaims that God "calls into existence the things that do not exist" (Romans 4:17). Through the prophet Isaiah, God Himself declares, "I am the Lord, who

2 See the description of St. Basil's understanding of Genesis 1 in Matthew Levering, *Engaging the Doctrine of Creation: Cosmos, Creatures, and the Wise and Good Creator* (Grand Rapids: Baker Academic, 2017), 128–34

made all things, who alone stretched out the heavens, who spread out the earth by Myself" (Isaiah 44:24). According to the witness of the prophets and apostles, God made everything *ex nihilo*, **out of nothing**. God did not have some preexisting matter at hand because nothing is eternally coexistent with God. This is difficult to describe. The writer to the Hebrews asserts it as best he can: God fashioned what is seen out of that which did not have appearance—literally, that which was not a phenomenon (Hebrews 11:3). We see the same belief confessed in the psalms: God "spoke, and it came to be; He commanded, and it stood firm" (Psalm 33:9). God's voice resounded, and space and time came to be, along with all of the energy and material within the cosmos. Nothing was until the Father spoke the Word by the Spirit that made all things come into being.

While Christians have always confessed the world to be the handiwork of God, for others throughout human history, the universe has not been considered creation at all—that is, the product of a divine, creative agent. Some ancient philosophers posited the eternality of matter and postulated various means of organizing this eternal "stuff" by an external hand or an internal force. Others in the ancient world contradicted the biblical view of the goodness of the material creation by defining matter as a corruption of the good, eternal spiritual essence. They believed that the visible, material world only exists because of a fall from original perfection, which was spiritual and invisible. Very few modern thinkers hold this second position as an origin story—though many elements of its worldview remain. Instead, contemporary scientists continue to theorize how matter, or energy, could be eternal. Whether there are infinitely many universes or an infinite cycle of universes, the motive remains the same: matter is not created but always is.

For the Christian faith, only God is, and the fact that God created all things from nothing is significant for two reasons. First, creation from nothing asserts the full and complete lordship of God, God's **sovereignty** and freedom. The creation is His. He made it and us. He is the Lord. Nothing can prevent God from having His way with His creation. This reality would be scary or frightening if God were anyone other than Jesus and His Father united in love by the Holy Spirit, revealed to us through the prophets and apostles. Because Jesus is one of the Trinity come in human flesh, it is good news that God is the King of all creation. God does not rule primarily by power but by love, the same love crucified and risen from the dead for the salvation of the world. If matter itself was eternal, God could be the shaper and molder of all that is, but He would not be its rightful King. God would be in charge only by virtue of His power. God, however, does not rule the creation like some tyrant who wants to do what is best for himself at the expense of his subjects. God rules for the sake of His creatures. God created in love and preserves all things in love so that His human creatures can be incorporated into the same love of the Father and the Son in the Spirit and reflect that love back to God and to other creatures. God is the true Lord as He created all things from nothing and continues to uphold the universe by His Word and Spirit.

Related to this, second, human creatures are not gods or lords in any sense. We are the clay, and God is the potter. He is the Creator, and we are the creatures. God is totally and qualitatively different from us as creatures. He is sovereign and free; we are dependent. He gives; we receive. Although the good news of the Gospel proclaims that even this wholly other Creator became a man and lived a fully human life in our place, we dare not forget the otherness of the Creator. That God made all things from nothing establishes a dividing wall between creatures and the Creator that we cannot pass. He is God; we are not. We are fully in His hands from our creation from nothing to our bodies turning back to dust, waiting for the great resurrection day. And in the hands of our gracious Creator and loving Giver is exactly where believers want to be.

The Character of the Creator

A commonplace observation among biblical scholars is that Genesis 1 and 2 are two distinct stories of creation. Although this observation can be misleading—we must recognize Genesis 1 and 2 as complementary accounts of God's creative activity, one focused more on the divine perspective and the other on Adam's perspective—distinguishing between them can portray more clearly the character of the Creator as revealed in Holy Writ. Genesis 1 discloses God in all of His power and **transcendence**. God is not a thing that is accessible in the creation. One cannot fly into space and eventually find the deity as long as one knows where to look. God is not an object to be put under a microscope, nor is divinity a category that human beings can grasp by nature. As the transcendent one, God is wholly other, outside of and beyond all created things, whether invisible or visible. This divine transcendence comes to the fore in Genesis 1 as God speaks the powerful Word in the Spirit that creates everything. God declares the Word that does what it says, bringing light, land, water, and all things into being from nothing.

Genesis 1 further reveals how God arranged His creation in **good order** as He fashioned the earth so that the great diversity of creatures would flourish. God has not proceeded arbitrarily in His dealings with creatures. He has shaped human life and the rest of creation with an inbuilt structure and design in order that all things prosper. In fact, the whole universe is structured with a sense of order so that animals, plants, and human creatures reproduce, receive nourishment, and flourish according to God's wisdom.

Genesis 1 unfolds God's creative activity by recounting what He brought into existence in orderly fashion on each of the six initial days that stand at the beginning of time. From the first day, God constructed the structures that order the lives of creatures: evening and morning, day and night. Believers, then, trust that there is an underlying order to the reality God created that persists beyond Eden. God created the world according to His good design and gracious will, and believers seek to understand and live according to God's wisdom.

Genesis 2 offers a necessary complement to God's transcendence in Genesis 1. The account of the second chapter of Genesis reveals God in His closeness and intimacy with His creation, in His **immanence**. In Genesis 2, God fashioned the man, Adam, from the dust of the ground, like a potter fashions a vase. Genesis 2 depicts God getting His hands dirty in the dust, pushing and pulling the dirt as He formed it into the first man. Even more intimately, God breathed into Adam His own breath, His own Spirit of life. We should not dismiss this biblical language here as merely **anthropomorphic**—attributing human characteristics to what is not human—or we will miss just how much God loves what He has made and how much He loves each of us. He has created us in His own image, theomorphic. Certainly, God the Father is no man with skin and bones, but God is the loving Father who so cares for His creatures that He sends His Son to get down and dirty with us on earth. This is our immanent God who is yet the transcendent Creator. After God formed Adam with His own hands and formed Eve from Adam's rib, God placed them in a good home, with plentiful food and water, bountiful beauty, and meaningful work (Genesis 2:8–15). God even walked with Adam and Eve in the cool of the day, in intimate relationship with His human creatures (cf. Genesis 3:8). Although God is the transcendent and all-powerful Creator, God did not remain distant from them. God fashioned Adam and Eve in love, sought deep and abiding relationships with them, and made them a home in which they could flourish in relationship to Him, to one another in marriage and other social structures fashioned by God, and to the rest of the creation in responsible service.

The Creator Fashions Human Identity in Relationship

In the doctrine of creation, *to be* is to be in relationship. God is never alone, being three distinct persons in perfect unity, and God's relational character is reflected in the creation as He made human beings to be with one another. Hence, in Genesis 2, God brought animals to the first man before He created for him a partner, the woman, to be his companion. The intertwined reality of the Three who are One is reflected in a small, analogous way in the reality of creatures being made for relationships. God made human creatures in particular to be in three central relationships: with God, with one another, and with the rest of creation.

People, especially in contemporary Western culture, have constructed a myth of the self-made individual. Almost all in the modern West think that our identities belong to us to shape how we will. We think that a person figures out who they are alone, as an individual, and it is the moral responsibility of society to give space for individuals to express their identities. Hence, contemporary North Americans often treat marriage and children as parts of an individual's story of self-identity, and institutions are treated as structures for each person to become who they want to be. In this perspective, marriage and children are good, if people want it, but everyone should be free to leave as soon as they want to write a different story and create a different identity. Although this notion that people are freely made individuals is ingrained deeply in American consciousness, we betray the truth of our relational existence in our desperate search for community, fulfilling our deep need to belong.

In the doctrine of creation, God's word that "it is not good for man to be alone" not only proclaimed the blessing of marriage but also spoke to the reality of human existence (cf. Genesis 2:18). As the poet John Donne wrote, no one is an island, even if it may take the tolling of funeral bells to make us realize how connected we are. Western society tempts us to think that my humanity belongs to me alone, but Scripture reveals that we are joined together in a common humanity by the God who has given us life and a common purpose: to love God, serve one another, and care for the creation.

The first relationship for which human beings were made is with God. To be made in God's image, which will be discussed more in the next chapter, is no less than to be made for relationship with God: to fear, love, and trust in Him above all things. God made Adam and Eve to listen to His voice, trust in His Word, and love Him, joining in joyful fellowship with their Creator. Human life thus functions best when we recognize God as our Creator and live in dependence upon Him through faith. This relationship has been broken by sin, but God has restored it through His Son's atoning death and vivifying resurrection and by His Spirit's work to make sinners part of the family of God, incorporated into the divine community of love. Human beings have been created to be loved by and to love the Creator.

The second relationship for which human beings were made is with fellow human beings. Nowhere is this clearer than Genesis 2. Having made the first man from dust and breathed into him the Spirit of life, God sought to create a "helper" for him. What Adam needed was not a lord nor a servant but a sustainer, a helper (Genesis 2:18), a companion to stand next to him in mutually supportive community. God thus made Eve from Adam's rib to be his equal and to be his complement, different from Adam and essential to human community precisely as a woman. Marriage is foundational for human community, but the human relationships for which God made us expand also beyond marriage. In fact, in the New Testament, both Jesus and Paul praise singleness as a holy vocation for the people of God (Matthew 19:11–12; 1 Corinthians 7:6–8). Christians do not need marriage to establish community since we are brought into God's family, the church, through Baptism, wherein Christians have opportunities and responsibilities to care for one another in love. Moreover, God places all of us in local communities and countries wherein every person is called to serve and care for neighbors in love that reflects God's own character. Whether in marriage or in singleness, in the church or the world, God made humanity for relationships, not to care for ourselves above all but to serve one another in love, putting others above ourselves.

The third relationship for which God created humanity is with our fellow creatures, the nonhuman creation. Christians tend to think of human beings as closer to divine than creaturely, but the Scriptures picture humans as dependent creatures, even as we are given pride of place in relationship to the Creator. As creatures ourselves, we dare not think of the rest of creation as mere objects to be manipulated according to human will. Instead, other creatures are *fellow* creatures, part of the Creator's design that also reflects His character, even if less so than human beings. In fact, Luther highlighted this relationship in the Small Catechism's explanation to the First Article of the Creed by using the word *samt*, "together with," to teach children that the "me" He created is together with all creatures. This third relationship is tertiary in comparison to the relationships with God and fellow humans, but it must not be ignored or belittled. As technology has increased, humanity has become increasingly capable of manipulating the creation. Pandemics, disorder, and natural disasters remind us of our ultimate powerlessness, inability, and dependence, but human beings still manipulate the natural world in ways unimaginable to your great-grandparents, let alone to people living several hundred years earlier. In recognizing nonhuman creatures as fellow creatures, called "good" by God Himself, humanity is responsible to serve the creation so that it flourishes.[3] We must care for creation as God does, not lording over it for mere economic advantages, but caring for its long-term welfare so that all human beings and the creation itself can thrive.

---

3 Commission on Theology and Church Relations, *Together with All Creatures: Caring for God's Living Earth* (St. Louis: LCMS, 2010), 30–38.

These three relationships constitute true human identity and purpose, showing God's design of human creatures as **eccentric**.[4] We encounter some whom we regard as eccentric because they are different from the norm, set apart by certain characteristics. In that sense, Christians are indeed eccentric since they have been made holy, set apart from their sinful ways, even as their Creator and Redeemer is holy. But all human creatures are eccentric in the sense of being turned outward from themselves, designed to find the center of their lives in others: first, in God, then in other human beings, and finally in the creation to which they have been called to attend. In this way, the whole of human life and purpose is given to each of us as a gift of the Creator. When we are born, we are placed on earth within an intricate web of relationships, and we must learn to see in them God's gifts to us that both sustain our lives and give us opportunity to serve in love outside of ourselves. These relationships make us who we are as dependent creatures made to trust in our Creator; follow His design to love fellow human beings in marriage, singleness, and friendship; and care for the creation that He loves, reflecting His own character of grace.

God's Claim on His Creation

As the doctrine of creation establishes that God is Creator and I am creature, it also establishes God's basis for evaluating me. His design, expressed in His Law, asks whether I have loved Him with my heart, soul, and mind and have loved my neighbor as myself (Matthew 22:37–39). If I have not fulfilled my humanity in accordance with the design of the Creator, I have placed myself under judgment. Sin gets its definition from the Law's design (1 Corinthians 15:56). Furthermore, the doctrine of creation establishes the basis for my re-creation. I am created anew in the image of Christ who, as the image of the invisible God, created all things and reconciles all things by making peace by the blood of His cross (Colossians 1:15–20).

The doctrine of creation also confesses my worth as a creature of God. It is blasphemy to blame mistakes on being "only human." God did not make junk. The problem with human living does not spring from our humanity. It springs from abandoning our humanity, centered in God and lived in service to the rest of God's creatures. The human creature stands high in God's design for His universe (Psalm 8:3–8). To love ourselves more than we love God—to listen to our own voice rather than to God's—eviscerates our humanity. To recognize ourselves as those loved by God, as His dependent children, confesses God's glory as our Maker and acknowledges our status as His creatures.

4 David H. Kelsey, *Eccentric Existence: A Theological Anthropology*, 2 vols. (Louisville: Westminster John Knox, 2009).

Furthermore, the doctrine of creation establishes the worth of all other human creatures. All prejudice, enmity, and hatred is ruled out by the worth that God has placed on the life of every human brother and sister, even when they are living apart from Him in unbelief. Total love, care, and concern for one another are ordained by God's placing us together with others in community. He has called us to love our fellow human creatures as we love ourselves. His verdict, announced by His Son, that we are His beloved children transforms us so that we see ourselves and others as who we really are: dearly loved children of God.

The Goodness of Creation

Having made the universe from nothing, God observed that the product of His creative Word was "good" on five of the six days of creation (Genesis 1:4, 10, 12, 18, 21, 25). At the end of the sixth day, "God saw everything that He had made, and behold, it was very good" (Genesis 1:31). Although Eden's gates are closed, God's "very good" still echoes, even if sometimes faintly.

Our own experience with material things can discourage us from recognizing materiality as very good, despite the claim of God's Word. Our bodies are the main place where we engage the material world, but we notice our bodies chiefly when they do not function well, in sickness, pain, and the throes of death. We see the corruption of our own flesh; we notice our bodies falling apart, no longer able to support or sustain us as they once did. We feel the temptations that surge through our emotions and desires. These negative experiences of our bodies as transient and corrupt can make some people, even Christians, conclude that the created order is not good.

When we experience disappointment with God's material creation, we need to remember that the nonhuman creation did not cause itself to fall. It was fallen upon. The ground is cursed because God's human creatures ate from the tree "of which I commanded you, 'You shall not eat of it.'" Human defiance and deafness to God's voice caused the ground to be cursed (Genesis 3:17). The entire creaturely order—including human bodies—groans now in travail, under the corruption of sin and the bondage of death. But the material creation will not be shucked off and thrown away, as the ancient Gnostics, a heretical group, claimed it would be. Nor do material things need to evolve into some higher plane, whether spiritual, organic, or cybernetic, as some contemporary thinkers suggest. The material world is good now, *as created*, and God will not destroy it for something different but will liberate it from sin and death and renew it for eternal joy in His kingdom. The ultimate Christian hope is that the whole material world will be freed from its bondage to decay and receive the glory of God's presence along with human creatures, the children of God, even in their bodies (Romans 8:19–23; 1 Corinthians 15).

Believers need to see the material world first and foremost as *creation*, the product of God's creative love and gracious will. Creation is good *because God created it*. Believers thus thank God for the entire material order, from their bodies to the farthest star. Believers praise God for the diversity of creatures, especially human creatures, that are good in their own right because God made them. In the diversity of creatures, God reveals the enormity of His love and the vastness of His creativity. Believers delight and wonder at the variety of bugs and birds, fish and fowl, creeping caterpillars, and cute koalas. Through the material world, God's generous goodness overflows to His creatures, giving us waterfalls at which to wonder, mountains at which to marvel, filet mignon to savor, friends in whom we can delight, and families to embrace. God has given manifold ways that we can express human love to one another and give glory to Him, not apart from our bodies or the material world but in and through them.

Moreover, out of God's limitless imagination, He offers us His immense love through the material world. Although the Creator transcends His creation, He condescended to enter it fully as a man in Jesus. Creation is so good that the Son of God Himself became a creature while remaining fully God. In taking on a human body, not only a human mind and spirit but our very flesh, under the corruption of death, aging, and temptation (Galatians 4:4), Jesus revealed just how good creation is, according to God's judgment. As if that were not enough already, the Holy Spirit, too, permeates material elements of creation to bring the saving grace of God in Christ to us human creatures, through words, water, bread, and wine. These are the very material of God's grace in the Sacraments.

In this light, Christians recognize the goodness of creation, seeing how God has designed the material world to be a realm where His love pervades all things and moves His creation to give Him glory. God has designed human sexuality, athletic ability, and taste buds for the fulfillment of our humanity and the glory of our Creator. In light of creation's goodness, believers can only join the psalmist in acknowledging: "O Lord, how manifold are Your works! In wisdom have You made them all; the earth is full of Your creatures. ... I will sing to the Lord as long as I live; I will sing praise to my God while I have [my] being" (Psalm 104:24, 33).

At the same time that believers confess matter to be good, Christians must be careful not to regard the creation in an idolatrous manner. In North American culture, the abundance of material goods tempts us to rely on them for identity, security, and meaning. Proper delight in human bodies can become lust, envy, or even a striving after immortality; wonder at and concern for the natural world can turn nature into an idol; and holy joy in good food and friends can become ungodly gluttony. This does not even mention how greed can transform the creation into a tool for gaining wealth and power. God made the material order, including ourselves, for relationship with Him and to reflect the divine love between Father and Son in the Spirit within the creation. He did not fashion the created order so that humankind could exploit it for its own purposes or refashion it into an idol.

Christians therefore can affirm the goodness of both material things and our bodies while at the same time confessing that a good life does not depend upon having stuff. For Christians, everything is a gift of the Creator who made it and holds it in His hands. We delight in the gifts that God has given us, but we also gladly give them away to others in need. As St. Augustine asserted, material goods are not to be loved, but to be used according to God's good will. When we love material goods, we are enslaved by them—we cannot serve both God and money (Matthew 6:24). When, however, we are moved to love God by His Spirit, we are free to love His creation, especially His human creatures, and delight in His creativity, using God's material gifts to care for others according to His good design and gracious will.

Challenges to the Biblical Teaching about the Creator

The Scriptures draw a sharp distinction between the Creator and His creation. All biblical teaching rests on the presumption that God is indeed "wholly other" than what He has made. The Creator makes all from nothing, and the creation comes to be according to the Creator's gracious will and good design. The Creator and the creation must not be confused.

Pantheism

Pantheism denies that God and creation are fundamentally different. Some pantheists spiritualize creation and try to draw it, or its essence, into the nature of God. Materialist pantheists project some divine force into nature and equate nature and its individual elements with the ultimate in divine power. In both cases, God is no longer the transcendent one, who is to be grasped by Word and promise. God instead becomes part of the universe—even if god is the whole of its complex, interconnected parts—and the earth or universe is attributed with characteristics of divinity. In pantheism, the creator and the creation mutually permeate each other whether in a spiritual or a material sense.

Ancient Hinduism had pantheistic elements. The early modern philosopher Baruch Spinoza denied a personal divine being; he taught that the divine substance extends itself in the form of nature and creatures of all kinds. Some mystics in Christian history have taught that our goal as human beings is to unite with God's being, diminishing or eliminating the distinction between God and His human creatures. Many common beliefs today have pantheistic elements, such as in some versions of meditation or yoga, wherein getting in touch with ourselves or the world through these practices is understood as connecting with ultimate reality, the most important truths about ourselves or the world, which is a kind of god.

Pantheistic belief denies God's uniqueness as Creator, and it often rejects the goodness of material creation. Pantheistic belief destroys a biblical understanding of both who God is and who we are. Any confusion of Creator and creation skews a proper understanding of the intended relationship.

Deism

During the Enlightenment, some Western philosophers put distance as well as distinction between the Creator and His created order. **Deism** teaches that there is indeed a Creator, but that He has little interest in the continuing life of the creation or its development. Some deists taught that God is totally absent from His world; He is like a clockmaker who, having created the clock, winds it up and leaves it ticking away on its own forever. Others taught that God exercises providence over the material world but has left the moral and spiritual order of things in human hands. Still others permitted Him a role in the spiritual realm but denied that He had created a future life for humankind.

Although deism no longer plays an important role in intellectual circles as it did during the formation of the United States—atheistic evolution is the more prominent position among mainstream thinkers today—a form of deism persists in American society. Sociologists have recognized that American religiosity tends toward a kind of deism. God is presumed to exist and to love us, but He is also absent from our lives unless we need Him.[5] Many contemporary Western people act as if God is a divine butler who stays out of the way except when we want Him to serve us.

Although deism might seem to protect God by keeping Him transcendent in heaven, not bothered by piddly human concerns, it in fact deeply reduces God and threatens the reality of the Gospel. Scripture shows us a God who is wholly other, who made us when we were not, yet this God also desires intimacy and love, wanting to redeem creatures who have fallen away from Him in sin. The God who loved Adam and Eve enough to clothe them with animal skins after their sin would never abandon His creatures.

5 Christian Smith, *Soul Searching: The Religious and Spiritual Lives of American Teenagers* (Oxford: Oxford University Press, 2005), 165.

God instead designed creation for our good, works through it to reveal His own presence and grace, and cares for it and us daily. If God were to ever take away His creative hand from the world, everything would no longer be. Only God's presence in His creation sustains its operation and preserves the human community in the midst of all woes. The Creator still preserves us.

Dualism

The mystery of evil calls into question the complete power of God over His creation. Therefore, some thinkers have from time to time suggested that two more or less equal divine powers must exist, and human beings must be victims of their continuing struggle, the struggle between good and evil. Different dualistic systems have described the final result of the struggle in differing ways. In some, the struggle is eternal. In others, good is supposed to win the final victory. In both approaches salvation is possible as the forces of good win individual human creatures back from the evil force or god.

The most famous proponent of **dualism** is the shadowy third-century figure Manes or Manichaeus.[6] He taught that light and darkness, as eternal principles, are locked in conflict. His "Manichaean" doctrine found significant following in the period of the early church. Its echoes are still heard in the twenty-first century in those searching for a logical explanation for the power of evil. Scripture teaches that God has asserted His own control of evil in the face of our perception of its seeming triumph. He claims His creation as His own even in the midst of its defiance of Him and its fall into evil. He remains Creator.

Gnosticism

Manes seems to have developed his views under the influence of a system of thought that scholars have labeled Gnosticism.[7] So called because its followers believed that they had the secret *gnosis* (Greek for "knowledge") of life, Gnosticism taught a dualism between spirit and matter. The varieties of this system of thought all rest upon the presupposition that spiritual things are more real and important than material things. The ultimate good was held to be an impersonal spirit, existing as the unknowable divine being beyond the grasp of mortal humans. In some way or other this divine spirit generated or emanated separate spiritual beings, among them by some

6 Jaroslav Pelikan, *The Emergence of the Catholic Tradition (100–600)*, vol. 1 of *The Christian Tradition: A History of the Development of Doctrine* (Chicago: University of Chicago Press, 1971), 136–37.

7 Pelikan, *Emergence of the Catholic Tradition*, 81–97; J. N. D. Kelly, *Early Christian Doctrine* (New York: Harper & Row, 1960), 22–28.

mischance a "demiurge" or "word" or creator. Through its agency, not the work of the supreme deity, creation came into being.

Created by this lesser deity, according to the Gnostics, the material order was entirely evil at worst or irrelevant at best. Gnosticism generally taught that sparks of the divine spirit were imprisoned in the material creation by falling from unity with the divine down the ladder of emanations to the worst possible circumstance, entrapment in a material body. Salvation was viewed as the liberation of the individual's soul or spirit from the material body, leading to progressive exaltation up the many levels of spiritual emanation. This exaltation would be completed in the loss of individuality, the absorption of the spark of soul that had once been individualized into the impersonal divine spirit at the other, highest, end of reality.

Gnosticism had much variety in the ancient world, often adapting worldviews of other philosophies or religions, retaining details of the old worldview while changing the foundation to fit with its dualistic view of spirit and matter. Today, Gnostic tendencies can still be found in popular thinking, sometimes feeding on a Christian understanding of the world. For instance, human identity is often understood as a matter of personal decision, elevating human will and freedom—things that can be considered spiritual—above the body and the embodied relationships that God has given to us by grace. In addition, sex is often treated in contemporary society as irrelevant to our spiritual, psychological, and emotional health because sex is just a matter of the body rather than the soul or spirit. As a third example of continued Gnostic influence, even Christians can mistakenly think of the soul as "who I really am" and believe that humanity's eternal destiny is merely to be spirits in the sky.

Gnostic beliefs deprecate God's good material creation, the incarnation of the Son of God, and human individuality. St. Paul criticized all three of these errors by teaching the resurrection of the body (1 Corinthians 15:42–44). For St. Paul, our bodily resurrection is assured because the Son of God Himself became a true man, was killed on a cross, and was raised from the dead in His physical body. Each individual believer has the promise of everlasting life with Jesus in a new resurrected body since Jesus has already been through death and promises new life by His grace and power. This promise of what we will be is the fulfillment of God's loving creative work that has been despoiled by sin. God has fashioned each human creature through His continuing care of His creatures (Psalm 139:13; Job 31:15; Jeremiah 1:5). He loves us as individuals, and He calls each person to trust in Him and obey His Word in body and soul. He continues to use His good material creation for the blessing of people, in both the horizontal and vertical dimensions of human life. And our resurrection as individuals is assured; we shall live with

Him as individual human creatures forever with Spirit-filled bodies in the new heavens and new earth.

Atheistic Evolution

The biggest challenge to Christian belief in the Creator in the twenty-first century is the teaching of atheistic evolution. Rooted in the understanding that Darwinian evolution has made God philosophically unnecessary, recent "new atheists" have revived many old arguments against the Creator with a new vehemence and absolute certainty that God does not exist (without the depth or the understanding of Christianity that many of the older thinkers had).[8] Despite its denial of traditional belief in the Creator, new atheism creates new divinities by trusting absolutely in human reasoning and certain kinds of empirical evidence even as their doctrine diminishes people to mere animals and rejects the Creator's wise design.

The chief problem with an evolutionary worldview is not the process of evolution but when atheistic evolution functions as a worldview to explain everything in terms of natural causes that can be verified by the scientific method. This **scientific naturalism** not only rejects supernatural causes as possible scientific explanations, but it even denies all spiritual and supernatural realities, presuming that everything real can be measured by scientific instruments. Scientific naturalism reduces human nature and relationships to organic processes, passionate urges, and a struggle for power. More egregiously, it acts as a religious worldview that has already determined ultimate reality. Just because scientific naturalism does not hold a traditional belief in a god does not mean it is any less of a religious philosophy, no matter how objective it claims to be.

Evolutionary dogma, under the constraints of scientific naturalism, must be distinguished from biological theories that use genetic, physical, or chemical information in tracing changes that fall under God's normal management of the created world. Adaptation and small-scale genetic change pose no challenges to the biblical teaching of creation. In the nineteenth-century battle against Charles Darwin's followers, some Christians tried to defend the doctrine of creation by asserting an immutability of biological species, but there are no biblical grounds to warrant such an assertion. God created the world to adapt and change and cares for it providentially through various mechanisms, including genetic variation and adaptation. The biblical writers, inspired as they were in their contexts, had no knowledge of contemporary genetic theory. (Even Darwin did not; the discoveries of his contemporary, the Roman Catholic monk Gregor Mendel, which began

8 David Bentley Hart, *Atheist Delusions: The Christian Revolution and Its Fashionable Enemies* (New Haven, CT: Yale University Press, 2009), 3–18.

modern genetics, were not published until after Darwin's death.) Genetic change and the development of new species may well be part of this plan of God. On the other hand, such theories may be surpassed by future scientific research and conceptualization. We do not need scriptural precedent to recognize, appreciate, and benefit from the work of scientists in this field.

Some scientists label the theories that work with evolutionary change at the level of gene and chromosome **microevolution**, which can be readily observed in laboratories. When evolutionary thought is extended from a working tool for research to a framework for ascertaining and interpreting the meaning of life and the universe, it becomes **macroevolution**. Macroevolution rests upon the same leap of faith as scientific naturalism—except in the case of theistic evolution, which presumes that God is the agent of evolutionary change. Confusion between the two levels of usage behind the term *evolution* has led some Christians to focus on the differences between evolutionary dogma and biblical faith in unhelpful ways.

This dogma's faith in human powers to determine and define reality is just as significant as its denial of the biblical account of the creation of the world. To understand the fundamental differences between the biblical teaching on creation and the evolutionist faith system, we return to epistemology, the manner in which people learn and know. The faith system of contemporary evolutionary theory claims that its beliefs follow the empirical, experimental, and scientific method of learning. This method relies on the human senses to evaluate data based on experiments devised by an experimenter. The method presumes that knowledge can be proven by repeated testing. It claims an objectivity to its findings because they can be submitted to trial by others, who can corroborate the findings through repetition. Objects that cannot be subjected to repeated testing lie outside the command of this approach to human knowledge.

Therefore, when the epistemology of human experiment tries to define the origins and bounds of reality, it has gone beyond the limits of its competence. Human experiment cannot reach beyond material reality and repeatable phenomena. That does not make nonmaterial things unreal, just as the authors' inability to see Rome from their current vantage points does not make Rome unreal. Human experimentation simply has limits. Ultimate causality lies outside its realms. Scientific experimentation cannot tell us what something is for, where it is going, or where it came from in any nontrivial way. Science has gone astray when it attempts to answer a different kind of question from the ones for which it was designed. It exceeds the acknowledged limits of the scientific method when it attempts to pierce the veil behind which lies the origin of all things and ultimate control of the universe. When evolutionary dogma attempts to formulate a general theory of the beginnings of creation and the meaning of life, it transgresses its own boundaries. The guiding mechanisms for creation's engines cannot be grasped by experiment.

Evolutionary dogma does not remain objective when it wanders into explanations that arise from leaps of faith beyond empirical testing. Neither origins nor one-time historical events are subject to repeatable experiments, which is required for the scientific method to confirm any explanation. Evolutionary dogma shows its religious assumptions when it seizes upon faith statements from a voice of authority regarding matters on which there is only conjecture. The guiding principles that drive nature and human history must lie outside the realm of scientific analysis since they cannot be subjected to the instruments of empirical testing.

Christians confess that God lies beyond the instruments of human authority. In fact, the ultimate power of the universe *must* lie beyond human control and definition, if the Creator is really God. Because of this, truly theistic evolutionism is impossible. True theism, that is, the faith in the God who reveals Himself in crib and cross, must abandon the empirical epistemology of experiment when it listens to its God.

God tells us first that He created all that exists, not with a big bang but with a still, small voice that said, "Let there be." Whether God's voice loosed a big bang is beyond our knowing. If such a theory can add to the human good, it would be fine. But like all theories we establish to serve our needs in the horizontal realm, such a theory is at best tentative human knowledge.

Christians do well to distinguish and properly use the contrasting epistemologies that must govern knowledge of God and knowledge of His creation, also when they address the issue of evolutionary dogma. The attempt to disprove evolution empirically is part of the way in which natural science proceeds according to its own rules. There are many more good, empirical, scientific arguments against some fundamental presuppositions of evolutionary dogma than the establishment in the Western scientific community admits—although believers should not be blind to the inner logic of its dogma. Therefore, Christian scientists may want to participate in the continuing testing of evolutionary theory through experimental argument.

Believers should recognize, however, that conducting the defense of the biblical teaching of creation on the turf of empirical epistemology may ultimately undercut the biblical position. Even if one could disprove evolution by empirical means, the source of that knowledge lies within human control. That refutation of evolution thus would not accurately reflect how believers come to know God as Creator. Such an approach would put our knowledge of creation always at the mercy of the next theorist, who could use empirical terms to express a different doctrine.

Christians also must recognize that their rejection of the system of dogma associated with the name of Charles Darwin must include rejection of **social Darwinism** as well. The views that arose out of Darwin's concept of the "survival of the fittest" made a significant impact on social thought in Western culture in the nineteenth and twentieth centuries. Racists, ruthless capitalists, and imperialists used popularized Darwinism to propagate inhuman and antihuman views of humanity.[9] Social Darwinism issued a scientific license to many in the late nineteenth and early twentieth centuries for exploitation and oppression of others. People—always the marginalized—were sterilized, experimented on, and murdered in the name of evolutionary progress and the survival of the fittest. The biblical doctrine of creation forbids inhumane treatment of any person the Creator loves and made—especially such treatment of the poor, the widow, and the orphan, the least of these.

Believers should also recognize that Darwin's interpretation of the natural world arose within the context of nineteenth-century Hegelianism and the broader currents of thought that embraced a doctrine of inevitable progress. Georg Wilhelm Friedrich Hegel (1770–1831), professor at the University of Berlin, codified the Enlightenment conviction that human history is moving in an inexorable drive upward—toward an ever better, more perfect form of life. Despite the age of the Enlightenment experiencing moments of discouragement regarding this doctrine, the technological and medical progress of the age encouraged high hopes for human progress.

The experiences of the National Socialist physician Josef Mengele's medicine and the applications of technology employed by Adolf Hitler and Pol Pot have somewhat dampened enthusiasm for the doctrine of progress. But hope springs eternal, and most North Americans still believe in the inevitability of progress. A closer look at ancient or recent history permits no such illusions. Therefore, Christians should recognize that underneath Darwin's thought lies an untenable presupposition: that earthly life will inevitably and inexorably improve, and do so on the basis of powers not defined as the power of Yahweh. From this presupposition some individual ideas of merit may proceed. Nevertheless, from such a presupposition proceeds a dogma that inevitably and inexorably opposes the biblical understanding of Creator and creature and the corrupting power of sin from which we need a Savior.

God is the presupposition of the entire creation. He began it with a Word, and He sustains and preserves it until that day on which He will bring

9 George L. Mosse, *The Culture of Western Europe: The Nineteenth and Twentieth Centuries, an Introduction* (Chicago: Rand McNally, 1961), 77–78, 200–205.

it to its consummation. He is our Creator, and we are His creatures. All life proceeds from Him. He is its starting point, its proper goal, and the one who cares for it from beginning to end. All biblical teaching proceeds from this beginning, which lies in God's hand and Word. Not we ourselves, nor any other forces of the universe, but rather God made us and all things, and He remains our caring Creator and loving Lord who wants to bring us into fellowship with Himself through His Son and Spirit.

CHAPTER 4
HUMAN CREATURES

"IT is He who made us" (Psalm 100:3). The fact that God created us and we did not create ourselves is such an obvious point that its significance is easily overlooked. At a minimum, this means there was a time when each human being was not—human creatures are not eternal. There were no humans until God created human creatures and blessed them—no human souls or bodies existed until woman and man became living creatures by God's power, modeled after His own image (Genesis 1:27–28). God formed the first human from the dust of the ground and breathed into this creature the breath of life (Genesis 2:7).

By God's grace and according to His wise plan, we were brought into this world *to be His*. Simply put, we were made for relationship with God. We are His people, the sheep of His pasture (Psalm 100:3). The breath that God exhaled into the first human creature in Genesis 2 points to the centrality of this vertical relationship. We were not designed to eat, drink, and be merry, but to depend on our Creator, walk with Him, listen to His Word, and converse with Him as dear children speak with their dear Father. What makes us right with God is not our performance, emotions, or activity. What makes us right with God—and fully human according to His creative intention—is simply our Spirit-driven response of trust and love to the gifts that He gives without any merit or worthiness in us, apart from all deeds we perform. God made Adam and Eve—and us—for Himself, breathing into them the breath of life.

While we dare not forget the breath of God that animates human bodies and sets us in relationship to Him, we must also remember that human creatures are truly dust. Made from the dust, we are not alien to the rest of creation. We are as much creatures as lions, hummingbirds, and even sedimentary stones. Although human beings are made in God's image, we are not gods. As those made from dust yet given dominion over creation, we stand as first among equals in the creation, first not because of our power or strength but because of God's command and promise. In fact, according to Scripture, human creatures were made to have a symbiotic relationship with the rest of creation: from its dust we are fashioned, yet until we were here to till the ground, no plant of the field sprang up (Genesis 2:5). In biblical perspective, human beings are good for the earth, as it is good for us. God thus did not issue a license for human exploitation of nature, but called human creatures to serve the creation in His stead. After all, the whole created order belongs to God and not to us. Nature is designed to protect itself against human abuse, and God stands in judgment over human misuse of His world and its resources. We experience this when the body falls victim to cancers caused by pollution, housing developments are flooded by a river in revolt against our attempts to channel it, and storms, fires, rising seas, and hurricanes seem to be strengthened in water and air newly warmed. The dust of the earth points to the horizontal relationships that human creatures are designed to have with the rest of His creation. What makes us right in the world, as the human creatures God intended us to be, is our proper performance of God's commands, our proper tilling of its ground, and our proper care for its creatures.

God's design of the human creature gives us a reason to praise. He sparks awe and wonder in us because we see how "fearful and wonderful" He is. His image in us reflects His care and concern in creating our inmost being, in restoring us to a proper relationship with Himself, and in knitting together the body that emerged from our mother's womb (Psalm 139:13–18). We learn to flourish as His human creatures when we live according to His Word, trusting in His promises and following His commands in obedience.

Dependent on the Creator

Being a creature means being dependent on the Creator. Such thinking about human creatures runs against the grain of modern Western thinking. After the fall, we quite naturally exercise our independence in rebellion against our Creator, but we were made to rest in dependence upon God. Human beings were created to fear, love, and trust in God above all things. As Luther's Small Catechism proclaims, we depend upon God for the material needs of daily life, for protection from every danger, and for preservation from all evil. All creaturely life is thus sheer gift. It is significant that Luther teaches God's pure, "fatherly, divine goodness and mercy, without any merit or worthiness in me" at this place in the First Article,[1] and not in the Second Article in regard to trusting in Christ for salvation. Our total dependence upon God is not just a spiritual matter since our whole being—material and spiritual, body and soul—depends entirely on the Creator. We live, move, and have our being only because of God's gifts of breath, life,

1 Small Catechism II 2 (*LSCE*, 16).

health, protection, and so much more (Acts 17:28). When we view life as our Creator shaped it and gifted it to us by grace alone, we recognize our total dependence upon Him.

North Americans want to believe that they stand on their own two feet. As our culture understands it, we are the most authentic, complete persons when we think for ourselves, feel for ourselves, act for ourselves, and determine our individual purpose for ourselves. Freedom, the highest of North American virtues, seems to demand complete independence from everything and everyone else. We are only free, we insist, when we do as we please. Each of us is the captain of my ship and the determiner of my destiny, or at least this is the story many tell.

The biblical faith confesses the opposite: we are dependent on God's goodness and mercy; we find our identity, security, and meaning in Him alone; and we are bound to thank, praise, serve, and obey God. Such dependence does not diminish our humanity but actually frees us to be who we were made to be. Just as children are not the happiest or most fulfilled when they are rebelling against their parents, but when they are finding their way according to parental wisdom, human creatures thrive when we follow God's wisdom, trust in His promises, and live according to His commands in the three types of relationships that constitute human life: with God, with fellow human creatures, and with the rest of creation, as discussed in the previous chapter. For the Scriptures, then, freedom does not mean independence from other people or from God, but it means to be what God has made us to be—no more and certainly no less. When human creatures are brought to faith in God through the Spirit, we can only praise our God: "Yahweh, our Lord, how majestic is Your name in all the earth!" (Psalm 8:3–8).

Biblical Anthropology

Anthropology refers to the study of human beings. In contrast to much contemporary anthropology that focuses on human culture and society, which tends to separate and divide various cultures and peoples, biblical anthropology focuses on human nature, describing things that unite all human beings as creatures of the Creator. Following the clues given in Holy Scripture, the Christian tradition has described human nature in two ways, **dichotomous** or **trichotomous**, two-part or three-part. Despite confessing both perspectives, the Bible is united that human beings are both physical and spiritual, made for relationship with God and for relationships with fellow creatures.

The Scriptures commonly talk about human beings as whole persons. The Hebrew word *nephesh*, commonly translated "soul" or "life," often carries the sense of the whole person, the living self who stands before God.[2] In addition, the Bible regularly speaks of the **heart** of a person, not referring to the bodily organ that pumps blood but to "the highest faculty of man," the source of a person's affections and desires that shape our emotions and our choices.[3] The heart is what is judged by God (1 Samuel 16:7; 1 Kings 8:39); the heart is the self in relationship with God and the source of what we feel, think, and do (Mark 7:21–22). This scriptural way of speaking reminds us that, though we can describe the various parts of human nature, we ultimately stand as whole persons before God, responsible for our lives in the body and promised forgiveness and eternal life by grace alone that transforms even our sinful hearts.

Scripture also uses the more common language of the Christian tradition for human nature: body and soul, or body, soul, and spirit. In Matthew 10, Jesus spoke of the destruction of body and soul (Matthew 10:28), incorporating all that is human into these two parts. The writer to the Hebrews distinguishes the soul from the spirit, parallel to dividing joints and marrow in the body, suggesting that in the unseen part of human creatures there are two subdivisions (Hebrews 4:12). Paul used this trichotomous, three-part, description of body, soul, and spirit in his benediction upon the Thessalonian church (1 Thessalonians 5:23). On the other hand, Mary's use of "soul" and "spirit" in the opening of her song of praise seems to make the two synonyms (Luke 1:46–47). Nowhere in Scripture does God clearly define whether there are properly two or three "parts" to human beings. The biblical writers worked with the cultural descriptions at hand in their societies, just as we do today. Therefore, we need not lock ourselves into one description even as we seek to remain faithful to Scripture.

Body and Soul

Because God is spirit (John 4:24), and thus unseen, and because our bodies fail us in their mortality, we inevitably think less of our bodies. The Scriptures, though, confess that our bodies are bound for resurrection and are essential to God's eternal plan of salvation (1 Corinthians 15:42–44). The human **body** came from God's creative hand, out of the dust, fashioned with the nonphysical human components in the image of God for physical and nonphysical functions (Genesis 1:26–31; 2:7). God included that body in what He pronounced very good (Genesis 1:31). In light of the creative and

2 A classic study on *nephesh* is Hans Walter Wolff, *Anthropology of the Old Testament*, trans. Margaret Kohl (London: SCM, 1974). The authors referred to a selection of this text found in Marc Cortez and Michael P. Jensen, eds., *T&T Clark Reader in Theological Anthropology* (London: Bloomsbury T&T Clark, 2018), 150–56.

3 Philip Melanchthon, *Commonplaces: Loci Communes 1521*, trans. Christian Preus (St. Louis: Concordia, 2014), 32–33 and 35.

redemptive work of God, human beings do not merely *have* bodies, but we *are* bodies. Our bodies are not a possession for us to use as we wish, but they are part of who we are, not only in this age but also eternally in the age to come, as is the incarnate Son of God. Therefore, God despises every kind of neglect or abuse of human bodies—of our own and of our neighbor's. He calls upon us to help and befriend our neighbor in every bodily need.

Whatever we may think of our physical components, we usually designate the rest of what we are as "nonphysical." That fact demonstrates how much we are bound to our bodies. The body provides the orientation point for our thinking about ourselves. We cannot imagine a life outside of the body; our "most spiritual" experiences of thinking, being loved, trusting, and feeling are experienced in the body and as bodies. At the same time that we recognize the importance of our material bodies, we must recognize that we are also more than physical beings. We speak of people who do not feel what we would like them to feel as people "with no heart," though the mass of muscle in their chest cavity continues to beat. There is something nonphysical about us that is essential. Our minds and thoughts, our emotions, and our relationships are as important as our bodies for our sense of identity. These things are experienced in the body, but they are more than body.

These unseen components are often lumped together and labeled **soul**. In the Christian tradition, the soul has been understood to include reasoning powers and the ability to feel; it includes will, conscience, and personality. The soul names the reality that God has made human beings specially, designing them to be different from other creatures: rational, moral, creative, compassionate, and social, to name a few unique characteristics. Other living creatures may have aspects of these things—there is no biblical reason for Christians to deny that animals have their own ways of thinking or feeling even if they are not the same as human rationality or emotion—but none has the God given combination that constitutes the human soul. In a more general sense, the soul includes whatever makes the difference between a living human body and a corpse; it embraces whatever God does that makes us alive. As intangible as all these things may be, they are real, and without them, we would not be the creatures God has made humans to be. In fact, just as we are bodies, so we *are* souls. Souls are not something we have or possess, but the soul constitutes a human creature who cannot be reduced to materiality. Evolutionary biology diminishes humans to mere physicality, animals who act on biological, genetic responses, stimulated by neurons. The Scriptures, though, refuse to reduce human creatures to twitching ganglia hooked up to the central cerebrum and cerebellum. We are soul and body, made for relationship with the Creator and to reflect God's character

Trust in the Creator Holds Life Together

Believers recognize that there is another essential "part" to being human, even beyond body and soul. Body and the several components of soul (mind, reason, will, emotion, etc.), which we have described, remain functional—though not whole—in the horizontal relationships of earthly life, even when sin and death reign in our lives. To be fully what God made us to be, however, we must be in relationship to God as well. The **trust** that binds us to God takes place in unseen functions of "brain" and "heart." That ability to trust God could be called a third component of humanity and labeled "spirit." If we use that way of speaking, such a label can remind us that trust in God is not something that makes us more than human but that fulfills God's wise design for our humanity, making us the fully human creatures that God intends us to be.

Just as body and soul do not label mere parts of a human being—as if they were possessions to take or leave—but rather name aspects of human nature that permeate whole persons, trust in God, too, is not simply one more component part of our humanity. We must not think of trust as a thing (what medieval Christians called a "habit") that could be reinserted in a fallen human creature like an organ transplant. Rather, proper trust is the relationship with God that grasps our whole being, body and soul, reason and will, mind and emotions. Trust fulfills our humanity by grabbing hold of the promises of God, which places us in proper relationship to Him as dependent on His mercy. Mistrust breaks that relationship; unbelief misplaces that core orientation. Unbelief seeks ultimate identity, security, and meaning elsewhere, not in Yahweh. Our spirit is not a component part, like will, emotion, or reason (although spirit can sometimes be used to describe these in another sense). Our spirit instead arises from our whole being—our heart—drawn forth to embrace the God whose outstretched arms create the spirit of our trust, our love, our childlike fear of Him who made us. *Trust* is a clearer word than *spirit* for the human end of the relationship with God, which is established by the Spirit.

Our spirit, our trust, rests in our Creator. The Hebrew word *shalom* sums up what it means to rest in God. The usual translation of that word is "peace," but it means far more than the cessation or absence of hostilities. The lexicon provides an array of definitions for *shalom*: completeness, safety, prosperity, health, tranquility, friendship, peace with God. The verbal form can mean "be complete or finished," "be sound or uninjured," "make whole or good; restore."[4] In the Garden of Eden, Adam and Eve did not

4 Francis Brown, S. R. Driver, and Charles A. Briggs, *The Brown-Driver-Briggs Hebrew and English Lexicon* (1906; repr., Peabody, MA: Hendrickson Publishers, 2004), 1022–23, s.v. *shalom* and *shalem*.

so much *have peace*, as a possession they had won for themselves, as they were *at peace*. There was true *shalom* as their existence was wrapped in the blanket of harmony and rest that God bestowed upon them as a gift. Such was their humanity. It was designed to be righteous, that is, in the right place, in the right relationship, first of all with their Creator. For them peace was having life all together, with all its elements in the right place. Peace was not inaction, but it was restful. Peace was being confident that all was well in the midst of existence itself and every human activity. At the heart of this gift of peace stood the favor and love of their God. Every moment for Adam and Eve was one of worship as they lived by trust in their Creator and praised Him with every breath, word, and heartbeat. For all their descendants, peace comes also in true worship as we trust that God presents us with the gift of His presence and preserves us as His progeny.

In the Image of God

What may be the most significant description of human nature comes in Genesis 1. On day 6, the divine Word changes from "Let there be" to "Let Us make" as God speaks the Word to create human beings "in Our image, after Our likeness" (Genesis 1:26). God is clear that He makes both women and men "in His own image" (Genesis 1:27). Human beings are indeed "fearfully and wonderfully made," as God "formed [our] inward parts" and "knitted [us] together in [our] mother's womb" (Psalm 139:13–14). The first thing that we should recognize about the scriptural teaching that human beings are made in **God's image** is this God-given value that is placed on all human beings. God so values human lives that He created us as part of His family. No matter what a person might look like, what culture they are from, what abilities they have or do not have, or what beliefs they hold, all people with human DNA are made in God's image and thus have infinite value in God's eyes. This understanding of being made in God's image challenges contemporary North American thinking to recognize the least of these in the womb as fully human as well as the inherent value of the homeless, poor, marginalized, and immigrants among us. To be made in God's image is no less than to be so valued by God as to have been created for relationship with Him, redeemed by the blood of Jesus, and sought out by the Spirit to be conformed to the image of Christ.

Recently, exegetical theologians—those who work closely with biblical texts—have emphasized that the Hebrew word *tselem* refers to an image or statue that a king or emperor might place in a faraway territory. For example, in the first century, Caesar might have placed in Philippi a statue of his image to remind citizens that Caesar was in charge in that place even if he was not visibly present. In this understanding of being made in God's image, human beings represent God's authority and rule on earth. They stand in God's place as they image Him to the rest of creation. This connection between rule and image illustrates also how God gives human beings, who have been made in His image, the charge to exercise dominion on earth, serving the rest of the creation in God's place.

Although the image of God does carry a sense of reflecting God's glory and authority to the rest of God's creation, that sense does not exhaust the meaning of the phrase. The Christian tradition has also interpreted being made in God's image in several other ways. The Lutheran Confessions emphasize that being made in God's image means to be in right relationship with God, reflecting the Creator's love and mercy by depending on Him in faith. Although sin deforms this sense of being made in God's image, that all human beings today are made for relationship with God reminds us that we were created to find our ultimate security, identity, and meaning in God, and our humanity is fulfilled as we live by faith. In addition, many in the early church understood that being made in God's image means to be made as rational creatures, created to know God. As long as we recognize this knowledge as holistic—head knowledge *and* heart knowledge, knowing the truth about God *and* knowing God as children know a loving father—the image of God as rationality helps us see that human beings were made specially by God to hear His word, know Him, and respond in prayer and praise. Many contemporary theologians insist that being made in God's image means to be free, able to make our own decisions and live for others in freedom. Other contemporary scholars stress the social or relational aspect of humanity as being made in God's image. Just as the one God is inherently social—three distinct persons united in love—so human beings are not created to be alone but to find ourselves, our identity and purpose, in relationship with others. Still others argue that other human characteristics, such as our creativity and ability to reproduce free selves of our own, must reflect God in some way. Finally, we must not forget that the one true "image of the invisible God" is Jesus Christ (Colossians 1:15). The Son of God is the "radiance of the glory of God and the exact imprint of His nature" (Hebrews 1:3). Jesus stands not only as the one who shows us the Father but also as the one who shows us ourselves. He is the most human one, the one who lived in perfect trust and love of the Father as well as perfect love of His neighbors, and He brings us into the same relationship with God by His Spirit.

What, then, is the image of God? Perhaps it is best not to insist on a single definition. In a variety of ways, human creatures reflect their Creator as we trust in God, love one another as fellow creatures with infinite value in God's eyes, and serve the creation so that it flourishes.[5] Human beings are designed to be **theophanic**, revealing their Creator and His goodness as "mobile shrines" that offer God's blessings to the world.[6] Faith in Jesus recreates us by the Spirit of God so that we "put on the new self, which is being renewed in knowledge after the image of its creator" (Colossians 3:10).

Exercising Dominion

One aspect of being made in God's image, namely, God's charge to human creatures to "have dominion over" the creatures of the earth and the earth itself, has been often misunderstood in the modern world. Humanity, in our horizontal relationships with fellow creatures, was designed above all to reflect to other creatures, particularly other human creatures, God's love, care, and concern. It is indeed wonderful to be God's child; it is also wonderful to live out the adult responsibilities He has given His human creatures through opportunities to serve others. These responsibilities are summed up in the word **dominion** in Genesis (1:26, 28). This word has been misunderstood in Western culture because readers of Scripture have translated this concept from biblical thought into economics.

Dominion refers to lordship or rule. In the structures of this fallen world, lordship usually looks like power exercised for the sake of the powerful. It is true that King Louis XIV claimed not only to be the state himself but also to be "first servant" of the people of France. In modern democracies, politicians are supposed to serve the people whom they represent. But, in fact, political structures set some people in charge not merely to serve but to be served. These power structures are easily manipulated for selfish purposes and for the exploitation of others subject to them.

Dominion has a strikingly different meaning in the language of God. Gentile rulers lorded it over their people, but Christ taught His disciples that "it shall not be so among you" (Mark 10:43). Whoever is great among God's people will serve others; whoever wants to be first among them shall be their slave. The model is clear: Christ Himself came not to be served but to serve and even to sacrifice His life as a ransom for many (Mark 10:41–45). This is dominion in the kingdom of God.

Dominion in the language of God looks like God lording it *under*, not over, His creation. God is a supportive and serving Lord, not exploitative or manipulative. He is in charge, but He exercises proper authority

5 The early church also described the image of God in a variety of ways. See Nonna Verna Harrison, *God's Many-Splendored Image: Theological Anthropology for Christian Formation* (Grand Rapids: Baker Academic, 2010).

6 John W. Kleinig, *Wonderfully Made: A Protestant Theology of the Body* (Bellingham, WA: Lexham Press, 2021), 95.

so that creatures flourish. He uses His power for the sake of His creatures, not for Himself. So it is with the dominion that humanity is to exercise. This dominion is designed to serve, to lord it in the sense of embodying the Lord's care and concern and love. This dominion exploits neither nature nor other human creatures for its own sake. It lords from below, supporting, uplifting, embracing, guiding, and directing as appropriate.

In Genesis 1, God relates dominion specifically to nature, to nonhuman creatures, but believers recognize that they are called to deliver this same service of reflecting God's love and care to other human creatures as well. In fact, caring for creation and caring for the least of these among human beings go hand in hand. It is the poor and marginalized who are most affected by pollution, the plundering of nature, and natural disasters. God calls all humanity, and believers especially in following Jesus, to serve the least of these by caring for the whole of creation: land, water, human, and nonhuman creatures.

For the exercise of the adult responsibilities of dominion in the horizontal realm of our lives, God has given commands to multiple arenas of life, different situations in which God calls us to serve. He designed human life to be lived in four distinct **areas of responsibility**: the church and the Word, family and home, work and culture, and society and government. In each of these situations God has given human creatures responsibilities—"response-abilities"—the ability to respond to human need in God's image, as His masks, behind whom He comes to provide and protect. Believers and unbelievers alike find purpose in their responsibilities, finding secondary sources of identity, security, and meaning. Unbelievers may view these responsibilities as opportunities or assignments, as delight or duty or dreary drudge. Believers recognize them as **vocations**, as callings from God to be His masks, reflecting His image in the incidental displays of love and concern that make daily life possible.

Free to Be God's Children

The predominant views of human freedom present a serious challenge to believers' understanding of our status as children of God. Two views of human freedom—determinism and voluntarism—are quite common. These are contradictory, but in the thinking of many, they can find an uneasy peace with each other.

Determinism

For the first time since the days of the early church, many in the culture around us have resigned themselves to a kind of **determinism**. Determinism places ultimate power for human decision-making outside the individual, setting the human creature at the mercy of something external. In the twenty-first century the powers and principalities of Paul's world (Romans 8:38) have been replaced by genetic determinism or environmental coercion. People are told—and thus often believe—that they are governed and trapped by their genetic makeup. They cannot be what their genes have not programmed them to be. They are condemned to the illnesses or behavior patterns that their genes impose upon them.

In addition, people are told that their upbringing and home environment have patterned habits that are next to impossible to break. They are victims of a social and economic system that has effectively marginalized them from the chief benefits of society, and there is little they can do about it. The human being exists, in the view of the determinists, "beyond freedom and dignity."[7] Enhanced by "proofs" from the natural and social sciences, determinism seems to confirm much of human experience. We often find ourselves in situations that we did not orchestrate and that we cannot control.

At the same time, determinism fails to account for both the complexity of human creatures and the lived reality of choices. Human beings are complex. Neither genetics nor environmental factors predispose people in one single way but in multiple directions that often come into conflict. In other words, we all have experiences and personal dispositions that could fit with many different ends. Genetics and environmental factors are too complex to be simple causes for what we do and who we are. More than that, normal, lived reality shows us that our choices matter, and some choices make a significant difference. Such freedom within limits is appropriate for a creature dependent on the Creator, but contemporary Western culture naturally rebels against creaturely limits.

Voluntarism

The opposite of determinism is **voluntarism**. Voluntarism is the belief that the individual human will is totally free to exercise its choices. Such a belief in a free will, or free human choice, stands at the center of many value systems today. In the words of Stanley Hauerwas: "Our task is to become free, not through the acquisition of virtue, but by preventing ourselves from being determined, so that we can always keep our 'options open.' "[8] Voluntarism's roots go back in part to ancient Greek thinking. At the pinnacle of Greek philosophy, in the age of Socrates, Plato, and Aristotle, the figure of a Creator God had retreated over the horizon of religious thinking.

7 In the words of B. F. Skinner, *Beyond Freedom and Dignity* (New York: Knopf, 1971).

8 Stanley Hauerwas, *The Peaceable Kingdom* (Notre Dame, IN: University of Notre Dame Press, 1983), 8.

Human beings were left alone to care for themselves. To think through the fundamental plan for human action in such an arena, it was necessary to posit a human will largely, if not totally, unencumbered by necessity, by outward force or condition. The Greeks built a successful society on the basis of this conviction. They found that encouraging at least the elite of society to act freely, according to rational standards, led to good government and benefits for the community.

During the age of the Enlightenment, eighteenth-century Europeans came to similar conclusions. Disgusted at more than a century of wars—sometimes fought because of religious differences but more often fought to expand a nation's territory while disguising it as religious strife—and increasingly self-confident because of technological and medical advances, modern Europeans sought solutions in the free exercise of human rationality. The Rationalist thinkers of this age reinforced the Greek heritage that defined the human being as a freely willing, thinking, self-governing individual. (Brakes were placed on many of the worst implications of such a view by the strong sense of community that tradition and the necessities of a more primitive economy placed upon them.) This view was part of the theoretical basis of the American Revolution, embodied in both the U.S. Constitution and the Declaration of Independence. The twentieth-century success of the American project has only enhanced this view of humankind.

The concept of such a free will, working independently of its Creator and governing itself on the basis of its own rationality, cannot be found in the Scriptures. Human freedom, as described by the Bible, does not consist of the absence of any conditions, confines, or constrictions for human action and attitude. Genuine human freedom is a gift from God, to be used within His design for His purposes. This is not an imposition or a deprivation. It is good for us because it is the way God has made us. He has made me "free to be me," but free to be the "me" whom He designed and defined.

The Biblical Concept of Freedom

Freedom within God's design brings blessing and fulfillment to human creatures, recognizing that **true freedom** liberates a person for good purposes. Just as a fish confined to water is not determined or trapped but free to live and move in a place conducive to its life, the biblical concept of freedom recognizes that human freedom involves living according to God's Word and *for* the neighbor. North Americans so often think that freedom means that we do not have to answer to anyone, but that just leaves us in a battle of wills, competing with everyone else to please the sinful flesh. In contrast, God's gift of freedom liberates human creatures, first, from everything that might threaten us. God's freedom permitted Adam and Eve to live without fear, safe and sure in His love. God's new gift of freedom in Christ bestows freedom from every evil that threatens fallen sinners: freedom from sin, guilt, condemnation, the power of Satan, and the threat of the grave. At the same time, God's new gift of freedom in Christ restores our freedom for service to God and to the rest of His creation. Living in *shalom*, in harmony and peace, with other creatures gives us the experience of true human freedom, resting in God's love and serving others as a reflection of the same love.

Bondage of the Will

Some today label as freedom the ability to exercise our wills against God. It seems that human creatures are so desperate to preserve a sense of control over their lives that we even call freedom the deliberate closing of our ears to God's Word and the hardening of our hearts to God's Spirit. Such an understanding of freedom is a confusion of the biblical concept of freedom in two ways. First, true human freedom does not consist of choosing between options but is the glad and free following of God's will by His Spirit. Hence, Jesus is the freest one precisely as He joyfully follows the Father's will to suffering and the cross. Many reason that human freedom is the ability to accept or reject God's Word, but that way of thinking embodies the wrong understanding of humanity, thinking of an individual striving toward God rather than a sinful, broken creature who needs God's gracious salvation in which we find freedom by faith. To be clear, human creatures absolutely make choices of their own wills, but our freedom is found in aligning our wills with God's, not in exercising independent authority. Second, in exercising our wills against God, as all do naturally in sin, we bind ourselves to a false source of identity, security, and meaning when we "freely" choose options that run counter to trust in God and to His design for our lives. We might make this choice autonomously, and it might be exactly the choice we want, but it is not free; such idolatrous, sinful choices reveal the **bondage of the will**. These choices turn us away from God. We cannot fear, love, and trust in Him above all things because our wills will not function to make that choice. We cannot on our own turn back from revolt and rebellion.

The alternatives for describing the possible shapes of human life are not exhausted by viewing the human creature as either a freely willing being or as a puppet. The third alternative reflects the biblical reality: God made us neither to be independent beings who fulfill themselves in free choices exercised according to our sinful desires nor to be automatons that run according to genetic programming. He created us to be His children. The mystery of the relationship between Creator and human creature is not described completely with this notion of being God's children. To be honest, it does not satiate many of our curiosities. But such is Christ's definition of those whom He has come to restore to the Father's family (John 3:3–8; Matthew 18:3).

Sin has bound the human will to turn its back on God. Instead of being free for God and others, we are captive to sin and the desires of the sinful flesh. We seek out substitutes for God, and we cannot turn to Him by our own power. Although we still experience the ability to make choices in the horizontal realm, we cannot choose to trust in the true God. Only the Holy Spirit can turn us from false sources of identity, security, and meaning to find in Him the one we can trust ultimately.

Freedom and Responsibility

The biblical view of the human creature shows the limits of human creatureliness, especially under sin, but it does not deny human responsibility. Instead of positing an individualistic human liberty as the essence of humanity, the biblical writers describe the human creature as able and mandated to respond. Our response takes place in relationships: response to God with trust and love, response to the rest of creation with acts of love and care. In the Augsburg Confession, Article XVIII, Philip Melanchthon sorted out this paradox by teaching that human creatures are bound in "things above," in our vertical relationship with God, but are free in our horizontal relationships, in "things below." Although this oversimplifies human experience, it expresses the fact that in our relationship with God we are born and reborn as God's children. We have no more sovereignty of action or control over our relationship with Him than infants have over their choice of parents and their status as members of their family. Melanchthon's definition also expresses the fact that God's Law absolutely holds us responsible for our own actions.

Even apart from biblical insights on the matter, human experience teaches vaguely something of this truth. Most people recognize, particularly at critical junctures in their lives, that they are unable to control the course of events as completely as they would like. Some things lie outside human control. At the same time, most people recognize that their decisions do affect the direction of their lives and often the lives of others.

The reality of human freedom and responsibility can be expressed simply, but it forms a challenging paradox that lies deeper than our own experience of decision-making. On the one hand, the Gospel assures us that each believer's life lies safe in God's hands and that He is responsible for all in His created order. On the other hand, God's Law demands responsible action from us at every turn. The truth of God and His Word thus lies behind human **freedom and responsibility**. In the Gospel, all we can do is trust in God's mercy and receive the creaturely freedom and good gifts that

He so graciously gives without our work or merit. In the Law, however, we are accountable for our life in the body, we are responsible for our failings and successes, and we must follow His order and design for human life. The paradox between Law and Gospel will not be resolved in this age but must remain, giving believers peace on the one hand and calling us to account for our sins on the other.

Therefore, the biblical view of human freedom and the human will does not fall neatly into the category of determinism or into the category of voluntarism. The whole of human life lies in the hands of God, but He does not impersonally manipulate human fate. Much of human life moves on the basis of human decisions, and we are convinced that our decisions matter. But evidence accumulates quickly to echo the biblical view that we are not the captains of our own ship nor masters of our soul. The biblical view of God's loving care and fatherly responsibility for us lies alongside its view of the necessity of human obedience and responsibility, exercised by our own wills, in an uneasy tension.

Modern psychology assists us in recognizing that the tension between free choice in things below and bound choice in things above is not the only distinction of importance for our analysis of sinful wills. Creaturely circumstances of various kinds limit the possibilities for choice in daily life. Not all people can be everything they want to be. Some will never have natural capabilities to perform certain acts or achieve particular accomplishments. In addition, sin complicates choices not only in the vertical realm but also in the horizontal realm. In things below we often experience the visitation of the parents' sins upon the children (Exodus 20:5). Households twisted by sin teach sins to their offspring and thus cripple the will of the next generation. Such crippled wills are often incapable of exercising free choice in things below. Many abused children, for example, seem nearly bound to abuse their own children, for they have had ingrained into them a model for parenting that knows no other pattern of behavior than abuse. Such wills seem bound in relationship to other human creatures, as well as in relationship to God.

Even if the will were completely free, freely chosen abusiveness would hardly be recognized as freedom. The very inhuman nature of the act would be seen by all as a form of bondage. So it is with every form of activity or attitude exercised against God. True human freedom lies only in acknowledging Him as Creator and ourselves as creatures. True human freedom enjoys being free from evil of every form, and it enjoys being free for service to God and others.

He is Creator, and we are His creatures, His children. His design for human life gives life as it can only be enjoyed. Therefore, the biblical teaching on creation challenges every way of thought that misleads people regarding the relationship between the Creator and His created order.

Other Challenges to Biblical Teaching

Individualism and Materialism

God created individuals in body and soul so that each human being is "wonderfully made" in His own image. The Creator cares deeply about human beings as whole persons, providing good gifts to all without any merit or worthiness in anyone. God promises to raise individual bodies on the Last Day and give eternal life to all people who trust in the Lord Jesus. In this way, Christianity recognizes both the value of individuals and the value of the material world.

In contemporary Western culture, both of these good gifts of God have become idols, sources of primary identity, security, and meaning for many. The two errors of individualism and materialism demonstrate how God's gifts become perverted in the minds of fallen sinners. When people rest their lives upon their own rights rather than on God's plan of mutual dependence, they turn their backs on fellow creatures and on God Himself. God created human beings not to be alone (Genesis 2:18) but for life in community. I am not an 'I'land. I am a part of the mainland of God's humanity. Human worth cannot be found in reckless assertions of individuality. Individuals find their true worth in the relationships that God designed for them with Himself and with their fellow creatures.

Likewise, individuals do not enjoy God's wise design for humanity when they depend on material blessings for their ultimate well-being. Advertising bombards contemporary people with so many things that claim to fulfill our needs and solve our problems. The reality is that consumer culture makes us treat good gifts as disposable and life as the ever-growing accumulation of stuff. This disposable culture is dangerous for our hearts—we often desire more and more instead of resting in our Creator—and it is dangerous for the environment—as natural resources are depleted and we pollute the earth and oceans. God gave material gifts for His creatures to enjoy in mutual service, not as ends in themselves. Human creatures live well when we recognize that what we own is not our own and when we treat the blessings of God as gifts to be used for the benefit of others.

Marriage and Sexuality

The assumption that individuals should be able to choose their identity and purpose directly opposes Christianity most visibly on the front of marriage and sexuality. God designed sex as a good gift to be enjoyed between a man and a woman who have made lifelong promises to each other for the adventure of marriage: building a family, raising children, and for Christians, being formed into Christ in sanctification. North Americans, however, see marriage as a matter of personal growth for those in love and sexuality as a tool for personal pleasure. Marriage, then, should be easy, just as easy as it is to fall in love, and divorce should be normal, as normal as intense emotions of love fade over time. Sex has even less ostensible meaning; it is just something people do for fun. All of this confirms the decades-old judgment of Lutheran theologian Gerhard Forde, who noted with a frown that Americans think they have a "right to life, liberty, and the pursuit of a satisfying orgasm whenever and wherever it may be found."[9] Marriage and sexuality have been divorced from the Creator and from the children that are the proper goal of both. Instead of seeing marriage and sex within the Creator's design, we claim them as individual rights for personal pleasure.

When conservative Christians talk about these developments in marriage and sexuality, they tend to criticize the "gay agenda," liberal politicians, or some other easy target quite different from themselves, but it is essential to understand that the problem with sexuality goes deeper. The issue is not just that the culture accepts LGBTQ+ lifestyles, but that sexuality is understood as the primary or sole component of personal identity.[10] In Western culture, we identify ourselves by our sexuality and increasingly by our gender identity.[11] The growing prevalence of personal pronouns points to how important sexuality and gender are to contemporary self-understandings.[12] Christians often decry these developments, but they fail to recognize how sexuality is an idol also in our own lives. Pornography, adultery, divorce, gay and lesbian sex, and masturbation are not new, but what is new is the cultural weight given to justify sexual sins. It is as if we—Christians too!—must justify our worship at the altar of Eros, as we seek identity, security, and meaning in sexuality and our own sexual practice, whether ascetic or libertine. For placing even God's good gift of sexuality—and certainly any abuse of it—at the center of our attention will only deform us before it fails us.

---

9 Gerhard O. Forde, "Human Sexuality and Romans, Chapter One," in *The Preached God: Proclamation in Word and Sacrament*, ed. Mark C. Mattes and Steven D. Paulson (Grand Rapids: Eerdmans, 2007), 210.

10 Carl R. Trueman, *The Rise and Triumph of the Modern Self: Cultural Amnesia, Expressive Individualism, and the Road to Sexual Revolution* (Wheaton, IL: Crossway, 2020).

11 For helpful discussion of the terms to inform this debate, see Preston Sprinkle, *Embodied: Transgender Identities, the Church, and What the Bible Has to Say* (Colorado Springs, CO: David C Cook, 2021), 29–48.

12 For a pastorally informed discussion of pronoun use with transgender people—broadly understood to encompass "the various ways some people experience incongruence between their biological sex and their gender (gender identity or gender role)"—see Sprinkle, *Embodied*, 199–212 (quote here at p. 49).

The Christian Church has a difficult challenge ahead of it in speaking and living the truth of God's Word. Let us offer five considerations for how to navigate this cultural moment. First, the church must emphasize the good of lifelong **commitment** in marriage. Every semester Hopkins asks his students what percentage of people would self-report being "very happy" in their marriages, and the vast majority of students—often all students—guess that less than 25 percent of married people are very happy. Even though many of these students want to marry, they do not believe marriage is actually valuable for human fulfillment and happiness. In reality, the National Marriage Project continues to show about 60 percent of people self-report as "very happy."[13] Marriage is good, even great, since God made woman for man and man for woman right from the beginning. Christians can go even further in recognizing that Christian marriage mirrors God's own heart—the relationship of Christ to His church (Ephesians 5)—by offering promises into the unknown future. Christian marriage most mirrors God's character and faithfulness when husband and wife remain faithful to promises made long ago in far different circumstances for better or for worse, for richer or for poorer, in sickness and in health.

Second, marriage is not static and boring, but a beautiful **adventure** on which many are placed by God. Too many today think of marriage as if it involved no movement or change, but the opposite is true. The only "static" elements of marriage are the promises to be faithful to each other. People and circumstances change continually, and the adventure of marriage involves a deepening of the relationship together for the goal of sanctification in Christ Jesus. The journey of Christian marriage also embraces the differences between man and woman. In Genesis 2, God creates Eve like Adam—a human made in God's image—but different from Adam, given complementary gifts that are not the same as his. These differences are essential to their marriage since children—who are "one flesh" from the two—are an expected and intended (though not guaranteed after the fall into sin) part of their marriage relationship. Married couples today inhabit the same divine institution of marriage, in which they have been called to serve each other, submit to each other, and help each other in doing God's will to the glory of the Creator (cf. Ephesians 5:21–33). Such work is hardly boring as wife and husband keep their promises, put each other first, and seek to have (or adopt, officially or unofficially) children in hope.

Third, **singleness** is a God-given vocation as well as marriage. Christians do not need to be married or in a romantic relationship to find meaning

---

13 Alan J. Hawkins et al., "State of Our Unions, 2022," National Marriage Project, p. 42. Accessed August 29, 2022, http://nationalmarriageproject.org/wp-content/uploads/2022/02/Wheatley_StateofUnions_020222_v1.pdf.

for their lives. After all, Christians have an extended family in the church that embraces every situation and relationship in life, and their primary identity and meaning is in God. Additionally, Paul called Christians in Corinth to remain unmarried, for he saw singleness as the clearer path of sanctification and service in Christ's name in view of the end of all things (1 Corinthians 7:25–40). To be sure, marriage is good, but in singleness Christians have a great calling to serve others and bring the Word of God in a breadth of friendships and relationships. It is not without reason that the Lutheran Confessions call virginity "a more excellent gift" than marriage.[14] A church that forgets the vocation of singleness as a divine gift is in danger of worshiping at the altar of Eros.

Fourth, the church must not confuse being male and female with masculinity and femininity. God made Adam and Eve male and female, but he did not make Adam into a football player and Eve into a seamstress. God calls each person to follow Jesus in holiness, but He does not demand that each male be strong and tough and each female be an emotionally responsive multitasker. In an age of sexual and gender confusion, the church should not add fuel to the fire by mixing biological sex with cultural categories of masculinity and femininity.[15] After all, Scripture describes God with plenty of feminine imagery: comforting His people like a mother comforts her child (Isaiah 66:13), concerned for His people as a nursing mother is for her infant (Isaiah 49:15), and protecting and nurturing Israel like a mother eagle her chicks (Deuteronomy 32:11). God gives every person the gift of biological sex, but He does not specify how each female, male, or intersex person is to live that out beyond the call of obedience to God's commands and responsible service to the neighbor.

Finally, people need role models to show the beauty of Christian marriage and the importance of healthy friendships. Popular media highlights the glamour and sexuality of celebrity; pornography furthers this kind of idolatrous display by projecting idealized naked bodies apart from real bodily presence.[16] In addition, an overemphasis on sexual purity can actually put sex on a similar pedestal so that sex is given inordinate importance in the Christian life. Instead of these idolatrous notions, the church needs to look again to those who embody healthy and holy sexuality. Christians should not avoid talking about romance—Song of Songs is not afraid to illustrate romantic love—or only speak about sex in a negative fashion. Sex is a good and helpful gift for marriage between a man and a woman, given by God Himself! Within its place in marriage, sex deepens intimacy, focuses

14 Apology of the Augsburg Confession XXIII 38.

15 See Sprinkle, *Embodied*, 79–94.

16 Kleinig, *Wonderfully Made*, 172–74.

each spouse on the other, and opens space for the future, for children. At the same time, Christians dare not give in to continual or raunchy discussion of sexuality, as if it were just another topic of public discussion. Churches should lift up holy, romantic love between spouses to help young people envision the adventure of marriage; also to be celebrated are healthy, holy friendships, which need no romance, to show that relationships do not need to be sexual to be important and intimate.

Spiritual Care for LGBTQ+ Persons

Holy Scripture teaches that sex between an unmarried man and woman, two men, two women, or more than two people is sin, as such actions transgress against God's intended design and direct commands for human sexuality (e.g., Genesis 2:21–25; Matthew 19:3–12; Romans 1:24–27; 1 Corinthians 6:9–11, 15–20). God's church must offer these clear, biblical teachings to its members and to the world. At the same time, believers must be willing to present these teachings in a winsome manner in the context of the Gospel and offer spiritual care for gay, lesbian, bisexual, transgender, and every other person who struggles with sex or gender in the church and outside of it.

Good spiritual care requires that Christians treat every case *individually*, listening to people, understanding their stories, and bringing God's word of both Law and Gospel to bear on their lives.[17] Many gay, lesbian, and transgender people have heard the condemning Law from the church and feel the guilt of their sin, but they have not heard often the Gospel spoken in the context of a caring community so that Jesus and His work is recognized as for them. No sin lies beyond the pale of Christ's atoning death and vivifying resurrection. Moreover, the church is a hospital for sinners, not a sanctuary for saints. People struggling with sin and its effects, including same-sex attraction and gender dysphoria, should not be alienated from the church, but given opportunity to hear God's Word, know His forgiveness, and follow Jesus as the church seeks to live together in repentance. The church must be a community that lives in Christ's forgiveness and offers it to all in love even as it speaks the truth of God's Word in a culture that no longer knows God's design for human bodies and life.

By attending to the uniqueness of people's stories, the church is playing the long game—cultures, nations, and societies come and go, but the Word of the Lord remains forever—and can afford to move slowly and recognize the humanity of each individual without trying to win the culture war in every conversation. In other words, Christians do not need to adjudicate

17 On the importance of valuing individuals in the context of the transgender conversation, see Sprinkle, *Embodied*, 58–62.

every instance of the culture wars with every person. It is far more important to hear an individual's story, affirm his or her humanity and the love of God in Christ for that person, inviting participation in a church community that is following Jesus in repentance and sanctification. In such a community, the reality of God's creation as male and female and the goodness of Christian marriage can take on flesh and make sense of God's Word among fellow sinners, who are confident in Christ and the Scriptures, yet still figuring out how to live faithfully in the messiness of the world.

One challenge in offering spiritual care for LGBTQ+ persons is ministry to same-sex attracted Christians. Many who grew up in the church, read their Bibles, and went to Sunday School will feel appropriate tension between their same-sex attraction and the will of God. Most important, believers must teach that same-sex attracted people are created in the image of God and dearly loved by Jesus. They are among those for whom Jesus died, and in Baptism, Jesus gave them His Spirit to make them holy. Their sexual attraction does not change the reality of God's Word that grants them their true identity as baptized believers and beloved creatures. Such Christians should be encouraged to live in singleness and pursue a variety of holy friendships as part of their sanctification in Christ. Those who pursue this chaste holiness should be held up in honor in the church (cf. Matthew 19:12; 1 Corinthians 7:38). Some, however, will think that they cannot handle chastity. For gay or lesbian Christians who cannot bear the weight of singleness, the church must be willing to take the time to listen to them, understand them and the place of their hearts, as much as is possible, and speak God's word of Law and Gospel to bring repentance and forgiveness of sins. Alienating or condemning LGBTQ+ persons who are struggling to live in God's will is just as bad as giving people permission to live in sin. This is challenging ministry that requires prayer, the Word, the guidance of the Holy Spirit, and grace from one Christian to another.

The most difficult issue today is probably not same-sex relationships but gender dysphoria and ministry to transgender people. Here too, the most important lesson is treating transgender people as human creatures, created by God and loved by Jesus to death on a cross. Ministry to transgender people will require much listening, compassion, and slow teaching to encourage and lead them to faithfulness to Jesus. The difficulty of this ministry is only compounded by the alternative doctrines of Western culture that conflict with God's Word.

The Scriptures teach that God made human beings male and female in the beginning. This was not a matter of culture or society, but sexual biology, the corresponding biology of man and woman necessary to produce offspring. Although many today speak of gender fluidity and gender as a cultural construct, the Bible speaks almost exclusively about biological sex, not gender. If we focus on the body rather than the psychology of the brain—which is far more fluid than most people admit[18]—the science also points in the direction of two biological sexes. Even intersex conditions prove the rule that biologically people are male or female or a blend of the characteristics of the two.[19] No distinctly third kind of biological sex exists other than female or male. The Scriptures confess our bodies and sex are created in God's image and made to be inhabited by His Spirit. We need to learn to see our biological sex as female, male, or intersex as a gift of God to use according to His will.

Today, a number of people, especially young people, are suffering from incongruence between their biological sex and their gender identity, called gender dysphoria.[20] The reasons are nearly as numerous as the number of people with the condition. Ministering to people with gender dysphoria will require patience and compassion above all to listen carefully and offer the truth of God's Word that prioritizes the Gospel. The first recourse for gender dysphoria for Christians should not be to change the body, but to talk with pastors, psychologists, and doctors about these feelings and how to be faithful to God's design and Word. More often than not, the problem is not the body—that is just the easier fix—but the whole person who needs to be healed so as to appreciate the biological gifts of maleness and femaleness that the Creator has given. This healing and recognition of God's created gifts will also happen in a community that cares for those struggling with their biology as it cares for each of us sinners who are yet redeemed by Christ the crucified.

No matter how much we try to determine our own lives or create our own identities, the doctrine of creation shows these self-driven paths to be narrow and lifeless. The full flourishing of human life is possible only when we recognize our dependence on the Creator and His mercy. "It is He who made us, and we are His" (Psalm 100:3). By His Spirit, we learn to see ourselves, our bodies, souls, and all our members—including our sexual organs—not as tools for personal benefit but as gifts of God to be used according to His design and for the good of our neighbors. Recognizing ourselves as God's creatures in faith, we are truly free, free to be the children that He has made and remade us to be, reflecting His image.

18 See Sprinkle, *Embodied,* 127–41.

19 See Sprinkle, *Embodied*, 122–23.

20 On rapid-onset gender dysphoria, see Sprinkle, *Embodied*, 159–77.

CHAPTER 5
GOD PROVIDES

THE good Creator does not forsake what He made. He has all life in His hands, and He graciously and generously gives good gifts to His creatures. He provides His human creatures with body and soul, limbs and senses, reason and faculties of mind, food and clothing, and everything else that we have and are. Our trust that God is daily and richly caring for us provides confidence for the Christian life even when suffering and need arise. Faith in God's providence also provides the framework in which we recognize God's good gifts in thankfulness, praise Him in joy, and act as instruments of His providence in words and deeds that touch the needs of others.

God Provides for His Own

God provides for all He has made, for everyone and everything in creation. He keeps it and us running. "In Him all things hold together" (Colossians 1:17). He upholds the universe by His word of power (Hebrews 1:3). The God who made the world and everything in it, Paul told the Athenians, fashioned every human nation on the face of the earth. He has allotted them periods of time and geographic boundaries for their lives. Paul then used the words of the ancient poet Aratus, and perhaps also Epimenides, in confessing that in God we live and move and have our being, and our existence stems from Him (Acts 17:24–28). God has promised to keep the seasons in their places (Genesis 8:22). God makes the sun rise on the evil as well as the good and sends the rain on the just and the unjust (Matthew 5:45). He preserves humankind and animal life (Psalm 36:6), and He provides for the interworking of all parts of His creation (Psalm 104:10–31).

Contemporary North Americans do not usually give God credit for His ordering and running of the universe. We prefer to point out the flaws and think that we are capable of fixing the issues—though our hubris often results in disaster. The fundamental problem with this view is that we think God only acts when we are not acting ourselves. In other words, we believe that if human beings are responsible for something, then God cannot be. Consequently, God only appears to provide through miracles or unexplained phenomena rather than guiding ordinary, daily life. In Scripture, however, God provides, protects, and preserves not only directly but also indirectly through human creatures and the creation, using the laws of nature, the help of neighbors, and the fecundity of the earth to provide. God's providence is the ultimate cause of these even though they are not recognizable as God's providential hand apart from faith.

Despite the way that God hides His directing of the universe, Christians are particularly conscious of His role in their lives from conception and birth (Psalm 139:13; Job 31:15; Jeremiah 1:5) to death (Matthew 10:28–31). He who keeps inventory of the hairs on our heads (Matthew 10:30) holds His thinking, willing people in His own hand and plan (Psalm 37:24; Proverbs 16:9). He keeps His people in His sight, delivering them from death and keeping them alive in famine and other adversity (Psalm 33:13–15, 18–19). Believers rest upon the assurance that God directs their lives for their good (Romans 8:28). That does not mean that everything they experience is good. In a fallen, sinful world, believers often wrestle with God about calamities and trouble He allows, and believers suffer under evils and sins that grieve God too. Yet God is close to the brokenhearted (Psalm 34:18), and His hand directs good and evil in their lives toward His good end.

God Receives the Complaints of His Own

God's governance of life is not always clear to believers. Christians often encounter misfortune and suffer evil at the hand of other human creatures or at the mercy of nature. Some believers shy away from complaining to God about such suffering. This shyness can be dishonest about our feelings. It may also deny the depth of God's love for us. It is not wrong to cry out to God in anguish and to lay our suffering and sense of loss before His loving heart. In fact, Holy Scripture is full of **laments**, cries of sorrow and pain directed to God in prayer, especially in the Psalms.

God did not create us to be angry with Him, but we do well to recognize the difference between the cry of faith, "God, I am angry with You," and the cry of unbelief, "I am angry with God," though the difference is not always apparent at first. The former shriek confesses God's lordship and our expectation of His goodness, even if in a negative way. It cries to God in the hour of need, turning to Him as the dear Father, even as it may betray sinful misapprehensions of how God is at work in our lives. In response to such a shriek of pain and anger, our heavenly Father is always ready to swoop up His children into His loving arms—even when they are throwing a temper tantrum—and cuddle them in His lap.

In the face of destruction and pain, God's people cried out in Isaiah: "The Lord has forsaken me; my Lord has forgotten me." In mock indignation

God replied, "Can a woman forget her nursing child, that she should have no compassion on the son of her womb?" Then He assured the Jews whose despair in the face of the devastation of Zion had overcome them: "Even these [mothers] may forget, yet I will not forget you! Behold, I have engraved you on the palms of My hands. … Those who wait for Me shall not be put to shame" (Isaiah 49:14–16, 23). The maternal instinct and compassion of God our Father never fails.

Thus, even in anger and frustration over God's apparent absence or His mistaken direction of the course of our lives, we can boldly and confidently approach Him as children approach a loving Father. Believers experience days in which Job's words can give voice to their thoughts: "God has cast me into the mire, and I have become like dust and ashes. I cry to You for help and You do not answer me; I stand, and You only look at me. You have turned cruel to me; with the might of Your hand You persecute me" (Job 30:19–21). Finally, however, in the midst of all their suffering, God leads His people to confess with Job: "I know that You can do all things, and that no purpose of Yours can be thwarted" (Job 42:2). This confidence, shaken and battered as it might be, permits God's children to throw a fit at His feet, but it is also the handle by which He lifts us to His lap.

God Is Lord over Evil

In this present age of sin and death, evil sometimes seems to triumph, and God seems to be absent. But God is Lord over evil. When His people were suffering oppression in Egypt, He liberated them by smashing Pharaoh's tyranny. When the angels left their proper positions, He chained them in the darkness. When Sodom and Gomorrah indulged in immorality and unnatural lust, He punished them with fire (Jude 5–7).

God's control over evil is so complete that He could even claim it for His own purposes. He claimed responsibility for light and darkness, for weal and woe, "well-being" and "calamity" (Isaiah 45:7). He could say, "Against this family I am devising disaster, from which you cannot remove your necks" (Micah 2:3). He causes blindness and deafness even as He gives sight and hearing (Exodus 4:11). Amos could console his hearers by explaining: "Does disaster come to a city, unless the Lord has done it?" (Amos 3:6). None of these passages offers an explanation for the origin of evil. None of these passages can be easily dismissed by saying that what we view as evil—for instance, blindness—may not really be evil from God's point of view. The message of these passages points to a deeper truth: God is Lord over evil. God has the whole world in His hands. God masters and moves all human history. Without piercing the mystery of evil, these passages affirm God's lordship over everything, even evil.

Thus, when evil assumes control of people, God is not absent. We often do not understand what God is doing, and we cannot penetrate the veil to see His mind outside of the cross. At the same time, Scripture testifies that God may be present in giving those steeped in evil over to their stubborn hearts (Psalm 81:11–12; cf. Acts 14:16; Romans 1:24). This does not mean that He does not want them to be saved (1 Timothy 2:4). It means that He retains control of His creation.

God grieves over the evil that afflicts His people. God sets limits upon the ills that afflict them. These limits may not fall exactly where Job and his kin would prefer them, but God does set limits (Job 1:12; 2:6). God never forgets His chosen people and is always sensitive to their limitations (Matthew 24:22; 1 Corinthians 10:13). He intervenes on their behalf and frustrates their enemies' plans (Psalm 33:10). He turns enemies into friends, a Saul into a Paul (Acts 9). Not always but often He takes the evil intentions of evil people and fools them; He brings good out of evil, as He did in Joseph's case (Genesis 50:20). God is the loving Lord of His people. He answers their prayers to keep them as the apple of His eye and hide them in the shadow of His wings (Psalm 17:8). He remains their Father and King.

God Preserves and Provides through the Created Order

God exercises His kingly, fatherly love by preserving and providing for His people. For instance, He feeds them: "The eyes of all look to You, and You give them their food in due season. You open Your hand; You satisfy the desire of every living thing" (Psalm 145:15–16). Usually He provides food through His ordered system of provision (Genesis 1:19–30; 9:3); sometimes He sends manna (Exodus 16:14).

Nature Works according to God's Pattern

Nature works according to God's plan, under His direction, exhibiting a fairly regular set of natural causes or "laws." Human nourishment proceeds from, among other things, His governance of the weather (Job 36:26–33). The discipline of meteorology may not have mastered God's program for rain and lightning, but the patterns of weather are plain enough for squirrels, farmers, and meteorologists to offer some wisdom. His plans regulate the course of seasons and days (Psalm 104:19–23). The "laws of nature" have been passed in the legislature of human observation and scientific analysis. Human investigators are always refining these laws and making better descriptions of the way that God has made creation function. But God has written into the script for His creation a normal, regular, quite reliable pattern of action. This enables human creatures to use and manage creation, to exercise dominion under it.

Miracles

God cares for His creation through miracles as well. The word *miracle* may refer to any event in the physical world that deviates from the laws of nature formulated by human investigators and superseding current knowledge of those laws. Although we define miracles as acts that break the laws of nature, as understood by human beings, miracles in Scripture usually do the opposite: they fulfill God's creative design and intention for the world and His people. For instance, Jesus' miracles of feeding the five thousand and four thousand should not be understood as rupturing or suspending the laws of nature. Rather, the creation's Lord made the bounty of the earth spring forth for the hungry as intended in the beginning. Throughout Holy Scripture, God's miracles do not merely wow; they restore and set right the fallen creation, as signs of God's word of promise and as actions that bring restoration, healing, life, truth, and abundance to a broken world.

Miracles are not self-interpreting. In other words, just because we see a miraculous event occur does not mean that we know the cause or the purpose. Miracles need interpretation, words, to tell us what they mean. After all, miracles may proceed from God's power, but they may reflect the power of Satan (Matthew 12:24). We are on sure ground when we talk about the miracles of Holy Scripture or when miracles lead us to trust in Jesus Christ or confess God's providential work in the world to care for His people in body and soul (compare 1 John 4:1–6).

The word *miracle* may be applied to any event that opens the eyes of human creatures to God. John recorded the "signs" Christ performed in order that his readers might believe that Jesus is the Messiah, God's Son, and that by believing they might have life in His name (John 20:31). Some miracles provide for God's children; all of them invite faith. From the perspective of human analysis three types of miracles emerge. Some may defy explanation for all time; they transcend the way in which God normally works in His universe. Commercial production of quality wine from water lies beyond our imagination (John 2:1–11). Other miracles may be explained with advanced human knowledge. During Kolb's university years, the friend of a friend, their group learned, had been miraculously cured of leukemia. Looking back, it seems likely that God used newly developed "miracle" drugs and the physicians who were experimenting with them in performing that miracle. The friend's remission still gave cause for praise of God; it remains a miracle, part of God's providence, even when explained. Third, some miracles may have a scientific explanation. The exodus was possible because God sent an east wind, and through its blowing all night long He drove back the sea (Exodus 14:21). Nevertheless, the circumstances and the timing of the exodus remain God's providential care no matter what the scientific explanation might be.

Believers must reject the claims of those who deny the possibility of miracles because they are enthralled with human control of the universe. In reality, God retains control. He makes this clear to us just at those moments when we believe we have mastered the technology to preserve life as we like it (Genesis 11:1–9). Believers must also avoid thinking that God provides for us only when He works through miracles. He is utterly faithful in meeting the need of His people, on His terms, not always on ours.

The Structures of Human Life Provide

God provides not only through the regular and irregular workings of the natural or physical world about us. He also provides through the structures for human life that He has woven into the warp and woof of human society. His structure arises out of the **four situations for human community**: home, occupation, societal relationships (both the formal relationships of the political sphere and the informal relationships of neighborly contact and associations for specific purposes), and congregational life. God provides through fellow human creatures, whom He uses as **masks** for His own presence and caregiving as He gives them roles and responsibilities to play. God's providence is not apparent to normal vision since He hides beyond His creatures that He uses as masks. Yet God truly provides through them as they function in fulfilling the responsibilities of spouse, parent, child; of supervisor or worker, of butcher, baker, and candlestick maker; of legislator or bureaucrat, taxpayer, or police officer, of neighbor or Little League coach; of worshiper and witness, of pastor, Sunday School teacher, or altar guild member. In the words of Charles Arand: "God does this work 'in, with, and under' his creatures." God provides through creatures, limiting Himself voluntarily so as to make creatures instruments of His Word and work.[1]

God calls Christians to responsibilities and roles that serve others; He appoints all human beings to such tasks. Through the exercise of these "response-abilities," He meets the needs of others in an orderly way. Different societies organize the four situations differently and sometimes define the responsibilities of each situation in differing manners. God actively supports and governs His world through all His human masks, whatever institutional forms their situations may take.

1 Charles P. Arand, "Back to the Beginning: Creation Shapes the Entire Story," *Concordia Journal* 40, no. 2 (2014), 134.

God Provides through Angels

If we weigh the biblical evidence, human creatures serve God as His primary means of meeting the needs of other human creatures. Nonetheless, the biblical writers occasionally noted the critical importance of God's angelic creatures in caring for His human creatures. The Scriptures give few details on the nature and none on the origin of the angels. Occasionally called "gods," assembled in God's council, in the Old Testament (e.g., Psalm 82:1; 138:1), they assumed the name "messenger" (Greek: angel) in the New Testament. In the intertestamental period, Jews elaborated their description of the angels with elements from neighboring peoples. This does not alter the fact of the angels' existence. Because the angels do not subject themselves to human analysis and control, some in the modern Western world have doubted their existence. The angels do not depend on human belief in their existence to continue to provide God's care as "ministering spirits sent out to serve for the sake of those who are to inherit salvation" (Hebrews 1:14).

God created the angels to praise and worship Him (Isaiah 6:3). They serve as His messengers (Matthew 1:20; Luke 1:8–20, 26–38; 2:8–14; 24:1–8). They will assist the Lord in completing human history (Matthew 25:31; 1 Thessalonians 4:16). God has commissioned them to have charge of His people and guard us in all our ways. They bear us up on their hands and protect us from stumbling (Psalm 91:11–12). They confront the enemies of God's people, whether these enemies are armies (2 Kings 19:35), lions (Daniel 6:22), or jailers (Acts 5:17–21; 12:6–11). Around those who live in God's family His angel has thrown up a line of defense and rescues them from evil (Psalm 34:7).

What we don't know about angels is far more than what we do know, but we can rest assured that God is in control of both the physical and the spiritual realms—the entire cosmos—and He employs His angels for His good purposes. Angels should point us not to explore them more deeply but, as fellow servants of the triune God, to fall before our Lord in trust, prayer, and praise (Revelation 22:8–9).

Providence in the Face of Life's Tragedies

Evil abounds, even in the lives of those who live in God's family. The most piercing question believers and unbelievers scream into the ear of God or the dark of the night is "Why?" "Why is there evil in the world if God is good and almighty?" This is the ultimate of human questioning in a fallen world. Variations abound. In the realm of eternal salvation, the question is phrased, "Why are some saved, and not others?" In the realm of daily life, the question takes the form of demanding to know why my brother died young, why my company failed just before my pension was vested, why my attempts to win the right spouse always end in shame. "What did I do to deserve this?" we cry out as we notice that worse scoundrels than we are getting off scot-free. "Why is life so unfair?" we shriek, but the concepts of fairness and equality provide inadequate protection against the onslaught of evil. Christians also have two special questions about forms of evil in their experience. "If the Holy Spirit is Lord of the church, why is the church always such a mess, divided by serious doctrinal differences or by trivial personal or political differences?" Beyond that, and perhaps more critical: "Why does the Holy Spirit not liberate me from sin and temptation, with which I continue to struggle and to which I often fall?" Paul's recognition that the messenger of Satan's harassment served to make clear that the apostle depended on God's power and not his own (2 Corinthians 12:9) offers assurance of God's faithfulness but not an explanation for why an evil bedeviling me does not go away.

Jesus' contemporaries posed the question to Him more than once. His disciples wanted to know whether the man who had been born blind had brought his condition upon himself or whether his parents were at fault. It is not clear exactly what Jesus meant when He replied, "It was not that this man sinned, or his parents, but that the works of God might be displayed in him" (John 9:2–3). The text does not clarify whether Jesus' "that" refers simply to the result of the situation or to its actual purpose. Jesus may have been refusing to indulge in speculation regarding the "why" of the situation and simply commenting: "Whatever the cause, the result of his blindness is that God's work is to be made manifest here." To the Jewish mind, however, with its utter confidence in God's control of all things, Jesus may have been saying, "God had a purpose in this man's blindness: to give the opportunity to show forth what God is doing in Me." We cannot be sure from the text. In any case, Jesus points away from human causality or blame to God's sovereignty and the relationship of human creatures with their God.

The same approach guided Jesus' address to two questions posed at another time by events around Him. He cited two examples of the seemingly unfair way in which tragedy strikes. Pilate's police had mingled the blood of some Galileans with their sacrifices. Jesus used this incident to meet the obvious question: "Do you think that these Galileans were worse sinners than all the other Galileans, because they suffered in this way?" "Or those eighteen on whom the tower in Siloam fell and killed them: do you think that they were worse offenders than all the others who lived in Jerusalem?" Jesus rejected the equation of these evils with a certain quantity of sin. Such a verdict stems from a false understanding of God's judgment. God's judgment is not designed first to punish but to call to repentance and bring about a right relationship with God by faith. "No," Jesus said. They were not the worst offenders; these Galileans had not sinned more than their fellow Galileans. The questions missed the point. The only point that Jesus drew from these incidents was the need for personal repentance by all (Luke 13:1–5). He wanted the whole life of all His human creatures to be lived in repentance, sorrow for sin and faith in God.

Theodicy

The question remains pressing today: How can evil exist if God is truly good and all-powerful? It is a deep and difficult conundrum. If God is good, why does He allow evil? If God is all-powerful, why does He not do something about evil? To make the problem even worse, this is one of the most common questions that non-Christians raise against the Christian faith: "How can your God be good, or even exist, if He allows injustice, murder, and all kinds of evil?" Christians should learn to recognize underneath this question and our own difficulties with the problem not merely a logical puzzle but an aching heart that cries out for help—"How could God allow this to happen to my child? my mother? my health?" In other words, although the problem of evil does need to be addressed as a cognitive matter, it is fundamentally an existential problem that makes all people—Christians, Muslims, and atheists alike—question the core of human identity, security, and meaning. The best solution, then, may not be a logical one, but the good news of a new relationship with the Father, through His Son, Jesus, in which we can rest secure eternally.[2] From that vantage point, the problem of evil takes on a new, less persistent character.

Although no logical answer has ever been formulated to this most unrelenting of human questions, the failure to solve the problem of evil has not been for lack of effort. In fact, the problem of evil may be "the guiding force for modern thought."[3] The attempt to solve it is haughtily called **theodicy**, literally, the justification of God. A German philosopher of the eighteenth century, Gottfried Wilhelm Leibniz, invented the term.

The modern world may have made the problem of evil its theme, but the problem has been well-known for millennia. In the Scriptures, the psalmist cried out: "For I was envious of the arrogant when I saw the prosperity of the wicked. For they have no pangs until death; their bodies are fat and sleek. They are not in trouble as others are; they are not stricken like the rest of

2 See David Luy and Matthew Levering, "Introduction: Evil in Christian Theology," in *Evil and Creation: Historical and Constructive Essays in Christian Dogmatics*, ed. David J. Luy, Matthew Levering, and George Kalantzis (Bellingham, WA: Lexham Press, 2020), 1–9.

3 Susan Neiman, *Evil in Modern Thought: An Alternative History of Philosophy* (Princeton, NJ: Princeton University Press, 2002), 2–3.

mankind" (Psalm 73:3–5). The preacher of Ecclesiastes recognized the same trouble: "In my vain life I have seen everything. There is a righteous man who perishes in his righteousness, and there is a wicked man who prolongs his life in his evildoing" (Ecclesiastes 7:15). Along with the recognition of the problem, the effort to vindicate God by explaining how He could ordain or permit natural and moral evil also predates Leibniz by millennia. But God refuses to permit His human creatures to justify Him, to remodel Him and refurbish His image, even in the face of evil.

Many people try to get God off the hook for the problem of evil, but the solution quickly becomes worse than the problem. Most often, God becomes less than God, not fully in control of the world. Such are the logical solutions that human beings construct to solve the problem of evil. Solving the problem according to syllogistic logic always ends in denying one fundamental truth or another.

Evil Is Not an Illusion. Some have tried to deny the first of the three points of the dilemma: that evil exists. In the nineteenth century, Mary Baker Eddy codified the wish that evil would prove to be an illusion into a religion, Christian Science. Much of Western culture since the Enlightenment has secretly hoped she was right. The Enlightenment itself thought that evil had been somewhat overrated. Its rationalism believed that human mastery of the world around us and human abilities to forge a new world would force the triumph of good over evil. Holocaust and Hiroshima, genocides and wars, pandemics and environmental catastrophes have discouraged many. Despite our best efforts, evil does not seem to be going anywhere.

The irony of rejecting evil's existence is that it actually destroys hope rather than creating a more hopeful people. Optimism about human abilities devastates hope when reality sets in—that we are not as powerful as we thought.[4] Instead of recognizing the real magnitude of evil, we soft-pedal the human experiences of guilt and shame, of tragedy, tribulation, and trouble, of despair, death, and damnation, and we put on a happy face. But that, too, ends in despair. Denying evil makes fools of us all.

If evil is real, then to solve the logical conundrum, God must be either too weak to do something about evil or unconcerned with human good. Pierre Bayle put the problem this way in his famous late seventeenth-century *Historical and Critical Dictionary* that inspired Leibniz's account of theodicy: "God is either willing to remove evil and cannot; or he can and is unwilling."[5]

---

4 Compare David Zahl, *Low Anthropology: The Unlikely Key to a Gracious View of Others (and Yourself)* (Grand Rapids: Brazos, 2022), 11–40.

5 See Neiman, *Evil in Modern Thought*, 118.

God Is Almighty. The contradiction must remain. Some, however, hang on to the hope that God is good and solve the problem of evil by conceding God's impotence. In his book *When Bad Things Happen to Good People*, Rabbi Harold Kushner offers a twofold "solution" to the question of theodicy.[6] First, we may hope that God is evolving toward being almighty. Second, we must forgive and love God despite the fact that He does not come up to our standards for the good. Rabbi Kushner offers a thoroughly human god, truly a god created in our own image. Furthermore, Kushner focuses only on the evils outside us, the evils over which we have no control. He avoids confronting the evil within. He proposes forgiving our limited, flawed god and remaining—as far as is possible in the face of bad luck, sickness, and cruelty—in control. The problem of evil is solved, but at what cost?

God Is Good. The drama *Amadeus* depicts the composer Salieri's struggle against evils directed at him from a god with a mean streak. Salieri had pledged God his whole life if God would give him fame. God went back on the bargain Salieri thought they had struck. The frivolous, impudent Mozart got the talent and recognition Salieri had wanted, as author Peter Schaffer weaves the script, and Salieri became bitter, despising God. (Who would not despise such a god?) Salieri's solution to the problem of evil placed all power in God's hands. But Salieri saw that power displayed in "the taunting of [an] unachievable, uncaring god."[7] Neither Kushner's god nor Salieri's satisfies. They satisfy neither the biblical description of God nor human longing and need.

The Biblical Approach to Theodicy

If God is almighty and God is good, why does evil exist? The question remains unanswered and unanswerable from the vantage point of the fallen human creature. Instead of offering a logical solution to the problem of evil, the Scriptures offer us a story that helps us understand evil in our lives and in the world, and have hope for what God will do to evil in the end. In other words, God does not tell us why evil exists, but He does tell us where evil is going and how to understand evil today. Evil is headed for its own tomb, led by our victorious Lord. Evil is not eternal, neither past nor future. Evil was not in the beginning and will not be in the new heavens and the new earth. For Christians, Jesus' empty tomb stands as the sign of His victory over death, hell, sin, and all evil, both inside and out.

In addition to giving us the hope of a future without evil, God also tells us where evil puts us today. Evil damages our relationship with God and alienates us from human community. Hence, God comes to combat evil

6 Harold S. Kushner, *When Bad Things Happen to Good People* (New York: Avon, 1981).

7 Peter Schaffer, *Amadeus* (New York: Harper & Row, 1981), 150.

every day through the presence of His people. They turn back evil with their love for the vulnerable and suffering, for those who suffer sickness, cruelty, pain, or their own guilt and shame.

Christian responses to evil must be careful to acknowledge the reality of evil. No one who is suffering the loss of a dear loved one too soon wants to hear how God works all things for good, no matter how true the sentiment is. At the same time, Christians should not call evil everything that causes suffering. Even experience shows how God builds character in our suffering so that trust and love are not diminished but built up through suffering. A longer look at life often shows how our stories are like Joseph's: what we assumed to be evil, "God meant it for good" (Genesis 50:20). All proper Christian responses to evil recognize God as God, refuse to shy away from the harsh reality of evil, and proclaim God's presence, goodness, and ultimate victory slowly but certainly to those in the throes of evil.

The Permissive Will of God. Christians may try to get God off the hook for evil by distinguishing His absolute will from His permissive will. We know that God does not want or cause evil, so we presume that He permits it against His own will. This "solution" tries to pierce the veil of the hidden God. It neither meets the logical criterion for analysis, nor does it meet the need of the sufferer. It may remind us that God does not want to harm us, but Job did not find God's giving license for evil a great comfort. Neither do many others. Even when we have posited a permissive will of God, we have not answered the question of why He would permit evil even if He does not cause it. The dilemma remains.

Reward and Punishment as Explanation for Evil. The Scriptures offer several partial solutions to the problem of evil that work within certain limits. For instance, the Bible recognizes that evil afflicts the guilty, for God visits iniquity upon those who perpetrate it (Exodus 34:7). God rewards good conduct and punishes sinful conduct. That is only just and fair. This answer has the strength of explaining a good deal of evil. We reap what we sow. We smoke, and we develop lung cancer. We drive dangerously fast, and we have an automobile accident. God's Law keeps close track of us, and it dispenses its judgments.

This view preserves a sense of order and regularity in the world about us. It preserves a sense of justice and fairness in the universe. But it does not explain "innocent victims." Some smokers live to a ripe old age; some young nonsmokers develop lung cancer. Some speeders never get caught, to say nothing of dying in an accident. Some pedestrians who never crossed against a light are struck and killed on their way to visit the sick or feed the hungry. Furthermore, too often this view of evil drives us to assess blame where none actually exists. We begin to think that human creatures are in control of their own fate through proper performance of God's Law. This approach to the problem of evil may bring some sufferers to repentance, but too often it will turn them in upon themselves, seeking a false explanation for suffering.[8] Those who have avoided evil will be tempted toward pride at their performance while those in evil's grasp may sink in despair.

Lament to God as a Reaction to Evil. At other times biblical writers turned to God in lament, as Habakkuk did when he cried out: "O LORD, how long shall I cry for help, and You will not hear?" (Habakkuk 1:2). Habakkuk looked to God for relief from suffering by calling down God's judgment against his enemies (Habakkuk 1:5–2:20). Jeremiah did the same: "Let those be put to shame who persecute me, but let me not be put to shame; let them be dismayed, but let me not be dismayed; bring upon them the day of disaster; destroy them with double destruction!" (Jeremiah 17:18). Such expression of negative feelings—outright hatred for the foe—seems too impatient and too self-righteous. It puts the burden on God's back, and perhaps the blame on Him for failing to deliver His people from their oppression. It may seem impious to put blame on God, but the Psalter is full of laments and cries. Praying laments honestly vents the believer's frustrations and fears. It correctly calls judgment down upon evil, putting the judgment in God's hands rather than our own. In addition, crying out in lament recognizes that God is the one who is ultimately in charge. It will not let Him off the hook for what happens in the world. In Dietrich Bonhoeffer's words, one who laments with the Psalms "sets out to do battle against God for God."[9] In lament, a child of God cries out to the heavenly Father in hope according to God's revealed promise even while suffering all kinds of evil that God has, according to His hidden will, permitted. In this way, lament expresses trust in God despite present circumstances and thus puts the lonely lamenter in community both with God[10] and all who pray "deliver us from evil."[11]

The Suffering Servant. One important response to evil in Scripture is the presence of God in the midst of suffering and evil. Throughout Scripture, God refuses to be distant from His people even as they experience all kinds of pain and suffering—"The LORD is near to the brokenhearted and saves the crushed in spirit" (Psalm 34:18). In fact, the Suffering Servant of Isaiah (42:1–4; 49:1–7; 50:4–9; 52:13–53:11) takes the importance of presence in the midst of evil one step further, suggesting that suffering can be absorbed

---

8 Daniel J. Simundson, *Faith under Fire: How the Bible Speaks to Us in Times of Suffering* ([San Francisco]: Harper Collins, 1991), 17–41.

9 Dietrich Bonhoeffer, *Psalms: The Prayer Book of the Bible* (Minneapolis: Augsburg, 1970), 48.

10 Simundson, *Faith under Fire*, 43–61.

11 Compare Bonhoeffer, *Psalms*, 27 and 49.

vicariously, that is, for others. On a human level, pastors, counselors, and church workers know a little of how this works. When someone shares their deep burdens and struggles, the one who shares feels a little better, and the one who hears the burdens bears them also and feels a little worse. However, the vicarious nature of suffering is only true to a point at the human level. Christ suffered vicariously for all human creatures caught in the trap of the ultimate evil, sin, and its corollary, death, but no other person can do what Christ did. On the individual level, suffering for others does not always deliver them from their suffering.[12]

At the same time, the Suffering Servant reminds us that God's people never suffer in isolation from God. Jesus became sin (2 Corinthians 5:21), took upon Himself the curse of the Law (Galatians 3:13), was tried unjustly, executed, and buried in a tomb. In whatever evil we suffer as God's people, we have the promise that we do not suffer apart from Jesus. "Who shall separate us from the love of Christ? Shall tribulation, or distress, or persecution, or famine, or nakedness, or danger, or sword?" Paul continues, "No. … For I am sure that neither death nor life, nor angels, nor rulers, nor things present nor things to come, nor powers, nor height nor depth, nor anything else in all creation, will be able to separate us from the love of God in Christ Jesus our Lord" (Romans 8:35, 37–39). Jesus, our Suffering Servant, will never abandon us no matter how evil the circumstances appear.

Job's "Answer." Perhaps the greatest treatment of theodicy in human literature, the book of Job presents an impressive array of attempts to answer the question "Why?" Although Job's "solution" hardly satisfies our desire for a logical answer, the book of Job recognizes the vacuity of most human responses in the face of profound suffering. Job's friends offer various reasons for why Job deserves to suffer, but Job helps us see how these answers do not solve anything but actually further the problem: alienating Job even more from God and human community. What Job yearns for throughout the book is the presence and voice of God as he alternates among lament, repentance, complaint, and hope. Job wants to know where he stands with the Creator: "I cry to You [God] for help and You do not answer me; I stand, and You only look at me" (Job 30:20). In this way, Job reminds believers that evil is not primarily a logical problem, but an existential one. People do not need the right answer to the conundrum of evil as much as they need relationships that solve the problem of alienation, as suffering and evil place all of us outside the camp, alone and afraid.

In the climax of the book of Job, God shows up in a way that both challenges Job's (and our) demand that God justify Himself and begins to solve Job's biggest problem, his relationship with his Creator. God does not speak

12 Simundson, *Faith under Fire*, 63–79.

flowery words of comfort, but reminds Job (and us) that He is God, and we are not. "Who is this that darkens counsel by words without knowledge?" God asks Job (Job 38:2). "Shall a faultfinder contend with the Almighty?" God continues. "Will you even put Me in the wrong? Will you condemn Me that you may be in the right?" (Job 40:2, 8). Job's final confession leaves the question of evil unanswered. He can only acknowledge that God is God: "I know that You can do all things, and that no purpose of Yours can be thwarted" (Job 42:2). He acknowledges his own unworthiness before God: "I despise myself, and repent in dust and ashes" (Job 42:6). Although God does not say much to reassure Job, God does say to Job's friends: "You have not spoken of Me what is right, as My servant Job has" (Job 42:7). In this way, Job receives the assurance that he is God's own even in the midst of suffering. God remains God, and Job remains His child.[13]

The Bible's "Answer." Job most directly addresses the problem of evil, but it, as the rest of the Bible, refuses to give us the logical answer we want. In fact, God does not tell us where evil comes from in the first place. Philip Melanchthon summarized the biblical material by stating that "although God creates and preserves nature, nevertheless the cause of sin is the will of those who are evil, that is, of the devil and the ungodly. Since it was not assisted by God, their will turned away from God."[14] But this response stops short of the answer we demand in our misery. What lies behind or beyond our own perverted will and that of the devil? It would do us no good to know.

There are really only two possible answers. It is either our fault, or it is God's fault. Neither answer gets us out of our own mess. What we need is God's answer to the questions about the present and future—where we are now with evil, and where we will be with it. Those questions God has answered in Christ, and that is enough. We need not and dare not chase after the hidden God for answers to the question of the origin of evil. We can rest assured with the answers that the revealed God has given us in the death and resurrection of His Son. We cannot justify God. God has justified us. He has justified our existence for eternity with Him and will bring all things to His desired end. He holds both the present and the future, and we are in His hands. That is all we need to know.

The doctrine of providence grabs hold of God. It climbs into His lap. "The doctrine of providence" is better said as "faith trusting a loving and providing God." The doctrine of providence leads us to reject faith as a good luck charm. Faith endures when evil seems to imply the absence of God. Faith clings to God's person and promise, even when no sign of blessing appears in our lives. At the same time, the doctrine of providence rejects

13 Simundson, *Faith under Fire*, 81–101.

14 Augsburg Confession XIX.

fatalism: faith does not sing "*Que sera, sera* ... whatever will be, will be." Faith reaches out in confidence for the extended hand of God, even when it reaches blindly. It rests assured that God's hand is there even when that hand is not evident.

In this way, believers are brought into chorus with Habakkuk. He began by rehearsing how human existence was severely threatened, how all had gone wrong (3:17–19):

> Though the fig tree should not blossom,
> nor fruit be on the vines,
> the produce of the olive fail
> and the fields yield no food,
> the flock be cut off from the fold
> and there be no herd in the stalls [in other words, not much more could go wrong],
> yet I will rejoice in the LORD;
> I will take joy in the God of my salvation.
> GOD, the Lord, is my strength;
> He makes my feet like the deer's;
> He makes me tread on my high places.

Paul, too, is part of our chorus: "Not that I am speaking of being in need, for I have learned in whatever situation I am to be content. I know how to be brought low, and I know how to abound. In any and every circumstance, I have learned the secret of facing plenty and hunger, abundance and need. I can do all things through Him who strengthens me" (Philippians 4:11–13).

Only the Lord can ultimately preserve His people. He is, in fact, our last resort. It is good when faith finds Him as our first resort. It then confesses that He has made us and still preserves us. It recognizes that—because of His providing love—it is our delight to thank and praise, serve and obey Him.

CHAPTER 6
SIN AND EVIL

THE existence of evil is not difficult to see. Things are not right; we are not right with the world. The harmony, order, and peace we would like to have vanished. We are discontented with how we have shaped our identities. We are uncertain about the security of our lives. We are worried about what it all means. We recognize that everything has somehow missed the mark from what it should be. Life is out of sync, off-kilter. One Hebrew word, *cha'ta*, has that sense of being off the mark and is best translated "sin."

Still, no one can grasp the depth and totality of the problem without the Word of God. All of us know that evil is real, but no one believes the problem is I myself. Evil lurks outside of us—Satan and the sinful world—but the most pressing matter at hand for Holy Scripture is not "out there," but in here, in my heart and soul. Hence, for Luther, the doctrine of sin is not about a concept but about us, as sinners, guilty and condemned before God.[1] The doctrine of sin implicates all of us in the unbelief, alienation, disobedience, and death that began in the garden with Adam and Eve. Their story is also ours.

The Original Sin

Adam and Eve were used to walking with God and chatting with Him in the cool of the day, like good friends. They were accustomed to being at His side, delighting in His voice and presence. They rejoiced in their bodies and souls, life, breath, and one another as gifts from their Creator. They served each other and the garden gladly, eating of its abundant and delicious fruits, except the fruit of the tree in the middle of the garden. One day, inexplicably, their trust turned to doubt, and the resulting broken relationship with God devastated everything, even the warp and woof of creation. The broken relationship with God is the origin and root of all sin and every evil. God had

1 Ľubomír Batka, "Luther's Teaching on Sin and Evil," in *The Oxford Handbook of Martin Luther's Theology*, ed. Robert Kolb, Irene Dingel, and Ľubomír Batka (Oxford: Oxford University Press, 2014), 233.

created trust and love between Himself and His creatures. When that trust was broken, peace fled as fear rushed into the hearts of Adam and Eve, and they tried to elude the Friend they once loved (Genesis 3:10).

It began when the old snake approached Eve (and Adam who was with her) and asked a seemingly benign question: "Did God actually say, 'You shall not eat of any tree in the garden'?" (Genesis 3:1). Adam and Eve had been living by the Word, talking with God, and trusting in His promises. There was nothing to question, nothing to doubt. Like young children sitting on the lap of their beloved father, they hung on every word from their Creator's mouth. Such is the trust that constitutes the core of our humanity and the right relationship with God, providing peace and purpose.

But Satan offered Eve and Adam a different disposition toward God's Word—"Did God actually say?" For the first time, Eve and Adam did not simply hear and believe their Creator, but were set over God's Word as judges to determine for themselves what God meant. And Eve began to play with the Word. God had said in Genesis 2:16–17: "You must not eat from the tree." Eve added, "You must not touch it" (Genesis 3:2–3). She tried to improve God's Word, perhaps to make it defend her in the way she wanted to be defended. She deceived herself into thinking she could take care of God's Word instead of relying on Him to take care of her. Her attempt at mastery of the Word produced the devil's mastery of her. The devil's deceit led Eve, and Adam with her, to doubt and mistrust God. That was the first, the original, sin.

Adam's Sin Infects Us All

Their sin is now ours. The Scriptures confess that before any of us did anything wrong, before we could understand sin or repent of it, each human creature's relationship with the Creator was already broken as soon as the person existed. In Adam we have all sinned (Romans 5:19). Every human being is conceived and born deaf to the Word of God, blind to God's grace, ignorant of God's mercy, and doomed to die eternally without His intervention. Not only are we lacking what we need in relationship to God, but we are also unable to produce trust in God's Word, open our eyes to God's mercy, or gain true knowledge of God.[2] In other words, **original sin** is a deep-seated disease within all of Adam and Eve's progeny, each of us, that makes us despise God, lack confidence in God, hate His judgment, and put trust in created things rather than the Creator.[3] Adam and Eve's broken relationship with God is ours.

---

2 Apology of the Augsburg Confession II 3.

3 Apology of the Augsburg Confession II 8.

We would never think that the problem of sin is so grave without the witness of the apostles and prophets. Babies seem so cute; they could not be broken sinners under a curse. According to our usual manner of thinking, we have made bad choices, but our sins are not that bad. We are all naturally **Pelagians**—followers of the fifth-century heretic Pelagius—believing that humans are basically good and free to make virtuous decisions. All we have to do is to make better choices, we think, and work a little harder, then sin will be nearly gone.

The Bible, however, diagnoses a far more extensive and far worse disease in us than we could ever guess. Paul writes: "None is righteous, no, not one; no one understands; no one seeks for God. All have turned aside; together they have become worthless; no one does good, not even one" (Romans 3:10–12). In Ephesians, Paul adds that we were once "dead" in "trespasses and sins," being "children of wrath" who followed after the devil in disobedience (2:1–3). David shows that this original sin is universal. It infects every single human being before we could even be conscious of our sin: "Behold, I was brought forth in iniquity, and in sin did my mother conceive me" (Psalm 51:5). Without faith in the Lord Jesus, all people have a broken relationship with the Creator that needs to be restored.

But, some object, why am I guilty of a sin that I never committed? Why am I blamed for Adam and Eve's disobedience? We protest that we did not ask to be born this way, guilty, on the road to death, caught in mortality and evil. Our protest, however, does not avail. Original sin is not a device the biblical writers used to pin the blame for sin on Adam and Eve. Neither does the doctrine point out how unfair life is. Original sin is a teaching that reminds us of the real impotence, guilt, and shame with which we are born: we have inherited a state of despising the Author of life and are doomed to die apart from Him, unable to fix the problem. In fact, we do not want to fix it. The doctrine of original sin impresses upon us that human creatures, since Adam, have lived under and experienced the curse—and tried to persuade themselves that they like it. This determination to master our own lives apart from God, and its concomitant mortality, is not the original human condition. Our humanity was designed not for this but for the Lord (1 Corinthians 6:13), yet Adam's curse belongs to all.

According to the teaching of original sin, not only is humanity guilty before God, but we are also totally diseased in our hearts and souls. It is not as if God counts us guilty of a sin, committed long ago, that has no continued influence upon us. Instead, every person is born an idolater with a broken relationship to God. Instead of having life abundantly through faith in the Creator, we are all focused on created things, desiring them more than the Creator. In reality, then, Adam's sin is our sin. He made himself judge over God's Word; he turned away from his heavenly Father; he trusted his own feelings and thoughts rather than living by confidence in God's voice. And we are all Adam. All of us are conceived and born in the same way, as idolaters who have turned away from the living God and trusted in ourselves rather than His Word. Hence, Luther comments on Psalm 51:5: David "does not say, 'My mother conceived me with sin,' but, '*I—I myself—I* was conceived in sin.' "[4] Our guilt is deserved.

Our biggest problem is not our sins—the bad choices we make and know about—but our sin, our sinfulness or original sin. We have this disease embedded deep in our hearts, minds, and souls that cannot be balanced with a few good works or forgotten by standing next to someone who appears to have it worse. To say it simply, we do not just commit sins; we are sinners. Without Christ and His Spirit, there is nothing in us except sin as we do not fear, love, and trust in God above all things, and we are constantly inclined to love ourselves above all. We must learn to say with David: "Declare me innocent from hidden faults" (Psalm 19:12); and with Luther: "Everything is pure sin with us,"[5] so that we can come without pretense or self-confidence to the One who promises: "I came not to call the righteous, but sinners" (Mark 2:17).

Alternate Views of Original Sin

All Christians offer an account of sin, but not all speak of sin or original sin in the same way as the Lutheran confession of faith. Some Protestants in North America talk less about original sin and more about sins. In this popular—seldom academic—view, sin is not the disease of the heart and soul that turns us against our Creator, but bad choices that transgress against God's commands. Some, accordingly, argue that babies are born pure and can sin only after they achieve the consciousness and rationality to make their own choices. This view ignores, however, the fact that what God demands of us is not primarily right actions but a right heart (Mark 7:20–23). Our problem of sin is not that we make wrong choices but that we are wrong people, idolaters, who do not fear, love, and trust in God above all things.

Even in the most innocent of human creatures, tiny babies, original sin makes itself visible—in their self-centeredness, which demands and expects that all else will serve them; in their low frustration tolerance; in their sense

4 AE 37:363 (emphasis added). Compare Oswald Bayer, *Martin Luther's Theology: A Contemporary Interpretation*, trans. Thomas H. Trapp (Grand Rapids: Eerdmans, 2008), 193.

5 Smalcald Articles III III 36.

of hurry and demand for immediate satisfaction.[6] Their mortality also reveals the curse. Babies die, and death comes from sin (Romans 6:23). This confirms the psalmist's confession: from birth unrighteousness has plagued us; from conception sin has grasped us (Psalm 51:5).

The view of Eastern Orthodoxy is more nuanced than the prior view, though it, too, fails to see the radical nature of original sin. Eastern Orthodoxy teaches that the human creature was created incomplete, though without sin, able "naturally" to "grow in divine life. Divine life is a gift, but also a task which is to be accomplished by a free human effort."[7] This view misses several important points. First, the "good" of Genesis 1 pronounced upon all creation posits a human creature truly good, in perfect relationship with God, without any need for further progress. In addition, the nature of sin is much more radical than this view suggests. The broken relationship has destroyed the ability of human creatures to work toward a better relationship with God. In fact, by our sinful flesh, we do not want to pursue God or the things of God: "The natural person does not accept the things of the Spirit of God, for they are folly to him" (1 Corinthians 2:14).[8] The fallen creature is not so easily reparable or improved. The fallen creature has died in the sin of breaking away from the Author of life.

Traditional Roman Catholic theology also fails to focus adequately on the brokenness of the relationship with God. Roman Catholic theology defines original sin as the "deprivation of sanctifying grace," which brings with it the necessity of submitting to suffering and death.[9] This quasi-quantifying of grace into a gift that God places inside the believer focuses too much on what the creature has and what it must do, rather than where the creature is in relationship to God. Human creatures doubt God's Word, which has ruptured the relationship of the children with their heavenly Father.

This ruptured relationship affects every part of every person. Lutheran theology teaches **total depravity**, that no aspect of human nature nor any human creature is free from original sin and its effects. Human beings remain valuable creatures of God, but every person's relationship with God is completely broken without faith in the Gospel, and we are unable to fix it. The term *total depravity* is often misunderstood as claiming that nothing

6 John E. Keller, "The Realities of Original Sin in Clinical Pastoral Counseling," Third Concordia Academy, Wartburg Theological Seminary, Dubuque, Iowa, August 12, 1975.

7 John Meyendorff, *Byzantine Theology: Historical Trends and Doctrinal Themes* (New York: Fordham University Press, 1979), 139, 143–46.

8 Thesis 17 of Luther's 1517 *Disputation against Scholastic Theology* states: "Man is by nature unable to want God to be God. Indeed, he himself wants to be God, and does not want God to be God" (AE 31:10).

9 *Canons and Decrees of the Council of Trent*, trans. H. J. Schroeder (St. Louis: Herder, 1941), 21 23.

in human life is good. Our sin, however, does not nullify God's goodness. God continues to give blessings to His own and to those who do not trust in Him. Many of those who do not believe in Him lead outwardly moral lives—reflecting their good creation by the Creator. Nevertheless, because all truly good actions flow from trust in God, they are not conforming to God's plan. Total depravity refers to that complete inability to correspond to our original design, grounded in trusting God as Creator and Deliverer. In contrast, Roman Catholic theology does not clearly confess the pervasiveness of original sin. It posits a part of humanity, the *synderesis*, the root of conscience, that naturally knows the good, the will of God.[10] The conscience is not perfect; it needs grace to do God's will, but it is not completely broken either.

The Scriptures are convinced that our problem of sin is so bad that the Son of God had to die at our hands and for us, who are the "ungodly" and "weak" sinners who need to be justified before God (Romans 5:6–9). Sin has infected all of us completely.

The Liar's Lie: The Origin of Evil

At one point or another, every Christian wonders from whence evil and sin came. At one level, the sin of Adam and Eve makes no sense. They were in perfect relationship with their Creator and the creation. From that perspective, Adam and Eve's doubt seems inconceivable—and thus without excuse.[11] Why did Adam and Eve fall for Satan's lie? We can only know that their hearts were deformed and imprisoned by their sinful desire to be their own gods. We cannot know why they rejected their caring Creator for devilish deceits.

One common solution among modern and contemporary theologians is to turn Adam and Eve into types of humanity rather than real, historical beings. Adam and Eve represent all of us, but they were not real individuals. In this way, Adam and Eve simply show us how we are already fallen, turning to disobedience, fostering division, and trusting in ourselves more than God. If, however, Adam and Eve are not historical beings who

10 Reinhard Hütter, *John Henry Newman on Truth and Its Counterfeits: A Guide for Our Times* (Washington, DC: Catholic University of America Press, 2020), 21–73. Following Aquinas and Cardinal Newman, Hütter speaks of the *synderesis* as "the rational creature's participation in the eternal law" (55). As an "innate habitus," the *synderesis* knows the proper moral end of humanity (56–59). Hence, Newman calls the conscience—actually speaking of the *synderesis*, which is the "theonomic root of conscience"—the "first vicar of Christ" because the *synderesis* is "the origin of the light that illumines reason by providing the natural *habitus* of the first principles of moral truth" (61). The *synderesis* can be ignored or stifled, but not wrong.

11 Compare the dictum in Robert Jenson, *Systematic Theology*, vol. 2 (Oxford: Oxford University Press, 1999), 134: "Starting from righteousness, sin is inexplicable."

doubted God's Word and revolted against the Creator in time and history, then human sinfulness must stem from nature. This only worsens our situation. The Creator must have built sin into the model of humanity. Sin would then be a necessary part of what it means to be human. Such a view destroys human responsibility for sin and human hope for God's restoration of human nature in the resurrection of the dead and the life of the age to come.[12] For the Scriptures, then, Adam and Eve, creatures of God, stand at the beginning of human history. Their doubt, defiance, and disobedience of God permeate this history.

The Scriptures trace the problem, the evil, back to the devil's murderous lies even though the devil does not provide a way out of our responsibility for sin. The Scriptures make clear that God is good. He is not the cause nor origin of human sinfulness. He created His human creatures, along with the rest of His creation, good (Genesis 1:31). He takes no delight in wickedness. He abhors human sin (Psalm 5:4–6; Zechariah 8:17). When Adam and Eve fled His presence, God, too, wondered why (Genesis 3:9–11).

Sin arises from the devil's deceit (1 John 3:8; Revelation 12:9). The devil's fallen nature drives him to deceive (John 8:44), and since the fall in Eden his lies have led human creatures astray from trust in God (2 Corinthians 11:3; 1 Peter 5:8–9). *Satan*, a Hebrew word that means "the accuser," is always questioning the goodness of God's human creatures and calling into question the propriety of their receiving His blessing (Job 1–2).

How did the devil become evil? Scripture says nothing about the fall of the angels aside from mentioning it (Jude 6). The devil took many with him apparently, for there are many devils (Mark 5:9). "From the beginning" of human encounters with him, the devil has been determined to take away the life that God has given us, that is, to separate us from God (John 8:44). The devils recognize that they are engaged in a war to the death with God (Mark 1:23–24). But God is God; He has won. He has condemned them to "eternal chains under gloomy darkness" (Jude 6), to that "eternal fire prepared for the devil and his angels" (Matthew 25:41). Nonetheless, they continue to practice their limited but formidable power in God's universe (Ephesians 6:11–12; Acts 26:18). They assault human bodies (Luke 13:16; 2 Corinthians 12:7), but above all Satan attempts to destroy the working of God's Word, the trust that forms the human side of the relationship between God and His human creatures. He does so by undermining confidence in the Word, just as he did with Eve and Adam: "Did God actually say?" (1 Timothy 4:1–4; Luke 8:12; Genesis 3:1).

---

12 On the connections of the historicity of Adam and Eve to original sin and Christian theology, see Hans Madueme and Michael Reeves, eds., *Adam, the Fall, and Original Sin: Theological, Biblical, and Scientific Perspectives* (Grand Rapids: Baker Academic, 2014).

For many in North America, the reality of a personal devil seems like child's play. Most of us imagine a silly figure, dressed in red, with horns and a sneer, and we put such a figure into the same category as Sasquatch or the Loch Ness monster. Our rejection of Satan, however, betrays both our indebtedness to modern Western thinking and our failure to know the Scriptures. We do well not to look for devils behind every tree stump, but to recognize the spiritual powers actually at work in the world. The devil "disguises himself as an angel of light" (2 Corinthians 11:14), and we must learn to see the rulers, authorities, and cosmic powers that pervade this present darkness, and against which we must stand firm in the armor of God (Ephesians 6:12–13). Christians in other parts of the world may be able to teach Western Christians much about spiritual warfare and the reality of demons.[13]

Judas's desire to betray Christ sprang from the devil's implantation of his evil plan into his heart (John 13:2). Yet the Scriptures never permit us to declare, "The devil made me do it." The existence of evil poses big questions as we wrestle with how to put life right again, as discussed in the prior chapter: Where is evil taking us? Where has evil put us today? Where did evil come from? The Scriptures do not give us complete answers to that last question, but at least we know that the devil does not bear the blame and consequences of our sin. We do.

Original Sin and the Bondage of the Will

The doctrine of original sin contradicts a concept of the freedom of the will, that human beings have autonomy and freedom to do good or evil on their own. The doctrine of original sin confesses that all people stand under God's judgment and are responsible to Him for who they are and what they do. Although original sin is inherited, it does not remove responsibility from the sinful heirs. In fact, each individual possesses the same sinful will as Adam, the desire to control his or her own life. In original sin, human creatures are turned away from God—no longer fearing, loving, and trusting in Him above all things—and are turned toward an idol, most often, the idol of the ego: me. Hence, Luther described sin as the *incurvatus in se*, being curved in upon ourselves, the self-enveloping fetal position, which is the opposite of the open, outward-facing, cruciform shape of life lived in Edenic peace. Otherwise stated, all of us in sin are closed off to God and our neighbors. We are worried about ourselves, our wants, our needs, our desires, and our lives, and we flee from whatever we cannot control or find a way to manipulate it for our own purposes.

13 On spiritual warfare, see Jon C. Furgeson, *The Sword and the Mask: Building an Antifragile Approach to Spiritual Warfare* (Eugene, OR: Wipf & Stock, 2022).

Our wills are bound to sin in this self-centered way, having an inevitable lust of the heart toward sin that the Christian tradition names **concupiscence**. Some think that the doctrine of the bondage of the will is deterministic—forcing human beings to do something they do not want to do—but the point of the bound will is the exact opposite. The **bondage of the will** is simply a diagnosis of what happens in our lives: we do exactly what we want, and we cannot do otherwise. What we want, however, and will always want—without the Holy Spirit's transforming presence—is sin. "The will does what it does because it wills to, and it will not do otherwise. The will is bound to will what it wills. After the fall, it is bound by sin, hence not free."[14] What we all do, then, is concur in Adam and Eve's doubt. Even when we claim freedom of the will—most of all, when we claim freedom!—we are curved in upon ourselves and will not choose God over alternative sources of ultimate identity, security, and meaning apart from His disruption of our lives.

Worse yet, bound to sin, human creatures are incapable of recognizing the depth of their corruption. Fallen, sinful eyes cannot pierce the mystery of human sin, the destruction of the Edenic freedom from evil and for service. When we glimpse its height and breadth, the terror of its consequences blinds us. Hence, we can muster the courage to admit how corrupt we are only when we are moved by God's Spirit to trust in Jesus Christ as the one who has intervened to save us. Jesus has come as a Second Adam to reverse the original Adam's desertion of Eden and restore our humanity as God fashioned it for Eden. Only through this Second Adam does the significance of the first Adam's folly and tragedy come clearly into view (Romans 5:12–21).[15] The corruption of humanity is absolute in the vertical relationship. In their relationship with God, sinners have lost it all. They cannot turn to God on their own. Their will automatically and instinctively chooses the alternative—any alternative—to their Creator, Yahweh.

Rebelling Upward

The traditional title for the events of Genesis 3 is "the fall." It refers to the fact that Adam and Eve were in right relationship with God until their sin destroyed the fear, love, and trust that characterize righteousness before God. Commonly, people think that Eve and Adam turned from the higher virtues of morality, religion, and philosophy to the baser lusts of the body: sensuality, gluttony, and greed. We think the fall is this downward

14 Gerhard O. Forde, *On Being a Theologian of the Cross: Reflections on Luther's Heidelberg Disputation, 1518* (Grand Rapids: Eerdmans, 1997), 54.

15 Gerhard O. Forde, *Theology Is for Proclamation* (Minneapolis: Fortress, 1990), 51; Smalcald Articles III I 3.

trajectory from virtue to vice, from the soul to the body. The Scriptures tell us something else.

After Satan sowed the seeds of doubt in Adam and Eve's heart, he tempted them not with sex, food, or things, but with divinity. "You will be *like God*, knowing good and evil" (Genesis 3:5, emphasis added). Eve reached for the fruit not only because it was attractive, but because the tree was "to be desired to make one wise" (Genesis 3:6). Adam and Eve's fall was not into lust and vice but into self-fashioned wisdom, knowledge, and the delusion of equality with God. In other words, the first sin was that Adam and Eve doubted God's Word and replaced it with their own judgment. As soon as they did not live by trust, they asserted their mastery over the Word, over God, and they aspired to usurp God's place.[16] They did not fall down; they rebelled upward as they pushed God off the throne and enthroned themselves in His place.

Here also, Adam and Eve's history has become ours. In the sinfulness into which we were born, we swept God from our lives, desiring to know good and evil for ourselves and take our lives into our own hands rather than living by faith in the Creator. With God dethroned, we needed to supply ourselves with a new source of identity, security, and meaning, and we moved to fill it. We were dissatisfied with being "merely" human creatures, and so we lifted ourselves up to be more than creatures. In the process we became, instead, less than the perfect creatures God had fashioned in Eden. Like Adam and Eve, our doubt becomes rebellion, shame, blame, alienation, disobedience, and death.

When Adam and Eve rejected God's Word for their own understanding, they recognized their nakedness and covered themselves, trying to hide their sin and shame from God and from themselves. Once vulnerable and open, not ashamed but at peace, they fell under the dominance of sin. This created insecurities and inadequacies as they recognized in themselves finitude and newborn mortality. Instead of running to God, their shield and very great reward (Genesis 15:1), they tried to cover their guilt behind fig leaves, concealing themselves in the thicket to avoid the presence of the Almighty (Genesis 3:7–8). When confronted by their loving Creator who wanted to walk with them and delight in them, they hid their shame behind blame and self-justification. When offered opportunity to confess, Adam admitted nothing. Rather, he blamed Eve and God: "The woman whom *You* gave to be with me, she gave me fruit" (Genesis 3:12, emphasis added). It is as if Adam had said, "I didn't do anything wrong. I'm justified. I only followed that woman. It's really her fault. In fact, You created that woman, God. Aren't You to blame for that?" Eve followed suit: "The serpent deceived me"

16 Forde, *Theology Is for Proclamation*, 50.

(Genesis 3:13). No longer receiving their righteousness from God and His Word, Adam and Eve tried to justify themselves, first hiding from their guilt, and then throwing blame at everyone else.

Once again, their story is ours. Our sin often begins with pride, but our pride is frequently a cover-up for guilt and shame, which we hide even from ourselves. Much of the Western Church has equated original sin with pride. John Milton eloquently described the devil's fall in terms of pride.[17] Like Adam and Eve, we lift ourselves above God and His Word in sinful pride, but even such pride stems from doubt that God can and will take care of us. Pride, then, seems quite similar to the psychologist and philosopher Alfred Adler's understanding of the superiority complex. According to Adler, no true superiority complex exists; each reveals an underlying inferiority complex, arising from the need to compensate.[18] In a similar way, sinful pride regularly reveals the vain attempt of the sinner to cover inadequacy and guilt. It indicates that we know our inability to control our lives better than we admit, but we hide it from others and ourselves. We need God to confront us, condemn us, and show us by His Word the reality that we are dust and to dust we shall return (Genesis 3:19) so that He might claim us again as His dust, His creatures, and be our Creator in whom we trust. But without the Spirit, we run in the opposite direction, deserting God's presence, driven by guilt, pride, shame, and fear.

The Hopefulness of the Doctrine of Original Sin

The teaching of original sin destroys all optimism in human performance. No human being can achieve something before God. No human performance is good enough to earn God's favor (Romans 4:1–5). This strikes many as depressing and even dangerous. If your works cannot get you ahead before God, then why would you ever do them? The question, though, betrays its own self-reliance and lack of trust in God's grace. If human sin is doubt of God's Word and all the ways that we try to use God and others for our own benefit, optimizing human performance does not lead us to trust in the Lord's mercy, but only to despair or pride. Unless we have already been broken by life to recognize our total inability—at which point we have given up in despair—we will disguise our sin, all the more to ourselves, under the cover of lawful righteousness, pious intention, authentic self-identity, or simply being better than others. All of these disguises are ultimately self-justification, ways that human creatures distinguish between good and evil

17 John Milton, *Paradise Lost* (1667; New York: Norton, 1975), e.g. I.36, p. 7; XII.25, p. 264.

18 Alfred Adler, *Understanding Human Nature*, trans. Walter Beran Wolfe (Garden City, NY: Garden City Publishing, 1927), 72–80.

and place ourselves on the good side.[19] Instead of bringing us to the solution, self-justification only leads us to blame others, avoid feeling our guilt and shame, and hide from ourselves the true reality of our broken relationship with God. Hence, the doctrine of original sin intends to cut down all attempts for human beings to save themselves by status, emotion, contemplation, or morality, so that we can receive the good news that "Christ Jesus came into the world to save sinners, of whom I am the foremost" (1 Timothy 1:15). In such faith comes real hope and real freedom.

The Root Sin: Unbelief

The root of all sin is human deafness to the Word of God. From lack of trust—the need to secure life on our own terms—proceed all other sins. Like roots of a tree that absorb the needed moisture and nutrients from the soil, making the tree to grow, blossom, and bear fruit, so unbelief and doubt corrupt and disease the roots so that human creatures produce not plentiful fruits of the Spirit but deadly deeds of the sinful flesh. After all, everything that does not proceed from a relationship of trust in Yahweh misses the mark for our humanity. St. Paul says it clearly: "Whatever does not proceed from faith is sin" (Romans 14:23). Breaking the First Commandment inevitably leads to loving and trusting some other god or gods. Since no single substitute for the Creator is ever sufficient to satisfy, we sinners are all polytheists. And without trust in Yahweh, we break each of the other commandments (Genesis 39:9).

Some Christians overlook the fundamental fact that doubt broke the relationship of trust between creature and Creator. It is easy to think of sin primarily as disobedience—as all parents and children know too well—but the heart of sin goes to the root of our relationship with God and our attitudes toward life. This is why Jesus says, "From within, *out of the heart* of man, come evil thoughts, sexual immorality, theft, murder, adultery, coveting, wickedness, deceit, sensuality, envy, slander, pride, foolishness. All these evil things come from within" (Mark 7:21–23, emphasis added). The Hebrew word for "obedience" also emphasizes the way that obedience stems from the heart that trusts in God. The word in Hebrew for "hear," *shama*, can also mean "obey." To hear God is to obey Him. We do not obey because we are not listening; we doubt His Word and turn to other gods. Sin is, at its root, being deaf to the Word of God, not trusting the Lord. We cannot fix this problem with our actions. We need to receive, hear, and believe the promise of the Gospel and have our hearts made new by the Spirit.

---

19 This definition comes from Ted Peters, *Sin Boldly! Justifying Faith for Fragile and Broken Souls* (Minneapolis: Fortress, 2015), 204.

Doubt Leads to Alienation, Defensiveness, Disobedience, and Death

No longer having life from God in His Word, we seek life in other things, which only further alienates us from the Author of life. We pursue **idols**, false gods, in which we attempt to find safety, purpose, and a sense of self. Even if we do not worship these things in a traditional sense, we put them on a pedestal, and they turn us into themselves. We carve out blocks of time, sacred time, for our golden calves. We prioritize spreadsheets over prayer, sporting events over Scripture, news over neighbors, and investments over relationships, becoming workaholics, fanatics, and full of anxiety. Our hearts chase whatever they fancy, and we become what we trust.[20] "Those who make [idols] become like them, so do all who trust in them" (Psalm 135:18). Instead of a life of faith, reflecting the Creator's love and grace as those made in His image, our idolatry sets us at odds with the one true God.

Our false trust in God-substitutes has also damaged, sometimes even devastated, all horizontal relationships between human creatures and in human communities. In Genesis 3, Adam and Eve came to be in conflict not only with God but also with each other. They recognized each other no longer as a divine gift to be loved and served, but as a potential threat to their own happiness and existence. They needed to cover their nakedness to protect their vulnerabilities from prying, judging eyes (Genesis 3:7–10). They did not admit fault, but blamed each other, exalting themselves over the other (Genesis 3:12–13). They were set against each other in a power struggle as bad as that imagined by the philosopher Thomas Hobbes: a war of all against all (Genesis 3:16b).[21]

Burdened by the same sin, human creatures continue to doubt that we can depend on God for how best to live, so we try to establish and safeguard ourselves over and against fellow creatures. To protect our identities, we use fellow creatures, manipulating and exploiting them instead of loving and serving them. In so doing we always abuse them. When our deeds and motivation are exposed, we grow angry, and we flee from them as well as from God. "That woman You put here with me" (Genesis 3:12), we say to God, recalling our alienation from Him and at the same time trying to protect ourselves by hiding behind someone else, using another to save ourselves. We only alienate ourselves further.

As we begin to feel our estrangement from others and our personal failings that contributed to it, we often become defensive. We do not always

---

20 See G. K. Beale, *We Become What We Worship: A Biblical Theology of Idolatry* (Downers Grove, IL: IVP Academic, 2008).

21 Thomas Hobbes, *Leviathan* (1651). Available at https://www.gutenberg.org/files/3207/3207-h/3207-h.htm.

recognize that sin exhibits itself in defensiveness. Sometimes that defensiveness takes form in hiding, fleeing from God's presence (Genesis 3:8) or running from the claims others have upon us, linked as we are in human community. Defensiveness can also drive sinners into the doldrums of apathy and withdrawal from human activities. At other times defensiveness takes form in rage, abuse of others, and self-justification. Sinners know that the best defense is a good offense, and so sinners are offensive. But we need to remember in dealing with sinners that their offensiveness arises out of fear, guilt, and shame.

This "defensive offensiveness" exhibits itself in division from one another. When the relationship with God—which gives us our ultimate sense of identity, security, and meaning—is broken, it is little wonder that we are also divided from our fellow human creatures in our horizontal relationships. Only when we are confident that God is protecting and providing, even in our sinful wretched state, can we open up our lives in that cruciform shape—arms outstretched to embrace and uphold others—the shape in which God made us.[22]

God's leash on the horizontal impact of human sinfulness often seems tragically and scandalously long. Fear and self-interest provide inadequate checks on the desire of sinners to secure their lives on their own terms. Nobility of purpose can turn quietly into exploitation and cruelty. Yet people who do not worship Christ can often do better rather than worse as they follow the structures and strictures of the Law in its social and political aspects (civil righteousness). They can construct good governments and practice a fair amount of decency among one another. Still, the need to shore up their own sense of identity, security, and meaning causes them to trespass on the neighbor from time to time. The corruption in horizontal relationships is limited—though it is always serious enough to prevent full enjoyment of life and often so serious as to institutionalize corruption, exploitation, and injustice. In contrast, Adam and Eve's doubt totally and completely destroyed the human creatures' relationship with God.

Although horizontal relationships are not completely broken, they are poisoned, rotting out because of the broken relationship with God and the resulting disobedience of His commands. Doubting His way of doing things, we do it our way, and breaking God's commands, we also trespass on the turf of others. We dominate and exploit others, blame them and justify ourselves, so that we can secure our own lives. This only encourages those we harm to strike back to protect themselves, deepening still

22 Hence, a "low anthropology" and a high view of sin enables kindness and love toward others. David Zahl, *Low Anthropology: The Unlikely Key to a Gracious View of Others (and Yourself)* (Grand Rapids: Brazos Press, 2022).

the division through mutual disobedience. It seems impossible to break the circle of doing it wrong.

We bring upon ourselves a sense of despair because we cannot do it right. We cannot do it right because at the core of our beings we are not right, that is, we are not right with God. We have no peace. We are restless. We wear out. We die (Genesis 2:17; 3:19; Romans 6:23). Death lingers over all of us as a result of our root sin; death is doubt's outermost, final branch in our diseased tree. Alone, angry, and afraid, Satan's murderous lie—"You will not surely die" (Genesis 3:4)—finally flowers. We die, and we are damned. From the original sin of doubt, with which we are born, the whole life of sin unfolds, and it keeps unfolding until we die.

The Fruits of Sin: Actual Sins

The root sin of unbelief stems into many different kinds of disobedience to God's will, which is another basic definition of sin (1 John 3:4). To help us understand and recognize our sins, the church has employed several classifications of the sins that plague daily human life. The purpose of the following analysis is to help Christians recognize sin more clearly and repent of both actual sins that flow from doubt and the original sin of our diseased hearts.

Original sin results in **actual sins**, sins of thought, word, and deed that stem from our lack of trust. When we no longer fear, love, and trust in God above all things, we discard God's will and secure life for ourselves by grabbing hold of other parts of God's creation, manipulating them for our own sake. Those acts that exhibit our mistrust of God by abusing His name or His call to worship fall under the "First Table" of the Ten Commandments, grouped there with the fundamental command to trust in Him above all else. The "Second Table" of the Ten Commandments, the Fourth through the Tenth, treat acts that harm other human creatures in a variety of ways.

Another distinction can be made between the commandments that treat attitudes (First, Ninth and, Tenth; toward God in the case of the First Commandment, toward others in the Ninth and Tenth) and those that treat actions (Second and Third against God, Fourth through Eighth against others). This distinction has been labeled the distinction between external sins of action and internal sins of attitude.

Sins of Commission and Sins of Omission. Another distinction can be made between sins of commission and sins of omission. Sins of commission include those attitudes or actions that offend and harm directly. They break God's Law by doing the opposite of what it commands. Sins of omission break God's Law by failing to do the positive it commands. They offend and harm in a passive or negative fashion.

Sins of commission are generally easier to identify. Sins of omission show us what God wants from His creatures, not merely avoiding evil but fulfilling our humanity perfectly, the way He designed it. Further, sins of omission can have a deeper impact on our relationships. Failing to "be there" with praise for God or for study of His Word deepens the alienation between Creator and creature. Failing to be present with God's love or care for human neighbors deprives them of the support God intended them to have through human community.

Distinctions in Motivation. The church has also distinguished sins in terms of motivation. Some sins we know we are committing; others are unknown, unwitting sins (Leviticus 4:2; Psalm 19:12). Our culture may blind us to the fact that certain actions are sinful. Holding another human being in legal bondage—slavery—inevitably leads to ungodly abuse. But cultural standards have obscured the wickedness of this sin from Christian slave owners at times in the church's history. In committing sins of which we are unaware, we are still guilty as we exhibit the deeply rooted and complex hold that sinfulness has upon all human beings.

That pernicious and permeating hold upon our wills is also to be seen in the distinction between "voluntary" or planned sins and "involuntary" or unplanned sins. Paul complained of doing evil he wanted to avoid and failing to do the good he wanted to do (Romans 7:15–19). This distinction does not lift responsibility from us; we experience the curse falling upon all our sins. Even when we protest that we did not plan to offend, offense is taken. When we felt trapped into doing what we "had to do," other people are still hurt. Even involuntary sins suffocate us.

Habitual Sins and Occasional Sins. The church has also distinguished occasional sins from habitual sins. Habitual sins are those that repeat themselves as part of our lifestyle; occasional sins are those we commit seldom, on specific occasions, or in specific situations. Again, each poses its own problems. The occasional sin reminds us of our weakness and the need to be on guard, fighting against all temptations to depart from God's will. Even habitual sins may be forgiven as we continue in the struggle against them. Their existence reminds us of the mystery of sin remaining in the life of the redeemed. Forgiveness does not always correct sinful habits. Believers must ask, "Why do you want to know?" as fellow Christians inquire about their relationship with God in the midst of their struggle against habitual sins. Only the Gospel can change sinful habits, but defiant, secure sinners will be unable to hear the Gospel and must first be broken by the Law.

Individual Sins and Communal Sins. The struggle against sin continues for us as individuals and as members of larger groups. We distinguish those sins that we commit as individuals from those we commit as members of society or of groups within society. Sharing blame with other members of the group, however, does not lift blame from an individual. We still feel responsible for sins with which we had nothing to do as individuals but from which we benefit. Our standard of living, possible only because some in Western society exploit other lands, places a burden upon us even though as individuals most of us have never consciously tried to exploit anyone from overseas. Indeed, contemporary white Americans did not personally hold slaves and did not invent a system that systematically deprives racial and other minorities of justice. But all Americans nonetheless suffer the consequences of this exploitation in a host of ways in which such exercise of racist injustice has twisted human relationships in American society. We suffer not only from our human solidarity in sin; we suffer as well from solidarity in sins committed by other members of groups of which we are a part. Such is the nature of human nature, as God made us in community.

Venial Sins and Mortal Sins. Some Christians have also distinguished sin into the categories of venial—the less serious, which are wrong but do not break the relationship with God—and mortal—the more serious, those that break the relationship with God. This distinction ignores the fact that each actual sin reveals the lack of trust beneath it. All sins are equal before God, for each betrays our corruption at the core, our doubt of God's Word and promise. What makes a sin truly deadly is our attitude toward it. As soon as we think a sin, even a small sin, is not a big deal, we are in danger of the fires of hell, but when we confess our sins, even the big ones, God "is faithful and just to forgive us our sins and to cleanse us from all unrighteousness" (1 John 1:9).[23]

At the same time, some sins have more serious implications or consequences for the neighbor than others. Most of us would rather be insulted than murdered. God sympathizes with His human creatures as they suffer evil. He is not indifferent to the differences in human suffering. But His heart is equally grieved by "small" and "big" sins. Each reaffirms our flight from Him, our abandonment of our childlike stance before Him. Indeed, we may label the sinfulness that places us in the jaws of death as "mortal" (John 8:24; Romans 8:13), for sin kills (Ezekiel 18:4). But no particular actual sin offends God more or less than another. Failure to fear, love, and trust in God above all things—the original and root sin—separates us from the Author of life.

The "Unforgivable Sin." Christ once referred to the "unforgivable" or "unpardonable" sin of blasphemy against the Holy Spirit (Matthew 12:31–32; Mark 3:29; Luke 12:10). He gave no details on what constituted this sin. Christians have speculated that it must be stubborn and unrelenting

23 Forde, *On Being a Theologian of the Cross*, 38–43.

resistance to the Holy Spirit in unbelief. The best response to questions concerning this sin is that the person who worries about committing it must not be. No profit can be found in pursuing speculation regarding this sin. Its mention should serve simply as a call to repentance and faith.

Brokenness and Evil, Without and Within

The brokenness of the creation began with Adam and Eve's doubt of God's Word, and it spiraled into every nook and cranny of the cosmos. Every aspect of human nature is poisoned with sin, and we need a Savior to bring healing salve as an antidote. Scripture reveals that not just human nature but the whole creation is diseased with sin. Adam and Eve's sin brought thistles and thorns that make cultivating the earth tiresome and troublesome; their sin made childbirth a dangerous and painful task (Genesis 3:16–18). Death and decay took hold of the fabric of the universe so that all things fall apart—what scientists call entropy. St. Paul refers to the creation as in "bondage to corruption" and "groaning together in the pains of childbirth," subjected to mortality and dissolution as it awaits its redemption (Romans 8:20–22).

With sin having infiltrated everything, we often experience the fallen universe descending upon us without warning to disrupt our lives. We regularly encounter evils that do not sort out easily as either our fault or the fault of someone or something else. We are both victims and perpetrators of evil. Commonly in North America, we label a variety of bondages to evil as illness or put the responsibility on systemic social factors, which takes the blame off individuals. For instance, few in our culture label alcoholism, substance abuse, pornography, or other addictions as sin. Nonetheless, those plagued by these forms of bondage feel the oppression of sin and its effects in their guilt and sense of responsibility. The point is not to lay blame, which only announces the verdict and provides no solution, but to recognize just how deeply sin goes and how deeply all people need the Savior. The Bible tells of the sins of parents being visited to the third and fourth generations of those who continue to live in defiance of the Lord (Deuteronomy 5:9). In fact, even experience—such as with abuse—shows how the sins of parents and children merge. Whether caused by genes, lack of social support, mental illness, past trauma, or bad choices, these addictions and patterns of sin remain a bondage and a disruptive, restless way of life. Bondage to evil holds people fast, and it visits various plagues upon them even though they cannot always help it. As corrupt creatures who live in a corrupted cosmos, sin holds both individuals and the social fabric of all human societies in its oppressive grip.

Death is the big evil that speaks its "no" upon every human effort to secure life apart from its Creator. Its mammoth grasp haunts us throughout our lives. Most evils, though, are relatively small. The concept of the "banality of evil" reminds us that evil pounces upon us most often in cheap and tawdry forms. Hannah Arendt first used this term to describe the nature of the monstrous evil of the Holocaust.[24] She found that the perpetrators of the "Final Solution," the attempt to eliminate the whole Jewish people, were people altogether too normal in their appearance and outlook. A combination of opportunities and pressures led them into the possibility of practicing self-defense at mammoth cost to certain others. In their origins they were like the grocery store clerk next door, which means that *they were like us*. Evil at its insidious worst arises from the little advantages we take of our neighbor, the small compromises with the devil's lie, the almost unnoticeable sacrifices of conscience we make. It surprises us to realize how nice evil people can be. It surprises us how easily nice people do evil. We are surprised when we recognize how easily we ourselves fall into evil. Evil grasps from within and without, from all sides.

Reacting with Guilt, Shame, Impotence, and Fear

As it dawns upon sinners that evil has struck again, they react in one of two basic ways. When we feel threatened or overwhelmed by evil outside ourselves, we feel impotent. When we recognize that the evil has arisen from within, we feel guilty and ashamed. Fear in the face of our powerlessness and shame nags our entire outlook on life.

Impotence acknowledges the loss of control. It may express itself in apathy, fear, or rage, an angry yet often fearful attempt to regain some sense of power. Such rage frequently begins a cycle of revenge that involves many victims. The boss's put-down may be met by an act of revenge directed against spouse, child, or friends, who then directs rage at another. In short, the rage of impotence incites us to foolish expressions of power, which only damage us further. The fist slammed against the wall neither reclaims one's power nor compensates for the loss. At best it vents the frustration. But the impotence remains. Only the victory of God's power in Christ crucified can put all human impotence in the proper perspective, the perspective of God's love in cross and empty tomb.

Guilt and shame condemn from within. It may be the acknowledgment of God's standard, but it often is the confession of failure to attain one's own standard. It poisons life, for it cuts away at our estimation of ourselves and of God. Guilt judges the self; we put ourselves on trial against our own aspirations or demands, and we find ourselves wanting. We must be careful, however, not to put our own judgments before God's. Even when we do not

24 Hannah Arendt, *Eichmann in Jerusalem: A Report on the Banality of Evil* (New York: Viking, 1964), 231.

feel guilty, we are guilty before God. Our sin goes to our core, and we always need His forgiveness and faith in His promise. More important, God has done something about our guilt even when we feel its verdict upon us. God has borne our guilt and paid our debt through the death and resurrection of His Son, and Baptism into Christ by the Spirit cleanses sin's stain. Guilt's agony leads many to avoid it or justify themselves, but Christians must let guilt lead them to the cross, the source of forgiveness and freedom.

Guilt is the very premonition of death, and one way or another, sinners must die. They must die forever in hell, or they must die in Baptism to be raised to new life in Christ.

CHAPTER 7
THE LAW OF GOD

GOD'S Law is among the most delightful, yet also the deadliest, of God's creatures. For those who love God, His Law is pure delight: "Oh, how I love Your law! It is my meditation all the day" (Psalm 119:97). So Adam and Eve in the garden received God's commandment—to not eat of the tree in the middle of the garden (Genesis 2:17)—not as a threat but as a way to exercise their dependence, love, and faith. The commandment was their joy, because the One who gave it was their ultimate gladness.

After the tremendous mystery of the fall into sin, the Law became a menace to Adam and Eve. In sin, the commandment's presumption of their dependence was no longer good news of a loving Creator and Provider, but it was a threat to their individuality, autonomy, and life. In this fallen world, also for Christians, "the law always accuses."[1] It moves from delight to diagnosis, and its report is "not good," the opposite of God's appraisal at the end of day 6 (Genesis 1:31).

Some Christians make this accusing function into a secondary feature of the Law in order to focus more fully on the actions that God commands for His human creatures. To be sure, God's Law reveals His will, showing us the structure of creation and how to live well in it, and God insists that His creatures follow the Law. Nevertheless, the condemnation of the Law is not accidental in this age. God uses His Law to expose the "utter depths" of human sinfulness, uncovering our deafness to God's Word, our trust in created things, and our pursuit of happiness in those idols.[2] God intends to kill sinners with His Law and put to death the old habits of hell, so that in dying to sin, we might live in Christ Jesus. Thus "the law brings wrath" (Romans 4:15), and this wrath intends to expose Adam's disease that inheres within every human creature.

Christians, being righteous and sinners at the same time, are both confronted by the Law in order to be led to repentance and taught by the Law how to live well in relationship to God and fellow creatures. The American

1 Apology of the Augsburg Confession IV 38 and 128 (Kolb-Wengert, 126, 141).

2 Smalcald Articles III II 4 (Kolb-Wengert, 312).

Lutheran theologian Mattias Loy confessed this twofold character of the Law in his hymn: "The Law of God is good and wise And sets His will before our eyes, Shows us the way of righteousness, *And dooms to death when we transgress*."[3]

God's Law Is Good and Wise But ...

God designed human life to be good. His design for life is a gift toward His creatures. This structure, the Law, gives us the gift of living out His gift of life in joy and peace. Adam and Eve doubted God's Word, however, and as a result of that doubt they broke out of His structure for created life. The commandment, which was once pure delight—more desired than gold and sweeter than honey (Psalm 19:10)—now condemned their failures to live according to God's will.

Human life was designed to be lived well within the area opened by God's Law. Like a child safety gate that gives a toddler free rein of a playroom, the Law makes space for human creatures to live peaceably and joyfully according to God's will. Where Adam and Eve once saw the room opened by the Law, Adam's progeny see only boundaries, and they look like prison walls. Wrapped up in ourselves, we are blind to the Law's goodness—and sometimes even to the Law itself—and we slam ourselves into its walls, whether in a vain attempt to break out of them or prove our own strength and self-sufficiency. In doing so we bruise and bloody the peace God gives, for the Law imposes upon us discouragement and dismay, disease and disillusionment, degradation and death.

Christ gave us a summary of the human life God designed for His creatures in His description of the two kinds of relationships that constitute humanity: "You shall love the Lord your God with all your heart and with all your soul and with all your mind. This is the great and first commandment. And a second is like it: You shall love your neighbor as yourself" (Matthew 22:37–39). In this way, God revealed His will for human creatures: love (cf. Galatians 5:14).

Some theologians designate the revelation of God's will as the wide or more general sense of the Law, since it is sometimes used in Holy Scripture in this broad way (cf. Isaiah 2:3). In the wide sense, the Law is nothing other than the communication of God's will for His creatures, including His desire and work to save them.[4] The wide sense of the Law thus includes within it

---

3 *Lutheran Service Book* (St. Louis: Concordia, 2006), 579, stanza 1 (emphasis added).

4 Compare Solid Declaration of the Formula of Concord V 17 (Kolb-Wengert, 584): "The law is a divine teaching in which the righteous, unchanging will of God revealed how human beings were created in their nature, thoughts, words, and deeds to be pleasing and acceptable to God."

God's promise of grace in Christ, which is the work of the Gospel, properly speaking. These theologians distinguish the wide sense of the Law from the narrow or proper sense, which designates how God's Word instructs us in "what is right and God-pleasing and condemns everything that is sin and contrary to God's will."[5] In this narrow sense, the Law is strictly distinct from the narrow sense of the Gospel, which neither requires nor demands anything but comforts sinners with the promise of the forgiveness of sins in Christ alone. As it functions in the narrow sense in Holy Scripture, the Law points out that when we are not loving God as the ultimate source of our identity, security, and meaning, and when we are not loving others as we love ourselves, we are separated from the Author of life. We are in death. And the Law reveals our alienation and demise.

Although Scripture does use the word *Law* sometimes in a more general sense, God's people dare not confuse Law and Gospel on this basis. The Lutheran Confessions do not make a distinction between a wide and narrow sense of the Law—only between the two senses of the Gospel—in order that the Christians would know God's Law as His structure for human life and as "everything that reproves sin" for "its proper function is to reprove sin and to lead to the knowledge of sin."[6] When we recognize the Law as such, we will run to—and lead others to—Christ Jesus and the promise of the Gospel, where we find comfort, life, and salvation in the word of the cross.

Whether it describes God's will for us or diagnoses our misdeeds and mistrust, the Law does not grant life nor create faith. Life in Christ and by the Spirit is the will of God for all fallen human creatures as we are brought to fear Him as our God, love Him as the self-giving Lord, and trust in His promises for salvation (1 Timothy 2:4). From this faith, we are led by the Spirit to follow God's commands and live according to His design for human life. God's design for our lives is no more—or less—than a product of God's creative hand. God made the Law, and He is its Lord. The Law reflects His wisdom, it functions according to His will, and it reveals His will to us. According to Holy Scripture, God has not given the Law power to give life. The Law can only describe and diagnose human life. God gives life by grace. Even before the fall, Adam and Eve lived by God's grace alone, not by virtue of their performance of His commands. Each day in Eden was sustained by the Creator's gracious care. Human performance has never been, nor will it ever be, able to secure human life.

The Law shows us God's good and wise design for humanity, but it neither gives life nor provides the power to follow it. The Law describes

5 Epitome of the Formula of Concord V 3 (Kolb-Wengert, 500).

6 Solid Declaration of the Formula of Concord V 17 (Kolb-Wengert, 584). See also above, p. 134 n. 4.

what life should be like, assessing, analyzing, and adjudicating whether we are alive in God or dead in our flight from Him. This assessment is its most important function for all people in this age. The Law confronts us with our failure to be God's children. In doing so it pronounces judgment. It condemns and kills, according to God's will for sinners.

Fleeing God's Law

Because God uses His Law first to confront sinners, expose their idolatrous hearts and selfish minds, and reveal their complete impotence to control their destiny, one of the basic reactions is to run from God's Law. Like the younger son in the parable of the prodigal, sinners often flee into a far country, trying to escape from God's design for human life (Luke 15:13). We squander God's gracious gifts, seeking pleasure, self-authenticity, and autonomy—making our own laws and our own paths for life's journey. It may work for a time, but eventually God's Law strikes back. A famine discloses the younger son's dire situation. Cancer brings with it the specter of death. We find ourselves at rock bottom, alone and lonely, having broken all the relationships of those who were close to us. God has so designed human life so that when we flee from His Law, life breaks in order that we find ourselves completely in need, recognizing our fundamental dependence as creatures who need God's grace given in the cross of Christ.

This first kind of running from God's Law is easily recognized, but a second type is more insidious. Instead of running from God's design for human life completely, sinners also flee from the Law by trying to keep it perfectly, "imagining that they can and do keep the law by their own powers."[7] Thinking of the Law as simple basic actions that we are capable of doing—"I haven't killed anyone. Look how good I am!"—we run from its accusing force by manipulating God's Law into a few rules we are capable of following. This kind of flight from God's Law fails to recognize that the Law is "not a means whereby one could bargain with or vaunt oneself individually or collectively before God. The Law is not a remedy for sin."[8] After all, God does not merely want people who do right things, but a people who *are* right, right with Him by faith (the First Commandment).

We must differentiate between a love of God's Law—which does not flee from its accusations but accepts its judgment, falls on Christ for His mercy, and seeks to do God's will—and our attempts to use God's Law for our own benefit. The latter attitude is a dangerous one in which we stay in control by avoiding sin. This is what the older son in the parable of the prodigal attempted to do with his father. The older son was convinced that

---

7 Smalcald Articles III II 3 (Kolb-Wengert, 312).

8 Gerhard O. Forde, *Theology Is for Proclamation* (Minneapolis: Fortress, 1990), 76.

he had done everything right and that he *deserved* a party and an inheritance because of his perfect performance (Luke 15:28–30). Instead of recognizing his dependence on the father, the older son tried to use the Law to avoid sin and get what he wanted.[9] Christians, in particular, are in danger of this kind of legalism, in which the Law becomes our "defense against the gift."[10] We can easily fall into the temptation of thinking that as long as we keep the Law, we remain free from its attacks, in control of our eternal destinies.

Although few Christians would espouse such an obvious notion of **works-righteousness**, our attitudes reveal the older brother in our sinful hearts that has, in reality, fled from God's Law for human traditions. When we feel that we have earned success and favor more than other messier people, we are measuring ourselves according to human standards. When we think that our prayers deserve an answer or we rage at God for not giving us our due, we have succumbed to human traditions instead of attending to the Word. When we believe that our church is better than others on the basis of status, wealth, or anything else, we have run from God's Law and substituted an idol for the living God.

God's Law intends to shut our mouths, stop our excuses, and compel us to recognize the truth of who God is. "Whatever the law says it speaks to those who are under the law, so that every mouth may be stopped, and the whole world may be held accountable to God" (Romans 3:19). In other words, God is God, and human beings are His creatures. More than that, we are full of sin, and we do not give Him the honor, trust, love, or reverence that He deserves and that fulfills our own humanity. By the Spirit, we must learn not to flee the accusations of the Law, but hear them in their fullness so that we might recognize our utter need and be opened to hear the Gospel of God that brings the solution: "For all have sinned and fall short of the glory of God, and *are justified by His grace as a gift*, through the redemption that is in Christ Jesus" (Romans 3:23–24, emphasis added).

Conscience and Natural Law

The channel through which God's Law is processed in human creatures is called the **conscience**. The Gentiles, Paul observed, did not have the Law of Moses written out for them as the Jews had. Nonetheless, they had a sense of what was right for human life. It was "written on their hearts," and it both accused and excused them as they made decisions for living (Romans 2:14–16). This sense of God's presence and Law does not bestow a

---

9 See Timothy Keller, *The Prodigal God: Recovering the Heart of the Christian Faith* (New York: Dutton, 2008), 37–44.

10 Gerhard O. Forde, *On Being a Theologian of the Cross: Reflections on Luther's Heidelberg Disputation, 1518* (Grand Rapids: Eerdmans, 1997), 27.

perfect knowledge of God, far from that (Romans 1:21). Apart from Christ, minds are darkened, hearts are hardened, and sinners become callous and indulge in all sorts of evil (Ephesians 4:17–19; Romans 1:32).

As noted earlier, some modern anthropologists have questioned whether any universal law or design can be read from the human heart. Moral standards differ significantly among cultures, they report. While this is true when investigators compare specific morals and mores, the large consensus on proper moral behavior among cultures suggests that all human creatures have not only an inborn sense that right and wrong exist but also some sense of the Law's content. We may not recognize injustice clearly when it happens to someone else, but we know injustice when it happens to us. In the Christian tradition, this notion is called **natural law**, which recognizes that God has built His design and structure for human life into the world. This design is not obvious to every individual, but the general consensus of human society shows a remarkable confluence on **moral law**, how human beings ought to live.[11]

The challenge of understanding natural law is that the conscience cannot be separated from cultural and personal experience. It is impossible to determine what instruction the human "heart" would give apart from cultural wisdom and experience, for all children grow up within the context of culturally determined moral instruction. That instruction, it should be noted, gathers the rational judgments of generations regarding what will make human life better or worse. From collective experience, societies frame and adjust their own values and standards. All human culture is a continuing laboratory, an ongoing experiment, on what shape human life ought to take. Such cultural experiments last a long time. Sometimes the experiment will continue for decades before a society concludes that it has made a false judgment on right and wrong regarding some area of human life. Without the guidance of Scripture, these experiments never produce the truth of God's design for human life fully, but they do approximate it in varying degrees. Christians, however, do not have to wonder about the content of natural law. God has given the Ten Commandments, which are the clear revelation of His will, describing how human life works according to His design and structure.

Because of human sin, including false cultural input, the conscience can err. Philip Melanchthon considered the conscience to be a "practical syllogism," that is, a comparison of the Law with one's personal behavior where

11 See Robert C. Baker and Roland Cap Ehlke, eds., *Natural Law: A Lutheran Reappraisal* (St. Louis: Concordia, 2011).

the conscience concludes guilt or innocence.[12] Despite the limitations of this definition, it does illuminate different ways the conscience can err. God's Law can be overshadowed by cultural norms so that the major premise of the syllogism—what God says or commands—is wrong. People can look at themselves inaccurately or dishonestly, excusing wrong behavior or accusing where God's Law does not. The conscience can also be dulled by experience so that the conclusion of guilt is not made. In short, human conscience does not always function as it ought because sin has blurred its vision.

Although the judgments of conscience are worthless in defining who God is, its judgments regarding right and wrong in the horizontal dimension of human life are generally right enough to preserve life. Conscience produces civic righteousness, the right kind of action for maintaining society. When believers struggle to determine their own best course of action, they may experience struggles of conscience. Sometimes this will be because of blurred or false judgments offered by cultural standards that govern the area of life under consideration. Sometimes it will arise from conflicts between two goods or between two evils, to determine which is preferable. Believers flee to Christ in the midst of such struggles. They plead for the Holy Spirit's guidance, and they take refuge in the forgiveness that Christ gives even when conscience errs.

The Use and Three Uses of the Law

The Law's content, summarized in the Ten Commandments, reveals the shape of human life as it is supposed to be lived according to God's will. The Law shows what human life should look like, both in relationship to God (commandments 1–3) and to other human creatures (commandments 4–10). Such an understanding of the Law, however, can confuse us into thinking that the Law is purely informational. This could not be further from the truth. God's Law does provide information, content, as to His will, but it does much more. Theologians designate this "more" as the **uses** or **functions** of the Law—*use* refers to the speaker's intention while *function* references the effect on the hearer.

In the Smalcald Articles, Luther designated two offices or powers of the Law: to curb or restrain sin by threat or reward and to reveal the total corruption of the human heart.[13] Later Lutherans, including Philip Melanchthon and the authors of the Formula of Concord, have generally described three ways in which the Law functions in human life, adding a

12 Melanchthon defined the conscience this way in all editions of his *Loci Communes* except 1521. Philip Melanchthon, *Commonplaces: Loci Communes 1521*, trans. Christian Preus (St. Louis: Concordia, 2014), 105 n. 15.

13 Smalcald Articles III II 2–4 (Kolb-Wengert, 311–12).

teaching function for those inhabited by God's Spirit. The different uses or functions of the Law help Christians understand that God uses His Law for three distinct purposes, and it helps us recognize that our words may be understood in these distinct ways too. Believers must be cognizant of how their words might be heard in order that they distinguish properly between Law and Gospel as they teach God's Word to others.

Those who hear God's Law from the lips of believers may or may not receive the Law according to the use intended. In fact, no Christian can control how the Law functions in the life of another, nor can we control how God's Word functions in our own lives. The Law, after all, belongs to God and contains His power. The true user of the Law, then, is God, and once the power of God's Law is loosed, it is not controlled by us. A parent or teacher may intend to curb a child's behavior, preventing that child from harming herself or others, but the child may feel cut to the heart, accused and condemned as a bad kid. We may think we have the perfect formula to convince an unbelieving friend that he is a sinner and needs the Gospel, but he may hear that accusation as pure threat of punishment. Accordingly, he may fall into line externally but without any internal conviction of his broken relationship with God. Or he may revolt with ferocity, rebelling against the condemnation in rage and disobedience. We may be engaged in Christian instruction on living according to the Spirit, but our hearers may feel the sentence of death.

Because Christian proclaimers have little control over how the Law is heard, we must always be sensitive to the effect the Law—whatever its intent—is having on the person to whom we are addressing it. We dare not forget that whatever use we intend, the Law always accuses. At its friendliest, this guide dog is a domesticated wolf,[14] and we cannot predict when it will spring on us with its deadly accusation and reduce us to guilt once again.

The Law Curbs and Regulates Life in the Horizontal Realm

The first power named by Luther in the Smalcald Articles is the Law's ability to restrain sin. In this first use, the Law coerces us or entices us into proper external behavior. It keeps us in line, on the right path, at least externally. This is the most common function of God's Law for sinners. We experience it every time a driver sees a police car on the road, or we decide against an action because of potential consequences. This first, curbing function of the Law is called **the political use** of the Law because it enables us to live together within the *polis*, the Greek word for "city or community."

14 James Arne Nestingen, *The Faith We Hold: The Living Witness of Luther and the Augsburg Confession* (Minneapolis: Augsburg, 1983), 38–39.

The political or coercive function of the Law keeps us in line by one of two methods. First, it entices us by offering rewards for good behavior. These rewards can be called promises of the Law, but they must not be confused with the Gospel. Being rewarded for good behavior is just as much a function of the Law as being punished for bad behavior. More important, performance of the Law, even perfect performance, does not make a person God's redeemed child, but such performance results from being His child. In addition to offering rewards, the Law also scares us into compliance by threatening punishment for disobedience. Often, but not always, the Law threatens us effectively, and we comply. Usually, we do so for our own sake, not for the sake of a neighbor. Sometimes, however, sinners catch a larger vision of life and act out of nobler motivations.[15] They come to see the good of society as the goal and believe that the common welfare of all compels selfless behavior. In this way, sinners can achieve a certain kind of **civil righteousness**, a status of righteousness according to human standards that does not count before God. Nevertheless, the curbing force of the Law cannot turn sinners to Jesus and produce fear, love, and trust in God or altruistic love of the neighbor for God's sake.

We should not minimize the importance of the Law's first use. Its force calls self-willed sinners back to some sense of the original, good order that God designed for human life. It thus serves to preserve and protect recollections of Eden among us who have strayed far from its gate. In so doing, what God designed as the vehicle for human freedom has become His agent for compelling human responsibility. Thus the Law makes life tolerable in a sinful world. It counterbalances the self-centered, destructive urges that beset me in my sinful arrogance and ignorance. It prevents me from doing some really stupid things to myself and other people. Furthermore, it prevents other people from doing stupid or evil things to me. By restraining evil and promoting justice in this way, God's Law befriends the victims of sinners and protects sinners from themselves.

In society, people may not be good or nice to me for the right reasons, but they are civil to me. They may be hypocritical as they smile and help me. But their compliance—*and mine*—preserve order in our community. I would rather have my neighbor love me, for her love would encourage her to be a helpful neighbor over the long haul. However, if she hates me but is afraid of the sheriff, and therefore does not try to hurt me, we can still live together safely in community. I never want to be hypocritical because

15 Lawrence J. Kohlberg, e.g., *The Psychology of Moral Development: The Nature and Validity of Moral Stages* (San Francisco: Harper & Row, 1984). Cf. the evaluation by Gilbert C. Meilaender, *The Theory and Practice of Virtue* (Notre Dame: University of Notre Dame Press, 1984), 75–99.

hypocrisy, a product of the Law's coercive force, is one of the sinful lies that perverts my life. At the same time, a hypocritical smile feels better than hateful words, even as that hypocrisy is just as sinful before God. Among sinners, hypocrisy makes the world go around.

Police use the coercive force of the Law to keep order in the part of society for which they are responsible. So do parents and teachers. That is part of their responsibility. They should not be afraid to face that responsibility and exercise it with a sense of joy in being God's agents for preserving what is better rather than permitting what is worse in a sinful world.

This civic or civil righteousness that the political use of the Law produces is a good gift of God in the brokenness of our sin-ridden horizontal relationships. Even at its best, however, the Law does not improve sinners. In fact, as Luther noted in his Smalcald Articles, the Law can make sinners more rebellious than compliant (Romans 5:20; 7:8–9).[16] Its threat of punishment can stir fires of resentment in the human heart, arising from our sinful desire to assert control and establish our identity apart from God. Bowing to God's Law is the last thing we want to do as sinners. It is essentially the "terrible twos" syndrome. We are not about to let God tell us what to do.

Worse yet, the curbing or political function of the Law can persuade sinners to confuse the two kinds of righteousness and believe that human performance of good works can achieve righteousness in God's sight. Such a plan is doomed to failure for two reasons. First, "there is not a righteous man on earth who does good and never sins" (Ecclesiastes 7:20). Everyone has sinned and fallen short of the glory of God (Romans 3:23). God demands *perfection* of both heart and hands (Matthew 5:48). Second, compliance with the Law's standards does not make creatures right with God; no human performance counts as righteousness that avails before God. Righteousness in God's sight lies completely in His favorable disposition, His grace, toward us. Even Adam and Eve in Eden found favor in His sight on the basis of mercy, not on the basis of their perfect performance of His Law.

The Law Accuses and Crushes in the Vertical Realm

The Law always evaluates sinners, shining light into human hearts and minds that reveals our total depravity before God. Luther called this reflective function of the Law the **theological use** of the Law. He considered it the Law's primary function because nothing could be more important for sinners than to know the "utter depths" of our fallen nature and "how completely corrupt it is."[17] Christians often picture this use of the Law by describing it as a mirror that confronts us with the awful truth of our corrupt hearts,

16 Smalcald Articles III II 2.

17 Smalcald Articles III II 4 (Kolb-Wengert, 312).

minds, and souls apart from Christ. It shows our sinfulness and brokenness that does not measure up to God's will for His creatures. The Law analyzes our actions, diagnoses our deeds, and scrutinizes our souls, revealing the doubt, false worship, and selfishness that permeate every human heart after the fall. Further, the Law illuminates the fallen nature of humanity, showing how human creatures lay in the bonds of death, Satan, and evil, unable to escape from their lethal clutches. The Law, then, announces God's verdict over fallen human beings without a Savior: death.

The Law Reveals Human Sinfulness. The Law teaches not merely that we commit sins but that we are sinners (Romans 3:20). Even Paul had to confess that his conscience had not sufficiently informed him of the full extent of sin. He had to encounter God's Law to appreciate how sinful his covetous thoughts were. He also confessed, however, that this only served to intensify his indulgence in coveting (Romans 7:7–8).

The Law reveals the reality of our brokenness, our perversion of human creatureliness. However else we may encounter the Law—as promises of blessing in return for obedience, as helpful suggestions for improving life, or as threats not to step out of line—the Law remains our adversary. Its accusation is undaunted and consistent. It places the burden and responsibility upon us. As long as human creatures remain under the Law's accusation, the Law's burden will crush us. Escape from its crushing condemnation comes only by shifting its burden to Christ.

The Law Reveals Evil Breaking Human Life. In addition to revealing human sinfulness, the Law also reflects the brokenness of human life as a whole. In this sense, the theological use of the Law not only accuses sinners but also reveals that we exist trapped in the general evil around us as well as in our own sin. The Law squeezes and chokes sinners whenever they encounter the inadequacy of their own power to make life ultimately good. The Law commands perfection (Matthew 5:48), but how can anyone achieve perfect holiness in a world full of sin and evil that we cannot control? The Law, thus, suffocates us and makes us gasp for life's breath—that which God breathed into us in Eden—as it reflects the failure of our own mastery over the course of our lives.

Natural disasters, epidemics and pandemics, wars, violent crimes, and more mundane human problems confront us with our inadequacy and failure. Estrangement and alienation from those we ought to love—and be loved by—spell out our deficiencies. Meaningless moments, stretching into months, write out on the lonely walls of our existence that our power is inadequate and our control has failed. We peek in the mirror of the Law whenever these shortcomings command our attention. We see no pretty sight. We see life unraveling in the direction of death, sometimes at a rapid pace.

The Law Reveals God's Wrath. God loves His human creatures so much that He will not stand aside while they ignore or rebel against His design for human life. Only within this design can His human creatures enjoy life fully. Only when they center life in Him and fulfill their humanity as He fashioned it will they enjoy true shalom. The Father of all boils in anger when His children are led astray and done to death, even when they do it to themselves. His jealousy (Exodus 20:5) reflects His love for us when we, caught in our sinfulness, cannot love Him back because we have brought upon ourselves the terminal blindness and deafness of our doubt.

God wrote into His Law the curse that would safeguard His perfect plan for His human creatures (Genesis 2:17; Exodus 20:5; Deuteronomy 27:26). Human experience recognizes that the curse works. We die (Ezekiel 18:20; Romans 6:23). Because God takes pleasure in His children's enjoyment of perfect peace, not of wickedness, He will not allow sinners to remain as they are, nor will God condone sins that harm His wise design for human life. God destroys sinners (Psalm 5:4–6) and then raises them up to new life in Christ. He reveals His anger against all ungodliness and unrighteousness (Romans 1:18; 2:5–9). Sins of every kind, at every level of seriousness in human eyes, offend God.

God hates the pious works of those who exploit the poor and needy (Amos 5:10–27). God has prepared vengeance against abuses of human sexuality, for the body belongs to Him (1 Thessalonians 4:3–8; 1 Corinthians 6:13–20). Those who are angry with others make themselves liable to judgment (Matthew 5:21–22). False witness shall not go unpunished, and propagators of fake news will not escape (Proverbs 19:5). God requires a reckoning for those who take life (Genesis 9:5–6). The writer of Proverbs wishes upon those who transgress the Fourth Commandment a horrible fate (Proverbs 30:17). Above all, God's anger burns against every form of idolatry (Hosea 8:5; Amos 5:6). God loves His children too much not to be filled with wrath against that which takes them away from Him.

Luther and the Lutheran Confessions call this work of the Law God's alien work, because it is alien to His nature as the God of the Gospel. Moreover, this work of the Law intends to make a highway in the desert for God's proper work of the preaching of grace and comfort to sinners through the good news of Jesus Christ. This understanding of the Law reminds us that God's ultimate goal with His people is a right relationship with Him wherein we come to love the Lord who first loved us.

Nevertheless, the experience of God's wrath remains problematic from the human standpoint on this side of Judgment Day. There His wrath will be expressed and experienced with crystal clarity when God condemns evil, visiting eternal punishment on those in league with sin and Satan, and makes all things new, re-creating shalom for His children (Matthew 25:31–46; Isaiah 25:6–12; Revelation 21:3–8). Short of the Last Day, human interpretations of evil and suffering remain fallible, often trying to explain the secret things of God rather than what He has revealed to us (Deuteronomy 29:29). After all, we cannot make sense of evil as a "fair punishment" for specific sins. Believers must avoid interpreting certain evils as an expression of God's wrath against specific sins and specific sinners, or unbelievers may have the impression that His wrath falls arbitrarily and God is unjust. Such a focus attempts to solve the problem of theodicy, but apart from faith, God will not be recognized as just.[18]

For this reason some theologians have suggested that God does not visit specific consequences upon sin. Rather, His structure for human life, the Law, collides with the human pursuit of freedom against this structure to produce the signs of His wrath. Otherwise stated, God has placed human creatures within His well-designed plan for life. When they try to break out of this plan, and live out possibilities that God has not fashioned for human life, they crash and smash into God's good structure, which bruises people in different ways depending on the specific rebellion against God's design. Further, human intelligence remains sufficiently effective—even in its fallen state—to avoid the consequences of living outside God's structure for a while. Thus the ways in which we suffer for breaking God's Law differ from individual to individual and case to case.

This apparent randomness reflects the reality of human experience, but we dare never suggest that God is absent from human life or condones human sin, whether He visits punishment directly and immediately or not. The Law, after all, is not a structure that stands independently of God, but it is His handiwork and part of His communication to His creatures (Psalm 19:1–3). At the same time, specific misfortune can seldom be attributed to specific sins. God may indeed use specific evils to call individuals to repentance, but no general theory of evil and punishment can be formulated from individual experiences. We usually confuse the issue when we attempt to correlate specific sins with specific ills in an individual's life. The general correlation between sin and judgment, however, reminds believers that God's wrath is real, even if its visitation cannot be perceived as clearly or regularly as we would like.

Thus believers should ask, "Why do you want to know?" when confronted with questions regarding the correlation of suffering and sin. When the agenda behind the question expresses concern about God's intention toward humankind, the answer will give assurance of His gracious love. When the agenda focuses on human activity and sinfulness, the answer will

18 See chapter 5.

give aid to a spirit that seeks repentance, affirming God's displeasure at the sin that disrupts the lives of His beloved creatures. The visitation of punishment should not be seen first of all as an assessment of blame but rather a call to repentance (Luke 13:4–5).

The Law Kills. Many forms of evil remind us not of individual sinfulness but of our common fragility and frailty in a world disrupted by sin. Attempts to tame the atom, for good and evil purposes, and attempts to increase food production to feed the hungry have both contributed to the spread of carcinogens in this world. Those who suffer cancer cannot be differentiated from those who do not on the basis of quantity or quality of individual sinfulness. In attempting to exercise responsibility and freedom, human creatures—even when doing their best—have fouled God's creation. Creation has turned back upon us, and it presses us in the trap that we fashioned as a means of improving life. Such failures remind us that God is grieved by our efforts to control and fashion life according to our whims and that we are absolutely dependent, despite our strongest protestations.

Thus God's Law reflects His judgment on our fallen and broken state. When sinners confront their own sinfulness or the frail nature of life, they recognize God's wrath toward sin and evil. Some sinners will harden their hearts in defense against the Law's observation; others will despair in guilt. But the Law cannot fix the problem. It can only tell us that things have gone wrong. The Gospel must follow the Law's diagnosis to bring despairing sinners to the God whose wrath arises from His love.

To hear God's gracious word of good news, sinners must recognize their need for the new life that the Gospel alone bestows. They must come to see that they are dead in their old way of life, living under false systems for finding ultimate identity, security, and meaning. This primary force of the Law, its second or theological function, produces corpses.

It does not make sense to argue with a corpse. We may have to tell the corpse that he is dead. We may have to announce time and time again that she has no life apart from Christ. But we do not use the theological function of the Law effectively as a club. The coercive function of the Law does work like a club, but the theological function works like a fine-tipped arrow, which pierces the heart. If the corpse will not listen to his own death sentence, we gain little by belaboring the point. We wait for a more opportune moment to press home again the Law's accusation and condemnation, its death notice.

Satan's Use of the Law. Satan, the accuser, also uses the condemning function of Law against believers.[19] In Satan's hand the Law becomes a weapon of deceit, a tool to undermine the Gospel. He approaches believers

---

19 Kolb learned this first from his Concordia College, St. Paul, colleague Stephen C. Stohlmann.

who have had their sins forgiven, and he attempts to persuade them that their guilt remains. When he uses the Law in this way, he is trying to drown out God's gracious voice and gift of new life.

Believers must resist this kind of accusation from the Law, for it takes away the comfort and power of the Gospel. Believers rightly hear the accusation of the Law, but they do not dwell on it or wallow in it. They are turned from its accusation to the Gospel, which becomes the complete focus for their lives. Depending on their emotional makeup and the kind of crisis of brokenness in which they find themselves, they may or may not "feel guilty" under its accusation. Such feelings are not the main point. Christians simply confess their guilt and flee from sin to the haven of the Gospel. Satan tries to interrupt that flight into the embrace of the Lord's forgiving arms by using the familiar notes of the Law's accusation as his siren song. The Gospel obliterates Satan's lie: "Who shall bring any charge against God's elect? It is God who justifies" (Romans 8:33).

The Instructive Use of the Law

The Law functions to keep all in line (first use) and to accuse and condemn human creatures for failing to be and act as God's beloved children (second use). But as believers encounter God's Law in daily life, they confront it as more than an enticing or threatening curb and a condemning mirror. We also turn to the Law for guidance and direction regarding how to live godly lives according to God's will, which is called the **third use** of the Law, the **instructive use**. This third use of the Law is not different in its content from the first and second uses—it is still God's commands and structure that express His will for human life. What is different about the third use of the Law are the hearts of those who hear it. In the language of the Formula of Concord, forgiven sinners, reborn through the Holy Spirit, liberated from the Law, do everything according to God's will "from a free and merry spirit," insofar as they are born anew.[20]

Insofar as Christians are born anew, the Law is not necessary to entice or threaten God's people to do His will. Christians are already transformed by the Spirit, regenerated by water and the Word, to love God and desire Him and His will. By the Spirit, a Christian's "delight is in the law of the Lord" (Psalm 1:2). Despite being made new by faith, believers' minds remain ignorant and infected, not knowing the entirety of God's will and structure for human life and in need of the Word's power by the Spirit to shape us ever more into the image of Christ Jesus (Colossians 3:10, 16). Believers, then, need not only the first and second uses of the Law, but also its third use that

20 Solid Declaration of the Formula of Concord VI 17 (Kolb-Wengert, 590).

teaches God's will and guides Christians to discern by the Spirit how to lead God-pleasing lives in the ambiguity of day-to-day life.

Some Lutherans deny that there is a purely instructive use of the Law. They teach that the Law guides Christian decision-making, but it always does so as it curbs the mind and will, which remain tainted by disdain for God's plan, and as it condemns such disdain. These theologians fear that an emphasis on the Law as a guide for the Christian can make the third use of the Law the central focus of Christian living, as has happened among some followers of John Calvin's theology. These Lutheran theologians rightly recognize that if the Law's third use becomes the heart of the Christian life, the power and comfort of the Gospel can be obscured. God's promises can be displaced by human performance, even if that performance is driven by the Holy Spirit. Hence, the Law's second use as the condemning and killing force of God must remain its primary and most important function, even for Christians, who remain sinners in this age (1 John 1:8), in order to drive us back to Jesus and what He does for us, apart from the Law (Galatians 2:16).

Christians should do nothing to refocus the Christian life from God's gracious action in Christ. As Christ's benefits are conveyed to us through the life-renewing Word, the Holy Spirit stands at the center of the believer's life. The Spirit produces the fruits of faith as a by-product of re-creating us as children of God. Yet in the mystery of our existence as both righteous and sinful people of God, the struggle against temptation does not cease in this age. The third use of the Law reminds believers that we need to know God's will since our minds are unclear on how to follow God's Word and commands in daily life. This is particularly true in an age that lacks moral clarity and hides sin under the guise of love, tolerance, and morality. The mind of the believer needs to be shaped by God's Word, Law and Gospel, to recognize sin in the world and "be transformed by the renewal of [the] mind" (Romans 12:2). To be sure, this is not merely a matter of receiving guidance by the Law, but it is not less than that either. The believer needs the Law's condemning force to put the sinful nature to death daily, the Law's curbing force to restrain our selfishness, and the Gospel that brings the Spirit and life. Believers' minds also must be conformed to the Word so that believers are truly *theodidacti*, those taught by God (John 6:45), as the third use of the Law does.

The instructive use of the Law recognizes that believers react toward the Law's curbing power in a different way, with different motivation, from those who stand outside the faith. At times, in their sinfulness, believers will be curbed by the Law's threats or promises. At other times, however, the Gospel will be directing their wills and thoughts toward serving God. Then believers will search the Law for God's counsel, rejoicing in being able to please Him through faith. As believers turn to the Law for instruction in living as God's beloved children, they will find in the Law more than guidance for their decision-making. They will also become more conscious of their past failures to live according to God's will, and they will sense the struggle that they will have to live out their righteousness in the future. However we may use the Law in dealing with others or ourselves, the Law will function as the Law in all its forms and make the impacts that the Holy Spirit wills it to make.[21]

As believers put the Law to use, they must avoid two extremes. On the one hand, Christians must reject **antinomianism**, the belief that believers can live without the Law. God's children do not focus their lives on their own obedience according to the Law but on God's gracious favor toward them. Nonetheless, believers—who are righteous and sinful at the same time—still need God's Law. It curbs their sinful nature, exposes their sinful desires, and provides information for their decision-making. On the other hand, believers must reject **legalism**, a dependence upon the Law and human performance of it for the assurance of God's grace. Legalists may claim to believe the Gospel, but their performance of the Law provides their security and gives life purpose.

We try to describe our actions according to God's plan with a variety of verbs. Some think that imperatives such as "you shall" or "do this" sound oppressive, and they prefer indicatives that simply describe what a believer "does" or "will do." These latter terms attempt to avoid the burden of expectation by simply describing the hoped-for reality of living out God's will with the Spirit's power. The fact is, however, that any verb describing what believers do or are supposed to do places the burden upon the Christian. God's Law—and its accusation—wells up within any focus on human performance and human creatures. Even indicatives and descriptions of the Christian life show us what we ought to do and how we fail to do them.

There is a related problem involved in Christian decision-making. Scripture rarely tells us how to act in specific situations. It tells us not to kill, but it does not tell us whether 60 or 80 miles per hour endangers the lives of others on the highway. It tells us not to commit adultery, but it leaves to us the evaluation of whether different styles of dress or dancing promote lust. It tells us not to steal, but it does not specify what constitutes fair profit in a capitalist system. It tells us to obey our parents and government, but it does not tell us when specific forms of obedience to legitimate authorities may cross the line and become disobedience to God (Acts 5:29). We are always compelled to make moral judgments.

21 Robert Kolb, "Wittenberg Uses of Law and Gospel," *Lutheran Quarterly* 37 (2023): 249–67.

In moral judgments, Christians do well to remember the simplicity of God's fundamental design for human life. We tend to rationalize and justify our actions to show why we were right instead of simply listening to God's Word and obeying Him. God's design for human life is quite simple: love God absolutely and love our neighbors as ourselves. Amazingly, even believers fail to recognize this simple solution to many—though not all—vexing moral dilemmas. Act as if someone else were doing the same thing to you in this situation (Matthew 7:12). The fact that this solution escapes our recollection so easily reminds us how thoroughly sin befuddles us.

The Law dogs the steps of believers and unbelievers alike throughout this life, and we must keep in mind that it turns easily from guide dog to wolf. But against its devouring jaws stands Jesus Christ, God in human flesh, delivered into the Law's paws and death's jaws so that He might give life to His children.

Controversies about the Law in Recent Lutheran Theology

Since the Law condemns and kills as its primary and most important use, one temptation for Lutheran theology is Gospel reductionism, also called Law-Gospel reductionism. **Gospel reductionism** refers to preaching and teaching that de-emphasizes the content of God's revealed Word in order to stress the accusing force of the Law as well as the comfort of the Gospel. In this view, the Law's importance is in its function, what it does to human creatures, not its content, what it says or commands. Similarly, the Gospel's content in the story of Christ is reduced to the forgiveness of sins that brings comfort and peace to the conscience. This view is often associated with a denial of the third use of the Law since the Law no longer teaches content of what God wills for human lives.

The true problem with Gospel reductionism, however, is more basic than a rejection of the Law's third use. Gospel reductionism focuses more on human beings and their psychological or emotional state than on what God says and does. In this way, cultural cues and social judgments, which shape our emotions, can become more important than the story of Scripture. For example, some Christians focus on the Gospel as God's love and acceptance of a person. Without the content of the scriptural account of the cross (1 John 4:9–10), love can be understood according to Western culture, which affirms and accepts all people, no matter their sin, leaving no room for repentance. In this way, God's commands and demand for justice are explained away or even condemned for not being loving enough. Instead of the Law revealing human sinfulness and teaching us the wise will of the Creator, acceptance and affirmation overcome the commandments of God.

In the process, the Gospel, too, is reduced to nice words for victims rather than forgiveness for sinners. Without the full truth of God's Law, people no longer have language to recognize themselves as sick with sin, and do not need a Gospel that speaks of a Savior who took upon Himself the world's sin that our terminal illness might be healed.

Ironically, a view that begins with a denial of God's commandments ends with harsher requirements than God's Law. Cultural virtues—such as tolerance, kindness, and acceptance—take the place of the Law, becoming sledgehammers with which to bash all who do not follow their demands. Such is the result when God's Law is denied. Antinomianism—denial of the Law—quickly becomes legalism—law without grace—when human living is divorced from God's good design for human life.

Since the turn of the twenty-first century, some Lutheran theologians have emphasized the eternality of the Law, *lex aeterna*, as a response to Gospel reductionism.[22] To establish the moral law and moral order of God as an unchanging reality, these theologians consider the Law to be part of God's essence rather than part of God's communicated will to His creatures.[23] All the commandments, in this view, originate in God's own triune nature as the love of the Father and the Son in the Spirit. In medieval theology, some went even further, understanding the Law as an eternal, built-in structure to reality. Thus God stood alongside His Law, not over it, and God—as well as human beings—had to conform to the eternal Law.

Luther rejected the scholastic theology that placed God and the Law side by side, understanding the Law as part of God's communicated will, a creature that reflects God's wisdom and goodness, not a structure that exists "prior" to creation. To be sure, the contemporary advocates of eternal law rightly confess that God's Law is not idiosyncratic or arbitrary. The Law is good and wise, and it describes the actual grain, the structure, of the universe. At the same time, the Law must be recognized and understood as part of God's speech, His communication to His creatures. God is a God of conversation and community, and the Law is part of how God talks to His creatures. It expresses how we relate to our God. It shows us where we have failed; it keeps us from harming one another; it helps us see how we live well as His creatures. The question "In what sense is the Law eternal?" is beside the point; the point is that God made us to hear His Word, and we must be taught and moved by His Spirit to listen, trust, and obey His will.

22 Jordan B. Cooper, *Lex Aeterna: A Defense of the Orthodox Lutheran Doctrine of God's Law and Critique of Gerhard Forde* (Eugene, OR: Wipf & Stock, 2017).

23 David P. Scaer, "Is Law Intrinsic to God's Essence?" *Concordia Theological Quarterly* 82 (2018): 7: "Law is what God is eternally in himself."

In the words of the Formula of Concord, the teachings of Law and Gospel "belong to this imperfect life."[24] Believers do not need to figure out the nature of the Law as such or reach into the hidden God to understand the inner workings of the Godhead and how those inner trinitarian dynamics shape our lives. Christians are to proclaim the Word that has been given to the church, the Word of Christ, the news of the Son of God who gave up His life for sinners that we might receive forgiveness, life, and salvation. All human creatures are to follow God's Law and design for human life, and the church must teach this Law as Scripture reveals it, but we dare not make the Law equal to God so that we do not hear it as His Word to us.

God has not only spoken His Word to us, but the One who is the eternal Logos, the eternal Word, has become flesh to bring grace and truth and make the Father known (John 1:16–18). In Jesus, the "fullness of God was pleased to dwell," and such fullness is seen in "making peace by the blood of His cross" (Colossians 1:19–20). In Luther's exquisite prose, Jesus is the "mirror of the Father's heart," showing us God's will for us, His grace and mercy,[25] which was given to Adam and Eve in Eden and will be forever apparent in the life everlasting with His Law written on our hearts and His forgiveness echoing in our ears (Jeremiah 31:33–34). Until then, we need the Law to curb our selfishness, reveal our corruption, and teach us God's wisdom and design for our lives as His children.

---

24 Solid Declaration of the Formula of Concord VI 24 (Kolb-Wengert, 591).

25 Large Catechism II 65 (Kolb-Wengert, 440).

CHAPTER 8

THE PERSON OF CHRIST

AT the center of the Christian faith is not an idea, a doctrine, or a practice, but a human creature, Jesus, who is the eternal God. Scripture speaks about Christ in this twofold way, as true God and true man. Jesus asserted, "Before Abraham was, I am" (John 8:58). John the evangelist wrote: "The Word became flesh and dwelt among us" (John 1:14). The apostle Peter proclaimed, "You killed the Author of life" (Acts 3:15). St. Paul wrote: "In Him all the fullness of God was pleased to dwell, and through Him to reconcile to Himself all things, whether on earth or in heaven, making peace by the blood of His cross" (Colossians 1:19–20). Time and eternity; flesh and Word; Creator of life and robbed of life; fully God yet shedding blood on the cross. Who is this Jesus?

In this chapter, we will examine the Scriptures to understand Jesus' person and identity, doing so in light of historical controversies regarding Christ's person. As we study Christology, we dare not think that the person of Christ is a mere academic matter. Jesus' identity strikes to the heart of Christian faith and worship; it affects how we interpret the Bible and whether we recognize the surety of His promises for us today. The essential issue can be stated simply: Did God come down to earth in Jesus to redeem sinners, or was Jesus' mission to lead humanity up to heaven, guiding us to God by learning His teachings and imitating Him?[1] Did God come down, or do we go up? Only one of these options is good news: one of the Trinity has become incarnate on earth as a true human being for us men and our salvation. In Paul's words: "When the fullness of time had come, God sent forth His Son, born of woman, born under the law, to redeem those who were under the law, so that we might receive adoption as sons" (Galatians 4:4–5).

---

1 This was at issue both at Nicaea and Chalcedon: Donald Fairbairn and Ryan M. Reeves, *The Story of Creeds and Confessions* (Grand Rapids: Baker Academic, 2019), 50–55, 77, 89–91, 101–4.

Jesus of Nazareth, True Man

To many conservative Christians today, Jesus' divine identity seems obvious. Those who have grown up in Christian churches are accustomed to confessing Jesus as God, praying to Him, and worshiping Him. It is easy, then, to recognize Jesus as true God and wonder what all the fuss was about for the first disciples: "Why didn't they get it?" we ask. "Didn't they see the miracles? Didn't they notice the knowledge, wisdom, and power Jesus possessed? How could they not understand that Jesus was true God?"

Two thousand years after Jesus walked the earth, contemporary Christians can hardly perceive the basic, material reality that the first witnesses saw, felt, heard, and smelled: Jesus' body. Jesus had no halo accompanying Him. His voice did not boom four octaves lower than average. His blood ran red, His sweat stung His eyes, and sometimes He stank. There was nothing special about Jesus' appearance at all (Isaiah 53:2). Consider His birth. The Bible teaches the doctrine of the **virgin birth**—that Mary conceived Jesus as a virgin through the power of the Holy Spirit apart from normal means—showing that Jesus was born in a unique and miraculous fashion (Luke 1:35). By the power of God, the eternal Son of God became a human creature in the womb of the virgin Mary. The wonder of wonders, though, is not that Mary was a virgin, but that *our God was born*. Mary's belly swelled with each passing month as the Son of God grew within her, and she endured the pains of childbirth as the Creator was born. This was not a sterile and idyllic birth; it was a normal, messy birth. Wonder of wonders! This was the birth of our God.

Christ's birth was attended by angels, it is true, but they came to a few lowly shepherds in the hills. The angels led the shepherds not to a palace but to a manger. Our God fed from His mother's breasts, as one dependent and in need, and He required regular diaper changes, like all of us. He was even under threat of death from the beginning of His life, and He had to be saved by His earthly father, Joseph, through an escape from jealous Herod's hooligan police (Matthew 2:13–16). During thirty years in Nazareth, Jesus showed no special power or ability, besides a profound love of God and His Word (Luke 2:41–52). Wonder of wonders! The Alpha and Omega had to learn the ABCs!

Jesus' ministry also revealed Him as true man. Jesus' mission began not with a bang but a whimper, a Baptism. At the Jordan River, Jesus was washed with water for repentance at the hands of John the Baptist and received the Holy Spirit to send Him on His mission (Matthew 3:13–17).[2] As true man, who not only represented all human beings but also took our place, Jesus

2 On the relationship of Jesus and the Spirit, see Leopoldo A. Sánchez M., *T&T Clark Introduction to Spirit Christology* (London: T&T Clark, 2022).

repented for our sin, the sinless one claiming human sin for Himself. When Jesus forgave the sins of the paralytic who was lowered to Him through a roof, a man was claiming divine authority to take away sins before God (Mark 2:1–12). When Jesus interpreted the Law—"You have heard it said … but *I say to you*"—a human teacher was declaring authority over God's Word (Matthew 5:17–48, emphasis added). When Jesus restored the withered hand of a man on the Sabbath, sound waves carried divine power as the voice of a human rabbi asserted authority over the Sabbath (Mark 3:1–5). We should not be surprised that the Pharisees and scribes looked to destroy Him (Mark 3:6). A man like them, with a mother, sisters, and brothers (Mark 3:31–32; 6:1–5), claimed authority over God's Sabbath and Law, and asserted the authority to do God's work, forgiving sins and bringing salvation. Christians believe that this man—a real flesh-and-blood human being with a history, a family, a body, and a soul—is our God.

What was extraordinary about Jesus includes His ordinariness as a human creature; He was and is the human being that all people were created to be. Jesus imaged God rightly, living by faith in His heavenly Father and serving others in the outward-directed, cruciform shape of humility and love for which all people were made in Eden. Hence, the Scriptures call Jesus the Second Adam (Romans 5:12–19) and portray Him as our brother who lived a fully human life under the Law and its constraints in order that we may receive adoption as daughters and sons of God (Galatians 4:4–5). This fully human person is the same Son and Lord Christians worship with the almighty Father and the Holy Spirit. This man is our God.

The Christ: Son of God and Son of Man

The question of Jesus' identity is not only a modern concern. Jesus Himself posed the same question to His disciples "Who do people say that the Son of Man is?" (Matthew 16:13). The disciples reported a number of rumors. Some thought that John the Baptist had come back from the dead. Others suggested that Jesus was Elijah, Jeremiah, or another prophet, who had returned to announce and participate in God's rescue of Israel from her enemies. Jesus then posed the most important question for believers, the question that cuts to the core of our existence: "'Who do *you* say that I am?' Simon Peter replied, 'You are the Christ, the Son of the living God'" (Matthew 16:15–16).

For many Christians, Peter's answer sounds like the Nicene Creed: You are "the only-begotten Son of God … of one substance with the Father," but that is not what Peter would have understood. Peter did not recognize the full truth of his own words! To understand Peter's confession, we need to step back into the Old Testament context. All Judea was waiting and longing for the Messiah, the **Christ**, the long-promised, anointed King from the house of David—*Christ* is the Greek word for "Anointed One" and a translation of the Hebrew title "Messiah." Throughout the Scriptures, God promised to send a deliverer to rescue Israel from its enemies and bring about the fullness of His reign. Already in Genesis, Yahweh cursed the old evil foe and pledged to send a Seed of the woman to bruise Satan's head (Genesis 3:15). To Moses, God promised to "raise up for [Israel] a prophet like you from among their brothers," who would have God's Word in Him and who would speak only this Word of God (Deuteronomy 18:18). To David, the God of Israel vowed to raise up one from David's household who would establish the kingdom and the throne of David forever (2 Samuel 7:12–16). This Anointed One would be powered by the Spirit of God, bringing God's justice and righteousness by His Word and ushering in the new age of shalom for God's people (Isaiah 11:1–9).

In the first century, though, Israel was hardly a place of God's justice and peace. In fact, most Israelites understood themselves to be in exile, far from the restored kingdom that God had promised through the prophets.[3] After all, Israel had no proper heir of David on the throne and was ruled by Gentiles, pagans, who did not acknowledge Yahweh as God. Israel no longer possessed the ark of the covenant and its mercy seat from which the God of Abraham promised to encounter His people and speak to them His Word (Exodus 25:22). These circumstances explain why Zechariah, John the Baptist's father, cried out upon the loosing of his lips by the Holy Spirit: "Blessed be the Lord God of Israel, for He has visited and redeemed His people and has raised up a horn of salvation for us in the house of His servant David, as He spoke by the mouth of His holy prophets from of old, that we should be saved from our enemies and from the hand of all who hate us" (Luke 1:68–71). Zechariah recognized that Israel lay in need of God's visitation by an Anointed One from the house of David to save His people from their foes, and the Messiah had finally shown up.

In his great confession, Peter acknowledged Jesus to be this Anointed One from the line of David. In fact, the two titles Peter used—"Christ" and "**Son of God**"—were different designations for the same promised deliverer of Israel, as used in Scripture itself (e.g., Psalms 2, 72, 89, 132; 2 Samuel 7:10–14; Isaiah 11; Ezekiel 34, 37; Micah 5).[4] The second psalm depicts Yahweh reigning with His Anointed at His right hand. Yahweh calls

---

3 N. T. Wright, *Jesus and the Victory of God* (Minneapolis: Fortress, 1996), 126–27, 202–9. For a more readable account, see Wright's *Simply Jesus: A New Vision of Who He Was, What He Did, and Why He Matters* (New York: HarperOne, 2011), 34–35.

4 Michael F. Bird, *Jesus the Eternal Son: Answering Adoptionist Christology* (Grand Rapids: Eerdmans, 2017), 15.

the Messiah His "Son" and His "King" who will "break [the Gentile rulers] with a rod of iron and dash them in pieces like a potter's vessel" (Psalm 2:9). Following this lead of Scripture, the Messiah was expected to be a special human Son of God and Son of David (2 Samuel 7:14), who would have the power of God behind Him and operate on the basis of God's Word as He crushed Israel's enemies.[5]

Jesus, strikingly, never used the title "Son of God" for Himself even though He also did not deny that He was indeed God's specially designated heir of David. Although Jesus did not call Himself Son of God, He did show Himself to be the long-promised King and Son of David. From the beginning of His ministry, Jesus proclaimed, "Repent, for the kingdom of heaven is at hand" (Matthew 4:17). Jesus preached that God's reign and rule—the **kingdom of God**—was imminent, and it was coming *in Him*. Hence, the controversial church father Origen rightly called Jesus the *autobasileus*, the kingdom of God in His own person. Jesus' miracles were signs that God's reign of justice and shalom was already present, even if only in part. His forgiveness brought near God's compassion and steadfast love for His people, central to God's promised rule (Jeremiah 31:34). Jesus not only gave signs of the kingdom, but He also revealed Himself as its King. Jesus appointed twelve men to represent Israel and its twelve tribes, and Jesus was not one of the twelve. Re-creating Israel in relationship to Himself, Jesus was calling Himself the King in the midst of Roman rule.[6] As the true King, Jesus reached out with justice and compassion to the poor, the lost, the widow, and the sojourner, feeding them and caring for them like David, the prototypical shepherd (Matthew 11:25–30; 25:31–46; Mark 6:34–44; 7:24–30; 8:1–10; Luke 7:11–17; 15:1–32; John 10:1–18).

Jesus' words, however, rarely referred to Himself as the true King—at least until the last week or so of His life—except in a hidden way by calling Himself the **Son of Man**. The "Son of Man" was Jesus' preferred title for Himself, probably because it was not well understood and thus lacked the overtones of power embedded in most messianic titles.[7] Jesus, then, called Himself the Son of Man both to conceal and reveal His identity at the same time. Such concealment might seem strange, but it parallels the theme

5 Georg Fohrer and Eduard Lohse, "*huios*," *Theological Dictionary of the New Testament*, vol. 8, ed. Gerhard Friedrich, trans. and ed. Geoffrey W. Bromiley (Grand Rapids: Eerdmans, 1972), 347–53, 360–62; Oscar Cullmann, *The Christology of the New Testament*, trans. Shirley C. Guthrie and Charles A. M. Hall (Philadelphia: Westminster Press, 1963), 270–305.

6 Wright, *Simply Jesus*, 85–86.

7 Larry W. Hurtado, "The Son of Man: Summary and Concluding Observations (2011)," in *Ancient Jewish Monotheism and Early Christian Jesus-Devotion* (Waco, TX: Baylor University Press, 2017), 396–97.

of the messianic secret as Jesus charges people to say nothing about Him (e.g., Mark 5:43; 7:36; 8:26, 30; 9:9). Consider what happens when someone begins to recognize Jesus as the Messiah. Peter rebukes Jesus for proclaiming His death immediately following Simon's declaration of Jesus as the Christ (Matthew 16:22–23), and crowds, miraculously fed by Jesus' power, try to make Him king by force (John 6:15). On multiple occasions, people misunderstand Jesus' mission as one of power and glory instead of suffering and obedience. Thus Jesus used the designation Son of Man that could be understood both in a generic way as a human being or mortal, concealing the fullness of His identity, and in a much different way in connection to Daniel 7.[8]

In Daniel 7:13–14, God showed Daniel "one like a son of man." This Son of Man came to the throne of God "with the clouds of heaven" and was given "dominion and glory and a kingdom, that all peoples, nations, and languages should serve Him; His dominion is an everlasting dominion, which shall not pass away, and His kingdom one that shall not be destroyed." Note that this "one like a son of man" has the appearance of a human being, but He rules as only God can and receives worship that only God deserves. Perhaps nowhere in the Old Testament's looking forward to the coming of God's deliverance is it clearer that God's redemption would be carried out by one who was human and yet part of the divine identity.[9] Among the fiercely monotheistic Jews, there is only one sovereign ruler, judge, and only one deserving of worship: Yahweh Himself.[10] In this way, Jesus' preferred term for Himself points to His ultimate identity as true God while avoiding many associations of power and glory assumed of the Messiah.

Jesus made the connection between the Danielic Son of Man and Himself most clearly in the last week of His life when He appeared the least like a powerful Messiah. During Passion Week, Jesus promised His disciples that He would return to judge the earth, echoing the language of Daniel: "They will see the Son of Man coming in clouds with great power and glory" (Mark 13:26). Early in the morning on the day of His crucifixion, Jesus confessed the same thing about Himself to the Jewish leaders who had put Him on trial. They wanted Him to admit that He was the Messiah so that they could take Him to Pilate as a political revolutionary. When Caiaphas

---

8 D. S. Russell, *The Method and Message of Jewish Apocalyptic, 200 BC–100 AD* (Louisville: Westminster John Knox, 1964), shows that "son of man" was used among some groups in connection to Daniel 7 and the Messiah at the time of Jesus.

9 The language of "divine identity" follows Richard Bauckham, *God Crucified: Monotheism and Christology in the New Testament* (Grand Rapids: Eerdmans, 1998).

10 Bauckham lists three items as central to the divine identity: the divine name; the sovereign activity of creation, rule, and eschatological salvation; and receiving worship exclusively. The New Testament attributes all three to Jesus in various ways. Bauckham, *God Crucified*, 9–16.

asked Him to swear if He was the "Christ, the Son of the Blessed," Jesus replied, in effect, "I am, and that's not the half of it. I am also the Son of Man, seated at the right hand of Power, and coming on the clouds of heaven" (Mark 14:61–62). In joining the language of Psalm 110:1—being seated on God's own throne at His right hand—with Daniel 7, Jesus identifies Himself as the Messiah, the Lord, and the Son of Man while also undergoing such suffering that clearly rejects the way of power and glory.[11]

When Jesus predicted His Passion and death, He combined the description of the Danielic Son of Man, which reveals Jesus as true God—doing the things of God and having the attributes of God—with the characteristics of the Suffering Servant of God, of whom Isaiah spoke in chapters 42, 49, 50, and above all in chapters 52 and 53 (e.g., Matthew 16:21; 17:22). The One acquainted with grief, who bore the sins of many, was to be the Son of Man who had dominion, glory, and an everlasting kingdom.

The Word Become Flesh: The Scandal of Christianity

The most scandalous doctrine of Christianity is the paradox of God becoming a man, the Eternal One becoming vulnerable to history and time, suffering and death. The doctrine of the Trinity may seem like a bigger scandal—how can three divine persons constitute one God?—but many monotheists, including Jews, have been able to recognize plurality and structure within God's essence, such as God's Word, Wisdom, and Spirit.[12] The true impossibility was that the Creator could become a creature, that the Provider of breath would have to receive oxygen into His lungs. Hence, Paul writes: "We preach Christ crucified, a stumbling block to Jews and folly to Gentiles" (1 Corinthians 1:23). The cross is the ultimate stumbling block. We would think that no God worthy of the name would show up in a crib, on a cross, or in a crypt, but these are exactly where the Bible leads us to see our God and know Jesus as our crucified and risen Lord and Savior.

Two Heretical Solutions: Docetism and Subordinationism

To avoid the scandal of the incarnation, the biblical idiom and story began to be interpreted by philosophy that kept God safe from time and history. In John's Gospel, the beloved apostle confessed the Word, who was God and with God, become flesh (1:1, 14). Paul proclaimed the crucifixion

11 Bird, *Jesus the Eternal Son*, 101; Ben Witherington III, *The Christology of Jesus* (Minneapolis: Fortress, 1990), 258–61.

12 Oskar Skarsaune, *Incarnation: Myth or Fact?* trans. Trygve R. Skarsten (St. Louis: Concordia, 1991), 47.

of the Lord of glory (1 Corinthians 2:8). Peter preached that the Creator had been murdered by ones He had made (Acts 3:15). But such biblical paradoxes seem to violate the **impassibility** of the divine nature—that the divine essence cannot suffer—and logical solutions were offered that would save God from the indignity of becoming human.

Although the following "solutions" are ancient heresies, they are hardly confined to the past. Contemporary thinkers continue to suggest that Jesus' significance lies in His teachings that can inspire us to find authentic existence and ultimate meaning for ourselves rather than in the promise that in Christ, God has come to earth to save sinners. We must recognize these teachings as heresies and learn to speak like the prophets and the apostles about the eternal God who has become flesh, Jesus the Christ, to save the world.

Docetism. One way to avoid the scandal of the incarnation is to deny that Jesus was really flesh and died on the cross at all. Adherents of Docetism—from the Greek word *dokeo*, which means "to seem"[13]—claimed that Jesus only appeared to be, seemed to be, human. It seems to make sense that God would not be caught dead in human flesh, particularly from the perspective of spiritualists, such as the Gnostics, who believed that the material creation was at best inferior and at worst downright evil. Even some Christians influenced by such cultural presuppositions were convinced that God could not come in human flesh. They could not understand how the infinite deity could be so closely linked with the material and created order as Paul and John had claimed. They had no problem with Jesus bringing messages from God, teaching us how to find our way up to God, but they could not believe that God would come down physically to earth. So they said that God's appearances as Jesus were not those of a human creature. He only seemed human, as would a ghost or phantom.

Today also, some within Christian denominations are embarrassed by the idea that God would show up in human form. They want to speculate about a hidden god rather than confess the God who has revealed Himself in the vagaries of birth, suffering, and death on a cross. They say that Jesus Christ was a great human being, an important prophet, but the truly divine in Jesus was His message, His idea of God's love.[14] Others may so emphasize Jesus as a divine miracle worker that they shortchange His humanity by focusing on His divine status and power to the practical exclusion of His human nature.

---

13 J. N. D. Kelly, *Early Christian Doctrines* (New York: Harper & Row, 1960), 140–42; Jaroslav Pelikan, *The Emergence of the Catholic Tradition (100–600)*, vol. 1 of *The Christian Tradition: A History of the Development of Doctrine* (Chicago: University of Chicago Press, 1971), 89, 173–74.

14 For examples, see Dietrich Bonhoeffer, *Christ the Center*, trans. John Bowden (New York: Harper & Row, 1960), 78–85.

They prefer to ignore the crib and cross as they glory in the God who looks like us but cannot really be like us—according to their presuppositions.

Indeed, Jesus of Nazareth, our fully human Brother, is not merely like us. He is true God, the Second Person of the Trinity. In Jesus, the infinite God assumed the finite flesh of His human creatures to accomplish their salvation. Wonder of wonders! Our God is a man! Inevitably, when we deny Christ's true humanity, we become less than human creatures, rejecting the good creation of our bodies and the promise of resurrected bodies in the age to come that are like Christ's own. Hence, the ancient church father Gregory of Nazianzus, one of the Cappadocian fathers essential to the promulgation of Nicene orthodoxy, asserted the famous dictum "What is not assumed is not healed."[15] In other words, Jesus saves sinners by taking on every aspect of our fallen human nature and healing it in His birth, life, death, and resurrection in the flesh. Jesus is true God who has become our fully human Brother to save us from death's dreaded disease and make us children of God. With Holy Scripture, we must proclaim the incarnation of God!

Subordinationism. In the first years of the church an opposite, yet often parallel, opinion to the docetic heresy arose among some who also would not believe that God could become human. Instead of denying Jesus' true humanity, subordinationism resolved the scandal of the cross by denying that Jesus was God in the fullest sense. By making the Son of God into a lesser deity, as Arius did, or turning God's Son into a role into which God called a good man, as the adoptionists did, the eternal, impassible God was kept safe from crib, cross, and crypt. All forms of subordinationism deny that Jesus is fully God, one with the Father—and in so doing they reject that God has become a human creature.

Adoptionism. Among the earliest of those who denied that Christ was true God seem to be certain Jewish Christians in Palestine that the Christian tradition has called Ebionites—meaning "poor ones." Whether these Jewish Christians actually taught an adoptionist Christology is open to debate, but the early church attributed to the Ebionites the view that Jesus achieved His status as Son of God through an exemplary life.[16] Eusebius, the early church historian, says that the Ebionites believed Jesus "to be a plain and ordinary man" who "achieved righteousness merely by the progress of his character."[17] Following this logic, adoptionism teaches that Jesus was not essentially God's Son. Instead, Jesus was a man who *became* God's Son at some point during His life: at His resurrection, His Baptism, or even His birth.[18] Christ's

15 Fairbairn and Reeves, *Story of the Creeds*, 84.

16 Bird, *Jesus the Eternal Son*, 112–15.

17 Bird, *Jesus the Eternal Son*, 115 n. 22, quoting Eusebius, *Historia Ecclesiastica* 3.27.2.

18 Bird, *Jesus the Eternal Son*, 7.

sonship, then, is not a matter of a unique ontological relationship between Jesus and the Father, but a "legal fiction" that elevates Jesus to a new status.[19] It is as if God looked down from heaven, saw the man Jesus, and said, "Jesus is such a great guy, fulfilling My Law so well. I'm going to make Him My Son." Jesus remained only human, but He exhibited God's will so perfectly He may deserve some kind of veneration. In the Gentile world, Paul of Samosata was among those who taught a similar doctrine, which was labeled dynamic monarchianism. It taught the unity of God as the monarch (one ruler), who had placed a special power (*dynamis* in Greek) upon the human Jesus, the power of an impersonal holy spirit of God.[20]

Although adoptionism has been condemned by church councils, some today continue to believe and teach that Jesus is no more than God's specially adopted Son. Most perniciously, the human Jesus earned His sonship by merit, suggesting that our status as sons and daughters of God is by merit too.[21] If Jesus is not God come down in the flesh for us, we are on the hook for the impossible task of making our way up to God. The Jesus invented by the adoptionists who inspires people to live a good life may be a good teacher, but such a Jesus can never save.

Arianism. The version of subordinationism that persistently pestered the fourth-century church originated with a priest in Alexandria named Arius. His explanation of who Jesus is has often been designated Arianism.[22] Presuming the Father alone as God, the one immutable, impassible, and unoriginated, Arius could contrast the Son and the Father, emphasizing the difference between Father and Son.[23] For instance, Arius writes: "He [the Son] possesses nothing proper to God, in the real sense of propriety, for he is not equal to God, nor yet is he of the same substance. ... The Father is other than the Son in substance because he is without beginning."[24] Unlike Nicene orthodoxy that confessed the eternality of the Son in relationship to the Father—for example, the Father is always Father because the Son is His only-begotten eternally—Arius believed that the Son was generated by

---

19 Bird, *Jesus the Eternal Son*, 7.

20 Kelly, *Early Christian Doctrines*, 115–19; Pelikan, *Emergence of the Catholic Tradition*, 175–76.

21 Bird, *Jesus the Eternal Son*, 129.

22 In using the label "Arianism," we follow a common tradition. Lewis Ayres names Arius's "theological trajectory" as "Eusebian" rather than Arian because of the two men named Eusebius who were prominent supporters of Arius's trajectory and more influential in the fourth-century debates: *Nicaea and Its Legacy: An Approach to Fourth-Century Trinitarian Theology* (Oxford: Oxford University Press, 2004), 52.

23 Ayres, *Nicaea and Its Legacy*, 54.

24 Rowan Williams, *Arius: Heresy and Tradition*, rev. ed. (Grand Rapids: Eerdmans, 2001), 102, translating Arius's *Thalia*.

the Father's will. Although this happened before creation—and thus it is impossible to speak properly about time—for Arius there was a *when* the Son was not. In other words, for Arius, the Son is not coeternal with the Father. Consequently, Arius believed that the Son could not fully know the Father or image Him, doing so only partially, as if behind a veil.[25] God did not come down to earth, Arius believed; only God's first and highest creature, the Son, did.

Arian beliefs were also bolstered by elements of Platonic philosophy that permeated much religious and popular thinking at that time.[26] St. John called Jesus the Word, or Logos, of God. This language was also used in Platonic and religious cosmologies not in alignment with the Bible. In some of these popular philosophies and cults, the "Word" was the first departure from the unity of the One. With the Word's separation from the One came the breakdown of ultimate unity, which these cults regarded as salvation. The Word therefore could not be perfect because it was one step removed from the One and subject to change. The Word was the beginning of the process of creation, so some thought that this comparison was what John had in mind in the first chapter of his Gospel. Although scholars debate the point,[27] Arius himself seemed to presume a similar Platonic worldview as he understood the Father as the only unbegotten, which meant that the Son as the Logos had to come into existence. This was no problem for Arius—as it was for Athanasius and the Cappadocians—since Arius considered the Son as the one who would guide us to God, not as the Savior sent from God who is true God.[28] Although Arius and others used a scriptural term, *Word*, they were expressing a pagan idea that Jesus Christ was a subordinate divine being, not fully God nor eternal, though close to God.

We find it harder today to construct a reality, a cosmology, of semigods and demigods, making it more difficult for our contemporaries to understand subordinationism. Nonetheless, a few North American Christian theologians in the past century have suggested such an idea. In their view, while Jesus Christ could not be God Himself, He certainly could be more than human, somewhere in between fully God and merely a man. As with adoptionism, if Christ is not God incarnate in history, the onus is put on believers to be like Jesus and gain sonship by merit.[29] A demigod Jesus will not save.

---

25 Ayres, *Nicaea and Its Legacy*, 55.

26 Cf. Ayres, *Nicaea and Its Legacy*, 56.

27 See Frances M. Young with Andrew Teal, *From Nicaea to Chalcedon: A Guide to the Literature and Its Background*, 2nd. ed. (Grand Rapids: Baker Academic, 2010), 45–47.

28 Fairbairn and Reeves, *Story of Creeds*, 55–57.

29 Cf. Ayres, *Nicaea and Its Legacy*, 55.

The Word Become Flesh: The Idiom of Holy Scripture

Against these heretical "solutions" to the scandal of the incarnation, Christians must learn to speak the biblical idiom of the prophets and the apostles, confessed also in the Nicene Creed, that proclaims Jesus as the incarnate God, a man who is the eternal Son. We should not run from the paradox of God become a human being, but let it lead us to praise the "depths of the riches and wisdom and knowledge of God" who sent His Son "in the likeness of sinful flesh" for the salvation of the ungodly (Romans 11:33; 8:3).

John framed his entire Gospel with a confession of the **incarnation**, that God has come into the flesh and become a true human being. In the first chapter, the apostle calls Jesus both God's Word who is with God and God Himself: "In the beginning was the Word, and the Word was with God, and the Word was God" (John 1:1). The Jews had always associated God and His Word very closely; the Word delivered God's power and served as His creative and preserving instrument (Genesis 1; Psalm 107:20; 147:18; Isaiah 55:11).[30] They were scandalized, however, by John's attribution of this designation to the human Jesus. But John was explicit and thorough in his claim that Jesus of Nazareth, the Word of God, had the attributes of God, did the work of God, and rightly deserves worship. He dealt with the mystery of the Trinity, using Word and Son to distinguish Jesus from the Father while still affirming that this Word and Son of God is truly God. Beginning Jesus' career as the re-creator of God's children (John 1:12–13), John set that career in the context of Genesis 1, echoing its "in the beginning." This Word made flesh was the true light who had glory "as of the only Son from the Father" (John 1:14). In the conclusion of this prologue to his Gospel, John again confessed: "No one has ever seen God; the only God,[31] who is at the Father's side, He has made Him known" (John 1:18).

The writer to the Hebrews repeated this concept of Jesus as God's Word come in human form as he opened his letter. God had spoken in many and various ways through the prophets, but "in these last days He has spoken to us by His Son, whom He appointed the heir of all things, through whom also He created the world" (Hebrews 1:1–2). This Son of God was indeed the creative Word: "He is the radiance of the glory of God and the exact imprint of His nature" (1:3). The Jews of Jesus' day believed that God's glory could assume a visible presence. They labeled this "dwelling" of God's presence

---

30 Skarsaune, *Incarnation*, 25–33.

31 Textual variants indicate that one must choose between "the only-begotten Son" and "the only-begotten God." It is difficult to see how the latter could arise from the former but not vice versa. Hence, the latter is more likely original, using the principle of choosing the more difficult reading.

among His people the *shekinah*—God's presence, abiding, or dwelling.[32] The writer to the Hebrews, in expressing the tremendous mystery of God in human flesh, used this image as John did (John 1:14; 2:21; 4:20–26). According to Hebrews 1, Jesus not only brought God's presence into the world; He also "upholds the universe by the word of His power" (1:3). The writer even ascribed to Christ a description of Yahweh's creating power and eternal nature found in Psalm 102:25–27 (cf. Hebrews 1:10–12). Here again, unique characteristics and activity of God are attributed to "Jesus, the apostle and high priest of our confession" (Hebrews 3:1), the human creature whom some of the original readers may have known as the rabbi from Nazareth. For these Jews, however, a rabbi with Yahweh's characteristics, who did what only Yahweh could do, must be Yahweh Himself, distinguished from the Father by the designation "Son," but nonetheless God.

Although the New Testament binds together the identity of Jesus and Yahweh in multiple ways so that they are inseparable,[33] relatively seldom did Jesus' contemporaries directly call Him "God." Thomas did, though, when he encountered Christ come back from the dead. "My Lord and my God!" he confessed (John 20:28). In this he used two titles that both linked Jesus' identity with Yahweh. The Jews had avoided letting the holy, divine name, which God revealed to Moses in the burning bush, pass between their unclean lips. So they substituted the word "Lord" (*Adonai* in Hebrew) when Yahweh's name appeared in the Scriptures. Thomas may have been using the Hebrew language's device of parallelism to emphasize that he recognized in Jesus God come in human flesh. Certainly, Thomas's confession, as well as the apostles' worship of Jesus (e.g., Matthew 28:17; Luke 24:52), only makes sense for monotheistic Jews if they believe that Jesus is one with the God of Israel. In fact, the apostle Paul attributes to Jesus language that Yahweh speaks about Himself (Isaiah 45:22–23) to confess that Jesus receives the divine name, Yahweh, and is to be worshiped: "God has highly exalted [Jesus] and bestowed on Him the name that is above every name, so that at the name of Jesus every knee should bow, in heaven and on earth and under the earth, and every tongue confess that Jesus Christ is Lord, to the glory of God the Father" (Philippians 2:8–11).[34]

The early Christian confession that "Jesus is Lord" also carried another reference in the context of Roman rule. Roman emperors used the title

32 Horace D. Hummel, *The Word Becoming Flesh: An Introduction to the Origin, Purpose, and Meaning of the Old Testament* (St. Louis: Concordia, 1979), 78–79.

33 C. Kavin Rowe, *Early Narrative Christology: The Lord in the Gospel of Luke* (Berlin: de Gruyter, 2006), 27, argues this with regard to Luke's Gospel. See also Bauckham, *God Crucified*.

34 Bauckham, *God Crucified*, 34–35 and 56–61.

"Lord," were worshiped during their lives, and were granted honor as divine after death.[35] In this way, proclaiming Jesus as Lord in the Roman Empire was a counterclaim to the lordship of the emperor and called Christians to a different kind of life, following Jesus, from those who were concerned with the economic gifts of a divine emperor. While this may have helped Gentiles understand Jesus as divine, the emperor's divinity was of a different sort than Christ's—the emperor is merely one divine being among many, and qualitatively different from the gods at that[36]—and the fullness of Jesus as Lord would need to be recognized in light of the prophetic and apostolic Word in order to confess Jesus as "the Lord of glory," not just a lord among lords (1 Corinthians 2:8).

Christians often call Jesus "Lord" and "Savior." We should never divide these words from each other, as if "Lord" refers to how Christ leads us today and "Savior" refers to how He rescued us in the past. An ancient Near Eastern secular lord, or king, was first of all the protector and provider for his people. To be lord meant also to save. Our Savior has saved us so that we can live under His Lordship as God's children, in everlasting righteousness and innocence, serving Him in joyful praise. When we confess Jesus as Lord by the power of the Holy Spirit (1 Corinthians 12:3), we confess Him to be our *saving* Lord.

Paul proclaims the faith of believers past and present: we await "our blessed hope, the appearing of the glory of our great God and Savior Jesus Christ" (Titus 2:13). As we have shown in a variety of ways, Scripture depicts the man Jesus as having the characteristics of God, doing the work of God—creation, preservation, and salvation—and being properly worshiped to the glory of God. Such a one can only be equal to God.

The Nicene Answer. In dealing with Arianism, the church gathered at the Council of Nicaea in AD 325 to affirm the unity of the Son with the Father. Although the Nicene fathers used elements of philosophical language to affirm Christ's divinity, Athanasius and the Cappadocians showed how the Nicene Creed followed the teachings of the Bible. The council chose the contemporary philosophical notion of nature, essence, or substance to express the biblical confession that Jesus of Nazareth is God in human flesh. Such language made it clear to Christians of the fourth century and all subsequent centuries that Jesus is one God with the Father (John 10:30). In the creed the church began to formulate in 325 (completing it in the 380s), it acknowledged that Jesus Christ is "of one substance with the Father." This term, *homoousios*, was reinforced with other anti-Arian statements. Jesus Christ is not subordinate; He is eternal. He is begotten of His Father not in

35 Bird, *Jesus the Eternal Son*, 39.

36 A spectrum of divinity was acknowledged in antiquity: Bird, *Jesus the Eternal Son*, 41–43.

a material way as a human father begets a child in time, but in a mysterious, eternal way. The Son was, is, and always will be the begotten one of the Father, and the Father was, is, and always will be the begetter of the Son. Jesus is "God of God, Light of Light, very God of very God, begotten, not made, being of one substance [*homoousion*] with the Father, by whom all things were made." The Nicene Creed thus confesses that the Christ is no mere creature. Jesus of Nazareth is the eternal Son, fully God, Creator and Savior with the Father and the Spirit, who assumed human nature and became a creature in the womb of the virgin. Christ condescended to human beings so that through His cross and resurrection He would reconcile sinners to the Father by the Spirit. With this confession, the church established its belief that Jesus was both of one substance with the Father and of one substance with humanity, 100 percent God and 100 percent human.[37] The Nicene Creed may have used more than biblical language, but it clarified biblical truth in a Hellenistic culture by confessing the doctrine of Scripture: one of the Trinity has come down into the flesh to save.

Chalcedonian Christology

The Nicene Creed affirmed the key doctrines of Holy Scripture with regard to the person of Christ: the one person Jesus is both true God with the Father and the Spirit and true man with human creatures. Nevertheless, what this entailed had to be worked out over successive generations. In doing so, the church fathers did not see themselves as adding to the creed but as bringing clarification in light of new challenges. Hence, the Council of Chalcedon did not offer a new creed but reaffirmed the 381 Niceno-Constantinopolitan Creed.[38]

The challenges that surfaced during these subsequent debates were a direct consequence of the Nicene confession that taught that Jesus Christ was one God with the Father. To be clear, Christian theologians had proclaimed the paradox of God becoming man before Nicaea. Melito of Sardis, for instance, preached in a second-century sermon on the Passover: "He who hung the earth in place is hanged. He who fixed the heavens in place is fixed in place. He who made all things fast is made fast on the tree. The Master is insulted. God is murdered."[39] Arian thinking had eliminated such paradoxes by making Jesus subordinate to the Father, but Nicaea reopened the paradox of God become a man. How many minds did Jesus have, just the mind of God or a human mind too? To whom was the eternal Son praying

37 See Kelly, *Early Christian Doctrines*, 223–69.

38 Fairbairn and Reeves, *Story of Creeds*, 104.

39 Melito of Sardis, "A Homily on the Passover," in *The Christological Controversy*, ed. Richard A. Norris Jr. (Minneapolis: Fortress, 1980), 34.

in the garden before His death? How could God suffer and die? Attempts to solve these challenges tended to fall in two heretical directions: denying Jesus' full humanity or separating Jesus into two persons.

The Controversies Leading to Chalcedon

One of the first controversies came from a theologian named Apollinaris, a friend of Athanasius and a staunch opponent of Arianism. Overzealous to protect the divinity of the Savior, **Apollinaris** claimed that the Logos of God replaced the human soul or mind in the incarnation. Jesus, then, had a real human body, but the intellect of Jesus was always and only the Logos. No human mind got in the way of divine thought or will.[40] Such a Jesus was one undivided person, but He was no longer fully human. God dwelled on earth among us, but He was not really one of us. The church contended instead that the Jesus who is one substance with the Father is also one substance with human beings, having not just a human appearance but being completely human.[41] In Gregory of Nazianzus's famous words, "The unassumed is the unhealed."[42] Our God became human to heal us from the inside.

One of the major responses to Apollinaris's misstep came out of Syrian Antioch, the most notorious of which was Nestorius, who became bishop of Constantinople in 428. For **Nestorianism**, the emphasis of Christology fell not on the single person who is God and man, but on the two natures as separate acting principles, the Logos and the assumed man. One issue was that a common, technical language had not yet developed—distinctions among "essence," "nature," "hypostasis," and "person" were unclear—creating additional complications in the controversy.[43] Nevertheless, deeper, conceptual differences did exist among fifth-century Christians. Nestorius's understanding of the two natures in Christ was closer to that of adoptionism—an adoptionism from conception—than to Nicaea's *homoousios* of the incarnate Son. Nestorius considered Christ to be a man uniquely indwelt by God.[44] The eternal Logos, thus, might be *said* to be a man, but God was not really the subject of the human life of Jesus. Later church fathers would rule out this notion with the doctrine of the **anhypostasis**, confessing that the Son of God did not assume a human person but human nature. Whether Nestorius was trying to guard the integrity of the human nature or the impassibility of the divine, he separated God and man in Christ. God and a

40 Norris, *Christological Controversy*, 16–17.

41 See also Fairbairn and Reeves, *Story of Creeds*, 82–84; Kelly, *Early Christian Doctrines*, 289–301; and Pelikan, *Emergence of the Catholic Tradition*, 228, 239–40, 248.

42 See above, p. 161 n. 15.

43 See the chart in Fairbairn and Reeves, *Story of the Creeds*, 87.

44 Fairbairn and Reeves, *Story of the Creeds*, 87–88; Norris, *Christological Controversy*, 18–19.

human being were one appearance, one persona, but not one acting, feeling, and thinking subject. Hence, Nestorius could preach: "The incarnate God did not die; he raised up the one in whom he was incarnate."[45] No real connection or sharing existed between God and man in Jesus. According to the later criticisms found in the Lutheran Confessions, the two natures of Christ for Nestorius are like two boards glued together, connected but not sharing anything.[46]

A festering controversy between Nestorius and St. Cyril of Alexandria erupted between 428 and 431 when Nestorius proclaimed that the virgin Mary should not be called "the bearer of God," the *theotokos* in Greek. Nestorius would call Mary "the mother of Christ," but not "the mother of God." The implication was that Mary's Son was not really God. The official Council of Ephesus in 431, presided over by Cyril, affirmed with St. Paul that Jesus, the Son of God, the Second Person of the Trinity, was born of a woman and, like all other human creatures, was born under the Law (Galatians 4:4). Mary is the *theotokos* because her Son is the eternal Son of God.[47]

Some churches of the East separated from the rest of Christendom after this Ephesian council. Sometimes called the Nestorian Church in the West, their Christology has some similarities to Nestorius's doctrine, but these similarities are also complicated by terminological differences from Chalcedonian Christology.[48] Their Christology needs to be evaluated based on their whole understanding of Christ's person, not necessarily their rejection of Chalcedon alone.

As often happens, in reaction against Nestorius, another theologian, named **Eutyches**, went too far in the opposite direction. He insisted in the 440s on using Cyril's older formula that Christ was one nature after the incarnation—even though the word "nature" no longer meant an active subject, Cyril's original meaning, but what someone or something is. What Eutyches meant by the formula is difficult to discern, but the belief has been attributed to him that the human nature of Jesus is like a drop of wine in the ocean of Christ's divinity. The divine nature, being so superior to the human, essentially swallowed up the human.[49] In effect, then, Jesus would no longer be really human, resulting in a docetic Christology.

---

45 Nestorius, "First Sermon against the Theotokos," in Norris, *Christological Controversy*, 96.

46 Solid Declaration of the Formula of Concord VIII 14–15.

47 Fairbairn and Reeves, *Story of the Creeds*, 91–92; Norris, *Christological Controversy*, 20–21; Kelly, *Early Christian Doctrines*, 310–30; Pelikan, *Emergence of the Catholic Tradition*, 231–33, 242, 245, 251–56.

48 Fairbairn and Reeves, *Story of the Creeds*, 95–98.

49 Fairbairn and Reeves, *Story of the Creeds*, 98–99.

Followers of the one-nature formula are called **Monophysites**, or "one nature-ists." The Coptic churches of Egypt and Ethiopia remain insistent on one nature of Christ to this day, having rejected the 451 Chalcedonian confession of Christ as one person in two natures, even though the differences from Chalcedonian Christology appear more terminological than theological.[50]

The Chalcedonian Definition and Aftermath

Chalcedon sought to solve the controversies by emphasizing the unity of the person of Jesus while simultaneously asserting Christ as both one substance with the Father and one substance with humanity. The council used the language of Jesus having **two natures** to say that Jesus is truly God and truly man at the same time. In addition, the council defined Jesus as having **one person** or *hypostasis*, one active subject, who is the eternal Son of God. The council's emphasis throughout was that the same eternal, only-begotten Son of God came down from heaven and was incarnate in the virgin Mary, becoming a true man for us and our salvation.[51] The eternal Son did not cease to be God in the incarnation. Instead, God assumed human nature; the Creator became a creature, neither the divinity obliterating the humanity nor the humanity diminishing the divinity.

This mysterious union is called the **personal** or **hypostatic union**. In the words of the Athanasian Creed, "although he is God and a human being, nevertheless he is not two but one Christ. However, he is one not by the changing of the divinity in the flesh but by the taking up of the humanity in God. Indeed, he is one not by a confusion of substance but by a unity of person."[52] The union of God and human creature in Jesus Christ thus brings together the nature of God and the nature of humanity in one person. This union does not blend the natures together nor diminish either of them. The two are fully united, inseparably and indivisibly, in the personal union even as the two natures remain distinct, unmixed and unconfused.[53] Nestorius had taught that Christ's divine and human natures are both distinguishable and quite separable from each other. Eutyches had taught that the two natures are not only inseparable but ultimately indistinguishable. The Council of Chalcedon confessed that the two natures are inseparable but remain distinct from each other. The eternal Son has assumed human nature, becoming a man while remaining fully God.

The Chalcedonian definition did not end the Christological controversies. Later theologians debated whether God suffered (Theopaschitism)

---

50 Fairbairn and Reeves, *Story of the Creeds*, 104–6.

51 Fairbairn and Reeves, *Story of the Creeds*, 102–3.

52 Kolb-Wengert, 25.

53 Using the four negations of the Chalcedonian definition.

and whether Christ had two wills or one (Monotheletism). Although these debates may seem merely academic, they illustrate at least two important matters. First, there is an ever-present temptation to deny that one of the Trinity suffered and died for us in the flesh. When we give up on the scriptural paradox that the Author of life was murdered, we give up on a real incarnation, that God has come down to earth to save. Either God came down truly in Jesus, or we are stuck trying to make our way to God. The confessions of Nicaea and Chalcedon thus led to the proclamation of the fifth ecumenical council of Constantinople in 553: Jesus is truly the Lord of glory, one of the Trinity, who was crucified in the flesh.[54] Second, we must in no way deny or reduce the humanity of Jesus. During the monothelite controversy of the seventh century, Maximus the Confessor insisted that Christ had two wills. Maximus was tortured to death for confessing that whatever is true of human beings is true of Jesus. If human beings have a will, the incarnate God must have a human will too. The Lord Jesus submitted His human will to the Father that He might heal our sinful wills by His obedience to death on a cross. Christ's two wills is an extension of Gregory's dictum: what is not assumed is not healed.[55]

The Communication (or Sharing) of Attributes

In the mystery of the personal union, the two natures constitute one person, functioning together in unity. Each nature shares its characteristics with the other within this union. The sharing of characteristics between the two natures is called the **communication of attributes**, or in Latin *communicatio idiomatum*. The following principles of the sharing of characteristics in Christ extend Nicene and Chalcedonian Christology, insisting that the eternal Son is the same one who was born of the virgin, fully God and fully man in one person. Lutheran theology further developed the sharing of attributes during and after the Reformation. The key for Lutheran theology is the personal union, recognizing that there is only one active subject, Jesus Christ, who is God and a human being in one person. The two natures cannot be separated from each other, and Christ's humanity must be understood in relation to His divinity and vice versa. Hence, Luther writes: "Wherever you place God for me, you must also place the humanity for me. They simply will not let themselves be separated and divided from each other. He has become one person and does not separate the humanity from himself."[56]

---

54 Fairbairn and Reeves, *Story of the Creeds*, 144–49.

55 Fairbairn and Reeves, *Story of the Creeds*, 153. Cf. above, p. 161 n. 15.

56 *Confession concerning Christ's Supper* (1528), AE 37:219. Cited in Solid Declaration of the Formula of Concord VIII 84.

Lutheran theologians of the sixteenth and seventeenth centuries worked out the sharing of characteristics through the formulation of three principles. The first principle, the **principle of properties**—named also by the Latin *genus idiomaticum*—stated that "the characteristic of each individual nature is not ascribed to that nature alone, as if it were separated from the person, but it is ascribed to the whole person, which is simultaneously God and human (whether he is called God or a human being)."[57] In other words, attributes characteristic of either nature are properly confessed concerning the person, who is both God and man. Thus, when Paul stated that they had crucified the Lord of glory (1 Corinthians 2:8) or Peter reminded his hearers that they had killed the Author of life (Acts 3:15), they were speaking of the human characteristic of mortality but designating Jesus as truly divine. This biblical language is not just a matter of speaking, but depicts the tremendous mystery of the incarnation. The eternal Son has taken on human nature and characteristics in reality. The second stanza of the hymn "O Darkest Woe," written by the seventeenth-century Lutheran hymn writer Johann Rist (1607–67), sounds forth this truth: "O sorrow dread! Our God is dead."[58] God cannot die, yet in the personal union of God and man that is Jesus, the Second Person of the Trinity died for us on Calvary's cross.

The second principle, the **principle of work**, the *genus apotelesmaticum*, teaches that in His actions each nature within Christ performed what is peculiar to itself, with the participation of the other. In other words, Christ does some things *because* He is a man—for example, be born, hunger, and suffer—and He does other things *because* He is God—for example, forgive sins, rise from the dead, and send the Spirit—but He does nothing without the active participation of both natures. Christ is our Mediator, Savior, Lord, and King not according to one nature or the other, but through, in, and according to both natures.[59]

The third principle, the **principle of majesty**, the *genus majestaticum*, teaches that the Second Person of the Trinity shares with His human nature all His divine characteristics for common possession, use, and designation within the one person of Christ. The point of this principle is apparent in the Lord's Supper. Because Jesus has promised to be present in His body and blood wherever His people gather to receive Him under bread and wine, Jesus makes His humanity present with His divinity in the Supper. Since the incarnation, the Son of God does not leave behind His human nature—He has made it His own. Where Jesus is, He is there as God and man because

57 Solid Declaration of the Formula of Concord VIII 36 (Kolb-Wengert, 622).

58 *Lutheran Service Book* (St. Louis: Concordia, 2006), 448. Text © Joseph Herl. Used with permission.

59 Solid Declaration of the Formula of Concord VIII 46–47.

that is who He is. In Luther's words: "If he is present naturally and personally wherever he is, then he must be man there too, since he is not two separate persons but a single person. Wherever this person is, it is the single indivisible person, and if you can say, 'Here is God,' then you must also say, 'Christ the man is present too.' "[60]

Lutherans regard the sharing of the characteristics of the two natures as an important insight into God's coming into human flesh. Christ's body and blood share with the divine nature the characteristic of being able to be present wherever, whenever, and in whatever form God wills. It is great comfort to know that He who shares our human nature sits in the councils of the Trinity. God not only knows our human experience through His omniscience but also through the human experience of the Second Person of the Trinity.[61]

In this human creature, Jesus of Nazareth, the fullness of God was pleased to dwell. Rather than shy away from the paradox of God in crib, cross, and crypt, Christians can delight that God loved His creatures so much that the eternal Son became a man, in every respect like us except without sin (Hebrews 2:17; 4:15), while remaining truly God. Only because God came down to earth do we have the promise that God reconciles all to Himself, restoring the peace of Eden, through the blood shed by the incarnate God, Jesus, on the cross (Colossians 1:19–20).

60 *Confession concerning Christ's Supper* (1528), AE 37:218. Cited in Solid Declaration of the Formula of Concord VIII 82.

61 For more, see "The Person of Christ in Sixteenth-Century Lutheran Theology," in *Common Places in Christian Theology: A Curated Collection of Essays from Lutheran Quarterly*, ed. Mark C. Mattes (Irvine, CA: 1517 Publishing, 2023), 159–92.

CHAPTER 9
THE WORK OF CHRIST

THE medieval theologian St. Anselm asked the burning question about the work of Christ: Why did God become man? (*Cur Deus homo*?) Why did salvation require a cross? The biblical response takes us to the heart of our faith, the core of our existence: Jesus Christ has reconciled God and His sinful human creatures through the blood of the cross and the empty tomb. God became a man so that He might right our wrong relationship with Him. God has entered into human existence so that He might restore shameful sinners to the status and life of His children. The Bible and the Christian tradition have offered a variety of other responses too that will help us understand all that God has done for His creatures in Christ.

No matter how we describe the work of Jesus, the fact of atonement—at-one-ment—must remain at the center. In this vein, Philip Melanchthon wrote: "To know Christ is to know his benefits."[1] We know Jesus rightly only when we know Him by faith as the one who has procured great benefits for me and all sinners. One could comprehend all the biblical information about Jesus and grasp the truth of His two natures, but if Jesus is not known as my Savior and Reconciler, the real Jesus is not known at all. Hence, Luther, too, put Christ's redemptive work front and center in his Small Catechism: "I believe that Jesus Christ … is my Lord, who has redeemed me … purchased and won me from all sins, from death, and from the power of the devil; not with gold or silver, but with His holy, precious blood and with His innocent suffering and death, that I may be His own."[2] The central message of Christ's work is thus summed up in the words of the apostle Paul: "Christ Jesus came into the world to save sinners, of whom I am the foremost" (1 Timothy 1:15).

1 Philip Melanchthon, *Commonplaces: Loci Communes 1521*, trans. Christian Preus (St. Louis: Concordia, 2014), 24.

2 Small Catechism II 4 (*LSCE*, 17).

Humiliation and Exaltation

The Scriptures tell the story of Jesus in two movements, usually called the two states of Christ, **humiliation** and **exaltation**. The former movement is that of the eternal Son condescending to earth, coming down to us graciously not just as a human being but as a beggar, a poor peasant, who shared human weakness, took on human sinfulness, and lived under the Law by faith. The latter movement is that of the Father restoring Christ to His rightful status as the Son He has always been so that Jesus reigns over the creation as its King and Lord.

Although humiliation proceeds to exaltation, we must not see the humiliation as giving way to exaltation, as if only Christ's exaltation matters now for the church. Instead, the exalted Lord is the humiliated one with the marks of the cross still on His hands and side (Luke 24:39; John 20:27). The enthroned Lamb is the one who has been slain (Revelation 5:6). The supreme glory of Jesus is His cross (John 12:28–33). Both movements are essential to Jesus' identity as Savior of the world.

In what may have been an early Christian hymn, quoted by Paul, the church sang of Jesus and His salvation in these two movements: "who, though He was in the form of God, did not count equality with God a thing to be grasped, but emptied Himself, by taking the form of a servant, being born in the likeness of men. And being found in human form, He humbled Himself by becoming obedient to the point of death, even death on a cross" (Philippians 2:6–8). Christ's humiliation from conception to death on the cross in obedience to the Father is the basis for His exaltation: "Therefore God has highly exalted Him and bestowed on Him the name that is above every name, so that at the name of Jesus every knee should bow, in heaven and on earth and under the earth, and every tongue confess that Jesus Christ is Lord, to the glory of God the Father" (Philippians 2:9–11).

Paul describes here the narrative of Christ's work on earth. The eternal Son of God came down from heaven and became incarnate as a real human, taking the lowly form of a servant, and joining humanity under the curse of death. This gracious movement from the bosom of the Father to the bosom of the virgin to the bosom of the earth renders Christ's identity as the Lord who is the Suffering Servant. To be sure, the humiliation is distinct from the incarnation, Christ's becoming human, for Jesus remains truly human after the state of humiliation culminated in His death. Rather, His **humiliation** consisted of being regarded as worthy of death, humbling Himself to be in the "likeness of sinful flesh" (Romans 8:3), coming under the constraints and authority of the Law (Galatians 4:4), and becoming sin (2 Corinthians 5:21) and a curse (Galatians 3:13) for the salvation of sinners.

Lutheran theologians often describe Christ's humiliation in terms of the use of His power. Thus the humiliation is defined as the Son of God giving up the full exercise of His divine power. This aspect of the humiliation recognizes the depth to which true God becomes a man. Jesus did not use His divine power to know the alphabet, but submitted Himself to the natural law of learning and growth, just as all human creatures must. In His ministry too, Jesus did not fully exercise His omnipotence: God's Spirit moved in Him to heal (Mark 5:29–30; Luke 5:17), Jesus did not know the time of His return (Matthew 24:36), and sometimes He was unable to do a great work (Mark 6:5). The eternal Son never used His divine power for Himself, giving up its use in obedience to the Father, in order to live in the place of sinful human creatures under the Law from conception and birth, through His suffering, death, and burial.

Christ's **exaltation** embraces the course of His triumph over the enemies of His people. Although some sixteenth-century Lutherans believed that Jesus completed His sufferings in the descent into hell, most Lutherans have taught that the descent into hell confesses Christ's victory over Satan, his powers and minions.[3] Lutherans usually acknowledge that in the descent into hell, Jesus "proclaimed to the spirits in prison" as a mark of His triumph over evil that He had won by His death and resurrection (1 Peter 3:19–20). The exaltation includes, then, His resurrection, His descent into hell, His ascension, and His sitting at the right hand of the Father as Mediator and King. His exaltation will be exhibited further in His return to judge all human creatures. This exaltation reveals that He is the Lord and invites the praise of Yahweh and Jesus together, as the name above all names (Philippians 2:9–10).

Just as the humiliation describes the Son giving up the full use of His divine power, the exaltation teaches that Jesus has received again the full exercise of His power. In the exaltation, Christ reigns as King over the entire cosmos. Our fully human Savior is the King who is in control of the whole earth and its history. To be sure, between resurrection and coming again in judgment, Jesus reigns in a humble way. King Jesus is the servant! He does not encounter His human creatures in bare power often but in grace through preaching and the Sacraments. When Jesus comes to judge all things, He will be revealed as the Lord in power and glory, but now He humbles Himself in the means of grace, the feeble community of believers, and the offer of forgiveness to be received by faith.

At the heart of humiliation and exaltation is that our God has entered fully the evil and sin that assault us, has taken our place in life and death, and has been raised to eternal life to eliminate evil, absolve sin, and destroy

---

3 Article IX of the Epitome and Solid Declaration of the Formula of Concord.

death so that Christ's fellow human creatures can receive His rightful status as child of God. The cross stands at the center of this work of Christ; it is the ultimate point of His humiliation which is His greatest glory as the Savior (1 Corinthians 1:18–31).

The Author of Salvation: Christ as Prophet, Priest, and King

The writer to the Hebrews called Jesus the one "for whom and by whom all things exist," whose mission was completed through His suffering so that He could be the founder and author of salvation (Hebrews 2:10). Salvation encompasses the harmony of Eden, God's efforts to defeat the enemies that thwart peace in this age, and the work that Christ does to restore the sinful world to shalom. The biblical writers describe God's effort in Christ and its results in several ways.[4] The most significant for Lutheran theology, which pierces to the heart of the matter, is justification, the subject of the next chapter. All scriptural ways of speaking of this salvation of God in Christ can help believers recognize the depth of God's love and share His message and gift of salvation with others.

In the Middle Ages, theologians such as Thomas Aquinas used a threefold designation of Christ's office as a summary of His work in behalf of sinners. John Calvin picked up this threefold summary of Prophet, Priest, and King to outline his treatment of Christ's work in his *Institutes of the Christian Religion*.[5] Contemporary Americans rarely use the word **office** to indicate someone's role except in a few limited cases, such as office of the president. An office is just this: a role or authority given by God and designed by Him, along with the proper exercise of this position or divine assignment. Christ's threefold office of Prophet, Priest, and King are central roles that God designated in the Old Testament. Jesus is the greater Prophet, Priest, and King, fulfilling the work that God began through His designees in Israel for the sake of restoring the creation.

Luther himself discussed Christ in these three ways—individually, not often as a group—and later Lutherans used the threefold office as an organizational principle to summarize the work of Christ. The title **prophet** expresses Christ's role as the one who stands in God's place, proclaiming God's Word and revealing God to His people. The title **priest** presents Jesus as the one who represents sinful people before the Holy One, and who makes sinners righteous by taking their place as the victim under the Law,

---

4 Jacob A. O. Preus, *Just Words: Understanding the Fullness of the Gospel* (St. Louis: Concordia, 2000).

5 John Calvin, *The Institutes of the Christian Religion*, trans. Ford Lewis Battles, ed. John T. McNeill (Philadelphia: Westminster, 1960), 1:494–503.

sin, guilt, and death. The title **King** embraces His reign of peace and His victory over every evil that prevents His people from enjoying the peace He provides. In connection to Christ's work as King, we will also describe how He leads His people to live under His reign in righteousness, innocence, and blessedness.

We might be tempted to think that only the work of Christ as Priest is truly salvific and atoning, but Scripture depicts the whole of Christ's work as reconciling the broken relationship between God and sinners whether Jesus is proclaiming repentance and forgiveness of sins as the Prophet, taking our place under the Law as Priest, or conquering death and the devil as the King. After all, we selfish idolaters need to be turned by Christ through the Word to know the depth of our sin, the reality of the true God, and the forgiveness that He graciously provides. We sick sinners need a substitute to heal our disease by taking on our illness and rectifying corrupt human nature from the inside. We helpless, broken creatures need a King to conquer the powers that hold us captive and free us for life in His kingdom. He is the author and founder of salvation, described in manifold ways in the Bible, which He will complete when He comes again in glory.

Christ the Revealer: The Prophetic Work

"No one has ever seen God; the only God, who is at the Father's side, He has made Him known" (John 1:18). Jesus claimed for Himself the status of an Old Testament spokesman for God, a prophet, that is, one who proclaims the Word of the Lord—Jesus "forth-tells" the Word, whether or not He foretells the future. Jesus' role of Prophet thus embraces His preaching and teaching that reveals who God is and announces judgment and repentance as well as the gracious forgiveness of sins in Him. Only God's chosen prophets had been able to speak the Word of the Lord with confidence. The rabbis of Jesus' time could say, "The prophets and rabbis have said of old," but they could not say, "Truly, I say to you …" (Matthew 5:18, 26; 6:2, 5). With this affirmation, Jesus announced that His voice revealed God's Word and will in a way that Israel had not experienced since the last of the Old Testament prophets, Malachi.

Prophet. Second Temple Jews were longing for the prophet of the day of the Lord, the one whom God had promised to Moses (Deuteronomy 18:15–18). God had pledged to complete His prophetic revelation of Himself on His Great Day (Joel 2:28–32). Early in His ministry, Jesus identified Himself with the prophet upon whom the Spirit of the Lord rested (Luke 4:16–21), the promised eschatological prophet (John 6:14), perhaps even the long-awaited Elijah (Mark 6:15). His contemporaries heard from His own lips that the Father had sent Jesus by the Spirit on a special mission of proclamation and revelation (John 4:34; 5:30; 6:38; 9:4; Luke 4:18). They heard in His words a new and distinct authority, even the voice of God Himself (Matthew 7:28–29; John 7:46).[6] They also saw miraculous signs that served to verify His authority and begin to enact the day of the Lord in Him. They experienced an inbreaking of the Holy Spirit through His miraculous signs and after His resurrection (Acts 2:1–21, 33) experienced the gift of the same Spirit by Baptism in His name (Acts 2:38).

Light. The titles that use the concept of light focus on Christ illuminating both who God is and what true humanity is. He enlightens us regarding our vertical relationship with the Creator and our horizontal relationship with others, for He bestows on us the gift of God's righteousness at the same time He exemplifies the righteousness of human life. He lights up the lives of His people (John 1:4) and opens the eyes of the blind (Matthew 11:5). He both illumines the pathway through life (Matthew 4:15–16; Isaiah 9:1–2) and is the pathway on which truth and life are found (John 14:6). Christ's light even challenges the darkness that threatens His people and chases it away (John 1:5; 8:12; 12:46).

Jesus as Medium and Message. Jesus Christ communicates the presence of God into the midst of the fallen creation. He served as God's prophet, the medium whereby God conveyed His message to His people. A well-designed medium God fashioned in Him! He translated the message of His ultimate love for His defiant creatures into human form and flesh.

This medium, Jesus of Nazareth, is no mere medium, no mere instrument for revealing God's Word. Jesus is the long-promised prophet, but He is also more. He not only brings a message from God, but He is the message itself, the Word of God (John 1). To hear Jesus is to hear the Prophet who is God in the flesh; to know Jesus' ministry, death, and resurrection is to know reconciliation between God and sinful humanity. For God was in Christ reconciling the world to Himself (2 Corinthians 5:19) by the blood of His cross (Colossians 1:20). He demonstrated His love for us in that while we were still sinners, Christ died for us (Romans 5:8). This message was both proclaimed by Jesus and enacted by Him through His incarnation, ministry, cross, and empty tomb.

To recognize the prophetic work of Christ as essential for our reconciliation, consider the fall of Adam and Eve. They were made to know God, but in sin they were exiled from the garden and could no longer know God and His presence directly. As the long-promised Prophet, Christ

---

6 Gerhard Friedrich, "*prophetes*, 'Jesus,'" *Theological Dictionary of the New Testament*, vol. 6, trans. and ed. Geoffrey W. Bromiley (Grand Rapids: Eerdmans, 1968), 841–48; Oscar Cullmann, *The Christology of the New Testament*, trans. Shirley C. Guthrie and Charles A. M. Hall (Philadelphia: Westminster, 1963), 13–50.

brings the true knowledge and presence of God to their idolatrous heirs, whose hearts and minds are warped with sin. As the prophet, Jesus exposes wickedness and threatens judgment in order to bring about repentance (e.g., Matthew 21:12–13, 28–46; 22:1–14, 29; 23:1–36). After all, sinful human creatures no longer know the Creator rightly, nor do they have the presence of God by the Spirit. Jesus' prophetic work unmasks the idolatry of the human heart, reveals true knowledge of God as the just judge and gracious justifier in the cross, and grants the gift of the Holy Spirit so that believers know God personally and intimately by faith (John 16:7–15).[7]

The message of the cross is a message of foolishness and weakness from the standpoint of fallen human creatures. God chose what is foolish and weak in the world's eyes to shame the wise and the strong (1 Corinthians 1:18–30). The crucifixion of the Lord of glory (1 Corinthians 2:8) reveals both the ultimate love of God and the innate wickedness of this sinful world and its inhabitants. Sinners tried to get rid of Christ, refusing to submit to the Lord or receive His grace as a gift, and threw Him into a tomb. Jesus, however, rose from the dead to end their existence as sinners. He came back to give them new life by the Spirit (Romans 6:3–11). Therefore, as Christ proclaims who God is to us in His own person, He pronounces the end of all fallen human endeavors to secure life on our own terms. In recounting God's love for us, He shatters every hope we have apart from Him.

Theologians have called God's revelation in Jesus Christ a "revelation under the form of opposites." His ultimate power is disclosed in the hiddenness of a helpless man bleeding out on a cross; His ultimate wisdom is uncovered in the folly of a crib. At this point, we can understand why the New Testament stresses the mode of Christ's death—crucifixion—and not merely the fact of His death. In many ways, contemporary Christians have "put roses on the cross" to make Christ's death look nicer—He died out of love—whereas the New Testament proclaims forcefully the shame of crucifixion. The cross stands for utter disgrace and degradation. Important people were not crucified; somebodies were killed in a more dignified fashion. But Christ was stripped naked, laid bare to all, and suffered the shameful death of "a nobody."[8] Jesus specifically identified with the lowest of the low, taking

7 The importance of the Spirit in Jesus' prophetic work became clear to Hopkins in a conversation with Mark Koschmann over Simeon Zahl, *The Holy Spirit and Christian Experience* (Oxford: Oxford University Press, 2020), especially: "To be saved is, among other things, to 'receive the Spirit'" (82). See also Raniero Cantalamessa, *The Holy Spirit in the Life of Jesus*, trans. Alan Neame (Collegeville, MN: Liturgical Press, 1994), 38–50.

8 Fleming Rutledge, *The Crucifixion: Understanding the Death of Jesus Christ* (Grand Rapids: Eerdmans, 2015), 76.

on the hideous suffering and shame of the cross to reveal the Father's heart and His gracious salvation for us.[9]

God did not send Christ to open the door into the presence of God and let fallen human creatures peer directly into the majesty of our Creator. God sent Christ through that door, shutting it behind Him, to reveal who God is for us in reality. God's reality contradicts what we imagine God to be like. In God's self-disclosure, life springs forth from death. Christ's sinlessness is displayed in His conviction for the worst of sins, blasphemy (Matthew 26:65). His omnipotence reveals itself in weakness. His wisdom takes form in the ultimate foolishness of the cross (1 Corinthians 1:18–2:8). His love is exhibited under the form of the Father's wrath, forsaking His Son on the cross (Mark 15:34). His presence moves into our lives through that ultimate forsakenness. His justice and righteousness triumph in the midst of supreme injustice. The Author of life dies (Acts 3:15). Precisely at the most fragile and frail point of His humanity, against all human expectations, Christ reveals the ultimate expression of who God is and how He acts toward us.

During the state of His humiliation, Christ directly exercised His prophetic office in His proclamation of God's Word and in His embodying of that Word in faith and obedience. Now, as the exalted prophet, He continues His ministry of proclamation through the Scriptures and through those who trust in Him by the Spirit—especially, but not exclusively, through pastors, teachers, youth leaders, and other church workers—as they spread the message of the Father who raised His Son from the dead, and of repentance and the forgiveness of sins in Him (Luke 24:47). Through the message of Christ's cross, the Spirit works renewal and new birth in sinful hearts and minds, as God pours out His abundant mercy in Jesus for our salvation (Titus 3:4–7).

Christ the Vicar and Victim: The Priestly Work

God sent His Son, born of a woman, born under the Law, to redeem those who live under the Law and make them His family (Galatians 4:4–5). Jesus Christ takes our place—serves as our **vicar**—in the presence of every enemy that threatens the lives of His people: guilt and the accusation of the Law, the devil, and death itself. He became the victim of all that assaults us, and as the stand-in for us, He received the full brunt of the Law's condemnation and death's icy chill.

The Suffering Servant. The figure of the Suffering Servant of Isaiah 42, 49, 50, and 52–53 offers the greatest depiction of self-sacrificing love. Jesus consciously chose the pattern of the Servant being "handed over" and being

9 Rutledge, *Crucifixion*, 74–87.

killed—and then rising—as the framework for understanding His own suffering and death (Matthew 16:21; 17:22; 20:17–19). In the fourth Servant Song (Isaiah 52:13–53:12), the Servant's substitutionary suffering stands at the center of His work even though the prophet references also the resurrection: the Servant will "see His offspring" and "prolong His days" (53:10). Above all, the Servant—despised and rejected, a man of sorrows and acquainted with grief; stricken, smitten by God, and afflicted—was "pierced for our transgressions … crushed for our iniquities; upon Him was the chastisement that brought us peace, and with His wounds we are healed" (53:5). "The LORD has laid on Him the iniquity of us all" (53:6). "He bore the sin of many, and makes intercession for the transgressors" (53:12). Isaiah does not explain how and why the Servant bore the sins of others except to proclaim that the Servant intercedes for sinners with His own body, takes on their sin, and makes many righteous (53:11).

Reflecting this pattern, Jesus emptied Himself, took the form of a servant, and humbled Himself to journey obediently to the cross (Philippians 2:6–8). He came not to be served but to serve, giving Himself as a ransom for sinners (Mark 10:45). He challenged death, dying in place of those who were still hostile to Him (Romans 5:6–8). Christ condescended to come "in the likeness of sinful flesh and for sin" to take human sinfulness upon Himself and carry it vicariously in the place of sinners and on our behalf (Romans 8:3; cf. 2 Corinthians 5:21).

High Priest. The most common understanding of Christ's work among Christians is that of Jesus as the sacrifice for sin. This concept is connected with the image of Christ as Priest or High Priest. The practice of sacrifice to appease or coerce gods of one kind or another lies deeply embedded in various religious systems. Sacrifices performed in the right manner could entice or compel favors from the divine and set aside the wrath of the gods in most of these systems. The Jews did not conceive of sacrifice as the ultimate meritorious work or a magical means whereby they could convince Yahweh to do what they wanted. They received their sacrificial system as a gift from God, as a means through which He reconciled them to Himself (Hebrews 10:1–10). Thus God's people in the Old Testament were not right with Him just because they performed sacrifices but because they trusted in Him and His promise to save through the appointed sacrifices as a means of grace (Psalm 40:6; 51:16–17).

In Christ Jesus, God's sacrificial system found its capstone as Jesus took the place of both the priest and the sacrificial victim. God Himself arranged and performed the **expiation**, that which takes away sin from His children, by becoming the **propitiation**, that which sets aside His own wrath, for them (1 John 2:2; Romans 3:25). How can the eternal Son both give Himself over as sacrifice and ransom and at the same time remain in charge of making the sacrifice? This mystery is expressed in His being the **priest** who offers Himself for the people and remains forever as their mediator.[10]

The writer to the Hebrews used the image of priest extensively. He described Jesus as the human high priest designated to make expiation for the sins of the people (2:17). Being without sin Himself (4:15; 7:26–28), He could complete the final, ultimate, all-sufficient sacrifice for sin (9:26; 10:10). He built the bridge between sinful humanity and God by becoming the sacrifice Himself (9:12–14, 28). As both priest and victim, He purified His people's consciences through the sprinkling of His own blood (9:13–14). As the holy lamb and priest, Jesus took away the sins of His people so that they may enter God's promised rest by faith (3:12–4:16).

Sacrificed on the cross in His humiliation, Jesus is the new Passover Lamb of God, without spot or blemish, who shed His blood to free His people from slavery to sin (1 Peter 1:18–20) and has been raised to triumph over every enemy of His people. Ascended to the throne of God, He continues in His exaltation to serve as mediator, bridge builder (Hebrews 4:15–16; 10:19–25). He continues to be a priest forever, after the model of the king-priest Melchizedek, the mysterious figure who appeared to Abraham with the name "king of righteousness" but was performing priestly duties (Hebrews 6:20–7:19; Genesis 14:17–20). Jesus now lives to make intercession for those whom He draws near to God, as the **mediator** (Hebrews 7:25). Only He who gave Himself as a ransom for all is able to mediate between God and human creatures, serving as our advocate and casting away the accusations of Satan (1 Timothy 2:5; 1 John 2:1; Revelation 12:1–12).[11]

Redeemer. Through the concept of **redemption**, the Scriptures teach that Jesus stepped into our place to save us in a distinct way from His role as High Priest. Behind the English word *redeem* stand several related but distinct concepts in the Old Testament world. One might redeem another from slavery by offering a gift of sufficient value to cover the debt or obligations, paying the price of freedom or even the price to buy back life itself—in the case of a capital crime. For redemption to be necessary, life's circumstances have become so dire that liberation will exact a tremendous toll. Thus redemption always has a cost, a ransom. When the prophets proclaim God as the Redeemer of His people, the cost is essential to the point: God is not distant, untouched by His people's tragedy and suffering, but is personally

10 Gottlob Schrenk, "*archiereus*," *Theological Dictionary of the New Testament*, vol. 3, ed. Gerhard Kittel, trans. and ed. Geoffrey W. Bromiley (Grand Rapids: Eerdmans, 1965), 274–83; Cullmann, *Christology*, 83–107.

11 Wilhelm Dantine, *Justification of the Ungodly*, trans. Eric W. and Ruth C. Gritsch (St. Louis: Concordia, 1968), 86–88.

involved in the deliverance of His people (e.g., Exodus 6:5–7; Isaiah 43:1–4).[12] When God redeemed His people from Egypt, Israel's kidnapper did not receive a ransom payment but rather was overcome and conquered by God's involvement so that His people would be liberated. The Greek word for "redeem"—ἀπολΰω—has at its base the word for "loosening bonds," and Luther used the German word *erlösen*, which employs the same base. Redemption in the Old Testament signified God's involvement in liberation to grant the freedom to be truly human again. The personal involvement of the redeemer is even more apparent in the **kinsman-redeemer**. As in the story of Boaz and Naomi (through Ruth), a kinsman-redeemer reclaims the freedom, life, or goods of a next of kin at a significant cost to himself.

The New Testament takes up the notion of redemption to describe the work of Christ. Jesus is the Son of Man who gives His life as a ransom for many (Mark 10:45). Paul proclaims Christ to be our "redemption" (1 Corinthians 1:30), as Jesus bore the cost to take away sin (Romans 3:25). For human creatures enslaved to sin, under the power of evil, and condemned to die, the eternal Son became our Kinsman-Redeemer. He took on our flesh and entered into our family, that we might be adopted into His, as children of God. To complete our redemption, the Lord bought us with a price, His own blood, to free us from our slavery and condemnation that we might be His own and glorify Him in His kingdom (1 Corinthians 6:19–20).[13] Jesus did not come as a merchant with gold or silver for a commercial purchase (1 Peter 1:18); He plunged into this world of conflict between God and Satan as a soldier who paid the ultimate price for the liberation of His people; He paid with His life.

Curse and Sin. To the images of Jesus Christ as Suffering Servant, Priest, and Redeemer, Paul added a further description of His substitutionary role. Jesus took upon Himself the curse placed upon all those who do not obey God's Law, becoming a curse for us (Galatians 3:10–14). He even became sin itself (2 Corinthians 5:21). Paul's understanding echoes the Gospels. Jesus identified with sinners from His Baptism where He repented for human sin, numbering Himself with transgressors (Isaiah 53:12; Matthew 3:13–17). Christ healed lepers and the sick, taking their uncleanness upon Himself to make them holy (Mark 1:40–45; Matthew 8:17). He touched the unclean dead to give them life (Mark 5:41). This pattern culminated in the cross where Jesus became sin and a curse that accursed sinners might know the mercy of God.

12 Rutledge, *Crucifixion*, 291.

13 Rutledge, *Crucifixion*, 291–94.

Luther found this "the most joyous of all doctrines and the one that contains the most comfort." He commented on Galatians 3:13:

> It teaches that we have the indescribable and inestimable mercy and love of God. When the merciful Father saw that we were being oppressed through the Law, that we were being held under a curse, and that we could not be liberated from it by anything, He sent His Son into the world, heaped all the sins of all men upon Him, and said to Him: "Be Peter the denier; Paul the persecutor, blasphemer, and assaulter; David the adulterer; the sinner who ate the apple in Paradise; the thief on the cross. In short, be the person of all men, the one who has committed the sins of all men. And see to it that You pay and make satisfaction for them."[14]

Luther continues with the Law's judgment upon Christ: "I find Him a sinner, who takes upon Himself the sins of all men. I do not see any other sins than those in Him. Therefore let Him die on the cross!"[15] The Law, Luther reports, attacked and killed Christ, thereby purging the whole world of its sins and liberating all from death and every evil. In this attack on Christ, a **wondrous duel** has taken place between the fury of the powerful, cruel tyrant, sin, and the righteousness of Christ. Christ won! The King, who took our place by becoming the victim, conquered, killed, and buried the curse by assuming it for sinners.[16]

Christ the Victor: The Royal Work

The offices of prophet and priest tend to highlight human guilt and responsibility for sin. We are idolators, we have broken God's Law, and we are reconciled to the Father only because Christ breaks through to us in His Word and Spirit—Prophetic office—and offers Himself as the sacrifice—Priestly office. In the office of King, what comes to the forefront is not so much sin as culpability but sin as frailty and helplessness. This, too, reflects scriptural truth. Without Jesus, we are "dead in [our] trespasses and the uncircumcision of [our] flesh" (Colossians 2:13). We are stuck in the kingdom of Satan, following his ways (Ephesians 2:3). We are strangers to the promise and aliens to fellowship with God and His people (Ephesians 2:12). We are slaves to sin and bound to death (Romans 6:16). As weak sinners, unable to free ourselves from our sinful condition or achieve life amid death, we need a hero, a King, to surmount sin and demolish death so that we might live in God's kingdom of joy forever.

Savior. Jesus' name means "savior" (Matthew 1:21). The title "Savior" occurs relatively seldom alongside the name "Jesus," but His personal name

14 *Lectures on Galatians* (1531), AE 26:280.

15 *Lectures on Galatians* (1531), AE 26:280.

16 *Lectures on Galatians* (1531), AE 26:280–81.

embraces it already. The angelic messengers defined Jesus' role as Savior, both to Joseph (Matthew 1:21) and to the shepherds (Luke 2:11). This Savior, born in David's city, was the Christ and the Danielic Son of Man—Messiah, yet one with Yahweh Himself[17]—come to save His people from their enemies: sin, death, and the evil one (Luke 1:71).

Throughout the Gospels, Jesus is constantly saving people: the sick from illness, the dead from the grave, tax collectors from greed, lepers from leprosy, the possessed from demons, prostitutes from destitution, sinners from guilt, and much more. Even when Jesus looked least like a conquering hero—when the principalities and powers of this present darkness took Him to the tomb—Jesus yet won salvation for His people. In the wondrous duel, Jesus is both victim and victor. In losing, Jesus wins. He conquered sin, death, and the evil one by His cross. He was put to death for the trespasses of sinners, but rose from the dead to give them righteousness (Romans 4:25). Death cannot hold Him. Satan cannot stop Him. Sin finds no weakness in Him. He is the conquering Savior come to rescue His people from their enemies (Psalm 44:2–7; 74:12; 80:2; Isaiah 33:22).

The title "savior" was frequently employed by the so-called mystery cults of the early Christian era. They forged saviors who would help adherents escape from the evils of the material body with its impurities and from mortality. Paul confronted these false saviors directly when he proclaimed the coming of the "Savior, the Lord Jesus Christ, who will transform our lowly body to be like His glorious body, by the power that enables Him even to subject all things to Himself" (Philippians 3:20–21). Elsewhere, Paul preached the good news of "our Savior Christ Jesus, who abolished death and brought life and immortality to light through the gospel" (2 Timothy 1:10). Believers wait for "our blessed hope, the appearing of the glory of our great God and Savior Jesus Christ, who gave Himself for us to redeem us from all lawlessness and to purify for Himself a people for His own possession who are zealous for good works" (Titus 2:13–14). Christians anticipate the return of the Savior, Jesus, so that He can complete the victory He won through His death and resurrection.[18]

Victor over Death. By His cross and empty tomb our Savior disarmed all the foes of His people and at the same time canceled the bill of indictment lodged against those whom He came to forgive. His people had been dead in trespasses and far from God's family, but God made them alive through the death and the resurrection of Christ (Colossians 2:11–15). As

17 See the prior chapter for the evidence for this claim.

18 Werner Foerster and Georg Fohrer, "*soter*," *Theological Dictionary of the New Testament*, vol. 9, ed. Gerhard Friedrich, trans. and ed. Geoffrey W. Bromiley (Grand Rapids: Eerdmans, 1971), 1003–24; Cullmann, *Christology*, 238–45.

the Word who made all things in the beginning, Jesus entered into death in order to triumph over it and reclaim life for sinners caught in its clutches (John 1:4; 1 John 1:2; John 11:25–27). He entered first into death in our behalf (Hebrews 6:20), so that He might be the firstfruits of death's end in His resurrection (1 Corinthians 15:20). As the Second Adam, He retraced Adam's steps into mortality so that He might lead Adam and all his heirs into eternal life (Romans 5:12–17; 1 Corinthians 15:20–23). In the language of the church father Irenaeus, Jesus recapitulated Adam's mortal life on earth so that Adam's progeny may receive the immortal life of the Son of God by faith.

Jesus' resurrection is essential to His victory over death. Sometimes, preachers can give the impression that Christ's death completed reconciliation with God and the resurrection is merely the proof. For the Bible, though, the resurrection is not a mere exclamation point on Christ's death! Instead, Paul asserts that we are justified because Christ was raised (Romans 4:25). In fact, if Jesus remained dead in the tomb, Christians should be pitied, for their hope and faith have no basis (1 Corinthians 15:14, 17, 19). But Christ is risen! Whereas the crucifixion epitomizes the human rejection of Jesus, the resurrection is the Father's response to the murder of His Son. God declared that Jesus is indeed the Son of Man and Messiah He claimed to be (Romans 1:4; Acts 2:36; 3:14–15; 4:10; 5:30–31). What Jesus said was God's Word! What Jesus did was God's work! What Jesus embodies is God in the flesh! So affirms the resurrection.

Christ's resurrection liberates His people from sin and death (1 Corinthians 15:54–57). Christ the victor has come back from the grave to deliver to His Father the complete rule over all creation once again. Between Christ's resurrection victory and the resurrection of the Last Day, we rest assured in the promise of His royal return as the Son of Man, who comes from the clouds to exercise God's dominion (Matthew 24:27–44; 25:31–46).

The Resurrection of the Lord and His People. Even in the New Testament, people raised objections to the possibility of bodily resurrection (cf. Acts 23:8). Ancient people knew that the dead do not generally live again. Since the Enlightenment, such objections have become more common. Some argue that Jesus did not really die while others suggest that the disciples who claimed Jesus has been raised only meant they had felt Christ's spirit come back again, not His body. Both suggestions fail. On the former, the Romans were expert executioners. They did not fail to kill someone they crucified—this is why they stabbed the dead Christ with a spear. On the latter, we must remember that the disciples, too, were skeptical that the One before them could be their Master. They knew that dead people do not live, at least not until the resurrection on the Last Day. Hence, the disciples wanted Jesus to eat fish and show them that He was not a ghost (Luke 24:36–43). Thomas needed to put His fingers into Jesus' hands and His side (John 20:24–28). All of them needed Jesus to open their still-deaf ears and break through their blind sight by the Spirit so that they could see Him as the crucified *and risen* Messiah. Christ's resurrection was no mere spiritual resurrection. This was a fleshly resurrection in which Jesus' body and soul were reunited, and the tomb was emptied. In fact, early Christians believed so strongly in the physical resurrection of Jesus on a particular day that they moved Sabbath worship from the commanded day, Saturday, to Sunday, the first day of the new creation.[19]

Although the resurrection of Jesus was an event in time, it was also a unique historical event that cannot be verified according to modern standards of empirical proof. On the one hand, if someone were to produce the dead body of Jesus, it would eviscerate the Christian faith. Our faith depends on the crucified Lord being truly alive in the flesh. On the other hand, tests cannot be devised to prove either Christ's resurrection or the resurrection of the body on the Last Day, according to scientific strictures. The church must simply confess the bodily resurrection of the dead—of the dead Lord and of His dead children—against all objections.

Contempt for the material order in various philosophical traditions, both in Eastern and Western religions, has tended to diminish the prominence of the proclamation of Christ's bodily victory over sin and death in His resurrection, even within the church. However, the resurrection of the body—Christ's and His people's—stands at the heart of the faith the church confesses (1 Corinthians 15:3–5). Our resurrection hope—hope of a new, resurrected *body*—depends on the resurrection of the Lord Jesus and vice versa (1 Corinthians 15:12–19). Jesus' resurrection happened in history, but it was also the irruption of eternity into time, the end-time resurrection come early for one man. Thus Paul calls Jesus the **firstfruits** of the resurrection of the dead (1 Corinthians 15:20–23). Just as a fruit tree or crop bears a few items early before the full harvest, so Jesus is the first fruit, a sign of the coming harvest of all the dead and the promise of eternal, resurrected life for all who believe. Because Jesus was raised from the dead, believers have confidence that death will not be the end of us either. Our royal Deliverer has conquered by His death and resurrection so that we will be raised on the Last Day with all the saints to live eternally with the King.

King. In His humiliation Jesus ruled as King from the cross, with a crown of thorns and the broken scepter of a reed. He reigned, but He did so in a different way from sinful, human kings (John 18:33–37). His central

---

19 For details and evidence supporting this paragraph, see N. T. Wright, *The Resurrection of the Son of God* (Minneapolis: Fortress, 2003), esp. 685–718.

concern was truth, which He both proclaimed and embodied (John 14:6). In this way He led the subjects of His kingdom through death into His triumphal kingdom of life, righteousness, and truth through His resurrection.

Theologians have sometimes divided Jesus' kingship into three categories. His **kingdom of power** comprehends His rule over all parts of the universe, including His providential care of human creatures on a daily basis and His final triumph over the principalities and powers that oppose Him. His **kingdom of grace** embraces His exercise of kingly rule through the Word during this time between His first and second coming, as He reigns by preaching and the Sacraments for forgiveness of sins and reconciliation between God and fallen human creatures. The **kingdom of glory** is His rule in the age to come when His people will enjoy His reign face to face. This glory is partly realized now for believers who are with Jesus in death, but it will not be fully realized until the dead are raised in their bodies and the whole earth is re-created as the temple of Yahweh, the place of His presence, permeated by the Holy Spirit.[20]

These kingdoms do not exist as three separate agencies in Christ's kingly rule. They simply represent a human attempt to understand how Christ's loving care embraces all that He has created, for He is King of all. As the Messiah, the Son of David and Son of God, Jesus assumed rule over God's people. That rule embraced liberating them from their enemies and bringing them into a good kingdom, full of peace and rest, the foremost messianic role. But He executed that rule in His own way, exercising His dominion from below, as the royal servant of His people (Mark 10:45).[21]

Life under Christ's Reign. As our providing and protecting King, Christ extends His rule into our daily lives. The resurrection of the Lord causes His people to "be steadfast, immovable, always abounding in the work of the Lord" (1 Corinthians 15:58), for they know that in Him their lives and work have meaning and purpose. As He bestows the fruits of His resurrection upon His people through their Baptisms, they walk in newness of life under His reign. They consider themselves dead to sin and alive to God in Christ Jesus. They yield themselves to God as people who have been brought from death to life, recognizing that all parts of their lives have been re-created as God's instruments of righteousness (Romans 6:4, 11–14). Having been raised with Christ in Baptism, believers seek Christ's will. They set their

20 Jeffrey A. Gibbs, "Regaining Biblical Hope: Restoring the Prominence of the Parousia," *Concordia Journal* 27, no. 4 (October 2001): 317.

21 Walter Grundmann, Franz Hesse, Marinus de Jonge, and Adam Simon van der Woude, "*chrio*," *Theological Dictionary of the New Testament*, 9:493–580; Cullmann, *Christology*, 111–36.

minds on things above, focusing on the One who is their life and awaiting His coming again (Colossians 2:12; 3:1–4).

In the midst of sin and evil that assail us in this age, Christ has assured us of His presence and power throughout our earthly pilgrimage (Matthew 28:18–20). His healing and feeding during His earthly ministry demonstrate His concern for His people's bodily sustenance and health (Matthew 4:23–24; 14:13–21). He promises to be present even in the smallest gatherings of His people (Matthew 18:20). He does not leave them as orphans but provides the gift of the Holy Spirit (John 14:16–18), by whom He liberates them for true freedom, a life of peace, joy, and service (Galatians 5:1, 5, 13–26). Above all, His presence both constitutes and sustains the vertical relationship with God that is the heart of human identity and meaning.

This relationship of the union of the believer and the Lord is described in countless images in the New Testament. It is depicted in terms of the relationship of bride and bridegroom (Matthew 9:14–15; Mark 2:18–20; Luke 5:33–35; 2 Corinthians 11:2; Ephesians 5:22–23; Revelation 19:7; 21:9). This image echoes what Hosea's marriage to the prostitute Gomer (Hosea 1:2–3) presented: God is faithful to His people even when they are unfaithful. Christ joins sinners to Himself, shares with them all His goods, and makes them His family. He sustains His people as the bread of life (John 6:32–35, 48–51). He heals them as their physician (Matthew 9:10–13). He guides and protects them as a shepherd and rescues them when they stray (Luke 15:4–7; John 10:11–17; 1 Peter 2:25). He cherishes them as a parent (Mark 10:13–16; Matthew 23:37). His work and His companionship continue throughout the lives of believers until He raises them from the dead and brings them into the fullness of His presence forever.

Proclaiming the Savior

When people ask Christians who this Jesus is, we first ask them why they want to know. It will do little good to talk at length about Him as Savior and Lord to those who need no savior and who love other lords. We must first help such people perceive, at least dimly, some need for becoming acquainted with God in human flesh. For those who know their need, we will introduce Jesus in ways that faithfully proclaim the Lord Christ as He has introduced Himself to us through the pages of Scripture. We will try to begin with those characteristics that meet the needs of those who are asking. We will help them understand that Jesus is indeed their Savior and Lord, their God, who announces the forgiveness of their sins, took their place under God's wrath to death on a cross, and conquered sin, death, and the evil one by His resurrection.

The Mystery of How: Atonement Motifs and Atonement Theories

We began this chapter with the central questions of atonement: Why did God become man? Why did our salvation require a cross? We have argued thus far that Holy Scripture answers these questions in multiple ways. Jesus reveals the Father's heart, inaugurates the Last Day, sends the Spirit, offers the perfect sacrifice for sin, takes the place of sinners under the wrath of God, assumes human sinfulness, becomes a kinsman of sinful creatures, bears the cost of the ransom, becomes a curse and sin, takes death to the grave, conquers the enemies of God, liberates His people from sin and death, and rises from the dead to give His people eternal life. Like the many facets of a diamond, the Gospel light shines forth in manifold ways to depict Christ as the author of salvation, who reconciled God and sinful human creatures by the blood of His cross.

Why atonement *requires* the cross is simply not answered in Holy Scripture with mathematical precision. Some try to create such precision by making God's holiness or demand for justice that which mandates the death of a perfect substitute. Such ideas can illumine aspects of the Gospel, but they can also reduce Holy Scripture to one logic, obscuring other facets of the good news. For instance, in Scripture, God's holiness and perfection are revealed under opposites. God's holiness is exemplified in Christ's humiliation as Jesus becomes a curse and sin to make sinners holy. The apex of God's perfection is Jesus spat upon and judged as a blasphemer, forsaken even by the Father. Contrary to all expectations, God's holiness and justice have a cruciform shape. Our point is this: When believers demonstrate according to mathematical logic why Jesus *had* to die, the full biblical account tends to be shrouded, and we are tempted to proclaim the Gospel in one way to everyone instead of listening and responding with God's Law or a fitting declaration of the Gospel.[22] What we *can* say comes from Paul's summary of our atonement in Romans 4:25: He died to take care of our sins, and He rose to restore our righteousness as children of God. Paul told the same church how Christ's elimination of sin and gift of a new identity as God's child came to them: in their Baptisms their old identity as sinful doubter and rebel had been laid in Christ's tomb, and they were raised to live a new life in Christ as one of God's own family (Romans 6:4).

While some are tempted to offer the right answer for why Jesus had to die, others are tempted to avoid an answer altogether, simply saying that Jesus died "because He loves us." God's love for His creatures in Jesus is essential to why Jesus died, but the Bible says far more than that. Theologian

---

22 See Preus, *Just Words*, 23–24.

Fleming Rutledge observes that the response focused on love fails to reckon with the dishonor of crucifixion, the totality and depth of creation's corruption, and the repeated insistence of the New Testament that Jesus died "for sin."[23] An adequate way of speaking about Christ's death must deal with these essential scriptural themes.

The church has described a few different "motifs" or "theories" for how God came to rescue us from our sinfulness. Since the early twentieth century, theologians have focused on three atonement motifs, two of them based on biblical material. These atonement motifs summarize much of the church's attempt to organize answers to questions of why the eternal Son became human and was crucified.[24] None of these descriptions can plumb the mind of God and give a perfect, scientific explanation, but the biblical-based motifs will bring aspects of Christ's work as Savior into focus.

Atonement by Christ as Victor

In the early church—although Luther also frequently spoke of Christ's victory—the emphasis fell on Christ's redemption through His victory over all the powers that opposed and plagued the believer: the devil, hell, and evil all around. Twentieth-century scholarship designated this atonement motif the **Christus victor motif**. This victory happened above all in the resurrection of the Lord from the dead.

This motif recognizes properly the eschatological sense of Christ's death and resurrection. Death is the *final* enemy, Paul says (1 Corinthians 15:26), because it will be completely vanquished last—when Christ raises all the dead in the sepulchral harvest—and because death is the Creator's enemy that shows its power over creaturely existence most universally and dramatically. Christ's resurrection, then, defeats death's reign by ushering in a whole new world, the age of God's shalom, so that our Savior holds sway over sin, Satan, and sepulcher. God has done what enslaved, weak sinners could not do by sending His own Son into the flesh to free us from sin and death (Romans 8:2–3). This victory focuses first of all on the threat to our life in God from outside ourselves—although Christ also conquered the guilt and shame within us.

The second-century theologian Irenaeus, a major expositor of this theme, emphasized Christ's entrance into the darkness in which the human creature was held prisoner. There Jesus destroyed sin as He was tempted and triumphed over satanic temptation; there He destroyed death as He was buried and triumphed over the liar. Irenaeus taught that Christ **recapitulated**

23 Rutledge, *Crucifixion*, 467–68.

24 Gustaf Aulén, *Christus Victor: An Historical Study of the Three Main Types of the Idea of Atonement*, trans. A. G. Hebert (1931; repr., Eugene, OR: Wipf & Stock, 2003).

Adam's movement from life into death—relived Adam's life in his place—so that He might pioneer the way out of death into life for all Adam's descendants. Christ's assumption of humanity because of our fallenness provided the setting for His duel with all the forces of sin and death. This engagement became a duel to the death—to Christ's death, but to the ultimate death of Satan's claim on sinners and of death itself. In this triumph, Christ won the gift of resurrection and life for sinners. This new life in the Spirit restores God's original gift of life with Him, bestowed first in Eden.[25]

The Christus victor motif is expressed in more ways than battlefield imagery. This motif may also employ the psalmists' description of God's victorious intervention on behalf of His people in the courtroom. The Jews often thought of God's judgment in terms of a court of justice. There Christ argues for them and wins their case against the false deities and demons that claim God's people as their own. Jesus proves the case that these sinners, forgiven and liberated from sin's dominion, owe nothing to the false gods and to Satan.[26] Christ the King has conquered our enemies and incorporated us into His kingdom through Holy Baptism. We are "more than conquerors," and no accusation, claim, or action can separate us from our King, because He is the victor by His love (Romans 8:33–39).

As believers use the Christus victor motif, they will remember that the mystery of the atonement is greater than even the sum of all atonement motifs. Christus victor is good news to the weak and helpless, reminding Christians of all that Jesus has done for His people. It should not so concentrate our attention on external enemies, however, that we forget the enemy within, our own sin and guilt. Christ came to conquer both the enemies outside us and to assume into Himself our internal enemies because of which we are responsible for our own sin and death.

Atonement by Christ as Vicar and Victim, the Vicarious Satisfaction

Contemporary scholars sometimes find the idea of Christ's substitutionary work deeply distressing. They wonder why forgiveness required such a cost. "Why could God not just forgive?" they ask. "Why did God have to take out His wrath on Jesus? Why is God so angry?" To be clear, the Gospels show us that God did "just forgive"! Jesus began His ministry by forgiving sins (Mark 2:1–12; Luke 7:36–50). He demanded nothing; He simply forgave sins by divine authority. It is not God, then, but we who are

---

25 Gustaf Wingren, *Man and the Incarnation: A Study in the Biblical Theology of Irenaeus*, trans. Ross Mackenzie (Philadelphia: Muhlenberg, 1959), 96–98.

26 C. S. Lewis, *Reflections on the Psalms* (New York: Harcourt Brace Jovanovich, 1958), 10; and Dantine, *Justification of the Ungodly*, 78–79.

the obstacle to God's salvation—we do not want grace and forgiveness on God's terms. We want to be our own justifiers. Why, then, is God wrathful? His creatures have alienated themselves from Him, and His forgiveness is not getting through to them. In this perspective, the Bible poses a far different question from the ones above: How will the gracious Creator save such a stubborn, hard-hearted people? The answer is the cross.

Although the recognition of Jesus' forgiveness and grace throughout His ministry is one way to respond to these challenges to Christ's substitutionary work, it does not yet strike the essential note of God's justice. God insists in the Old Testament that He intends justice for the poor, the orphan, the widow, and the sojourner (e.g., Deuteronomy 10:17–19; Psalm 72; Isaiah 11:3–5). God will not allow injustice and exploitation to go unpunished (e.g., Isaiah 59:15; 61:8; Jeremiah 21:14; Hosea 7:2; Micah 2:1–5; 6:10–16). Contemporary people often overlook justice in divine things since we do not recognize how wrong the world is. Because of our first parents' sin and our own complicity in their wrongdoing, "in our world, something is terribly wrong and cries out to be put right."[27] Injustice and evil are systemic in our world, and the gravity of sin and the weight of injustice place a serious burden on creation and all human life. The weight of sin grows exponentially as we explode with wrath on others who take out their indignation on yet more. How does this cycle end? It ends by one who willingly bears the cost rather than taking it out on others. For all people, God Himself bore the cost in Jesus Christ so that justice is realized in Jesus' death, resurrection, and the consummation of His work on the Last Day. Hence, Paul proclaims that through Christ's atoning death God is both "just and the justifier of the one who has faith in Jesus" (Romans 3:24–26).

This discussion of God's justice brings us to the **vicarious satisfaction motif**, articulated by St. Anselm in the Middle Ages. Although Anselm and vicarious satisfaction are often maligned among modern theologians, Anselm rightly recognized the importance of God's justice done in Christ's death.[28] This atonement motif speaks of Christ as vicar, substitute, for sinners and victim in their behalf. Anselm observed that we are unjust, needy sinners, who will not have peace unless our relationship to God is put right.[29] God has righted our wrong by forgiving sins through His Son's willing death on the cross.

Anselm's context was the feudal system of medieval society. The system was based on a series of interlocking oaths between people higher and lower than each other in the societal hierarchy. Peasants swore oaths of loyalty

27 Rutledge, *Crucifixion*, 122.

28 Rutledge, *Crucifixion*, 147.

29 Rutledge, *Crucifixion*, 150–51.

and obligation to nobles, nobles swore them to dukes, dukes to kings and emperors. In turn, the emperor swore to the duke his oath of protection and justice, and the duke swore a similar oath to the noble, as the noble did to the peasant. Anselm viewed reality from the point of view of the feudal system, as did his European contemporaries. He believed that God and human creatures had a relationship of a similar sort. When humanity broke the feudal oath, satisfaction of the obligation was necessary, as it would be in a feudal court hearing a dispute between peasant and noble. Luther sometimes echoed this explanation, but often he asserted that God became human because only God had the power to take our sin in hand and crush it.

Anselm's understanding of reality may seem hopelessly archaic, but the idea of satisfaction is quite contemporary. We, too, recognize that deep injustices and crimes must be paid for. Innocent people incarcerated for crimes they did not commit deserve compensation. Restitution must be paid to innocents who have been wronged and hurt by companies that polluted a neighborhood's water for greater profit. Anselm's thought, then, is not obsolete. He recognized that justice requires confession of crimes and restitution so that human sin is "exposed, named, and renounced."[30]

How can human beings pay restitution to the Most High for their crimes? Anselm knew from Scripture that human creatures are separated from God in sin, dead in their trespasses, enslaved to the powers of darkness, and unable to save themselves. In short, no human creature could render proper satisfaction to God to effect reconciliation.[31] Since human beings are unable to satisfy the requirements of God's Law, Anselm taught that only God could render the proper satisfaction to realize righteousness and justice in the fallen creation. At the same time, it is right for human beings to make that satisfaction, since human beings, not God, are the obstacle to justice. Therefore, God became human—and a human victim—for only God could perform the satisfaction demanded by the Law, yet it was just for the satisfaction to be performed by a human being.

Although Anselm's theory and similar explanations do not rely solely on biblical concepts, Anselm's thought proceeds on biblical ground regarding both the problem of sin and Christ's substitutionary work. Anselm acknowledged the problem of sin as both our guilt before God and our captivity to sin—our inability to save ourselves—just as Scripture does (e.g., Romans 3:9–20; John 8:34). In addition, Anselm followed the Bible in speaking of Christ's work in relation to Old Testament sacrifices (e.g., John 1:29; Hebrews 9:11–14). Scripture teaches that Christ came to stand in our place under the Law (Galatians 4:4), to suffer on

30 Rutledge, *Crucifixion*, 152–53.

31 Rutledge, *Crucifixion*, 153–55.

our behalf (Romans 3:21–26), and to die the death that has fallen upon us (Romans 5:6–11). Christ came to take our place, to be our vicar, to give His life as a ransom for many (Mark 10:45), as the Suffering Servant was to do (Isaiah 53:6, 10, 12).

Some modern people find Christ's substitutionary work to be not just distressing but unjust, akin to divine child abuse. How could God the Father put such an unjust burden on His beloved Son? Anselm anticipated this modern question and provided a helpful answer. The Son does not go to the cross unwillingly but lays down His life of His own accord (John 10:18).[32] "For the joy that was set before Him [Jesus] endured the cross, despising the shame" (Hebrews 12:2). We must not think of atonement, then, as the Father punishing the Son out of anger, but as one of the Trinity willingly accepting the judgment upon sin that belongs to His human creatures, becoming a curse and sin itself, so that by grace sinners might receive adoption as daughters and sons.

Thinking of Christ as the sacrificial victim who took our place reassures us that our Lord not only defeated the enemies outside us, but He also has taken away the guilt and shame inside us. He has assimilated our guilt and shame into Himself and buried it in His own tomb, so that we stand righteous before the Father by faith. By taking our place—or by taking our sins into another place, His own body—Jesus has established Himself as Lord over sin. He alone has the capacity to eliminate our past faults and flaws. By absorbing them into Himself, He consumed them in the fire of His own Passion. We cannot control our past; it is set, done as we have fashioned it. But Jesus changes even our past. Jesus carried our sins to His tomb and forgot them there; He never goes back to find them, and He does not want us breaking into His tomb to find them again, either. God alone turns our flaws and faults aside and obliterates them from His own memory, where ultimate reality exists (Jeremiah 31:34). If our sins are not real to God, how can we treat them as if they define us, doubting God's forgiveness? We must trust the reality of God's Word—a reality given to us concretely in the word of absolution and in the body and blood of Jesus at the altar—even when it is contrary to our experience.

As we teach the vicarious satisfaction, we must be careful that the Law does not appear more powerful than God. We dare not obscure God's unconditional love by making it seem as though the Law could demand a price from God. The Law's demands fall on us, God's creatures who were made to live according to His design, as His loving and trusting children. He paid the cost of His own Son, who gladly paid the ransom with His own blood and life (1 Peter 1:18–19; 1 Corinthians 6:20). The price must not be reduced to

32 Rutledge, *Crucifixion*, 162.

a commercial calculation. It involves a matter far more profound than mere payment in the usual sense. God did not pay this out of obligation or requirement, but by grace, because He loved us, His children, and reconciled us to Himself, making peace by the blood of His cross (Colossians 1:20).

"Atonement" by Moral Example

Soon after Anselm, the theologian Peter Abelard attacked Anselm's notion of atonement and offered another explanation of how Christ saves, sometimes called the subjective theory of atonement. Abelard believed that satisfaction for another was impossible—if Adam's sin required satisfaction, how much more the sins against Jesus?—while yet thinking that the fundamental human problem was internal and not external. Abelard emphasized Jesus as teacher and example, who could awaken love that could change sinners into saints.[33] If sinners could follow Jesus' teaching and example, roused by His love and work for them, they would find the good life as God had made it.

Abelard's theory of "atonement" is not about God reconciling humanity to Himself at all. Because Abelard did not take sin as seriously as Anselm had, Abelard placed the working-out of salvation largely in human hands. We must find a way to make ourselves right with God, inspired by Jesus, but not saved by Him. While the Bible teaches that Christ is our model for the proper performance of human identity according to God's design, it does not teach that we are saved by following the model. Abelard confused the two kinds of righteousness and tried to make the righteousness of the horizontal realm operative before God. Scripture teaches that we are able to follow Christ only because He has saved us through His Passion, death, and resurrection. Christ must be first the sacrament and gift who saves us by His Spirit before we ever follow in His footsteps.

Atonement by the Joyous Exchange

Martin Luther often employed another image that connected the Christus victor and vicarious satisfaction motifs and provided Luther with his own motif. (Luther never attempted to explain the atonement; he used the full range of biblical descriptions as he found them appropriate in context.[34]) With an eye toward the marriage relationship of Christ and His church, Luther proclaimed the **joyous exchange** of Christ's innocence for the sinner's guilt and sin. Just as husband and wife become full partakers of everything that each other possesses, so Christ makes believers His

33 Aulén, *Christus Victor*, 96.

34 Ian D. Kingston Siggins, *Martin Luther's Doctrine of Christ* (New Haven, CT: Yale University Press, 1970), 108–13.

beloved, taking their sin and death to Himself and giving His beloved His own righteousness and life. Luther also spoke of the exchange of place and role when Christ became the criminal, "the greatest thief, murderer, adulterer, robber, desecrator, blasphemer, etc., there has ever been," while the believer becomes God's righteous child.[35] He also spoke of the exchange of residence as Christ ushered His people out of Satan's dumpy domicile into the magnificent mansions of His own governance.[36]

Thus in His Passion and death Christ absorbed into Himself all the evil that clings to His people. Substituting Himself for sinners, He gathered onto His own back the sin and guilt that condemns them to death. He took the entire evil of each individual into His tomb and deposited it there. This tomb is the only place in creation into which the Father does not look. Having assumed our suffering and death upon His own person, Christ traded them for life itself. In His resurrection triumph He won for all sinners the gift of life, as it had been fashioned for God's human creatures in Eden. His Easter victory claimed true human life in God's sight for humanity once again. He restores life by incorporating sinners into His death and resurrection through Baptism, and He shapes them for the Christian life of sanctification in the Spirit (Romans 6:3–11; Colossians 2:11–15). In this way, Christ is both the victor and the one who took sin and death upon Himself as victim.

The work of Christ cannot remain a mere historical datum. The One in whom God dwells bodily has made peace by the blood of the cross so that all hostility between God and His human creatures, and among His human creatures, might cease (Ephesians 2:11–18; Colossians 1:15–22). He came to rescue all people so that we might live out our humanity in the shalom for which He designed His human creatures in Eden. The joyous exchange summarizes this good news by connecting Christ's atoning work to the baptismal language of justification by God's grace through faith in Jesus Christ.

Why did Jesus die? Why did God become man? We dare not eliminate the mystery of God in Christ. Believers are to proclaim and teach the multifaceted reality of atonement as testified in Holy Scripture. Christ gave Himself on the cross for us so that God would be just and the justifier of the one who has faith in Jesus (Romans 3:23–26). Our Lord became man to take our place under the Law and heal our disease from the inside (Galatians 3:10–14; Romans 5:12–21). Christ was murdered because our wickedness and sin was so great that sinners could do nothing else when visited by the Creator (Acts 3:14–15). Jesus died to be the perfect Passover

35 *Lectures on Galatians* (1531), AE 26:277, compare 276–91.

36 *Sermons on John 14–16* (1533–34), AE 24:25–31.

lamb that turns away the wrath of God (John 1:29; 1 Peter 1:18–19). Christ was crucified to destroy sin, Satan, and death (2 Timothy 1:10; Colossians 2:15; Ephesians 2:14–16). The Son of God was killed because He assumed our sins and our sinfulness into Himself to its proper end (Isaiah 53:4–6, 10–12; 2 Corinthians 5:18–21). Jesus was executed because He took our curse so that we could have His blessing (Galatians 3:10–14; Romans 5:6–10). Christ died because the Father forsook His Son that human creatures might have God's presence forever (Matthew 27:46; 28:20). None of these may satisfy the human thirst for solutions to this awesome, divine mystery, but all of them proclaim the reality of atonement that is the heart of the scriptural story: "God so loved the world, that He gave His only Son, that whoever believes in Him should not perish but have eternal life" (John 3:16), for He died to bury our sin in His own tomb and rose to restore us to the family of God (Romans 4:25).

CHAPTER 10
JUSTIFICATION

THE standing of sinful mortals before the Creator runs like a silver thread through the Bible. In the midst of his misery, Job asked the essential question: "How can a man be in the right before God?" (Job 9:2). Although God's sovereignty and control over all things makes sinners weary and wary about their place before Him—when they get around to asking the question—Holy Scripture reveals the good news of justification. God endeavors to make His human creatures, who are lost in themselves as godless sinners, right before Him, saving them by His Word and Spirit and restoring their identity as God's children. The Lutheran reformers recognized that justification was not just another topic taught by Holy Writ, but was *the topic* of the Bible *sine qua non*, without which there is nothing. For the reformers, if we do not know ourselves as justified before God for Christ's sake, we have missed God's essential message to us.

More than five hundred years after the Reformation, justification seems like a quaint religious idea. Who believes in a final judgment, that all will stand before the Judge for who they are and what they have done? This might have been a common belief in the past when people were dogged by guilt, but contemporary Westerners have convinced themselves that guilt is unnecessary, a construct of a former age. Westerners rarely take God's judgment seriously, perhaps mentioning it in jokes and clichés about the pearly gates. After all, most insist that judgment is a bad thing. The newly fashioned god of love does not judge but affirms and accepts all—except for a few miscreants. How can justification still make sense in such a world?

Despite contemporary claims that people need not feel guilt, our persistent protestations against all judgment suggest guilt is, in fact, top of mind. Why do people feel judged so often by others if their own guilt is not close at hand? Why are we continually justifying ourselves to our parents, children, spouses, bosses, employees, neighbors, and friends if we feel secure? Why are the affirmation and agreement of the entire society so important on personal issues such as identity, autonomous choice, and sexuality? Contemporary people may claim that justification is irrelevant, but that is only because we have convinced ourselves of self-justification. We are persuaded that as long as I accept and forgive myself, I am accepted and forgiven objectively. My self-justification is all that matters. But our bones know a different reality that we cannot escape. We are on a perpetual search for a firm sense of identity and the confidence to express it to others. We cannot handle judgment because we do not stand on a firm foundation. We reject guilt because we cannot deal with our deep insecurities and failures. We reject God's justification because we are afraid that we might not be justified unless we are in charge. Sometimes, we become petrified or paralyzed by the feeling that we have no worth and have lost the respect of everyone else and ourselves.

The biblical understanding of justification is thus both relevant to our contemporary culture and offensive. It begins with the fact that we are not right, not right with others and not right with God. Paul writes about us in Romans: "None is righteous, no, not one; no one understands; no one seeks for God. All have turned aside; together they have become worthless; no one does good, not even one" (3:10–12). We are accountable to God for everything: who we are in our inmost being, our feelings and attitudes, our thoughts, what we have done, and what we have failed to do. And the verdict is in: our deeds are corrupt, our words are perverse, and we in ourselves are not good before God. Worse yet, we cannot do anything to correct the problem. Human performance does not and has never produced human righteousness before God, not even in the shalom of Eden. "By works of the law no human being will be justified in His sight" (Romans 3:20). This final point is the deepest offense: we are not in control of our status or place before God, our full human identity. We can only *receive* from Him our righteousness, our right standing with Him, by grace, without contributing anything. We cannot justify ourselves; "It is God who justifies" (Romans 8:33).

Justification comes from the Latin word *iustitia*, which can be translated both "righteousness" and "justice." In its biblical sense, justification is always relational. Justification defines the right relationship between God and His human creatures. It tells how God restores fallen sinners to that right relationship with Himself, rescuing them from sin and death, restoring them to life itself. The right relationship with God is essential to our being as human creatures, and a human life of shalom embraces this right relationship with God. When God justifies me, He does not explain what I have done wrong; He restores me to my proper place before Him, giving me righteousness in His sight, which is life itself.

By Grace Alone

Justification is God's act. He re-creates fallen sinners by forgiving their sin. He transforms them into His chosen children by bestowing a right relationship with Himself. Sinners cannot use God's Law as a guide for repairing their relationship with Him. Even without sin, Adam and Eve were in right standing with God through His effort, not their own. Sinners, too, return to that place solely through His effort, not our own. His effort is grace; His effort stems from His grace.

In the Middle Ages, the church taught that grace was a gift that God placed within the human creature, a psychological "component part," which added to the sinner what went missing when another component part, original righteousness, had been lost in the fall.[1] In this way, grace was something that came from God but was *in* the human person. Luther rejected attempts to analyze grace in terms of something added internally to the fallen creature. He defined **grace** as God's favor, His attitude of mercy, His lavish love, and His favorable disposition toward human creatures. God is gracious in pouring out His love and regarding fallen sinners as His own children.

God's grace is not compelled; nothing forces God to love His creatures. Nothing created can put its claim upon the Creator. He is indeed sovereign over all that He has made. In relationship to His creatures, God is always in the right. There can be no "unrighteousness" in God. Paul, in fact, posed the question: "Is there injustice on God's part?" The answer reflects the faith of all God's people: "By no means! For He says to Moses, 'I will have mercy on whom I have mercy, and I will have compassion on whom I have compassion' " (Romans 9:14–15). Not only is God always in control, giving mercy and grace according to His will, but God's grace is also never conditional on nor conditioned by human action. God's grace and favor are free: freely conceived, freely fashioned, and freely given.

In this freedom, God sent His only Son: "At the right time Christ died for the ungodly. For one will scarcely die for a righteous person though perhaps for a good person one would dare even to die—but God shows His love for us in that while we were still sinners, Christ died for us" (Romans 5:6–8). At the right time, God acted in grace by sending Jesus for sinners. God was not enticed by good human behavior, nor was God compelled by necessity. Instead, by grace alone Christ entered human existence, suffered, died, and was raised for ungodly sinners. Because of Jesus' life, death, and resurrection, we are justified, right with God on account of His blood, and have the promise of eternal salvation from God's coming judgment. "Since, therefore, we have now been justified by His blood, much

1 *Canons and Decrees of the Council of Trent*, trans. H. J. Schroeder (St. Louis: Herder, 1941), 29–46.

more shall we be saved by Him from the wrath of God. For if while we were enemies we were reconciled to God by the death of His Son, much more, now that we are reconciled, shall we be saved by His life" (Romans 5:9–10).

Even God's wrath expresses His love for His human creatures. God's final judgment is not wrath against His creation as such but wrath against all that fouls His handiwork and opposes creation's shalom. Just as remedying a crime requires judgment, the fallen nature of creation is such that judgment is necessary to make wrongs right and restore its broken and diseased character to the perfection of Eden. Thus God's anger is not ultimately directed against His creation but for it, for its ultimate happiness in Him. In a similar way, God's wrath experienced now by human creatures is anger against them, which is yet on their behalf. God's wrath is directed against the destruction of their trust in Him, the heart of human existence. His anger is like the anger that parents feel toward their children when the children endanger themselves or impair their future. God's grace sets aside His wrath by restoring the righteousness lost in sin.

This righteousness before God is the righteousness of trust in Him. Thus, in humankind, the opposite of God's grace is not His wrath, but self-justification, the attempt to recoup righteousness by human performance. Human actions, even perfect performance of them, can never put a claim on the Creator. The righteousness of human performance measures our standing only in active righteousness, not in the passive righteousness that avails before God. Christians live well in relationship to other creatures in love and service and in relationship to God in prayer and praise not as the cause but as the result of being right with God. In relationship to the Creator, we are right, righteous, only because He has re-created us as His children. In addition, as we consider our own deeds, we must recognize that our performance of God's Law is always imperfect. As sinners, even our best attempts at righteousness are like filthy rags (Isaiah 64:6), permeated with a lack of perfect faith in Yahweh. Even the most righteous of human creatures stands needful before God at every moment, as a poor beggar who can only trust in God's mercy in Christ.

Thus the whole Christian life rests on God's gracious disposition, the attitude and expression of His favor, toward us. His grace is sufficient for us. His power is made perfect in our weakness, and in our weakness His power and the favor of His love are revealed (2 Corinthians 12:9). God's grace causes Christian behavior, effecting in us a godly and sanctified life (2 Corinthians 1:12; Romans 12:6). All believers confess with St. Paul: "By the grace of God I am what I am, and His grace toward me was not in vain. On the contrary, I worked harder than any of them, though it was not I, but the grace of God that is with me" (1 Corinthians 15:10).

Grace to the Undeserving

The whole Bible can be seen as a testimony to God's justification of His broken, human creatures, but the apostle Paul offers the clearest witness to justification by grace through faith because of Christ. According to St. Paul, God's grace in Jesus Christ has turned everything upside down. The cross of Jesus has revealed the vacuity of wealth, education, race, occupation, and even religious status—all human markers of distinction—as bearers of value before God, and He has replaced them with grace. "God chose what is foolish in the world to shame the wise; God chose what is weak in the world to shame the strong; God chose what is low and despised in the world, even things that are not, to bring to nothing things that are" (1 Corinthians 1:27–28). Throughout his epistles, Paul "parades not the match but the mismatch between the act of God and the value or condition of its human beneficiaries."[2] The apostle insists that God's grace is given to those who do not deserve it, even to him, the chief of sinners (1 Timothy 1:15). God justifies those who fall short of His glory by grace (Romans 3:23–24). Even Abraham was promised forgiveness by grace, not offered it because he did something to earn it (Romans 4:13–16). Jesus was not sent to die for good people but for weak and ungodly ones, for sinners (Romans 5:6–8). Nearly the entire book of Galatians strives to show how God's promise cannot be earned by keeping the Law but is given through Jesus Christ, to be received by faith.

In recent years, some scholars—often labeled as the New Perspective on Paul—have interpreted Paul in a different way from the traditional Lutheran understanding of justification. One influential essay argues: "Where Paul was concerned about the possibility for Gentiles to be included in the messianic community, his statements are now read [by Luther-influenced Christians] as answers to the quest for assurance about man's salvation out of a common human predicament."[3] Reading Paul in the light of Second Temple Judaism, these scholars highlight that Paul is concerned with Jewish and Gentile relations, and not with the assurance of an individual's salvation. They criticize the notion that justification is about cleansing an individual's conscience of guilt, focusing instead on how Christ has opened the way for Gentiles to become part of the people of God without first becoming Jews. Although the New Perspective rightly seeks to understand Paul on his own terms, especially in the recognition that Jesus has paved the way for Gentiles

---

2 John M. G. Barclay, *Paul and the Gift* (Grand Rapids: Eerdmans, 2015), 490. On Paul's theology of justification, see also Mark A. Seifrid, *Christ, Our Righteousness: Paul's Theology of Justification* (Downers Grove, IL: IVP, 2000).

3 Krister Stendahl, "The Apostle Paul and the Introspective Conscience of the West," *Harvard Theological Review* 56, no. 3 (1963): 206.

to become heirs of the promise of Abraham, these scholars tend to downplay the radical newness of God's grace revealed in Christ. In emphasizing Paul's continuity with Second Temple Judaism, they tend to obscure the irruption of God's kingdom come in the Lord Jesus.

New Testament scholar John Barclay shows how St. Paul stressed the "incongruity," the total mismatch, between God's grace and sinful humanity. Despite contemporary assumptions that grace is defined as that given to the unworthy, Barclay demonstrates that grace was understood in six different ways—usually a combination of them—in the ancient Mediterranean world: as superabundance (excess and extravagance), singularity (pure goodness), priority (coming first), incongruity (given to the unworthy), efficacy (purposeful effectiveness), and noncircularity (given without expectation of return).[4] In fact, Barclay observes that the notion of grace given to the *undeserving* was deeply problematic in the ancient world. They thought that good people were given grace; evil people would not receive such a gift. For God to do otherwise would "threaten the justice and rationality of the universe."[5] In the midst of such assumptions, Paul maintained that human creatures cannot and do not deserve God's grace at all—to deserve it would make it something other than grace (cf. Romans 4:4). For the sake of Christ, God promises and gives grace to dying, broken rebels and trespassers who deserve the opposite. Everything has been turned upside down through Jesus: Gentiles are heirs of Abraham; sinners are forgiven by Christ's blood; the ungodly are righteous by faith; the dead are alive by Baptism into Jesus' death; the poor are rich through the Son of God; strangers are children of God by grace.[6]

Paul's testimony to the incongruity of grace—the way that God lavishes His love upon sinners—challenges all attempts to make human life, actions, or attitudes some part of salvation, no matter how small. Despite the biblical witness that makes salvation dependent on God's grace from first to last, Christians sometimes speak about grace as one part of salvation alongside the human component. For Tridentine Catholicism—the sixteenth-century council that set the course of the Roman Catholic Church until the twentieth century—God's grace supplied the necessary power for human beings to be converted and live a God-pleasing life. What will count on the Last Day will not be grace alone but human works produced by grace. Protestant Christians, too, sometimes think that sinners need to choose God and His grace, commit their lives to the Lord, pray the right prayer, or produce faith in their hearts in order to be saved. Instead of confessing grace alone as the

4 Barclay, *Paul and the Gift*, 70–75.

5 Barclay, *Paul and the Gift*, 563.

6 Compare Barclay, *Paul and the Gift*, 490–91.

cause of salvation, they focus on human responses to God's grace, suggesting that these count as righteousness—even if just a smidge—before God. In contrast, the Formula of Concord confesses: "The righteousness of faith consists *alone* in the forgiveness of sins by *sheer* grace, because of Christ's merit *alone*."[7] Because God's grace alone makes sinners right with Him, we can confess with the apostle Paul: "Far be it from me to boast except in the cross of our Lord Jesus Christ, by which the world has been crucified to me, and I to the world" (Galatians 6:14).

In short, human beings can do nothing to acquire God's grace and nothing to deserve it. We do nothing in justification; God's grace does it all (1 Corinthians 15:10). Hence, Luther and the Lutheran Confessions say that human creatures are **purely passive** in justification. The point is that human beings do not contribute to their salvation by their works, being, or attitude, but are acted upon by God to grant salvation from beginning to end.[8] That "we do nothing" means death for the person who presumes that doing something secures God's grace.[9] God is Creator, and for us to be in relationship with Him presumes that He remains the one who gives and sustains life by grace without any merit or worthiness in us.

Justified by His Gracious Word

God created the cosmos by His Word. He spoke, and all that exists came into being (Genesis 1). Likewise, God bespeaks sinners righteous. He declares rebels forgiven and re-creates fallen sinners as His own children through His Word.

The term *to justify* had at least two different shades of meaning, both in the Greek of the New Testament and in the German of Luther's day.[10] Usually, Lutherans define **justification** as "to pronounce righteous." God acts as gracious judge in pronouncing the fallen sinner innocent. In the word of justification, the Last Day's final judgment is heard in time as Jesus issues the ruling of what He will say in eternity. Jesus judges sinners "innocent" and "forgiven" because He took their sins upon Himself. This is God's promise for both who we are today by faith in Christ and who we will be forever. Thus justification in the biblical sense is labeled **forensic justification**. *Forensic* means "belonging to, used in, or suitable to courts of judicature or

7 Solid Declaration of the Formula of Concord III 39 (Kolb-Wengert, 569, emphasis added).

8 Solid Declaration of the Formula of Concord II 89.

9 Gerhard O. Forde, *Theology Is for Proclamation* (Minneapolis: Fortress, 1990), 136.

10 Gottlob Schrenk, "*dikaios*," *Theological Dictionary of the New Testament*, vol. 2, ed. Gerhard Kittel, trans. and ed. Geoffrey W. Bromiley (Grand Rapids: Eerdmans, 1964), 211–19; Wilhelm Dantine, *Justification of the Ungodly*, trans. Eric W. and Ruth C. Gritsch (St. Louis: Concordia, 1968), 21–36, 55–123; Werner Elert, *The Structure of Lutheranism*, vol. 1, trans. Walter A. Hanson (St. Louis: Concordia, 1962), 73–90.

to public discussion and debate."[11] It refers to activities of public speaking, and specifically to judgments rendered in court. God's word of justification, which bestows righteousness as a pronouncement of innocence and as a re-creative act, can be called forensic.

Just as the word of a courtroom judge determines reality for the defendant, so the Word of the Judge determines our reality. The person guilty of serial murder may for all practical purposes roam the streets freely once a judge has pronounced him innocent. The person who has committed no crime experiences the reality of guilt—prison, fines, probation—if a judge has pronounced her guilty. God's Word determines reality in an even stronger sense. When God pronounces the sinner innocent, the sinner does not remain a sinner. The sinner is righteous. God's regarding us as His children means that we are His children. He has said so. Just as God's "let there be light" resulted in creation's illumination, so God's promise of justification bespeaks sinners righteous. God's Word is reality. We must learn to believe it and live in it.

"To justify" means not only "to pronounce righteous, in the manner of a courtroom judge," however. It also means "to do justice to." When God justifies the sinner, the sinner receives justice. Most believers would protest: "No, sinners receive mercy and forgiveness. We don't get what's coming to us when God justifies us." Paul, though, describes justification in precisely such terms. Paul reaches the climax of his description of justification in Romans 3–8 with his affirmation that as God justifies the sinner, in Baptism, the sinner is baptized into Christ's death (6:4). We have been united with Him in a death like His (6:5). "We know that our old self was crucified with Him in order that the body of sin might be brought to nothing, so that we would no longer be enslaved to sin. For one who has died has been set free from sin" (6:6–7; cf. Colossians 2:11–15).

Sinners must die; it is what they have earned from their sin (Romans 6:23). And sinners do die. God does justice to them in justification. He buries them, but He buries them with Christ. Jesus has taken the sins of the world and hidden them in His tomb, the only place in His universe where the Father's glance never falls. Sinners do not exist before Him any longer, for Christ has let His grace overflow into their lives, as He shows them mercy (1 Timothy 1:15). Those who were sinners before His justifying Word did justice to them are now His saintly children. Christ's blood shed for His people has blotted out their sins, forgiving them in the riches of His mercy and grace (Romans 3:25; 1 John 2:2; Ephesians 1:7; Colossians 1:14, 20).

---

11 Merriam-Webster, s.v. "forensic," https://www.merriam-webster.com/dictionary/forensic (accessed March 27, 2024).

Lutherans sometimes debate whether it is proper to translate *justify* as "make righteous" as well as "pronounce righteous." Both definitions can be problematic when misunderstood. On the one hand, if we think that God has pronounced sinners righteous as merely a "legal fiction," by which God pretends we are something we are not, then even a true translation of justification as God declaring sinners righteous will be misconstrued. Some have thought of the Lutheran view of justification in this unreal way: "God says I am righteous, and we will let Him believe that. But that is not really the case. The fact of the matter is that I am a sinner. But I will be glad to let God think otherwise even if His view of me is wrong." This fictional understanding of justification places human consciousness at the center rather than God and His Word. Luther placed the highest level of reality in God's Word and grace in Christ. God bespeaks rebels righteous, and His Word is no fiction. We still experience how sin permeates our thoughts, words, and deeds, revealing the weakness of our best work on our own (Isaiah 64:6), but that experience does not determine the ultimate reality of our life, even here and now. Nothing could be more real than God's Word, which has re-created us through its pronouncement of our forgiveness to be His children. This Word is the supreme reality of our lives.

On the other hand, some have understood justification as "making righteous" in the sense that righteousness is empirically evident in the lives of all true believers. Instead of recognizing righteousness as a matter of God's Word and promise that directs believers outside of themselves to Jesus and the Gospel, justification as "making righteous" can make believers think they should be able to find holiness within. Such is the main danger with understanding justification as **theosis**, which refers to salvation and sanctification as human participation in the being and life of God.[12] The temptation to turn inward to find holiness and righteousness is a pernicious lie of the evil one! In order to direct believers to the certainty of the Gospel which is always *extra nos*, outside of ourselves, Lutherans often emphasize that the better translation of justification is "to pronounce righteous." At the same time, however, the Word of the Lord *is* acting in justification. It creates as it speaks; it does what it says. It makes sinners righteous as it pronounces them righteous. We truly are what God declares us to be; we are refashioned as children of God when His Word creates the new reality of sins forgiven and the gift of life in Christ for us. The more we recognize and delight in what God says about us, the more confident we become in

---

12 For criticism of theosis in Lutheran theology, see William W. Schumacher, *Who Do I Say That You Are? Anthropology and the Theology of Theosis in the Finnish School of Tuomo Mannermaa* (Eugene, OR: Wipf & Stock, 2010).

God's word of forgiveness and the more we will demonstrate that forgiven, restored nature.[13] As God's children, we cannot help but pray to our gracious God, desire to follow His will, and tell others about His grace.

This message of forgiveness of sins stood at the heart of the message of the first believers, a message of liberation from guilt and from sin's wages, death (Luke 24:47; Acts 5:31; 13:38–39; 26:16–18). God had raised them from the dead with Christ to newness of life, for He rose—having obliterated their trespasses by absorbing them into His death—so that they might become righteous (Romans 4:25). Believers consider themselves dead to sin and alive to God in Christ Jesus because they know that in His death and resurrection they have the assurance of everlasting life (Romans 6:8–11).

The fundamental reality of the life of believers lies in God's gift of death as a sinner and resurrection as God's child and heir (Romans 8:17). God's Word, which kills and makes alive, stands at the heart of both the understanding of justification as God's pronouncement and the understanding of justification as God's re-creating through His Word. God's Word effects the verdict of innocent. God's Word effects death and life.

By Faith Alone

Few religious topics have as much crossover into daily conversations as faith. For instance, a prominent television program in the 2020s features a poster that says "believe." The point is simply to believe, not to believe something or someone in particular, but just believe. Many are convinced of the import of faith in and of itself, without any value attached to what is believed in. This is part of why many Western people think that all religions are the same. Faith is faith, and they cannot perceive that the object of faith defines and structures one's faith. When the object of faith does come to the fore in popular understandings, the object is inevitably the self. Popular speakers emphasize self-worth, self-confidence, and faith in oneself for self-improvement: "Believe in yourself, and you will have success."

In such a culture, Christians must first confess not faith's significance but faith's worthlessness apart from Christ. In Mark 9, Jesus came down from the Mount of Transfiguration to find His disciples struggling to heal a boy oppressed by an unclean spirit. The father brought the boy to Jesus, crying for help: "If You can do anything, have compassion on us and help us" (9:22). These are not the words of a strong believer, but of someone at wit's end, trying anything to find help for his son. Undeterred by the man's lack of faith, Jesus confronted the father with his own answer: "'If You can'!

13 Cf. Oswald Bayer, *Living by Faith: Justification and Sanctification*, trans. Geoffrey Bromiley (Grand Rapids: Eerdmans, 2003), 42–73; and Gerhard O. Forde, *Justification by Faith: A Matter of Death and Life* (1982; repr., Mifflintown, PA: Sigler, 1991), 36.

All things are possible for the one who believes" (9:23). The father shouted out immediately in desperation: "I believe; help my unbelief!" (9:24). For this father, who did not have strong faith or much faith at all, his proximity to Jesus was far more significant than the strength of his faith. He was at the feet of Jesus, and Jesus' strength overcame his weakness and healed his son. Elsewhere, the Bible recognizes the weakness of the Twelve, their anxieties and doubts (Matthew 28:17; Mark 4:40–41; 6:51–52; 8:32–33; 9:32; 10:35–45; John 20:24–29), yet Jesus worked in them both saving faith and a heart to carry out His mission. It was not the strength of the Twelve's faith that made them great missionaries of the Gospel, but it was the strength of Jesus the Lord. Faith, on its own, is nothing.

At the same time that we recognize faith's inherent weakness, we must also recognize the importance of **faith** as the instrument that receives the Gospel, bringing peace and comfort to sinners. God Himself has promised forgiveness, life, and salvation in Jesus Christ through the Holy Spirit. The Faithful One, who promised Abraham descendants as many as the stars in the sky and brought it to pass through impossible circumstances, promises sinners salvation in the Gospel. This is where faith becomes essential. "A promise cannot be received in any other way than by faith."[14] In fact, God's promises do not merely require trust; God's Word elicits trust. God's promises are not only true, but they are also powerful to create the faith that receives the promise. It is that faith, inspired by the Spirit through the promise, that grasps the gift of justification by God's grace through the redemption God put forward in Christ Jesus by His blood (Romans 3:25).

The nature of a promise is that it cannot be proven. A promise rests not in the one who receives it but in the one who gives it. A promise is only as good as the promisor. The task of the receiver of the promise is not to prove it, but to trust in the reliability and faithfulness of the one who promises. We know of God's faithfulness because He made His promises come to pass in the history of Israel, the word and work of the prophets, and ultimately in Jesus Christ, the crucified and resurrected Lord. Because we know of God's love in Jesus, we can confess with all of God's people: "The steadfast love of the Lord never ceases; His mercies never come to an end; they are new every morning; great is Your faithfulness" (Lamentations 3:22–23).

Human faith, as expressed earlier, stands at the very core of human existence.[15] The original relationship of Adam and Eve with God in Eden rested upon the free exchange between Him who loved them and them who trusted Him. Christ has come to restore that relationship of trust so that God's children live by faith. Trust in God and His promises in Christ constitutes and

14 Apology of the Augsburg Confession IV 112 (Kolb-Wengert, 139).

15 See chapter 1.

sustains their entire life. Real faith cannot be coerced. It can only be drawn forth by a reliable object.

Faith is—at one level—a psychological phenomenon. It combines a knowledge of its object, a knowledge that can grow and develop, with an emotional commitment to that object. Faith in a person always involves a relationship. Faith indeed is a relationship. Yet the Christian faith is different from other faiths. It has a different object, a different content—Jesus of Nazareth and the God who He is and reveals. Such faith originates not merely in the knowledge and emotion of the human creature; it arises out of the Holy Spirit's working upon an individual in both mind and body, thoughts and emotions. Thus faith's very nature is receptive. It receives the gift of life in Jesus Christ.

Faith in Jesus Christ is elicited by Him, by His promise, because He is reliable. The Holy Spirit creates our trust in Him and His reliability. God graciously grants us the ability to believe in Christ, just as He grants us the ability to suffer for His sake on the basis of that faith (Philippians 1:29). Only through the Holy Spirit's power can sinners come to recognize in faith that Jesus Christ is their Lord (1 Corinthians 12:3).

The Holy Spirit re-creates the relationship between God and the fallen sinner by putting His claim upon the sinner through His Word, as He does in Baptism. Whether baptized as adults or infants, all believers must be dependent children before God, receiving from Him our being, life, and salvation, trusting in His grace. In addition, our relationship with Him grows on the human side as people hear God's word of forgiveness and life, and as they gain an understanding of Him through that Word. For those who do not know Jesus, the Word of God whistles through the ears in the power of the Spirit, often creating faith and bringing peace and comfort to troubled hearts. Faith grows out of hearing, and hearing springs from the sharing of God's Word (Romans 10:14).

Faith may not fully comprehend the mystery of God's speaking to us. Faith cannot always explain everything about God's attitude and action in our behalf. Faith is the assurance of things for which we hope; it is the conviction of that which we do not see (Hebrews 11:1). Faith knows God as a good Father and us as His children even if it does not know everything else. Fundamentally, faith is the relationship with the God who cannot be fully comprehended by His creatures, particularly when their minds are still suffering the damage of sin.

This trust in God is, of course, more than "mere knowledge" or "mere faith." Mere knowledge is possible in things that do not matter to us. We can have mere faith, a purely intellectual recognition, of the fact that Augustus Caesar ruled the Roman Empire two millennia ago. It is impossible, however, to have mere faith in a person. The emotional aspects of a personal relationship demand more than intellectual knowledge. When the Creator of all says, "I love you," it is impossible to treat these words as mere information. God's approach to us in the death and resurrection of Christ may cause some sinners to laugh, flee, or simply deny such an absurdity. It may cause other sinners to quake in fear before a God who found it necessary to die for us. But mere knowledge in reaction to God's message will turn quickly to an emotional reaction of one kind or another. God turns it to loving trust that comforts sinners with His love.

Thus simply at the word of Jesus, the official from Capernaum "believed the word that Jesus spoke to him," confident that Jesus' promise of healing for his son was reliable (John 4:50). The centurion at Capernaum was not used to relying on other people; he was used to being in charge. But he had confidence that Jesus' word was trustworthy. He said to Jesus, "Say the word," and that was sufficient for him (Luke 7:1–10). The Canaanite woman was not put off by Jesus' silence or the disciples' nastiness. She trusted that Jesus would want to throw her at least a crumb. Jesus did, with admiration for her faith (Matthew 15:21–28). All who trust in Him join these believers and Paul in confessing, even when suffering tests faith: "I know whom I have believed, and I am convinced that He is able to guard until that day what has been entrusted to me" (2 Timothy 1:12).

From God's perspective this relationship of faith is of one piece. It exists, or it does not exist. It is not a matter of degree. The relationship with God stands on the basis of His promise, and the psychological characteristics of that faith do not alter the nature or strength of the relationship. God is faithful even when we are not, "for He cannot deny Himself" (2 Timothy 2:13). He is faithful and will sanctify us wholly (1 Thessalonians 5:23–24). When we are failing, He is faithful and strengthens us and guards us from evil (2 Thessalonians 3:3).

From the human perspective, we feel the knowledge of God and His Gospel message for us grow—or escape our memories. While saving faith in Jesus Christ brings with it a change of heart and mind that stills troubled consciences and gladly offers prayer to God in difficulties,[16] our emotional commitment to God regularly waxes and wanes. We must be careful not to confuse our feelings about God with the faith that the Holy Spirit creates in our hearts and that grasps hold of us through the Word. The father of the boy with an unclean spirit was full of doubt (Mark 9:24). Christ observed Peter's "little" faith (Matthew 14:31), and He commented on the Canaanite woman's "great" faith in Him (Matthew 15:28). Such fluctuations in an

16 Compare Apology of the Augsburg Confession IV 45–47 and Simeon Zahl, *The Holy Spirit and Christian Experience* (Oxford: Oxford University Press, 2020), 118–31.

individual's experience do not indicate that God's relationship with us is stronger or weaker. The variations in the internal and external expressions of faith among individuals do not signal that one believer is closer to or further from God than another. Human experience of strength or weakness of faith does not determine the faithfulness of God. As vital as faith is to our life as God's children, it is the God of peace, not we, who equips us so that we may do His will. He is the one who works in us what is pleasing in His sight through Jesus Christ (Hebrews 13:20–21).

Righteous and Sinful at the Same Time

Faith is confidence in divine things promised but not experienced. In this sinful age, believers often experience their own sin and the power of evil in their lives. The fullness of the trust Adam and Eve knew in Eden escapes us. Because sin bites at our heels, we do not yet enjoy life fully even though, from Baptism on, we have eternal life. Our eternal life is assured in Christ (John 17:3), but we are not so sure. We focus on our own daily failures and wonder if God's Word can be true for sinners like us. This phenomenon of faith led Luther to teach that we are fully righteous and fully sinful at the same time—*simul iustus et peccator*. Luther's point was not that believers are partly sinner and partly righteous, seeking to grow in sanctification and decrease in sin—though this perspective has a place in the doctrine of sanctification. With the *simul*, Luther meant that in God's sight we have become *wholly* righteous, without any guilt or fault, because our sins have been taken away from us by Christ and we have been covered with His perfection. At the same time, in ourselves without Christ, we are nothing but sinful. Not only are our best works imperfect because of sin (Isaiah 64:6; Romans 7:15–20), but we remain utterly dependent on the mercy of God for daily life and eternal salvation. With Paul, every Christian rightly cries out: "Wretched [person] that I am! Who will deliver me from this body of death? Thanks be to God through Jesus Christ our Lord!" (Romans 7:24–25). Despite our sins, God does not hold them against us, but He holds us as His children. This is the promise of His Word, and we can be confident that the Lord's Word about us—that we are righteous—remains forever (cf. Isaiah 40:8).

Because God's Word is the deciding factor in our identity and relationship to Him, we must confess that we are in sin when we wallow in guilt or let potential guilt immobilize us as we try to make godly decisions. Instead, we will repent from focusing on ourselves rather than God's word of promise and rejoice that God has liberated us from our sin. He has freed us from every evil, including the evil that paralyzes us by making us doubt that we are free to praise God by loving our neighbor.

Some say that it is impossible for Christians to see double: the discord of seeing yourself as pleasing and displeasing to God at the same time can seem absurd.[17] But that is Luther's point: we hear God say, "You are My righteous child," while simultaneously recognizing how shabby and tawdry our thoughts, words, and actions are. Sinners repent of their sin while at the same time trusting in God's promise of complete righteousness in His sight. Luther's double perspective on the Christian life helps believers in two ways. First, we can be brutally honest about our own sinfulness. We can confront it and confess it without fear. Acknowledging its existence does not separate us from God. In fact, it is the first step in daily dying and rising as His children, drawing us ever to our God and to fellow sinners, our neighbors. Confessing sin forms the backdrop to trust in our gracious God, for He regards sinners as His righteous children for Christ's sake.

Second, the acknowledgment of our sinfulness is made always with the consciousness that sin is only half the story, and the smaller half at that. Better, the acknowledgment of sin is the foreword to the Word of God, which re-creates us fully in the image of His Son, dead to sin and risen to new life. Thus even when we are experiencing imperfection and worthlessness, we look to Jesus to know the truth, that we are daughters and sons of God. In Jesus, we can press on toward our own resurrection, in which we shall obtain the fullness of God's grace and our own perfection—because Christ Jesus has made us His own (Philippians 3:8–12). As God's own, we like to act like one of His children, proud of our family.

God Assures Us That We Are Righteous

In 1518, Luther met with the greatest Roman Catholic theologian of his time, Thomas de Vio, who was known then as Cardinal Cajetan, at Augsburg. Cajetan's one task was to make Luther recant. One of the stated reasons for Luther's required repentance was that Luther taught the Lord's Supper offered assurance of salvation. For Luther, Jesus' own presence was not a matter of ambiguity or question, but a certain promise from God Himself. Hence, Luther could reassure Christians of their forgiveness and salvation simply because the Lord Jesus promises to give Himself in the Supper. Cajetan thought assurance of salvation would make people arrogant and licentious. For Luther, though, forgiveness of sins in the Lord's Supper was something to grasp and believe. We are righteous because Jesus has promised.

---

17 Doubleness is a common feature of human life, however: David Zahl, *Low Anthropology: The Unlikely Key to a Gracious View of Others (and Yourself)* (Grand Rapids: Brazos Press, 2022), ch. 3.

This episode between Luther and Cajetan shows two contrasting understandings of the Christian faith that continue today. Some, like Cajetan, think that it is dangerous for Christians to be fully assured of their salvation. They rightly note that a Christian might fall away from the faith, and human creatures never know the future. What this view fails to recognize, however, is that the future belongs to God, and He speaks our future into the present by His promise in Christ. For Luther, Christians can take refuge in God as our mighty fortress because our eternal salvation is certain in Him. When we stop worrying about ourselves and focus on Jesus, *extra nos—outside of ourselves*—there is no uncertainty in the Christian faith, no "maybe yes, maybe no." After all, the promise of God does not waver between "yes" and "no" but is always "Yes" in Christ. "That is why it is through Him that we utter our Amen to God for His glory" (2 Corinthians 1:19–20). The Hebrew word "amen" confesses "that's the way it is." It expresses the confidence believers have in their utterly faithful God, to whom we cling, knowing that our place in God's family is secure in Jesus.

Why can believers be certain about salvation? In His abundant grace, God has designed three ways of reassuring us that nothing can separate us from His love in Jesus (Romans 8:38–39). To be clear, Christians should not constantly take their spiritual temperature as if introspection could cure spiritual anxiety.[18] Instead, Christians can live assured in the freedom given to them as children of God (Galatians 5:1). The key is that Christians should never look inward to know where they stand before God. They will find only sin and uncertainty in themselves. We must always direct our eyes outward to Jesus, known in Scripture, the ministry of Word and Sacraments, and the community of the church, where we can find comfort and confidence of God's love and mercy. And He who began His good work in us will complete it on the day on which our Lord comes to bring the reign of God fully and visibly to earth (Philippians 1:6).

God gives us assurance, first, as the Holy Spirit brings us to faith and keeps us in faith. The Spirit accomplishes His life-restoring work through the tools of His re-creating trade, the means of grace. We know that God forgives us as individuals because we have been baptized. "For as many of you as were baptized into Christ have put on Christ" (Galatians 3:27). We know that God loves us because we individually receive Christ's body and blood for the forgiveness of our sins. We know we are right with God because we hear His forgiveness through the proclamation of the Word and the absolution our pastor pronounces and His people share with us. Because these words are how God assures us of status as His children, we must not hesitate

18 Compare Dietrich Bonhoeffer, *Life Together*, vol. 5 of *Dietrich Bonhoeffer Works* (Minneapolis: Fortress, 1996), 38.

to share Christ and His love with our fellow sisters and brothers. As Dietrich Bonhoeffer wrote, the Christ in our hearts is always "weaker than the Christ in the word of other Christians."[19]

We also know that God loves us because He has invested Himself in our humanity. The incarnation of the Second Person of the Trinity is the second source of our confidence. We know that the eternal Son of God has taken human flesh into Himself not to reject sinners but to bring sinners to Himself. And He has not become incarnate in vain. We are certain that Christ's death and resurrection have swooped us up individually into the family of God. We are confident that Jesus died for each one of us, giving Himself as a ransom for all, for God wanted every human creature to be saved and come to a knowledge of the truth (1 Timothy 2:4–6). Christ died not only for "our sins" but for the sins of the whole world (1 John 2:2). In deepest despair, struggling faith can look to this assurance of the cross: the circle cannot be drawn in such a way to exclude me from those for whom Christ died.

Third, God assures us that we are righteous in His sight by remaining in control of our salvation from first to last. Nothing we can do determines whether we are His righteous children. He has chosen us before the foundation of the world, in the mystery of His love in Christ Jesus. No further reason is needed or given. God's election of His own family is a mystery, but the promise is clear: God foreordained us to be His children, and nothing can separate us from His love in Christ (Romans 8:29–39). When we appear before His throne, He will not be holding a checklist in His hand. He will be opening His arms to embrace His beloved children.

The Proper Distinction of Law and Gospel

The extravagant riches of God's good news seem to set Him up for abuse. The unconditional Gospel of Jesus almost invites sinners to say, "Let us sin the more that grace may increase." This is part of what Cajetan feared with the assurance of salvation. Paul, however, tells us that such an attitude is impossible because we are baptized, dead to sin with Christ (Romans 6:1–3). Nonetheless, it happens that sinners turn the Gospel into a license to sin. The solution comes not in placing conditions on the Gospel but in distinguishing Gospel from Law, and in distinguishing arrogant or secure sinners who would abuse the Gospel from broken sinners who can hear it and receive life through it. Secure sinners cannot understand the Gospel any more than the typical American can understand Swahili. Secure sinners understand only rewards and threats of the Law, and they think they deserve the rewards. What secure sinners need is the accusing, crushing force of the Law; it alone

19 Bonhoeffer, *Life Together*, 32.

confronts their arrogant self-confidence in language that can crack and demolish the sin.

Broken, despairing sinners, on the other hand, understand the Law's obligations and allegations altogether too well. These have heard the Law and know their sins and failures thoroughly. What they are missing is the Gospel. For them, the unconditional word of grace ushers in a whole new existence that does not depend on performance. Such free grace transforms them, offering free and full forgiveness in Jesus alone and the concomitant peace and freedom of the Gospel (Romans 5:1–5; Galatians 5:1, 13). Grace connects them into Christ's death, and it gives them new life with Him in His resurrection. In relationship with God, the re-creating word of justification obliterates their sinful record before the Father. It sets them completely righteous and innocent before Him, their names recorded in indelible ink in the Book of Life (Philippians 4:3). In their horizontal relationships, that word of re-creation begins to put to death the habits of hell and cultivate the habits of heaven.[20]

Because the struggle goes on between sin and faith within the Christian (Romans 7), the continuing dialogue between Law and Gospel dare not cease in this life. Believers must be reminded daily of their need to die to sin and be raised again to newness of life. The Law must continue to condemn desires in us that oppose God. The Gospel must continue to restore our flagging and failing consciousness of God's presence in our lives and His love for us.

Believers talk with one another and with those outside the faith on the basis of their estimate of whether the neighbor needs to hear some form of God's Law or God's Gospel. The first task of such ministry is not to speak but to listen. In listening to our neighbors, the Spirit will lead us in understanding whether they need Law or Gospel and in applying the word of repentance or the word of promise to their lives as we have opportunity. "We should listen with the ears of God, so that we can speak the Word of God."[21]

Christ Alone

This Gospel, and all that justification means, is comprehended in Jesus of Nazareth, the Second Person of the Holy Trinity. When you have said *Jesus*, you have said it all, Paul was convinced: "For I decided to know nothing among you except Jesus Christ and Him crucified" (1 Corinthians 2:2). In Christ alone Paul found all there is in life that gives ultimate identity,

20 C. F. W. Walther, *Law and Gospel*, trans. Christian Tiews, ed. Charles P. Schaum (St. Louis: Concordia, 2010); Bo Giertz, *The Hammer of God*, trans. Clifford Ansgar Nelson (Minneapolis: Augsburg, 1973).

21 Bonhoeffer, *Life Together*, 99.

security, and meaning: "But far be it from me to boast except in the cross of our Lord Jesus Christ, by which the world has been crucified to me, and I to the world" (Galatians 6:14). Death and life are all comprehended in Jesus alone.

Children of God are those who simply trust in Jesus the Messiah (1 John 5:1). They are those who have died and have their lives hidden with Him (Colossians 3:3). God chose us to be His children through Jesus Christ. In Christ we have redemption through His blood, the forgiveness of our trespasses, according to the riches of His grace, which He lavished upon us. God set forth His purpose for us in Christ and unites us to Himself in Him (Ephesians 1:3–14). For we have life in the name of Jesus the Messiah (John 20:31).

Living the Justified Life

Since we are justified through faith, we have peace with God through our Lord Jesus Christ. Through Him we have obtained access to life in God's favor. Faith in Jesus thus brings us joy as we live in the confidence and hope that we shall share in the glory of God. That joy is present even when we are caught in the midst of daily sufferings because God's love has been poured into our hearts through the Holy Spirit (Romans 5:1–5). Christ bestows peace upon us by putting us to death as sinners and raising us up to newness of life. That peace recognizes that God is relaxed with us, His children. If He is relaxed with us, we need no longer be uptight about ourselves. We can relax, rest, in His presence, and we can turn our focus to the lives of our neighbors, where He wants us to focus, so that we can carry His love and care to them. Thus our trust in His love inevitably produces deeds of love for others.

We are righteous in God's sight because of His grace and favor, because Christ has given us His own righteousness and innocence. What makes us right in the vertical relationship is always God's grace, always the righteousness of another, of God in Jesus. Therefore, this righteousness is called **alien righteousness** or the righteousness of someone else—*alienus* is the Latin word for "another." What makes us right in our horizontal relationships is the righteousness of our own performance. This righteousness, since it takes form in our own actions, is called **proper righteousness**—*proprius* is the Latin word for "one's own."

The confusion of these two kinds of righteousness can have disastrous results for our understanding of salvation. Too often Christians have understood righteousness one-dimensionally and presumed that proper righteousness is necessary to make sinners acceptable in God's sight. They have thus invented ways of defining grace as that which makes our deeds righteous enough to please God. God is pleased, however, not with ostensibly good fruit but with a good tree. He is pleased only with those whom He makes His children, apart from their performance. At the same time, alien and proper righteousness are inseparable in the life of the believer. The former is always producing the latter, imperfect though the latter may be. But the two must be kept distinct in our understanding if we are to comprehend rightly God's grace and His justification of sinners through the death and resurrection of Jesus.

Christ Died for All

Christ's death and resurrection have objectively covered the sins of all people. He is the propitiation for our sins, and not for ours only but for the sins of the whole world (1 John 2:2). God reconciled the entire world to Himself in Jesus (2 Corinthians 5:19). God sent Jesus because He loved the whole world (John 3:16). Just as Adam's trespass led to condemnation for all people, so Christ's act of righteousness offers acquittal and life for all (Romans 5:18). Objectively, Jesus has won righteousness for all. We must never limit those to whom Christ came and those for whom Christ died. Jesus is the Lord and Savior of all.

Subjectively, Jesus comes through the one whom He sends, the Holy Spirit. The Spirit teaches us all things (John 14:17, 26), bearing witness to Christ (John 15:26) even as the Spirit convicts the world and guides God's people into all truth (John 16:7–15). The Holy Spirit re-creates and renews them by pouring out God's mercy in the washing of regeneration, which conveys the benefits of Christ's death and resurrection to the baptized, justifying them and making them heirs in the hope of eternal life (Titus 3:4–7).

By the work of Christ conveyed to us by the Spirit in the Word, sinners are right with God. We are justified by grace alone, through faith alone, because of Jesus Christ alone. If we forget this, we have lost everything.

CHAPTER 11

GOD'S ELECTION OF HIS OWN

Note: This chapter could be part of the previous one because election should not be separated from justification. Since, however, election is especially challenging for beginning theologians, we have made it a separate chapter. Nevertheless, the doctrine of election only functions properly in unity with the atonement of Christ and the free gift of justification by grace alone delivered in the promise by the Holy Spirit.[1]

FOR many, few things are scarier or more offensive than the concept of election. The idea that God chooses His people for Himself before they are ever born seems wrong to Western thinking. It feels like God spins a spiritual roulette wheel to see whether the ball will fall on heaven or hell. Also called **predestination**—because one's eternal destiny is determined beforehand—the idea that our eternal fate is settled before all worlds seems arbitrary and unjust. For those who do not love God, election can cause a rebellion by taking their lives out of their hands: "Am I not in charge of my own life? Don't I decide what I believe?" Without trust that God has elected them *in Christ* through the Spirit-breathed external word of the Gospel, sinners are determined to keep their fate in their own hands—which Lutherans call the bondage of the will[2]—rather than trusting their lives to the hands of a choosy God who will have mercy on whom He has mercy (Romans 9:15; Exodus 33:19).

For Christians too, the idea of predestination can be terrifying. If God chooses His people for Himself before the foundation of the world (Ephesians 1:4), human reason concludes that God must reject others at the same time. Such logic places a burial shroud over faith's certainty. While some are hardened to think they can do whatever they want and still be saved, many are hounded continually by predestination: "Has God elected me or rejected me?" Luther himself was haunted by this question. Writing to a woman suffering a similar fear, Luther assured her that these worries are "the suggestions and fiery darts of the wretched devil." Knowing "all

1 Solid Declaration of the Formula of Concord XI 14.

2 See chapters 4 and 6.

about this affliction," Luther pointed her away from the internal struggles of her mind to Jesus Christ and His cross.[3] To another troubled by a similar demonic affliction, Luther wrote: "You should regard the Word as greater, more important, more powerful, more effective than these fleeting, vain ideas [regarding predestination to damnation] prompted by the devil, for the Word is true and human thoughts are vain and empty. So remember that God the Almighty did not create, predestine, and choose us to perish but to be saved, as Paul gave witness to the Ephesians."[4]

Luther's spiritual counsel goes to the heart of the matter. The doctrine of election must never set aside or qualify the Gospel. God wants all to be saved and come to a knowledge of the truth (1 Timothy 2:4). Hence, Lutheran theology teaches that Christ's atoning death and resurrection was not just for a few but for sinners, for all, which is called **universal atonement**. Further, the Holy Spirit delivers this message of salvation in Jesus through the word of promise in preaching, Baptism, the Lord's Supper, Christian conversation, and the Holy Scriptures, bringing death to sin and new life in faith where and when He wills.[5] God's word of justification is not a lie or a joke, but a promise of the Creator and Savior, a certain promise because He is trustworthy. In this light, the doctrine of election remains a mystery in terms of why some are saved and not others, but God's love for sinners and earnestness in saving them are not mysteries. The doctrine of election assures believers that our salvation is in God's hands from beginning to end, from before the world was created through eternity in the new creation, preserving us from conception to death and resurrection. "Those whom He predestined He also called, and those whom He called He also justified, and those whom He justified, He also glorified" (Romans 8:30).

Chosen by God

Westerners find the **scandal of particularity**—that God's love for all comes through particular people at particular points in history—deeply problematic, but Jews had less of a problem with God's sovereign choice of His own people. In this regard Paul echoed the Law and Prophets when he affirmed that God has the right to have mercy upon those whom He wants to have

3 Letter of April 30, 1531, in *Luther: Letters of Spiritual Counsel*, vol. 18 of Library of Christian Classics, ed. and trans. Theodore G. Tappert (Philadelphia: Westminster, 1955), 115–17. Cf. Stephen Pietsch, *Of Good Comfort: Martin Luther's Letters to the Depressed and Their Significance for Pastoral Care Today* (Adelaide: ATF Press, 2016), 269–72.

4 *D. Martin Luthers Werke: Briefwechsel* (Weimar: Hermann Böhlaus Nachfolger, 1947), 10:492.128–39 (no. 3956).

5 Augsburg Confession V 2 (Kolb-Wengert, 40, German text): Through Word and Sacrament, God "gives the Holy Spirit who produces faith, where and when he wills, in those who hear the gospel."

mercy (Romans 9:6–33). After all, God chose Abraham from all the peoples of the world, Isaac not Ishmael, Jacob not Esau, Israel not any other nation. But God did not choose these because they deserved or earned it but because of God's own love and faithfulness to His promise, a promise that would go through Abraham, Isaac, Jacob, and Israel to the world. "It was not because you were more in number than any other people that the LORD set His love on you and chose you, for you were the fewest of all peoples, but it is because the LORD loves you and is keeping the oath that He swore to your fathers" (Deuteronomy 7:7–8).

In the same way, the doctrine of election is not a choice God makes apart from His grace in His Son and Spirit, but election is the outworking of divine grace. In terms of human chronology, election precedes the work of Christ, but theologically, election can only be understood as election by grace *in* the crucified and risen Christ, sealed by the Holy Spirit. Hence, Paul writes: "In love He predestined us for adoption to Himself as sons through Jesus Christ, according to the purpose of His will" (Ephesians 1:4–5). Because we are elected for adoption in Christ, we should never seek to understand election apart from Jesus and the love of God revealed in Him. "Our election to eternal life does not rest upon our righteousness or virtues but solely on Christ's merit and the gracious will of his Father, who cannot deny himself [2 Timothy 2:13]."[6]

God's gracious will is shown to His people in the means of grace. By Word and Sacrament, God assures us that He has chosen us in Christ, and we are secure as His children. The Lutheran reformers thus insisted that Christ Himself is the Book of Life.[7] Whenever Christians are burdened with their status before God and their eternal destiny, "they should listen to Christ, who is the 'Book of Life' and the book of God's eternal election for all God's children to eternal life."[8] To know that God has adopted them as His children, Christians should not pursue secret spiritual knowledge, peering into heaven to comprehend the mind of God. Instead, Christians must keep their eyes and ears on Jesus, who gives Himself by the Spirit in preaching, Scripture, the Sacraments, and Christian community. Apart from Christ in the external word of the Gospel, there is only despair or arrogance, the first being dangerous and the second deadly to Christian faith.

Christians, however, sometimes seek assurance of their place in God's family in a variety of false ways. Some look to their own good works. They believe that if they are doing God's will, they can be confident that they

---

6 Solid Declaration of the Formula of Concord XI 75 (Kolb-Wengert, 652).

7 Solid Declaration of the Formula of Concord XI 13, 66, 70. See also Philippians 4:3; Revelation 3:5; 20:15.

8 Solid Declaration of the Formula of Concord XI 70 (Kolb-Wengert, 651).

are God's children. Such self-confidence will not last. If human actions and attitudes are required for certainty of salvation, how does anyone know when they have been good enough? When illness, death, or failure strikes, assurance vanishes because good works are sinking sand. Others trust their own feelings about God for their confidence that they remain His children. Feelings are fickle. Assurance rooted in feelings will shipwreck genuine faith in Christ. Faith is founded on the faithfulness of our Father, not our feelings. Some try to count external blessings as God's assurance that they are truly saved, thinking that success, happiness, and comfort are markers of God's blessing. Christ, however, says, "Take up [your] cross and follow Me," showing that God's assurance comes under the cross (Matthew 16:24–25). If we could count on anything external (apart from God's promise), it would be more biblical to be confident in God's presence because of a lack of blessings. But neither earthly fortune nor earthly misfortune can assure us of His love. Not even our own faith can give us that guarantee. Only the Word of the Lord ensures that we are His children. His Word, as it comes to us in the various forms of the means of grace, tells us that each believer belongs to God.

In Ephesians 1, the apostle Paul confesses the good news of the biblical doctrine of **election**: God in grace has chosen His people to be His own children in Christ Jesus. Before the foundation of the world, He chose us to be holy and blameless before Him. Because He loved us, He predestined us to be adopted as His children through Jesus, simply on the basis of His good pleasure—because He wanted to have us as His children. Through Christ He freely bestowed on us His glorious grace. In Christ we have redemption through His blood, the forgiveness of our trespasses, according to the riches of His grace which He lavished upon us. In preaching the Gospel to His people, He makes known the mystery of His will; in the means of grace, He presents His purposes, which He executed in Jesus. Christ is His plan for the fullness of time as He unites all things in Him. Thus in Christ, according to God's purposes, as He carries out His will, we recognize that our hope in Christ springs from God's plan for predestining and appointing us to live to praise His glory. To carry out this purpose the Holy Spirit brought the Word of truth, the Gospel of salvation, to us, and He brought us to trust in Christ (Ephesians 1:3–14). Paul confesses the unity of God's gracious election, the work of Christ, and the Holy Spirit's efforts through the means of grace. By grace, the Holy Trinity does it all to make sinners children of God.

Paul also discussed God's election of His people in Romans 8:28–39. There he noted that in everything that happens in their lives God works for the good of those who love Him. Those who love Him, by Paul's definition, are those whom He has called according to His plan or purpose. Refusing to separate God's call by His Word from His election by grace, Paul adds that those whom He has called are those whom He has predestined to be conformed to the image of His Son, the ones whom He intended from before the foundation of the world to incorporate into Christ's death and resurrection. The predestined are those whom God foreknew.

God's **foreknowledge** differs from the kind of foreknowledge human creatures might have. You, as you read this book, might "peek ahead" to chapter 17 to read about the doctrine of the church. A student could come into a professor's office, find a printed examination, and "peek ahead" to see the questions beforehand. God, however, did not "peek ahead" into human history to check on who might believe or who might do good works. As authors of this book, we know we will be writing about the doctrine of the church in chapter 17. We have the book outlined, and our intentions are set before they are ever executed with the words of the chapter. When professors foreknow that students should study a certain topic for the test, that foreknowledge creates what will exist on the exam. When students "peek ahead," their foreknowledge comes from a glance at what the professor has already designed and executed. God is the author of the new life of His people. His foreknowledge of His elect designs their salvation and executes His decision to choose His people for His church, to be His own children. God's foreknowledge is not the kind of foreknowledge that depends on its object. It creates its object.

Paul traced the process in Romans 8. In the mystery of His loving purpose and plan for us, He foreknew us. By His foreknowledge, He planned to make us His own, without any reference to our faith or our performance. He referred only to Christ as He designed our re-creation. Out of that creative foreknowledge came His election of those who would be His children.

God our Father not only created us but designed the shape of our lives. Those whom He predestined, He calls through the Gospel, and those whom He calls, He justifies. This is the way His plan unfolds. Those who have received this gift of righteousness anew through Christ will be glorified. Thus no charges can be brought against those whom God has chosen in Christ. God justifies those whom He foreknew and predestined through Christ's death and resurrection. Christ now intercedes for us at the Father's right hand. Therefore, nothing shall separate us from God's love in Jesus our Lord. We are more than conquerors through Him who loved us (Romans 8:28–39).

Paul was convinced that God's power resides in the Gospel of the God who saved us and called us. Its power rests not on the basis of what we do, but on the basis of His plan and the grace He began to bestow upon us before time began. This grace He made known with the appearance of our

Savior Christ Jesus (2 Timothy 1:8–10). Paul accumulated Old Testament witnesses to that understanding of how God has acted in behalf of His people in Romans 9. From Malachi 1:2–3 he cited God's sovereign choice of Jacob, not Esau, to fulfill His purposes. For, Paul observed, Rebekah's two children had not even been born. Neither had done anything good or bad when God elected Jacob. Paul confessed that this was so "in order that God's purpose of election might continue, not because of works but because of Him who calls" (Romans 9:11). Paul cited Exodus 33:19 to reinforce his claim that God will have mercy on those whom He chooses for mercy; "so then it depends not on human will or exertion, but on God, who has mercy" (Romans 9:16). After all, Paul knew from Isaiah 29:16 and 45:9 that God regards Himself as a potter who molds one vessel for beauty and another for menial use (Romans 9:19–24). Further, God has created His beloved people out of those who were not His people, according to Hosea (2:23; 1:10). As Isaiah 1:9 testifies, He distinguished Israel from Sodom and Gomorrah only on the basis of His free choice, His grace (see also Romans 9:25–29). God has chosen His own. Thus Luke could recognize that when the Gospel was proclaimed in Antioch of Pisidia, "as many as were appointed to eternal life believed" (Acts 13:48).

The Scandal and Promise of Election

The doctrine of election, too, often confuses and discourages people, particularly in Western culture, where human creatures are supposed to function responsibly and control their own destiny. But God has given us the gift of being His children—just as God through human parents bestows the gift of body and life—without any contribution from us children. God intends this teaching regarding election to comfort us, assure us, and carry us beyond any doubt that something can separate us from His love in Jesus. We properly use this teaching when it bestows such comfort and assurance.[9]

Nevertheless, God's election of sinners by grace raises a thorny question: Why are some saved and not others? This question is a special form of the issue of theodicy: why a good and almighty God permits evil among His creatures. Ultimately, creatures are unable to pierce the veil and understand the inner workings of the Creator. God alone is in charge of salvation. He saves; we do not. Thus this thorny question is called "the cross of theologians," the *crux theologorum*. The crux is so called because it crucifies all pretensions of those who want to be able to supply all the answers about God. This most crucial question cannot be answered, reminding theologians, and all of God's people, of their limits and killing their pride.

9 See Romans 8:18–39. See also Solid Declaration of the Formula of Concord XI 89–90.

When someone asks a question about why one is saved or another is not, Christians must carefully distinguish between Law and Gospel, seeking to understand why the questioner wants to know. Most of the time, the question is asked by those in despair for themselves or in terror for a loved one, and they need to hear the Gospel. Sometimes, however, it is asked by those who want permission to do whatever they want, and these need to hear the Law. For those in despair, an academic disputation about the nature of election or God's sovereign right over His creatures will not do, no matter how true the content. At the same time, we dare not suggest that human free will provides the distinguishing factor in why one is saved—God alone saves from beginning to end, as the doctrine of election confirms and clarifies. The only proper response, then, is not explanation but proclamation: speaking the good news and bringing the gift of Jesus Christ through the Word to those in need so that the Holy Spirit may work faith when and where it pleases God. As in the case of a beloved who wonders where she stands with her husband, the only solution is for the husband to speak the promise of love and give the gift of himself. As servants of the church's Bridegroom, Jesus, Christians stand in Christ's place to give the Gospel, God's own promise of love that bestows the crucified and risen Savior by the Spirit to those in despair. After all, those who fear they have so offended God that they can never be or become His children are crying out for assurance that God has chosen them to be His own. The crux may not be answered logically by the Gospel, but the Gospel offers a better solution: "God wants you and your loved ones to be saved. He sent His only Son to give up His life out of love for you and to rise from death to defeat the grave on your behalf. The crucified and living Savior, Jesus, has chosen you; trust in Him and rest in the strong hands of the Good Shepherd who will never let you go, in life or in death" (cf. John 10:11–16, 28).

As a doctrine intended to provide comfort for those in despair and give God glory for His salvation, election dare never become an invitation to speculate about whether we or others are truly elect children of God. The means of grace answer that question definitively. By Word and Sacrament, the Holy Spirit "does His choosing" in effecting God's eternal plan by calling us and covering us with Christ's righteousness. Using the doctrine of election as an entryway into speculation substitutes poison for potatoes. It can only harm faith by directing us away from the cornerstone of faith, Jesus. God chose us so that He might build faith.

This faith justifies, as the Spirit drowns sinners by burying them with Christ Jesus and raising them to new life in Him.[10] Such Spirit-given faith

10 On the importance of the Holy Spirit in the doctrine of election, see Paul R. Hinlicky, "How the Holy Spirit Disappeared in Lutheranism," in *The Person and Work of the Holy Spirit*, ed.

is not an idea or concept but a lived reality, experienced by God's human creatures in a real transformation. At the same time that faith is created by the Holy Spirit alone through the Word, human creatures are responsible for fearing, loving, and trusting in God above all things. We only love God because of God's work in us, but we do really love God and love our neighbors as ourselves through the Holy Spirit. This is the new birth that the Creator Spirit produces in believers through faith in Jesus. Human beings are not logs or rocks but creatures made in God's image with intellect, will, and emotions, who experience the gift of faith in their lives.[11] Luther thus confessed: "Faith, however, is a divine work in us which changes us and makes us to be born anew of God, John 1[:12–13]. It kills the old Adam and makes us altogether different men, in heart and spirit and mind and powers; and it brings with it the Holy Spirit. O it is a living, busy, active, mighty thing, this faith." Luther adds in the next paragraph: "Faith is a living, daring confidence in God's grace, so sure and certain that the believer would stake his life on it a thousand times. This knowledge of and confidence in God's grace makes men glad and bold and happy in dealing with God and with all creatures. And this is the work which the Holy Spirit performs in faith."[12] As the Formula of Concord insisted, the doctrine of election cannot be divorced from the work of Christ or the means of grace by which the Spirit works faith, drawing sinners to die and rise with Jesus.[13]

Hence, believers cannot use the doctrine of election as a false kind of assurance that permits them to "go on sinning so that grace may increase." The doctrine of election dare not be offered as comfort to someone claiming that his status as elect permits him to sin. What Paul said regarding Baptism in Romans 6:1–3 pertains to the doctrine of election. When someone tries to use the excuse that he can sin without worry because he is elect, this one instance permits us to turn election into condemning Law. He will not sin precisely because he is elect. Those who wish to use the doctrine of election as an excuse or license for sin do not understand what it means to be God's chosen children. People in such circumstances need to hear God's Law as it crushes their sinful pretense.

Although the doctrine of election might turn into Law by one who misuses it, God's election by grace is good news. It announces God's unconditioned love from first to last. It contradicts every despairing attempt to

---

Orrey McFarland, R. David Nelson, and David S. Yeago (Delhi, NY: ALPB Books, 2020), 161–65.

11 See Solid Declaration of the Formula of Concord II 68–72, which balances the reality of the Holy Spirit's work in our lives with the recognition of our continued sin and weakness.

12 *Preface to Romans* (1522, 1546), AE 35:370–71.

13 Solid Declaration of the Formula of Concord XI 14.

abandon hope in Christ on the basis of deductions about past performance or future failures and potential apostasy. The biblical teaching on God's unconditioned choice of us to be His own assures us that He who has begun His good work of re-creating us as His own will bring it to completion at the day of the Lord Jesus (Philippians 1:6). For nothing can separate us from God's love in Christ (Romans 8:39).

The Conundrum of Election

Martin Luther understood God's unconditioned choice of His people as a word of Gospel. It is good news that our being God's children stands completely apart from anything in us. In us uncertainty reigns, but God gives assurance that we are safe in His hands and shall remain so. At the same time, Luther steadfastly resisted the temptation to pierce the mystery of election and answer the question why some are saved and not others. Instead, he focused on the specific and immediate need of the sinner. To the secure sinner the Law—not the doctrine of election—must be presented. Secure sinners need to hear God's word of Law, which holds them responsible for their mistrust and misdeeds. The Law reminds all that the condemnation of sinners is not God's fault but our own. Each human being is lost and broken in sin by our own most grievous fault. For broken and despairing sinners, for those who recognize their condemnation and fall before God in need, the Gospel of comfort comes, assuring them of their forgiveness and eternal life in Jesus Christ. The doctrine of election is designed to bring such words of comfort, according to Luther and the Lutheran Confessions.[14]

The Lutheran doctrine of election is sometimes called **single predestination** because it insists that election runs only one way. God has chosen sinners to be His own children, but He chooses no one for perdition. Although this logic appears broken to human reason, it is the logic of Holy Scripture and the logic of justification. The God who desires all to be saved and come to a knowledge of the truth (1 Timothy 2:4) has not elected anyone to damnation. Instead, human creatures are responsible and accountable for their selfishness, perfidy, and disobedience. When we are condemned, it is our own fault. At the same time, the Scriptures testify that God has chosen His people for salvation (Ephesians 1:3–14), and God alone is responsible for saving His people from first to last (Isaiah 43:11). Thus, when we are saved, it is only by God and His grace. For Lutheran theology, then, election is understood not to answer the crux—Why are some saved and not others?—but to support the proclamation of God's Law and Gospel. Others, though, have tried to find an answer more acceptable to human reason.

14 *Lectures on Genesis* (1535–45), AE 5:42–50; Solid Declaration of the Formula of Concord XI 89–91.

Double Predestination. John Calvin, who learned much from Luther and Melanchthon, recognized the importance of the doctrine of election, but he followed human logic to a conclusion that Scripture never makes. For Calvin, if God chooses some for salvation, then He must necessarily choose others for damnation. This is the doctrine of **double predestination**. Calvin believed that God fashioned some human vessels to receive mercy as His children and other human vessels to be destroyed in hell.[15] In this way, Calvin separated the doctrine of election from the proper distinction of Law and Gospel. Calvin's understanding of election has the potential to obscure the necessity of offering the Gospel promise to the despairing. Furthermore, some secure sinners may use the doctrine of double predestination to avoid hearing the proclamation of the Law. In Calvin's view, election may cease to function as a doctrine of comfort in Christ. It has the potential to confuse Law and Gospel because those searching for confidence in Jesus may not be given the assurance of God's promise in the external Word while those certain in themselves may find reason for their self-security.

According to Scripture, God loves the world and sent His Son to save it (John 3:16). God gave Christ to be the expiation for the sins of the whole world (1 John 2:2). God wants all to be saved (1 Timothy 2:4). A doctrine of double predestination, however, adjusts the scriptural logic of Law and Gospel to make election sensible to human reason. In so doing, it fails to deal with the tension involved in the mystery of evil in the presence of a gracious, omnipotent God. This doctrine denies universal atonement, that God's saving grace in Christ covers all. Further, it makes it difficult to deal sensitively and properly with the difference between secure and broken sinners. Thus the doctrine of double predestination not only leaves itself open to offer security to arrogant sinners who bank on their status as elect to cover their willful sins, but it also may crush despairing sinners who cannot determine whether they are chosen or damned by God's decree. Such sinners only deepen their despair when they hear about election.

Synergism. Another logical solution to the crux is expressed in the view called synergism, which can also be called cooperationism. Synergists assert that God saves by His grace, but that the human creature ultimately either accepts or rejects that grace. God's choice of His children cannot become effective without human acceptance, according to this cooperationist view.

Some Lutherans among Luther's students and much of later Protestantism, particularly in North America, accepted this explanation. Sometimes called **election in view of faith**, they taught that God's foreknowledge did not create but merely saw what choices the human creature would make in the future.

15 John Calvin, *The Institutes of the Christian Religion*, vol. 2, trans. Ford Lewis Battles, ed. John T. McNeill (Philadelphia: Westminster, 1960), 920–64.

Instead of God being the sole cause of salvation, this view sees human action as the origin of one's redemption. Rather than election being the cause of faith, this view sees the human work of faith as the true cause of election. The crux appears to be solved—one is saved because she chose to accept the Gospel; another is damned because he rejected it—but at the expense of God's effort of grace. This view also places the burden of the Law squarely on the back of the believer. Each believer's eternal destiny rests upon the individual's decision. This recipe for uncertainty only superficially solves the problem, for it places a condition on God's grace at the key point at which it begins to operate in human creatures' lives. The ability of God's grace to draw believers to God depends on whether they permit it to work or not. Such a view contradicts the Lord's explanation that new birth, not human decision, brings God's children into His family (John 3:1–12). By offering an explanation why one person is saved and another not, it also implies that one person is better than another—having made the right choices—contradicting Paul's repeated injunction against boasting (Romans 3:27–28; 4:1–5; 1 Corinthians 1:28–31; Ephesians 2:8–9). Worst of all, this limited grace fails to deliver the comfort despairing sinners need.

Universalism. Others have solved the problem of why some are saved and not others by denying a basic premise: that some are not saved. In several eras of church history, universalists have taught that God will save all. In recent years some have argued that "love wins" or "anonymous Christians" will be saved apart from direct faith in Jesus.[16] The apostles taught that only through the name of Jesus can sinners be saved (Acts 4:12). Only Christ is the door that leads into the presence of the Father (John 10:7). Jesus alone is the way, the truth, and the life (John 14:6). Jesus is the gate through which all people may come to the Father, but no one will receive God or His salvation without receiving Jesus (John 14:7).

The Scriptures testify to this grace for all in Christ as well as God's judgment against every evil and all human creatures who are in league with it. Christ will separate those who have trusted in Him from those who have not. The latter will depart from Him into eternal punishment (Matthew 25:46). There they shall experience weeping, wailing, and gnashing of their teeth (Matthew 8:12; 22:13; 24:51; 25:30). The motivation for universalism may be admirable, but it denies Holy Scripture and builds a religious philosophy apart from Christ and His revealed Word. Such a foundation cannot stand.

---

16 Respectively, Rob Bell, *Love Wins: A Book about Heaven, Hell, and the Fate of Every Person Who Ever Lived* (New York: HarperOne, 2011), and Karl Rahner, "Christianity and the Non-Christian Religions," in *Theological Investigations*, vol. 5, trans. Karl-H. Kruger (Baltimore: Helicon Press, 1966), 115–34.

The certain foundation of the Christian faith is in Jesus, who is "wisdom from God, righteousness and sanctification and redemption" (1 Corinthians 1:30). Reminders of God's judgment warn us of the seriousness of God's wrath against all that disrupts the life of His human creatures. God has arranged to restore them to righteousness. He has done so according to His plan, which He set down before the foundation of the world. That plan brings death to sinners and restores life to them through the life, death, and resurrection of Jesus Christ. Through us, His people, He calls others to be joined to the chosen family of His elect people. As instruments of the Holy Spirit, we bring God's saving, re-creating, justifying Word to those around us.

CHAPTER 12
THE HOLY SPIRIT, THE WORD OF GOD, AND THE NEW LIFE OF FAITH

FOR most Lutherans, the Holy Spirit is the least discussed and least understood person of God. As the principal character of the New Testament and subject of the liturgical Church Year, Jesus the Son receives much attention. The Father, too, is recognized among the faithful as the Father of the Son, to whom Jesus taught His disciples to pray. The Holy Spirit, however, is often relegated to Pentecostal and charismatic traditions of Christianity that emphasize spiritual gifts, such as speaking in tongues. This should not be! The Lutheran Confessions follow Scripture in confessing the Holy Spirit as one of the Trinity who is continually at work through the Word of God in all of its forms—oral, written, and sacramental—as the church delivers the Word. Through this Word, the Spirit creates faith and saves sinners, killing them with Jesus to raise them anew in the Savior. The Holy Spirit is Lord and Giver of life, who brings new life in fallen human creatures through the Gospel.

The Self-Effacing Spirit

At one level, the lack of attention given the Holy Spirit is understandable. Throughout the Bible, the Holy Spirit never reveals, or even gives us a glimpse of, Himself. Like the wind, He only leaves traces of what He has been doing.[1] The Holy Spirit points ever to Jesus, like John the Baptist on the bank of the Jordan River, proclaiming: "The Lamb of God, who takes away the sin of the world!" (John 1:29). The Spirit overshadowed Mary for the unborn God to grow in her womb. The Spirit rested on Jesus in His Baptism, sending Him on the mission of salvation from the Father at the right time. Throughout Christ's ministry, the Spirit moved in Jesus, driving

1 See Frederick Dale Bruner and William Hordern, *The Holy Spirit: Shy Member of the Trinity* (Eugene, OR: Wipf & Stock, 2001).

Him into the wilderness to be tempted (Mark 1:12), empowering His preaching (Luke 4:18–21), healing the ailing (Matthew 12:28), and raising Him from the dead (Romans 8:10–11; 1 Peter 3:18). Additionally, Jesus promised that the Spirit will remind the church of who He is and lead them into all truth, which is Jesus Himself (John 14:6, 26). After the resurrection, Jesus breathed out the Spirit on the apostles, giving them authority to forgive sins on His behalf (John 20:22–23). Later, Jesus promised that the Spirit will be sent upon the Twelve to continue His ministry in Jerusalem, Judea, Samaria, and to the ends of the earth (Acts 1:8). Throughout Acts, we can see that the Holy Spirit and the Lord Jesus work in tandem, moving ahead of the apostles, sending the church on mission, breaking down barriers between people, bringing health to the sick, and creating faith through preaching and teaching Christ crucified and risen. Holy Scripture reveals that the Spirit is always active in working salvation for sinners, in unity with the Father and the Son, but the Holy Spirit never directs attention to Himself. Instead, the Holy Spirit directs the world to Jesus, the Savior.

The Holy Spirit's self-effacing character is of one piece with the humility of the Father and the Son. The Scriptures depict the Father as condescending to His creatures through His two hands, the Son and the Spirit.[2] The Father lowers Himself for the sake of His creatures, giving space for His beloved Son and the Spirit of holiness to create, save, and bring about His will. The Father places Jesus at the center of the plan of salvation, sending the Holy Spirit upon Him, so that God may be known as the loving Father that He was, is, and always will be. The Son's humility is the most obvious, as the Son refused to use His own divine power for Himself but lived a vulnerable life as a creature. Jesus did not direct attention to Himself either, but focused on the Father who sent Him, desiring to bring God glory. The Spirit's work, then, is similar to the Father and the Son as the Spirit brings human creatures to know Jesus by faith to the glory of the Father.

Two dangers must be avoided in our teaching and understanding of the Holy Spirit. On the one hand, we must avoid a practical binitarianism that elevates the Son and the Father to the throne and describes the Spirit as effectively subordinate to the two. Sometimes Christians speak as if the Spirit is superfluous since Jesus can do everything the Spirit does, but better.[3] Instead of confessing the Spirit as true God, without whom there is no Father or Son, the Spirit is quietly ignored. On the other hand, we must

---

2 On the language of God's hands, especially in the early church, see Killian McDonnell, *The Other Hand of God: The Holy Spirit as the Universal Touch and Goal* (Collegeville, MN: Liturgical Press, 2003).

3 Eugene F. Rogers, *After the Spirit: A Constructive Pneumatology from Resources Outside the Modern West* (Grand Rapids: Eerdmans, 2005), 19–44.

also avoid understanding the Spirit apart from the creedal confession of Christ and the story of God in Holy Scripture. When the Spirit is unmoored from the story of Jesus, religious experience can overshadow scriptural teaching so that the Spirit is understood as much through personal experience and emotion as the Spirit is understood biblically as one sent by the Father on the Son, borne by Jesus, and sent by Jesus for the mission of God. The danger in a pneumatology disconnected from the Bible's main story is what Luther and the reformers called **enthusiasm**. Enthusiasm literally means God-within-ism. In its framework, God's commands, grace, and revelation are known from internal resources rather than externally through the Word of God. In the Smalcald Articles, Luther defines enthusiasts as those who teach they have the Spirit without and before the Word, thus judging the external Word according to their internal sense.[4] Luther considers Adam's first sin as an example of enthusiasm in which Satan tempted Adam to turn away from God's external Word to his internal ideas and feelings about God.[5]

The biggest danger in the doctrine of the Holy Spirit, then, is to isolate the Spirit's work from the external Word and the Gospel of Jesus. According to the Augsburg Confession and its Apology, two central documents of Lutheran teaching, preaching and the Sacraments are not human works but are the work of the same Spirit of God who was poured out on all flesh at Pentecost to bring Jesus to the nations.[6] Just as the Son of God cannot be known apart from Jesus of Nazareth, God made flesh, so the Holy Spirit cannot be known apart from the means—the Word, personal, proclaimed, and sacramental—by which the Holy Spirit promises to make Himself present for the salvation of sinners. Hence, the Augsburg Confession declares:

> To obtain such faith God instituted the office of preaching, giving the gospel and the sacraments. Through these, as through means, he gives the Holy Spirit who produces faith, where and when he wills, in those who hear the gospel.[7]

The Lord and Giver of Life

Sometimes people talk about the Holy Spirit as a power or a feeling of God, not unlike "the Force" in the Star Wars franchise. The Scriptures, however, reveal for us the Holy Spirit who is personal, loving and caring for His

4 Smalcald Articles III VIII 3.

5 Smalcald Articles III VIII 5.

6 The importance of the Holy Spirit in the Augsburg Confession and its Apology, as well as Luther, has been observed recently by Simeon Zahl, *The Holy Spirit and Christian Experience* (Oxford: Oxford University Press, 2020).

7 Augsburg Confession V 1–2 (German text, Kolb-Wengert, 40).

creatures—not an "it" but a "He"—and is worthy of worship and praise as God.[8] The Holy Spirit does God's work in re-creating us through the washing of regeneration and renewal of Baptism (Titus 3:5). Against the Holy Spirit people can commit blasphemy, the sin of insulting or defaming God (Matthew 12:31). Christ (Matthew 28:19) and Paul (2 Corinthians 13:14) placed the Holy Spirit on the same level with the Father and the Son. In the Upper Room on the night of His betrayal, Jesus clearly distinguishes among Himself, the Father, and the Spirit, while giving the Spirit personal and divine characteristics (John 14–16). In fact, it is better for the apostles that Jesus die, rise, and be ascended because the Helper, the Spirit of truth, will come to them (John 16:7). The early church confirmed this teaching of the Bible: the Holy Spirit is true God, a distinct but inseparable person of the Holy Trinity, as it condemned the contrary belief of Macedonius at the Council of Constantinople in 381.[9]

The Holy Spirit does what only God can do in restoring fallen human creatures to their original relationship with God, so that they might live again in righteousness as heirs of eternal life (Titus 3:3–7). The Spirit accomplishes this re-creation through Baptism (Titus 3:5) and through the hearing of the Gospel (Galatians 3:2, 5). God's instrument of His creation at the beginning of all things was His Word as the Spirit hovered over the primordial waters. His instrument of re-creation at the beginning of the renewed relationship with individual believers is again His Word as the Spirit also moves through water. This Word takes various forms as the means of grace. Through His appointed means, the Holy Spirit delivers forgiveness of sins and the gift of faith to acknowledge Jesus as Lord, as the primary source of identity, security, and meaning (1 Corinthians 12:3).

Trusting in Christ as Lord enables believers to live the kind of life God designed for them in the beginning. The Holy Spirit pours the love of God in Jesus into believers by which He also dwells in them Himself, making them right with God through Christ (Romans 5:5). The Holy Spirit dwells in God's chosen people and makes them His temples. Their lives serve and praise God (Romans 8:9–11; 1 Corinthians 3:16; 6:19; 2 Timothy 1:14). Believers do not find the Spirit. They do not take possession of Him and hold Him as their own. The Spirit comes to us, takes possession of us, and takes up residence in us. He comes as a gift (Acts 10:45; 11:17). He is present

8 Jörg Frey, "How Did the Spirit Become a Person?" in *The Holy Spirit, Inspiration, and the Cultures of Antiquity*, ed. Jörg Frey and John R. Levison (Berlin: de Gruyter, 2014), 343–71, shows how the divine and personal nature of the Spirit is depicted in Holy Scripture.

9 J. N. D. Kelly, *Early Christian Doctrines* (New York: Harper & Row, 1960), 258–63; Jaroslav Pelikan, *The Emergence of the Catholic Tradition (100–600)*, vol. 1 of *The Christian Tradition* (Chicago: University of Chicago Press, 1971), 211–20.

in our lives as the first installment—the seal or guarantee—of God's pledge that we belong to Him (2 Corinthians 1:22; 5:5; Ephesians 1:14).

Righteous before God through this faith, believers practice the fruit of the Holy Spirit's presence in a life of love, joy, peace, patience, kindness, goodness, faithfulness, gentleness, and self-control (Galatians 5:22–25). He functions as our Helper or Advocate, the one who stands by us and who brings us the truth (John 15:26). When we do not know how to pray, the Spirit lifts up our voices to cry to God as our Father, our Abba, and intercedes on our behalf with groanings too deep for words (Romans 8:15, 26). The Second Person of the Trinity became God's Word in human form and flesh. The Third Person of the Trinity bears the forgiving and re-creating Word of God, and He always does so in Christ: in the person of Jesus Himself (Matthew 3:16–17; Luke 4:14–21), in His Body as a whole (1 Corinthians 3:16; Ephesians 2:19–22), and in each member who belongs to Christ (Romans 8:1–17; 1 Corinthians 6:19–20).[10] The Holy Spirit might not have His own flesh as the Son does, but He is embodied in Jesus, the church, and individual believers as He borrows our lips and hands, our voices and loving touch, and so accomplishes His work. Believers become the tools of His work in the world.

When we describe the work of the Holy Spirit, we often label it with the term **sanctification**. Christians usually use this term, which means "making holy," for the human response to God's Word. In his Small Catechism, Luther, however, did not define sanctification as the result of the Spirit's work in us. He defined sanctification as the process of the Spirit's work for and in believers. The Holy Spirit calls, gathers, enlightens, and sanctifies us within God's family, His church. He does so through the Gospel. He sanctifies us as He forgives all our sins, and He will complete this task as He raises us from the dead and grants eternal life to believers in Christ.

The term *sanctification* may be used in either sense, with the believer or with the Holy Spirit as its subject. Each respective emphasis focuses on the same fact of daily life. The Spirit takes those who have been bought with a price and re-creates their entire lives as temples in which the praise and honor of God is conducted (1 Corinthians 6:19–20). The Holy Spirit always points our lives to Christ and centers them in Him. Thus Paul can say that our lives are lived with Christ dwelling in us; it is He who lives in me, and not I myself, who lives out the life of faith (Galatians 2:19–21).

10 See Leopoldo A. Sánchez M., *T&T Clark Introduction to Spirit Christology* (London: T&T Clark, 2022), esp. 57–91 and 151–72.

The Holy Spirit Works through the Means of Grace

The Holy Spirit re-creates, as God created in the first place, through His Word. The Word comes in several forms, collectively called the means of grace. Some Christians put less stock in the power of the external Word than do Lutherans. Lutherans believe that the Gospel of Jesus does not merely share information about God. Lutherans believe that the Word we convey with our words, in various forms, actually conveys God's power for saving His people (Romans 1:16).

God Works through Selected Elements of the Created Order

Some Christians have followed ancient Platonic philosophy in regarding anything material, or created, as merely a shadow of a heavenly reality. For them, the best that human language or sacramental elements can do is direct our spiritual gaze toward heavenly realities. Lutheran theology, however, teaches that the Holy Spirit takes residence in bodies, using the material creation, to express His will and power. He has selected certain elements of His created order to be the instruments of His salvation. God's power and presence do not rest in the strong wind, which tore up the mountains in Elijah's sight as God led him to a cave (1 Kings 19:9–18). There he learned God's power is not to be experienced in earthquake or fire. It rests in the still small voice. God's voice comes to us externally, not from within our own murky emotions or imagination. It comes from outside of us. It speaks to us from God's mouth. As God's Word, it comes with power, and it shall not return to Him empty. God's Word accomplishes His purposes, and it prospers in the matter for which He sends it (Isaiah 55:11).

Some people have sneered at those who believe that God has revealed Himself in the human language of Scripture. They say that those who trust Holy Scripture put God in a box. The Bible, of course, is not a box. Its natural position is open, so that the Word flows out of it with power. God has placed His power in the Bible's words, from which the Holy Spirit springs, using its texts as specially crafted tools for killing sinners and bringing them to new life in Christ. The Word takes other forms as well, in certain created elements that He has chosen to make us truly alive. He began that process by choosing to come in human flesh. The fully human Jesus of Nazareth is the Second Person of the Trinity. In Him God's presence and power is enfleshed. As one who is fully human, like us in every respect but our sinfulness, Jesus reveals God's Word. He shows us who God is in His mercy and love.

God chose human language as His tool to be present among us. After all, God is the speaking God, who is in communication with us and calls and gathers us through His Word into His family. God also chose certain elements to link with His Word to convey His power to save in a more extravagant fashion. He loves to bombard us with His love in many and various ways. He comes to touch us with water and feed us with bread that bears Christ's body and wine that bears His blood. In these forms He re-creates, restores, and empowers His people through the Word. Through them He renews believers in His own image as forgiven children of God.

Finally, God has also chosen human creatures to bear the Word and share it with one another, standing in His place. In the preaching office, He has selected some to be special bearers of His Word, to speak by His own authority to bring repentance and forgiveness to the world (Luke 24:47). In addition, He has called every reborn member of His family, the church, to witness to the wonders of His love. As we bear the Word to others, we are agents of the Holy Spirit, who works saving faith through that Word.

The Word in All Its Forms

Often the means of grace are summarized with two words: *Word* and *Sacrament*. In the Smalcald Articles, Luther listed five ways in which God offers the richness of His grace and help against sin: first, through the spoken word (the sermon), by which the forgiveness of sins is preached to the whole world; second, through Baptism; third, through the Sacrament of the Altar; fourth, through the power of the Keys; and, finally, through the mutual conversation and consolation of Christians with one another.[11] Surprisingly, Luther did not mention the Bible itself. There are three possible reasons that might explain why Luther left the Scriptures off his list. Above all, the Bible is present in all five of these means by which God conveys the power of His forgiveness. The Scriptures stand at the heart of preaching, and they reveal how the Lord Jesus has given authority to His church to baptize, forgive, feed, and provide words of encouragement from God Himself to offer one another in Christian community. Second, many people in Luther's day were illiterate and had to depend on hearing Scripture, not reading it. Third, Luther was deeply convinced that believers need to be applying God's Word to the lives of others directly, with all the sensitivity they can bring to the task.

There is no magical power that arises simply from the words on the Bible's printed page. The content of the Gospel contains and delivers God's power for salvation as the Holy Spirit creates faith and speaks through the Bible. Just as we have great difficulty in removing the speck from the eye of another yet do not notice the log that is stuck in our own eye, so we often need a fellow believer to apply the good news of Christ's death and

11 Smalcald Articles III IV.

resurrection to our hurts and aches. Flipping through the pages of the Bible and chancing upon one verse or another may deliver the wrong message. If we would just hand the Bible to someone under the assaults of God's Law, he might open by chance to a passage such as Ecclesiastes 4:1–3 and concur altogether too quickly with its judgment that "the dead who are already dead [are] more fortunate than the living who are still alive" (4:2).

The Living Voice of the Gospel

Luther called the personal delivery of God's Word "the living voice of the Gospel." It involves a lovingly fashioned response of a part of God's Word that applies to our hearers. That Word will often need to be the Law. It will finally be the Gospel. That Word of God will be individually fitted and fashioned to be most effective and appropriate.

Therefore, Luther steered his readers toward oral expressions of God's Word of love when he wrote the Smalcald Articles. That does not mean that the text of Scripture itself or other written forms of conveying its message cannot deliver God's salvific power. The inspired Scriptures and the published works of Christians who guide our encounters with God's Word deliver its forgiveness and power effectively. Nonetheless, Christians must be aware that God has called them to converse with others and console them with God's good news in Christ. Christians neglect their call from God and the promise of the Spirit to work through them if they refer people to the Bible rather than offering the Gospel from their own lips.

Those forms of the Word through which God lavishes His love upon us can be classified in several ways. The means of grace can be summarized in one word: the Word. They can be listed as the five Luther mentioned in the Smalcald Articles—the sermon, Baptism, the Lord's Supper, absolution, and Christian conversation—and written forms of the Word, both the inspired Scriptures and other Christian writings derived from them. And now, within the last few decades, electronic media have joined these other channels of conveying the biblical message as new ways to proclaim God's Word. However we classify the means of grace, we recognize the three basic forms in which God's Word is conveyed by the power of the Holy Spirit to us: written, oral, and sacramental. God bombards us with His love, as it comes to us in His Word. He wants us to use this Word in all its forms as much and as best we can.

The Oral and Sacramental Forms of the Word

Oral forms of the **Word** include preaching—the sermon—Confession and Absolution, and the consolation of Christian brothers and sisters. The sacramental forms are Baptism and Holy Communion. The lines between oral and sacramental forms of the Word are neither hard nor fast. The oral forms are sacramental, offering forgiveness, life, and salvation as a gift of God's Spirit through means of human voices and people. The sacramental forms are oral, offering promises of God that strike the ears as a tangible element also touches the other senses. All forms of the Word are means of grace, expressions of God's love, signs of His presence, and forms of His verbal power by which the Holy Spirit takes residence and does His powerful work of salvation. God takes His oath and pledges His faithfulness to sinners in Christ in all forms of the Word.

The Sermon. "We preach Christ crucified" (1 Corinthians 1:23). Although the cross of Jesus may not seem like much in the eyes of the world, St. Paul insisted that Christ crucified and risen be the center of Christian preaching. After all, faith comes by hearing, and specifically hearing the Word of Christ (Romans 10:17). Hence, the task of preaching a sermon is not first about being relevant, but about bringing the Word of God to people in a manner they can hear. In fact, preaching is most relevant when it focuses on the Scriptures and the good news in Jesus, declaring the Word that God wants to share with His creatures.

Preaching thus builds bridges between God's Word and the hearers, through which the Spirit creates faith by the proclamation of Law and Gospel. Preaching—as well as Christian conversation—must be cognizant of the situation of the hearers and their spiritual needs. Are the hearers taking pride in themselves for their success or performance? Are they anxious or fearful? Are they enthralled with idols that give them security or purpose? Are they guilty or ashamed? Building bridges between God's Word and hearers requires that Christians pay attention to the state of those listening in order to proclaim God's Law to secure sinners and God's Gospel to shattered sinners. Believers are called to do their best in sensitively applying the Word. They dare never forget, however, that the Holy Spirit controls the witnessing and preaching process. The Spirit uses us to do His work, but we are never in control. The Holy Spirit works through us when He can and despite us when He must.

The sermon conveys God's power to save (Romans 1:16) to the assembled body of believers. They are commissioned as priests to carry that message to others informally as is appropriate in all situations of life. The several Great Commission passages (Matthew 28:18–20; Luke 24:46–49; John 20:19–23; Acts 1:8) give the charge to share the word of repentance and the forgiveness of sins to the whole church. Called pastors exercise that charge publicly; all believers are also called by God to share His Word, wherever they have opportunity.

Confession and Absolution. God has called His church to serve as His hit men, to deliver the death-dealing Law to secure sinners. God has called His church to serve as His midwives, to deliver life to despairing sinners through the Gospel. Christ has commanded this process of dealing death and dispensing life, calling His people to retain and remit the sins of others (John 20:23). Its power lies in the Holy Spirit's use of believers to speak under Christ's authority. He has selected believers as specific elements of His created order to carry out these tasks that restore sinners to God's family. Jesus commissioned His church to bind sins and loose them (Matthew 18:18), to open or shut heaven for others through the Word (Matthew 16:19). This exercise of the Keys of the kingdom of God is entrusted in the formal, public life of the church to pastors. At the same time, all believers use the Word to do this work individually, leading sinners to repentance and offering the forgiveness of sins in Christ to the repentant. The Office of the Keys is exercised in the various forms of Confession and Absolution.

Confession of sins is a dirge of death. Confession of sins opens the darkness of the soul to God's penetrating and piercing light. Confession of sins admits the justice of God's condemnation, or the correctness of the observation that we are dead without the Author of life.[12] In confession of sins, the Holy Spirit repeats our burial with Christ in Baptism.

Absolution looses or frees us from condemnation and eternal death. Absolution brings us to life in Christ. Absolution washes us by dissolving all that threatens us—sin, guilt, shame, alienation, the Law's verdict, death itself. The Holy Spirit restores sinners to being children of God caught up on the Father's lap, there secure from all evil and relaxed in His glorious light.

The church practices the confession of sins in a variety of ways. Most often Christians practice the secret confession of the heart: laying their sins before God and placing their lives at His mercy. The problem with such secret confession is that it is difficult for individuals to identify the log or speck in our own eyes, and it is even more difficult to hear comfort from an internal absolution. Hence, the Lutheran Confessions declare the importance of "private absolution" in the Christian life, which is usually called "private confession."[13] Private absolution allows people to hear God's Word of forgiveness from the outside—ordained pastors vow to keep confession private, though other Christians can also act as confessors—in order to receive God's Word directly without doubt that the promise of forgiveness is theirs, grasping to the absolution as a certain sign of God's love.

12 See Apology of the Augsburg Confession XII 107–108.

13 Apology of the Augsburg Confession XII 101 for the language of "private absolution." See also Apology of the Augsburg Confession XI; XII 98–112; Augsburg Confession XXV.

Confession of sins may also take place in small groups of believers who come together for Bible study and prayer. The practice of Confession and Absolution in such groups may bring the power of the Gospel to His people in a special way. In addition, Christians confess their sins in public. On rare occasions a matter of offense may be confessed by an individual before the congregation. When such an offense has taken place, caution must be used that the public confession be an experience that edifies, not a spectacle the sinner can use for self-justification or the congregation for self-congratulations. Much more widespread is the common confession of the public worship service, in which believers confess their sins and receive absolution together.

The advantages of the common confession in public worship and of the secret confession of the heart center around their accessibility. They are necessary because they provide confession and absolution at a minimal expense of time and travel. But ideally every believer would confess sins to another believer and receive from that person forgiveness and the assurance of God's love in Christ.

Absolution tailors the Gospel to the individual. In private confession of sins, the one who hears our confession comes to understand our personal battles against temptation and can apply Law and Gospel to those struggles with an insight and an objectivity that we often lack ourselves. When our pastor, or a believing friend, also knows about the sin to which we are tempted, we confront that sin no longer alone, but with the knowledge that our confessor's prayer and God's Word of strength stand alongside us in the battle against evil. Our confessor can also give voice to the Word of God's forgiveness and support that we, in our discouragement or despair, may be unable to sound for ourselves. Thus the comfort of the Gospel is immensely strengthened by the practice of private confession and absolution.

Christian Conversation. In the Smalcald Articles, Luther included the "mutual conversation and consolation" of Christians with one another as a form of the Gospel by which God offers counsel and support against sin.[14] Luther expected that the daily lives of Christians—at home, in the workplace and school, in the neighborhood and social groups, in the congregation—would include conversation that conveyed God's good news in Jesus. Luther presumed that believers would console one another with the forgiveness of sins in Christ as they went about their daily lives.

This consolation takes place most often as believers live out their callings in daily life. Such conversation demands that believers are engaged with the Bible, hearing and reading God's Word. Living out the consolation of the brethren also requires prayer, both for the Spirit's guidance and for His

14 Smalcald Articles III IV (Kolb-Wengert, 319).

help for our needs and the needs of our sisters and brothers. This task necessitates no sophisticated knowledge or training. It simply expresses the faith in the normal and everyday contacts of the believer's life and lets the Holy Spirit work as He has promised.

Through such conversation and consolation God brings His loving presence to His people. He repeats His baptismal claim upon them as they speak the Gospel to each other. He reinforces all that He accomplishes through public preaching, absolution, and the Supper as He lets His Word loose through everyday encouragement.

Christian Witness. In the course of life, believers also witness to their faith in the presence of those who do not know Jesus. Christians are called to build bridges that convey the Gospel into the lives of those around them. This witness can take place in formal evangelism programs in the congregation, but it always occurs as believers live their normal lives, connecting with others outside the church.

Christians do not choose whether to witness or not. To those who know that we are believers, we are always making some statement about our faith in Christ, even when our silence about Him reveals how important He is for us. We may witness to the wrong thing: our faith's lack of importance to us or our indifference to Jesus for daily life. But our words and deeds always say something about our faith. Those who get to know us, but do not know we are Christians, also receive a witness regarding our faith. They soon form an estimate of what holds our lives together, what is most important for us. They sense quite quickly what provides us with an ultimate sense of identity, security, and meaning. Therefore, believers do not choose whether to witness; they choose either to sharpen their witness or to let it convey a misimpression of the Lord.

Christian witness can happen in any situation. The Holy Spirit can use a hit-and-run speaking of His Word to good effect. The Gospel is most easily heard, humanly speaking, when believers have created a climate of trust in a relationship with an unbeliever. Those who do not know the Gospel may need to see that the Christian faith makes sense when lived in a family or community. In Dietrich Bonhoeffer's terminology, Christian community and lives often need to be "credible" to those who do not know Jesus before they grasp the relevance of the Gospel for them.[15] Although many will not know that we are Christians by observing the good deeds we do, the Holy Spirit builds a foundation not on words or actions alone but on the Gospel spoken in a community living in Christ's love.

---

15 Dietrich Bonhoeffer, "Contemporizing New Testament Texts," in *Theological Education at Finkenwalde, 1935–1937*, vol. 14 of Dietrich Bonhoeffer Works, trans. Douglas W. Stott, ed. H. Gaylon Barker and Mark S. Brocker (Minneapolis: Fortress, 2013), 433.

Believers must listen carefully to ascertain whether those with whom they are speaking need to hear Law or Gospel. They need to listen sensitively to determine how to formulate their words effectively, in a form a person who does not know the Bible can hear and understand. Believers must show tremendous patience as they convey the Word of the Lord. They must be willing to speak and then wait in silence, repeatedly and for the long haul, as the Holy Spirit reveals to the sinner that reliance on other sources of identity, security, and meaning spells death. Then, as our hearers test the truth of God's Word—and test us and our patience—we plant the seeds of the good news in Jesus and count on the Spirit to create new life and bring growth (1 Corinthians 3:5–7), not on our schedules but when and where He pleases.

To these tasks of being God's hit men and midwives we are called. We give His Word its living voice. The Holy Spirit gives believers the blessing of serving as His instruments in bringing sinners into death and children of God to life once again.

Sacraments. The sacramental forms of God's Word are not grouped together in the New Testament. The church has fashioned the category and chosen the term for the tangible gifts of God's Word on the basis of biblical teaching. The Latin word *sacramentum* referred originally to the oath that Roman soldiers took, pledging their faithfulness to the state. Christians used the term to translate the Greek word for "mystery." Sacraments are indeed mysterious as the infinite Creator is present in and offers His forgiveness through finite means that human creatures can grasp and believe.

Lutherans have also followed Augustine's understanding of sacrament as "gift."[16] God gives His forgiveness to His people in the Sacraments. He does so under external forms or means through His Word. The Sacraments are practiced because Christ has given them to His apostles and church and commanded us to use them. These three elements—promise of forgiveness, tangible or physical element/means, and Christ's command—constitute the Lutheran definition of a **sacrament**.

Sacraments convey God's Word of power, the Gospel of the forgiveness of sins. They do so regardless of the character of the person who administers them. In the early church, some Christians challenged the validity of the sacraments if they were performed by people who did not fit a certain definition of what a proper priest should be. The church rejected this view, that of the **Novatians** and the **Donatists**, because God's power lies in His promise delivered by the Spirit through the sacramental Word despite the

16 As Luther understood Augustine's broad definition of this term; cf. Ian D. Kingston Siggins, *Martin Luther's Doctrine of Christ* (New Haven, CT: Yale University Press, 1970), 156–64, on Luther's use of Augustine's pairing of "sacrament" and "example" for Christ.

sinners who preside over the mysteries.[17] The pastor does not determine the presence of the power of God; the Word does.

Indeed, if those who receive the Sacraments reject the promise of God, or dismiss it in unbelief, the Sacraments continue to offer forgiveness of sins. Like the hearing and reading of the Word, receiving God's promise sacramentally works faith and works through faith. Without faith the benefits do not penetrate our lives; without trust in God's promise, we receive condemnation (1 Corinthians 11:27–29). Thus we must distinguish the benefits of the Sacraments—and other forms of the promise of forgiveness—from their nature and their validity. God's Word remains His reliable promise whether faith receives it or not. The Sacraments do not depend on faith for God to offer His promise of forgiveness and new life. At the same time, the Sacraments do not work magically. The medieval church taught that the Sacraments functioned ***ex opere operato***, simply by virtue of the human participation of the priest and/or people in performing the sacramental act. As long as one was present and participating, then one received sacramental grace, regardless of faith. For Lutheran theology, God's Word is true even if no one believes it, but for us to benefit from God's grace, we must receive the Word by faith through the Holy Spirit.

Christians have disagreed on the number of acts that should be designated with the term *sacrament* because they have not always shared a common definition. In fact, at the time of the Lutheran Reformation, the reformers were exasperated at the Roman Catholics who insisted on following Peter Lombard (ca. 1100–60) and defining seven sacraments: Baptism, confirmation, the Lord's Supper, penance (called reconciliation today), extreme unction (or Last Rites), holy orders, and marriage. In one of the cheekier articles of the Apology of the Augsburg Confession, Philip Melanchthon argues that government, prayer, almsgiving, and afflictions could all be called sacraments, if defined in a certain way.[18] Melanchthon's point was that what makes a sacrament important is not a human definition but God's promise. "The sacraments are signs of the promises," Melanchthon wrote, adding "a promise is useless unless it is received by faith."[19] God's promise tied to an external sign: this is the center of how the Lutheran reformers understood sacraments. The Sacraments are signs that God gives of His forgiveness and salvation to be received by faith through a visible means, "a picture of the Word."[20]

17 Kelly, *Early Christian Doctrines*, 409–17; Pelikan, *Emergence of the Catholic Tradition*, 308–13.

18 Apology of the Augsburg Confession XIII 15–17.

19 Apology of the Augsburg Confession XIII 20 (Kolb-Wengert, 221).

20 Apology of the Augsburg Confession XIII 5 (Kolb-Wengert, 220).

In the Reformation era, Protestants generally rejected all but two or three of the seven mentioned above as sacraments. All Protestants retained Baptism and the Lord's Supper, although some redefined them as symbolic rites rather than sacraments that convey forgiveness of sins. Luther initially taught that Confession and Absolution is also a sacrament but then changed his mind and called Confession and Absolution a continuation of Baptism rather than a separate sacrament.[21] Since his time, Lutherans have differed on whether Confession and Absolution should be considered a third Sacrament or the continuation of God's baptismal action of killing and making alive.

The Sacraments remind us that God uses selected elements of His created order to save us. Their material character anchors salvation outside of ourselves. God's still, small voice is not a feeling welling up within us but is the voice of the living God, coming to us from the outside. "The self is a bottomless pit, a black hole, endlessly sucking everything within and crushing it. The internal self constantly defeats and swallows"[22] what we might call the "mere words" of proclamation and Christian consolation. The Sacraments keep the Word from being swept into the "black hole" of the self. These mysteries refuse to allow the Word to dissolve into our own feelings. The promise of God in Baptism remains, no matter how the bedraggled spirit of the Christian feels about it. The sustenance of the Lord's Supper wakes the Christian from the coma of doubt and despair as the sacramental elements cross the lips. They open the ears to the promise of the Words of Institution: "Given for you" and "Shed for you."

According to Luther, the object of faith "must be external so that it can be perceived and grasped by the senses and thus brought into the heart," and both the Word and Sacraments provide such external objects to which faith may grasp. In fact, Luther continues, "whatever God does and effects in us he desires to accomplish through such an external ordinance."[23] If faith does not cling to the Gospel on the outside, it turns inward to cling to itself and feed on itself. Such inward-focused faith may suffocate or starve. God must come externally. Nowhere is that clearer than in the Sacraments and in their external, material elements through which the Holy Spirit offers the promise of the Gospel.

The Holy Spirit Re-creates Believers

No one can confess faith in Jesus Christ as Lord apart from the Holy Spirit's power (1 Corinthians 12:3). The Holy Spirit regenerates and renews

21 *Babylonian Captivity of the Church* (1520), AE 36:81–91, 124.

22 Gerhard O. Forde, *Theology Is for Proclamation* (Minneapolis: Fortress, 1990), 159.

23 Large Catechism IV 30 (Kolb-Wengert, 460).

believers through the washing of Baptism (Titus 3:5) and other forms of the Word. Sinners enter the kingdom of God as little children (Matthew 18:3); they must be born again (John 3:3–8). God changes or converts sinners into His newborn chosen children. God takes the dust of those who are dead in trespasses and sins, those who have turned their backs on the Author of life, and He breathes into them the forgiveness of sins through His re-creative Word (John 20:22–23). This is all the work of the Holy Spirit, but it happens through material things (the means of grace) and in material things (the bodies of believers).

Not by Our Own Reason or Strength

The sinful human desire for autonomy and independence asserts itself again in relationship to the work of the Holy Spirit. Just as we must learn that we are dependent creatures, not the free Creator, and that we are bound sinners, not the gracious Savior, we also have to learn that we are not masters of our own bodies. We cannot muster saving faith by our own resources; we cannot bring ourselves to God by our works or thoughts. In short, we cannot be right with God without the Holy Spirit's work in us. In the words of Martin Luther, we must come to "believe that I cannot by my own reason or strength believe in Jesus Christ, my Lord, or come to Him."[24] In sin—apart from the Holy Spirit—people do not receive the gifts of God's Spirit. God's way of thinking, and our trust in the God revealed in the cross, seem folly to all sinners, apart from the Holy Spirit. Only through the Spirit can God's truth be discerned (1 Corinthians 2:14). Those who live apart from the Spirit set their minds on their own agenda; only those who have received life from the Spirit set their minds on His agenda (Romans 8:5).

The thrust of much of Western thought has opposed a biblical understanding of how God saves. We often insist that individuals must stand on their own two feet and take care of their own needs. Even Christians have fallen into the trap that thinks we can take care of ourselves. We act as if salvation depends on our proper mission methods and evangelism programs rather than the Word of God. After all, God's responsibility for our lives seems to contradict human responsibility. Since we would never deny our own authority, God's responsibility is pushed aside.

Pelagianism. Historically, the most important heresy that asserts human responsibility for salvation is named for the fourth-century monk Pelagius. Pelagius believed that human beings were essentially good and that they simply needed to make good choices to bring about their salvation. Against Augustine he advanced the view that believers take the initial and fundamental steps toward salvation by their own efforts. Once they have

24 Small Catechism II 4 (*LSCE*, 17).

begun the process, God adds His grace to bring these efforts to perfection. Pelagianism fails to see the depth of the problem of sin and the totality of the work of God for salvation.[25]

Semi-Pelagianism. Trying to balance God's grace and human effort, Semi-Pelagianism teaches that grace is always necessary to complete, if not to initiate, the process of becoming righteous. It mixes grace and human effort in various measures, trying to preserve some role for grace and some role for humans. The distinction between the two kinds of righteousness is simply lost in this view.

Synergism. Synergism confesses that sinners are saved by grace alone as long as they are willing to receive it. Sinners must reach out their hands to receive the gift. They must stop by the post office to pick up what God sends, even though He sends it without cost. Synergism thus operates with an adult model for the interaction between God and the sinner, presuming that God delivers His gift of grace according to the pattern by which adults receive gifts. This view, along with Pelagianism and Semi-Pelagianism, sets aside Christ's description of our entry into God's kingdom as "new birth" (John 3:3–8) and our need to become children to enter God's kingdom (Matthew 18:3). It also sets aside the judgment that sinners are not merely sick or in a state of disrepair when we live apart from God. Indeed, we are dead in trespasses and sin, in need of the Spirit to make us new (Ephesians 2:1–3).

In contrast to the synergists, conversion as Christ describes it is a matter of new birth, not of concluding an agreement or reaching out a hand, however weakened by sin it might be, to receive the gift. Such descriptions were available to Jesus and Paul. They chose instead to assert our need to die and be reborn (Romans 6:3–11; Colossians 2:11–15); they chose to describe our coming into the kingdom of God as new birth (John 3:5). The Holy Spirit re-creates—regenerates and renews—the human creature who has been dead in sin when He gives the gift of faith, the relationship of the child with the heavenly Father (Titus 3:5–8).

Conversion: God's New Creation

The mechanics of how sinners return to fearing, loving, and trusting God above all things must remain a mystery in the final analysis. Nonetheless, the parallels between God's creation of Adam and Eve and His re-creation of those who are mired in sin help explain the conversion of sinners. God took the dust and breathed into it the breath of life, and Adam became a human creature. God was the sole subject of the action. No pile of dust volunteered to become human. God did not seek out one healthy heap

25 Kelly, *Early Christian Doctrines*, 357–72; Pelikan, *Emergence of the Catholic Tradition*, 307–18.

of humus that would make a decision to accept God's offer and commit itself to the task of receiving God's breath. God created by His own power, without any help from the dirt. Similarly, using Christ's description of the new birth, no sinners contribute to the decision of their own salvation, any more than they contributed to the decision to be conceived and born physically. Our parents did not invite us to join them in discussing our own conceptions. They did not ask us whether we wished to be born. They gave us the gift of life without our request or help.

To return to the analogy between creation and re-creation, God's sovereign action transformed dust into humanity through His breath. The difference between dust and a human creature is quite obvious. Nonetheless, the elements of both are the same physical elements. The dust was transformed, but its material reality remained in the newly fashioned human creature. When adult humans are re-created, God fashions His own children from those who were dead in trespasses and sins. Nonetheless, the psychological elements of His human creatures do not disappear. They remain a part of the person who is converted, and God's Spirit moves in and through the human body in conversion.

For this reason, the preachers of God's Word proclaim, invite, and command repentance. They know that this re-creative Word works through the imaginations, minds, and wills of those who are dead in trespasses and sin. Just as Christ commanded the dead Lazarus to come forth from his tomb (John 11:43–44), so the language of command can be used as God converts or re-creates sinners. He does not void or ignore our humanity. He works with us as the psychological beings He created. Just as metal has characteristics that allow it to be melted and refashioned but does not have the ability to melt and refashion itself, so sinners already are the human creatures who can be reborn as God's children, but they do not have the ability to give themselves new birth.

God is in control of conversion. He re-creates by His sovereign act as He shapes our minds, emotions, and wills to receive the gift of His favor and love. The Holy Spirit reforms minds and hearts that were set on created things instead of on Him (Romans 8:5–11). The Holy Spirit leads sinners out of self-centered lives focused on pleasure into true life, which produces the fruits of the Spirit. Sinners thus die to the old way of thinking and living, crucified to the passions and desires that rule human flesh apart from God's Spirit (Galatians 5:16–24; cf. Ephesians 2:1–10). The old way of thinking and willing is set aside as the Holy Spirit moves our psyches, forming them in Christ's image. No one experiences this change, this conversion, unless Christ draws us out of unfaith into faith (John 6:44). Only by God's power do those who have fled from His presence become His children once again

(John 1:12–13; Jeremiah 31:18). He raises those dead in trespasses and sins to new life (Ephesians 2:1–10; Colossians 2:12). In desperation over his own weakness, Paul could cry out: "Wretched man that I am! Who will deliver me from this body of death?" His answer is ours too: "Thanks be to God through Jesus Christ our Lord!" (Romans 7:24–25).

Although God does it all, that does not mean that believers are uninvolved in the work of the Spirit. We experience a change in our bodies, our minds, and our emotions when we come to faith. By the Spirit who works through the Word, we move from guilt over sin to comfort in the Gospel. We change from fear of death to assurance of eternal life in Christ. We gladly pray to God as our Father who loves us in Jesus instead of seeing God as a terrifying Judge. In the Apology of the Augsburg Confession, Philip Melanchthon insisted that Spirit-wrought faith brings consolation and comfort to terrified consciences.[26] For many who do not know a time before Christ, this change may not be so apparent. For those who come to the faith later in life or come back to Christ, the experience of the Holy Spirit's work is often more obvious. To be clear, we are not saved because of our emotional or mental changes, and we should never look to our personal experience to have confidence in salvation. Instead, we must always look to Jesus whose Word moves into our hearts, minds, and soul by the Spirit to bring us to saving faith in the crucified and risen Savior.

Because Christians experience the work of the Spirit in our bodies, some may experience "accepting" Jesus Christ as their Lord and Savior while others may feel more like they fell in love and faith just happened to them. Some believers will articulate their faith as "committing" to Jesus in mind and will. Two things must be remembered here. First, far more important is God's acceptance of us as His children and His commitment to be our God and Father. Second, the Holy Spirit enables and empowers our minds and hearts to accept and commit. He always chooses us first and loves us first (John 15:16; 1 John 4:19).

From Death to Life in Christ

The Holy Spirit raises the dead to life through His re-creative Word, as it comes in all forms of the means of grace. In adults, God first works a sense of death. Sinners perceive the seriousness of their situation before their wills are moved by the Holy Spirit to want to do anything about it. God's plan for human life, His Law, reveals that life apart from God has failed (Romans 3:20; 1 Corinthians 15:56). The Law breaks the spirit of self-sufficiency and rebellion, often without directly accusing and condemning.

26 Apology of the Augsburg Confession IV 36–47, 62; see also Zahl, *Holy Spirit and Christian Experience*, 118–36, on "Philip Melanchthon's Soteriology of Consolation."

A slowly growing sense of inadequacy can bring people to recognize their desperate need for change, for conversion, just as effectively as a sudden crisis, in which old ways of life fall apart. Both may be more effective than the direct accusation voiced by Christians.

That direct confrontation is sometimes necessary, but it can also make sinners rebel even more. "Some, who are enemies of the law because it prohibits what they want to do and commands what they do not want to do, become worse because of it. On account of this, insofar as they are not restrained by punishment, they act against the law even more than before."[27] In whatever form the Law puts the squeeze on life lived in reliance on false gods, it attacks the sinner's falsely placed sense of identity, security, and meaning. It calls into question a way of life based on false gods and false goals. It ultimately challenges the idolatry that pretends we can secure life on the basis of someone or something God has made, not on God Himself.

Paul noted that this confrontation with the Law "grieves" sinners. He rejoiced in that, not because the Corinthians grieved but because they "were grieved into repenting. … For godly grief produces a repentance that leads to salvation without regret" (2 Corinthians 7:9–10). In this passage, Paul spoke of the repentance that believers experience, but the grief of sinners who repent for the first time is similar. The Holy Spirit Himself uses the Law, in its various forms, to convict sinners of their false belief and of their false conduct (John 17:8–11).

People may be tempted to ask—in one last attempt to contribute something to their own rebirth—what they have to do to be worthy of God's grace. The biblical answer is "nothing," both in the realm of the Law's doing the sinner to death and in the Gospel's bringing the person dead in trespasses to life again. Some Christians believe that they must at least muster a sufficiently sincere sorrow to make themselves look pitiful enough to attract God's mercy. **Contrition**—sorrow over sin—is necessary in the life of the new child of God. But the destruction of our old mind-set, our old idolatries, requires nothing but that fear the Law induces. A certain psychological level of terror is no prerequisite; neither is a certain quantity of grief or sorrow. "Contrition is not even a good work. For contrition that comes before faith is nothing but suffering on the part of human beings. It consists of anguish, pain, torment, and a feeling of being crushed—all of which God has caused in human beings with the hammer of the Law."[28] Sinners do not generate this fear in themselves. Life as God has created it hems, squeezes, and finally crushes those who try to break out of its form. That hemming,

27 Smalcald Articles III II 2 (Kolb-Wengert, 311–12).

28 C. F. W. Walther, *Law and Gospel*, trans. Christian Tiews, ed. Charles P. Schaum (St. Louis: Concordia, 2010), 276.

squeezing, and crushing brings sinners into the consciousness of their own death. That suffices to open them for the Holy Spirit's delivery of the Gospel.

The Holy Spirit can use the wide variety of human experience with flaws and failures to convict unbelievers of the inadequacy of their old gods. He comes with the Gospel revealed in Jesus Christ and conveyed through the Scriptures to raise those dead in trespasses to new life in Christ, lived out in trust in Him (John 15:26; 16:14–15). God has made the dead come to life by exchanging their death and His, by substituting His reclaimed, resurrected life for theirs (Ephesians 2:1–10). He has taken those who were "not a people" and through the blood of Christ has brought the alienated and strangers, the dead, into His own living family (1 Peter 2:10). There they find peace as the Holy Spirit makes them His dwelling place (Ephesians 2:11–22). This He does by proclaiming a word, which bespeaks them righteous. He re-creates as He created, through the power of His Word, which announces new life in Christ (Romans 10:17; 1 Peter 1:23). "For God, who said, 'Let light shine out of darkness,' has shone in our hearts to give the light of the knowledge of the glory of God in the face of Jesus Christ" (2 Corinthians 4:6). Thus He opens hearts through preaching (Acts 16:14). When it seems that we are working out our own salvation through the acts of our minds and hearts, it is God who is at work in us (Philippians 2:13).

The Holy Spirit's Work and Our Rhythm of Law and Gospel

The Holy Spirit works through the Word proclaimed and shared by believers. Christians, therefore, must attend to the Scriptures diligently so that they know God's message well. They must be sensitive to the needs of their hearers to speak both Law and Gospel. At the same time, the Holy Spirit is in charge of the entire witnessing process, guiding both speaker and hearer. He works sometimes despite His people more than through us. Believers must avoid not only a synergism of believing but also a synergism of witnessing. Believers must acknowledge the total sovereignty of the Holy Spirit over the one who is witnessing. We are indeed the Spirit's tools and even co-workers (1 Thessalonians 3:2), but we contribute nothing to the conversion of the other person (1 Corinthians 3:7). God is working in, with, and under us as we speak His Word.

The conversion, re-creation, of the sinner is instantaneous, yet it lasts throughout human life. God establishes His relationship with us through His sure promise. Yet the psychological weaning from false gods and the dawning of knowledge and the emotional commitment that builds on the knowledge of Jesus Christ continue throughout life on earth. "When our Lord and Master Jesus Christ said, 'Repent,' he willed the entire life of believers to be one of repentance."[29] When Christ calls us, "His call leads us to death."[30] Some who stand on the promise struggle with doubts, believing that they might not believe. Others lose some confidence or knowledge in Christ and question whether they are still in a faithful relationship with their Lord.

Our responses to those caught in such quandaries must be exercised within the distinction of Law and Gospel. We will respond to their questions only when we know why they want to know. For those who are resisting faith, the Law must be used to remind them that there is no God but Yahweh, and that our whole lives must rest in Him. For those who are broken in their confidence, losing their sense of ultimate identity, security, and meaning, the Gospel must bring reassurance of God's love and favor in Christ. Only in and through this Word does the Holy Spirit promise to produce faith.

The Word springs from the Holy Spirit as it comes in Baptism and absolution, in preaching and Christian conversation, in the Lord's Supper and in books, blogs, and electronic media of all kinds. These channels convey what God has revealed in Jesus Christ, as we learn from the Scriptures.

---

29 *Ninety-Five Theses* (1517), Thesis 1, AE 31:25.

30 Dietrich Bonhoeffer, *Discipleship*, vol. 4 of Dietrich Bonhoeffer Works, ed. Geffrey B. Kelly and John D. Godsey (Minneapolis: Fortress, 2001), 87.

CHAPTER 13
HOLY SCRIPTURE

IN the Bible, God speaks to His creatures. Nothing is more central to the doctrine of Holy Scripture than this fact: the Spirit moves through the pages of the Bible so that God's voice resounds and His purpose in Christ is accomplished. The God whose voice created light in the void bespeaks the new creation through the words of Holy Writ. The Word who became flesh for the redemption of the corrupted creation presents Himself to His people in the text of the Bible. The Spirit who delivered the Gospel to the nations blows through the pages to convict of sin and beget faith in the Savior. Martin Luther wrote: "Nowhere can the Spirit be found more present and more active than in the very holy letters which he wrote."[1] While the doctrine of Holy Scripture says more than this, nothing dare overshadow the reality of the Bible as God's living and active Word to His people.

The central "shape" of the Word is Jesus Christ, the incarnate Word, God in the flesh (John 1:14). All forms of the Word—oral, written, and sacramental—are God's Word because their content is the Lord Jesus. Thus Holy Scripture in both the Old and New Testaments finds its center in Jesus Christ, which is termed **Christocentricity**. In the Spirit, Moses proclaimed the Christ even if he did not consciously realize it. David witnessed to the One who is both his Lord and his Son. The prophets testified by the Spirit to the coming Messiah. The Old Testament speaks about Jesus less directly than the New, but its witness to Christ is no less central to its character. In fact, the Old Testament's importance in the church may not be diminished because its witness is less direct. God's people find eternal life in Holy Scripture, both Old and New Testaments, because it testifies to Jesus, who is life (John 5:39–40).

The Holy Scriptures that the church has today are God's authoritative, reliable Word through which we have access to the preaching and teaching of the prophets and apostles. We must learn to see the Bible as the book of the church, to be read in Christ's church and as a member of His Body. Only then do we learn to interpret—better: be interpreted by—the Scriptures as the

1 *D. Martin Luthers Werke* (Weimar: Böhlau, 1883–1993), 7:97.2–3.

words of the human prophets and apostles that are yet the living and breathing Word of God, judging, convicting, saving, and re-creating by the Spirit.

The Book of the Church

Holy Scripture's proper context is the church of God gathered under the triune name, with words of confession on believers' lips, words of forgiveness ringing in their ears, prayers for the broken world on their tongues, the bread which is Christ's body in hand, the wine that is Christ's blood in the throat, and praise of the God of Israel echoing in the sanctuary. Holy Scripture is read properly when it is read in this setting with these people of God—living and sainted—confessing the faith that has been received.

Context makes all the difference when it comes to interpretation. Imagine hearing the confession "Jesus is Lord" for the first time from someone coming at you with a sword on the battlefield compared to hearing it from a friend praying for you at the hospital or a preacher after the Gospel reading and acclamation. While Jesus is the same Lord regardless of context, each confession will be understood—interpreted—differently because the battlefield depicts Jesus as a very different Lord from the church in worship. The same is true about biblical interpretation. If one considers the university as the Bible's proper context, Holy Scripture will seem like an object of research—historical, religious, and/or anthropological—subject to the questions and concerns of modern scholars rather than the Spirit's purpose through the prophets and apostles. Some modern Christians treat the Bible as if its proper context is me, my individual story and life. Construed in this way, the Bible appears as a repository of ideas, by which the individual is told what things she must believe, or a guidebook for life, by which the individual reads the Bible for tips on how to live. Although the Bible contains both true doctrine and God's commands for human living, reducing the Bible to merely true ideas or divine advice does not grasp the fullness of God's Word.

As the book of the church, Holy Scripture is properly understood within the story of God—creation, salvation, sanctification, and consummation—for the purpose of making sinners "wise for salvation through faith in Christ Jesus" and equipping men and women of God for good works (2 Timothy 3:15–16). The church is the community that confesses this story and seeks to live under and in the Word of God that is life and truth itself.

The Story of Scripture: The Gospel at the Center

When Hopkins was learning Greek, he once asked his professor how he knew to translate a particularly thorny Greek sentence correctly when another option was also grammatically accurate. The professor responded: "Once you know what it says, then you can translate it correctly." It seems counterintuitive that to translate a word properly the translator must know what the sentence says, but interpretation—reading and understanding texts—always moves in two directions. The words themselves help the reader to understand the text, but the whole story also illumines the words, what each part means. What is true about translating Greek is also true about interpreting Holy Writ. Once we know how the story runs—the identities of the characters and the major plot points—we are able to understand Holy Scripture properly. To be clear, the point is not that God cannot speak through the Scriptures to new Christians or non-Christians—He most certainly can and does!—but scriptural understanding tends to take wisdom and growth in maturity (cf. Hebrews 5:12–14). Those who have been taught the whole story of God by the Spirit—creation, fall, calling of Abraham, redemption of Israel, and the culmination of God's promises in the death and resurrection of the Messiah—are more likely to read the Scriptures as the Word of the triune God, see themselves as sinful creatures in need of redemption by Christ, depend on the promise as children of Abraham through Jesus, pray boldly to the Father in the Spirit, and follow God's Law, all at the direction of the Spirit through the Word.

The story of Scripture thus acts as a guidebook or map—often called a **hermeneutical key**—to help in interpreting the Bible. Just as a map indicates how a city is connected to other locations via highways, byways, and waterways, so the story of Scripture provides the logic to connect the identity of the one God—Father, Son, and Holy Spirit—and God's salvific work with His creatures to each book of the Bible and its contents. For example, the book of Esther is not just a dramatic narrative of intrigue, poetic justice, and courage. Esther depicts the providential work of God who refuses to abandon His people, saving them in the midst of their darkest hour and prefiguring the messianic history of the cross—even though the book never mentions God directly. Like all books of Holy Scripture, Esther finds its meaning in relationship to God, His work and promises, as portrayed in the whole scope of the Bible.

The church has called the summaries of the narrative of Scripture for public teaching the **rule of faith** (*regula fidei* in Latin). St. Irenaeus, a second-century church father, articulated the rule of faith against Gnostics who claimed Jesus and the Gospel for themselves while denigrating the body and the Old Testament. Irenaeus showed their heresy by pointing to the basic story, what he called "the canon of the truth."[2] This canon essentially stated the content of the Apostles' Creed: The Father created all things. The same Father sent His Son by the power of the Spirit to be born of the virgin Mary in the flesh. Jesus suffered under Pontius Pilate, was crucified, died and

2 J. N. D. Kelly, *Early Christian Doctrines* (New York: Harper & Row, 1960), 37.

buried, raised from the dead on the third day, ascended into heaven, and is coming again to raise all flesh and usher in the new age of the kingdom of God through the Spirit. Gnostic interpretations of the Gospel were thus ruled out by the rule of faith since the rule confesses that salvation in Christ is part of the same work of God who created all things and who will raise all human flesh on the Last Day.

Different forms of the rule of faith appeared in the early church. Anchored in the ancient creeds—which themselves are summaries of the apostolic teaching found in Holy Scripture—different forms of the rule of faith address pressing needs of the time, helping the church confess the Gospel against false teachings. The rule of faith, then, provides fence posts to show what kinds of biblical interpretation fall outside the bounds of the scriptural narrative. For example, Christians cannot understand the Bible in such a way that it teaches material creation to be evil or irrelevant. Neither can Christians interpret the Bible to say that Jesus is not one God with the Father and the Spirit nor to say anything other than that Christ was crucified and killed in Palestine of the first century and raised from the dead on the third day. The rule of faith rules out false interpretations before they ever happen.

Reformation theology added an additional element to the rule of faith that was present in the church fathers' thinking but not always in their articulations of the *regula fidei*. The Lutheran Confessions insisted that salvation in Christ alone—the good news of the free grace of God in Jesus, the Gospel—is another fence that cannot be crossed. Lutherans are Christians who insist that the Gospel is the central and ultimate Word of God. The Scriptures certainly speak Law too, but God's final and most important Word is not command or accusation but promise in Jesus Christ. If the Scriptures are read without understanding the text in relationship to the God who justifies the ungodly by faith in Jesus apart from all human performance, that interpretation will be mistaken.[3] Additionally, the Bible cannot be read to teach that God's salvation is contingent on human activity or status. Instead, what Luther insisted in light of a coming church council applies equally to interpreting the Bible: "Nothing in this article [of justification by faith] can be conceded or given up, even if heaven and earth or whatever is transitory passed away. As St. Peter says in Acts 4[:12]: 'There is no other name ... given among mortals by which we must be saved.'"[4] Whenever the Scriptures are read apart from Jesus as our justification, they are misinterpreted as a book

3 The distinction between the formal principle—Scripture as the final source and authority for Christian faith and practice—and the material principle—God's justification of the ungodly apart from works—of Lutheran theology should be understood in this way.

4 Smalcald Articles II 5 (Kolb-Wengert, 301).

full of ideas to understand or rules to live by rather than the piercing Word of God that cuts to each person's heart, discerning thoughts and intentions and carrying out God's salvific will (Hebrews 4:12). In Reformation theology, the rule of faith tells the story of God's restoration of His fallen creatures, in which the forgiveness of sins is promised by grace alone as the Holy Spirit creates faith in the only-begotten Son to the glory of the Father.

Scripture's Purpose: Saving Faith and Maturity in the Community of Faith

The re-creative Word of the Lord is the text of Holy Scripture. St. John admitted that he could have written more about Jesus' life. What he did write, however, was enough. It was written so that its readers "may believe that Jesus is the Christ, the Son of God, and that by believing you may have life in His name" (John 20:31). Similarly, the apostle wrote his first epistle so that his readers "may know that you have eternal life" (1 John 5:13). "You have been acquainted with the sacred writings, which are able to make you wise for salvation through faith in Christ Jesus" (2 Timothy 3:15). "Whatever was written in former days was written for our instruction, that through endurance and through the encouragement of the Scriptures we might have hope" (Romans 15:4).

The primary purpose of the Scriptures is to bring fallen sinners to salvation. They do so by bringing sinners first to repentance, leading us to recognize our idolatry, all of our false sources of comfort and meaning. The Bible shows just how lost we are without the grace of God in Jesus. The Word, then, acquaints sinners with Christ, and the Spirit uses the Word to cultivate God's gift of faith through the Gospel. As Luther asserted about what constitutes Holy Scripture: each book "preaches and drives Christ home."[5] In so doing it functions as God's power in the lives of believers (Romans 1:16).

Alongside this central purpose of making believers "wise for salvation," the inspired Scriptures are useful "for teaching, for reproof, for correction, and for training in righteousness" (2 Timothy 3:16). Believers use them to learn more of God's gracious will and wondrous ways. They use them to rebuke and correct false ideas, which interfere with a proper understanding of God's Word. They use them to grow in the practice of godly living. The goal of the church's use of the Bible is that believers may enjoy the fullest renewal of their humanity possible—that they may become complete or mature—and thus be equipped for every good work (2 Timothy 3:17).

As the biblical message comes to believers through apostles, prophets, evangelists, pastors, and teachers, the saints of the church of God are

5 Quoted in Oswald Bayer, *Martin Luther's Theology: A Contemporary Interpretation*, trans. Thomas H. Trapp (Grand Rapids; Eerdmans, 2008), 82. See AE 35:396.

equipped for the work of ministry. The church is edified so that the saints might become one in their faith, in their knowledge of God's Son, and thus that they might be mature by the measure of Christ. This means that the Scriptures will prevent them from being tossed to and fro with every wind of cunning, crafty, and deceitful views of life. Instead, they will grow up in Christ, joined together as they are in Christ's Body, and they will speak God's truth to one another in love. Christ is conforming His people to Himself through the Spirit by the power of His Word to make sure that His Body continues to grow (Ephesians 4:11–16). The Scriptures do not have in view only the purpose of fostering individual faith and sanctification but also the purpose of building up the Body of Christ as a community of faith, called to deliver the Gospel and serve their neighbors in Christ's stead. The Scriptures gather God's people together to join with angels, saints, and martyrs in confessing the faith and giving praise to God and the Lamb, prefiguring the age to come (Revelation 7:9–12; cf. Mark 8:35–38).

Christian maturity and unity of faith, which the Scriptures cultivate, is grounded in trust in Jesus and the sure hope in His continuing presence. "For whatever was written in former days was written for our instruction, that through endurance and through the encouragement of the Scriptures we might have hope" (Romans 15:4). The Word of the Lord, as conveyed by apostles and prophets, forms the foundation of the whole church and of its individual members' lives. Thus this Word from God binds believers together in God's temple (Ephesians 2:19–22). The "apostles and prophets" mentioned by St. Paul are likely the apostles of the New Testament and the prophets of the Old Testament.[6] Their message is delivered to Christians in the twenty-first century through the Scriptures. Although sainted long before, the apostles continue to exercise their office as ambassadors of the Lord through their writings.[7]

Holy Scripture's Priority over the Church

Like the perennial chicken-and-egg question, theologians often ask, which came first, the Bible or the church?[8] On the one hand, the Bible clearly precedes the New Testament church. Moses himself was the first we know to have written down God's Word for His people (Exodus 34:27), more than a

---

6 It is possible that the passage may refer to two New Testament offices that were bringing the Word of the Lord to Paul's contemporaries. If so, these offices were yet rooted in the message of the prophets of the Old Testament and the apostles of the New.

7 Oscar Cullmann, *Peter—Disciple, Apostle, Martyr*, trans. Floyd V. Filson (Cleveland: World, 1953), 215–23.

8 For a helpful discussion that differs from ours (Hopkins and Kolb), putting the Bible and the church on relatively equal terms, see Brad East, *The Doctrine of Scripture* (Eugene, OR: Cascade Books, 2021), 9–36.

millennium before the birth of Jesus. The Torah, the prophetic writings, and the Psalms were stored together in Solomon's temple, indicating their sacred status (cf. 2 Kings 22:8).[9] In the first century, then, Jesus and His apostles knew the Holy Scriptures, having heard and read the Tanak—the Torah, prophets (*Nevi'im* in Hebrew), and writings (*Ketuvim* in Hebrew), the three traditional divisions of the Jewish Scriptures. In fact, Protestant rejection of the **deuterocanonical** books—the so-called second canon books that are included in Roman Catholic and Orthodox Bibles, often labeled "the Apocrypha"—followed a distinction made in the fourth century by St. Jerome and should be understood from this perspective. Jesus knew and used the Old Testament Scriptures as the Word of God, but the authority and status of the deuterocanonical books for Him and the apostles are not so clear.[10] If the deuterocanonical books are to be used by Christians today, they should not be accorded the same authority as Moses, the prophets, or the apostles—as Luther did in reading these texts as helpful wisdom but not as the inspired and authoritative Word of God.[11]

On the other hand, the nascent Christian Church existed without any New Testament books for at least a generation. The apostles preached, the evangelists witnessed, and Christian believers told their neighbors and friends about the coming of the King, who was murdered and buried but left the tomb behind. The witness of Jesus Christ took place without the New Testament Scriptures—while the experiences of the first generation of believers still guided the testimony—and the church blossomed and grew (Acts 2:42–47). The apostles had to make decisions about challenging issues in the church (Acts 15), and they had to write scathing letters in the Spirit to call the church to repentance and back to the free grace of the Gospel of God (Galatians). Nevertheless, many will point out that the church continued without a New Testament canon for centuries.

Scholars who emphasize the priority of the church will add that the church itself decided on the **canon**—the list of authoritative books for the Christian faith. The church had to choose which books would count as Holy Scripture and which would not. The Council of Nicaea in AD 325 literally voted to consider some texts as authoritative while others were rejected. Skeptical scholars, such as Bart Ehrman, argue that the divinity of Christ was at issue, indicating that the Nicene fathers voted for texts that confirmed

---

9 See Andrew E. Steinmann, *The Oracles of God: The Old Testament Canon* (St. Louis: Concordia Academic Press, 1999), 13–85.

10 Steinmann, *Oracles of God*, 109–10.

11 Robert Kolb, *Martin Luther and the Enduring Word of God: The Wittenberg School and Its Scripture-Centered Proclamation* (Grand Rapids: Baker Academic, 2016), 94–97.

their beliefs in Christ as God while rejecting those that said otherwise.[12] It seems like the church decided on the canon.

The historical reality, however, is much more complicated (and orthodox) than the prior paragraph suggests. Three things must be kept in mind. First, the fathers at Nicaea were not voting on all religious books as if any religious text had an equal chance to be considered Christian Scripture. Heretical writings had already been discarded by the church on the basis of the Gospel and the rule of faith. No Gnostic text—or any that denied Christ's identity as the incarnate Son of the Father, who made all things—could be considered Holy Scripture by a church that received the Old Testament as God's Word and the rule of faith as its confession. The council was only voting on *Christian* books that confessed Jesus Christ in accordance with the rule of faith. The question at issue was not whether these books confessed the truth of Jesus by the Spirit but whether they had the authority to serve the church catholic in the stead of the apostles.

Second, the canon formed much earlier than Nicaea. Already in the second century, the four Gospels were collected in one codex, one bound volume, as well as the epistles of Paul.[13] Like the Old Testament books placed together in the temple, the collection of texts in one book indicate they were understood as a unified, authoritative witness to Christ and apostolic preaching, and these writings were publicly read in worship as such. The church's collection of these texts was not political or arbitrary; it was led by the Holy Spirit as He inspired faith in Jesus, guided pure proclamation of the Gospel, and cultivated holiness and love in the church through these apostolic words. Already in the first century, certain documents, Gospel accounts and epistles, won a place alongside the Old Testament Scriptures in the public reading of the church. In so doing, the canon was being formed organically as the church confirmed these texts to be apostolic witnesses to the Gospel and a vehicle of the Spirit to create faith in the Savior. As the process continued, the canon came to be recognized by the church, but it was not created by the church. The Spirit, whom Jesus promised would lead the church into all truth, led also the process by which the texts of the apostles and evangelists came to be seen as that which they really are, the Word of God (John 16:13; 1 Thessalonians 2:13).[14]

12 For a detailed argument against this position, see Ben Witherington III, "Why the Lost Gospels Lost Out," *Christianity Today* (June 2004): 26–32.

13 Witherington, "Why the Lost Gospels Lost Out," 28–29. See also Harry Gamble, *Books and Readers in the Early Church* (New Haven, CT: Yale University Press, 1995).

14 The Holy Spirit's work in guiding the process by which God's Word has come to the contemporary church through canonization and translation is emphasized in East, *Doctrine of Scripture*, 32–36. East concludes, however, that the church should accept the

Third, we should not understand the formation of the New Testament canon on a human level as an act of the church trying to consolidate its power—after all, the church without power, under persecution, began to collect the Scriptures together through the Spirit as God's authoritative Word. Instead, the formation of the New Testament canon *on a human level* became natural and necessary as soon as the apostles began to die. While the apostles themselves were alive, no texts were necessary to record their words. Their witness was part of their everyday communication with the church of God. As the apostles began to fall asleep in the Lord, however, putting their words to the page became necessary so that the church might continue to be built on the witness of the apostles to the Lord Jesus (Ephesians 2:20). In fact, the officially adopted canon arose out of the usage of texts in congregations for worship, catechesis, and devotion, and that usage arose because the books that were being heard and employed convinced believers that they bore God's voice to them, the same voice they had heard in the apostles. For the church today as well, the Scriptures are the continued witness of the prophets and the apostles, grounding the church on the cornerstone which is Jesus Christ.

For Lutheran theology, the church can never be understood as primary over the Scriptures. While the Holy Spirit led the Body of Christ in forming the canon (and in translating the Bible), and the Bible's proper context for interpretation is the believing, tasting, and praying community, the church always kneels before the Word of God, looking to receive from Him through the Bible. Hence, in worship, some bring the Gospel into the center of the congregation, venerate the Gospel, and cross lips, head, and heart to show that the church stands beneath the Word of God. Other congregations may simply stand in honor of Christ and the Gospel. No matter what practices adorn the reading of the Word, the point is not to worship a book but to worship the God who inspired the prophets, apostles, and evangelists and speaks through the Bible. Therefore, God's Word must stand ever as the judge, standard, and center of the life of the church, calling it to repentance, incising any false teachings, shaping its proclamation toward the Gospel, forming it into Christ for His mission, and edifying it for maturity and good works.

The Nature of Holy Scripture

Scripture is quite modest about itself. It mentions itself seldom, and it never explains the mechanics of its origin. Its occasional references to its origin and nature assure us, however, that its writings, like Jesus, are fully divine

---

deuterocanonical books as Scripture. This conclusion does not follow necessarily from East's premise.

and fully human, completely God's Word and completely human language. In the Bible, the Holy Spirit speaks the authoritative Word of God through and as the human words and witness of the apostles and the prophets.

The Human Nature of Scripture

In human history, God's Word took shape first in oral form, in human language, a created element that God has chosen as the instrument of His re-creative speaking to His human creatures. The prophets "spoke from God as they were carried along by the Holy Spirit" (2 Peter 1:21; e.g., 2 Samuel 23:2; Isaiah 6:8–10; Jeremiah 1:7–8). How the Word of the Lord came to the prophets is not explained. False prophets also spoke, but somehow the Holy Spirit guided the people of God to recognize true prophets while many followed false prophets (Jeremiah 23:9–40; cf. Deuteronomy 18:20–22). Then, God turned the prophetic Word to written form. God commanded Moses to write down God's Law (Exodus 34:27). He commanded Jeremiah to record all the words that He had spoken to the prophet, for He wanted His Word, delivered to Jeremiah, to be at the disposal of His people when He later restored their fortunes in the land (Jeremiah 30:1–3). Jesus is the Word become flesh who also preached the Word and sent out His apostles to do the same (Luke 24:46–49). The apostles' message was consequently recognized as God's Word (1 Thessalonians 2:13), not only in its oral but also in its written form (Ephesians 3:2–6; 1 Corinthians 14:37; 2 Peter 3:15–16).

Many conservative Christians are predisposed to treat the Bible like a divine Word from heaven, ignoring its historical character as a human word. The contrast between the Qur'an, the Islamic holy book, and the Bible is instructive. The Qur'an was delivered by the angel Gabriel directly from heaven to the prophet Muhammad. Muhammad did not include his own thoughts or experiences in the Qur'an at all. It is purely a divine message, not at all contingent on time or history. Thus the only true Qur'an is in the original Arabic, for any translation would change the perfection of the text. Christian Scripture is different. The Holy Spirit inspired the prophets and apostles in history, through their experiences, not apart from them. For instance, Jeremiah wept, wailed, and lamented, proclaiming the Word of the Lord as one who was a laughingstock and reproach among the people (Jeremiah 20). Isaiah's vision of the Lord filling the temple happened in the year of King Uzziah's death (Isaiah 6). Because the Bible is not timeless truths but the prophetic and apostolic witness to the triune God who creates and redeems in history, the Bible has been translated into hundreds of languages across the world. The Yale Divinity School missiologist Lamin Sanneh, born into a Muslim family in The Gambia and converted to the Christian faith in his youth, argued that God is a translating communicator as we encounter Him in Scripture. The Second Person of the Trinity translated Himself into human flesh. We have very few of His own words in His native tongue, which was probably Aramaic, but we have them instead in Greek. Hence, Christians coming into another culture immediately learn the language and begin translating Scripture and other important witnesses into the native tongue.[15] The Spirit works through the Word of Christ in any language and culture to bring about faith (Romans 10:17).

The Bible is God's own Word, but it is cast in human language, composed under the Spirit's direction by human beings who wrote in the same way as other ancient documents were written. This coheres with the basic reality of the triune God: God acts in history. He revealed Himself by sending "a strong east wind" to divide waters and thereby save His chosen people (Exodus 14:21–29). He directed His people's exile and their return from exile (Nehemiah 1:8–9). The eternal Son was born as a fully human creature, a Jew, at a specific time in human history to be "crucified under Pontius Pilate," as believers regularly confess. God also reveals Himself in Scripture's pages in a totally human way. He has taken human language written in normal human fashion, set in specific contexts in human history, as the means by which He conveys His saving truth and power to us.

The writers of Scripture, therefore, give us glimpses of the human side of the process by which they wrote. John wrote to his fellow believers on the basis of what he had heard, seen, and touched (1 John 1:1), and he wrote because it gave him pleasure to share the Word of life with others (1 John 1:4). The process of writing the Gospel of John included selection of certain materials from a vast array of accounts to report (John 21:24–25). Luke turned eyewitness reports into an orderly narrative based on his research (Luke 1:1–4). The biblical writers used appropriate Hebrew, Aramaic, and Greek grammar and syntax. They used specific literary genres from their time periods, aware of how their message could be framed for their hearers and readers and how their ideas could be effectively conveyed. They wrote aware of their historical situations and bound by them, even as the Holy Spirit gave them words to convey the mysteries of God.

In its original expression in Hebrew, Aramaic, and Greek, and in any good translation, what God has written is apprehensible to readers. God's writers did not use any mysterious code. There is no secret about God's identity, character, or salvation that cannot be recognized by the average reader of Holy Scripture who attends to the words on the page to hear the God of Israel speak in His Son and by His Spirit. The language of the prophets and

15 Lamin Sanneh, *Translating the Message: The Missionary Impact on Culture* (Maryknoll, NY: Orbis, 2009).

apostles is plain, straightforward human language even though it is not our native tongue.

Despite the use of plain, human language by the authors, God's revelation of the mystery of His love is not so readily comprehensible. The human mind can understand that the author was claiming that God has come in human flesh (John 1:14). But the human mind cannot grasp or believe this to be true, apart from the Holy Spirit's aid (1 Corinthians 12:3).

Nonetheless, God's use of human language is not magical even if it conveys mystery. It is not some special "Gnostic" revelation that lies outside human apprehension. The Holy Spirit inspired the authors of the books of the Bible to write within their times, with the knowledge available to them, in forms that were used in their cultures to convey information. It is wrong to dismiss the Scriptures as merely human words. It is just as misleading to assert their divine nature but trap the inspired texts in some literalistic theory of language that reduces their words to symbols for any stray thought a believer may have. Fundamentalist interpreters of Scripture make it into a wax nose when they ignore the historical circumstances in which the biblical writers were inspired. Such interpreters reduce the Bible's words to their own playthings when they impose meanings upon the biblical language that it did not have in the author's use of the language of his time.

Thus believers strive to know as much about the world in which the biblical authors wrote as possible. Archaeological and linguistic studies remove obstacles to God's Word that come to our minds so that we attend to the Holy Spirit's voice as it comes through the message of the writers whom He inspired. At one level, we must read the Scriptures as if they are any other book, for they are plain human language, but we must also read them as they are unlike every other book, for they are the witness of the prophets and apostles to the Lord Jesus, inspired by the Spirit and the very voice of our God.

The Divine Nature of Holy Scripture

"All Scripture is breathed out by God" (*theopneustos*) (2 Timothy 3:16). St. Paul, or any other inspired writer, does not describe the nature or process for how God inspired the words of Scripture. It is simply presumed. Many Jews believed that God's Word spoke to them from the Mosaic and prophetic scrolls in the days after authoritative oral prophecy ceased. They knew that Scripture is the Word of God, as He delivered it to His people. The doctrine of **inspiration** simply teaches this truth: the human words of Scripture are God's own words, breathed out by His Spirit. Some Christians have posited theories of how inspiration might have worked. These theories can direct attention and trust to the process rather than to the Lord who speaks. Speculation about God's means and methods is unnecessary. Human speculation will not secure God's Word. God Himself has made His prophetic word more sure through the revelation of Himself in Jesus Christ (2 Peter 1:19).

Believers simply trust God as He speaks through every word of the Bible. They remember that the Bible, because it is God's Word, is not their own playground, and they dare never turn His Word into a wax sculpture, which they shape according to their own inclinations. In fact, God did not inspire merely the ideas, but the very words of the author—called **verbal inspiration**. The Holy Spirit does not speak in ideas or feelings, but in words that convey Christ and the Gospel. Hence, the apostle writes that "no prophecy of Scripture comes from someone's own interpretation" (2 Peter 1:20). The Holy Spirit moved those whose prophecies are conveyed to us in Scripture's pages; human activity—human thinking, speaking, and writing—was involved, but the impulse for the words lay with the Holy Spirit (2 Peter 1:21).

Some Christians are uncertain that God has really selected elements of His created order to convey His re-creative power and serve as His instruments. They believe that the Word of the Lord may be sought *in* the Scriptures but that the entire Scripture is not God's inspired Word. They believe that God would have no interest in telling us, for instance, that Nimrod was a mighty hunter (Genesis 10:9). The significance of this fact in Genesis is unclear to the authors of this book, but that does not make it any less the Word of God. Whatever the reason for this inspired piece of information, it need not serve some greater purpose in the vertical realm to be the Word of the Lord. God the Creator takes an interest in all of His creation.

God is present in the pages of Scripture. God is not imprisoned or boxed up in these pages, but God is there, waiting for readers who encounter His power in Law and Gospel. He condemns sin and expresses His wrath from its pages, although fallen human creatures encounter the crushing or irritating power of His Law throughout life. He bestows His promises, and through them life, in its pages as well, as the Scriptures testify of Jesus Christ (John 5:39). God bursts forth from the pages of Scripture to do His work. God's presence not only stands behind the words of the Bible by virtue of the Holy Spirit's inspiration; God's presence remains *in* the Scripture as He works through it to deliver the power of salvation in the Gospel to all who use it in their own lives and in the lives of others. Scripture does not merely contain the Word of the Lord; Holy Scripture *is* the Word of God.

Because the Scriptures are the Word of God, who does not lie, many Christians confess the inerrancy of the Bible. The problem with a doctrine of inerrancy, first, is that it delivers the text into human judgment on its "accuracy" or truth. Second, it focuses on the text itself, not the person who is speaking to us from the text. The reliability of God the Spirit establishes the text as that on which we can depend completely for the truth. By stressing the text over the speaker, inerrancy tends to focus believers on unimportant details, such as whether the biblical writers ever contradicted each other or made mistakes of fact that are immaterial to the Gospel (e.g., the chronology of John versus Mark in the story of Jesus' life).[16] Complicating this question is the fact that the cultural and literary expectations of the Gospel writers were far different from our own. No one should think that mistakes were made if the writers followed the expectations of their time for writing a truthful, historical account of Christ's life. Furthermore, inerrancy only applies to the original autographs—the first written manuscripts by the inspired authors—which have been lost to history. Therefore, the real point of the doctrine of **inerrancy** is not to focus Christians on proving the Bible to be right in all details, but to trust in the Bible as the Word of God. Believers must never treat Scripture as if it has errors. Believers attend to the Bible wherein the Spirit speaks the Word of life, the Word of Christ.

Interpreting the Scriptures

To understand the Holy Scriptures as God's Word is one thing, but to interpret Holy Scripture for the church is another. Interpretation is not a science but an art, or better, an act of faith. Interpretation of Holy Scripture happens properly in the midst of prayer, letting God's Word lead believers to come before the Father with all boldness and confidence. Good interpretation takes place in conversation with the assembly of the saints—living and dead—to converse together about what the Word means in life and ministry. Proper Christian interpretation makes connections within the canon, to the story of Scripture, to the doctrine of the church, and to the lives of believers.

Although Christian interpretation of the Bible is a function of faith led by the Spirit, believers proceed from certain fundamental principles to interpret the biblical message. Out of the Lutheran Reformation and Luther's practice of the task of biblical interpretation arose an approach to reading the Scriptures embraced in four principles.

The Clarity of Scripture

First, the Scriptures are clear. This principle of the Bible's **clarity**, also called perspicuity, is not always apparent to those who read it. The principle intends to posit that the Scriptures contain no mysterious language.

16 On the relation of scriptural authority to Christ and the Gospel, see Peter Nafzger, *"These Are Written": Toward a Cruciform Theology of Scripture* (Eugene, OR: Pickwick, 2013).

There is no secret code that has to be broken to understand God's Word, as noted above. Its words are apprehensible to the average reader, even when its message can be received only as a gift through the Holy Spirit. God's wisdom is foolishness to those who operate apart from faith, with a rationalistic or empirical epistemology (1 Corinthians 1:21–25). Paul acknowledged the necessity of destroying arguments and obstacles to the knowledge of God so that the thoughts of believers might be held captive to Christ (2 Corinthians 10:5). Nonetheless, what the biblical writers convey is available to the apprehension of the average reader.

That does not mean that a believer will understand and master every passage of the Bible. Sometimes the diction of an ancient language or the necessary context of a long-lost societal practice makes a text difficult to comprehend. More significant, the wisdom of God is deep and unsearchable, even inscrutable at points, for believers also (Romans 11:33). Peter found some of what Paul had written difficult to understand (2 Peter 3:16). Believers do not trust in their own mastery of Scripture for their ultimate sense of identity, security, and meaning. They trust in the Lord who is present in His Word as it is found in the Bible's pages. They place their lives in the hand of the Lord who is speaking in His Word even when they cannot explain every phrase to their own satisfaction.

Despite the challenges of reading the Bible, Scripture is clear because it is written in plain human language for all to know the triune God through His self-disclosure. In fact, God's gracious message is abundantly clear: "God so loved the world, that He gave His only Son, that whoever believes in Him should not perish but have eternal life" (John 3:16). As Paul writes, sacred Scripture is able to make us wise to salvation through faith in Christ Jesus (2 Timothy 3:15).

The Sufficiency of Scripture

In regard to the knowledge of God and the salvation of human creatures—and there can be no other chief concern for the believer who approaches the Word—Scripture is **sufficient**. Jesus observed, as He put words in Abraham's mouth in telling the story of Lazarus and the rich man, that "they have Moses and the Prophets; let them hear them" (Luke 16:29). God has given human creatures dominion to learn how much of life works in the horizontal realm, which He does not disclose in the revelation of Himself. He comes to us in the Word with the specific knowledge we need to be restored to our relationship with Him. He tells us everything that we need to know about Him as our God and about ourselves as His creatures. For this, the core of human life, the Bible contains all we need to know, even if it does not contain all we want to know.

The Power of Scripture

Third, Scripture is **powerful**, for it instructs us in salvation through faith in Jesus Christ. The word of the prophets could be compared to fire and to a hammer that breaks a rock in pieces (Jeremiah 23:29). The words of Scripture rise from the page to pierce the heart (Hebrews 4:12). John's words about the Word made flesh were written to bring life to those who read them (1 John 5:13; John 20:30–31). They continue the creative speaking of God as they bring sinners to new life in Christ.

Scripture Interprets Scripture

Finally, **Scripture interprets Scripture**. Although this is often understood to mean that unclear passages should be interpreted by clear passages in Scripture, that helpful, practical advice is not the main point. Instead, when Luther spoke about Scripture being its own interpreter, the point was that the Lord alone governs how His Word is to be understood, and He does it by means of the same Word.[17] The Christian can never remove himself from the Word to judge its truth or falsity from the outside. Instead, God's Word remains an authoritative voice outside our control. The Spirit speaks through the Word, accomplishing His purposes (Isaiah 55:10–11). Therefore, the words of Scripture must be read as human words, but their content and significance cannot be judged by human criteria. The Scriptures are interpreted rightly not when they have been explained, but when they have been heard in the condemning force of the Law that exposes human idolatry and in the comforting promise of the Gospel that brings Christ's salvation to sinners. When we are killed and made alive by the Spirit through the text, the text is understood according to God's intent. Hence, theologian Oswald Bayer writes about Luther's view: "The interpreter does not interpret Scripture, but Scripture interprets the interpreter."[18]

To be clear, all sorts of historical and literary research enrich our understanding and apprehension of the text. If the texts of the Bible are not viewed in their historical context, they will be misunderstood. A wooden, overly literalistic use of biblical language does not listen to God but twists the words of the biblical page around the cultural preconceptions informing the reader. It fails to see the Scriptures not only as God's Word to me now, but as God's Word to His people then, of which I am a part in the Body of Christ.

The reader always stands under the biblical text, not over it. Human judgment cannot be exercised against the meaning and message of the text; human judgment can be exercised only in its service. This, of course, is a

---

17 Bayer, *Martin Luther's Theology*, 68–72.

18 Bayer, *Martin Luther's Theology*, 72.

difficult line to draw, even among believers who in good faith wish to place themselves under the text. Cultural presuppositions ambush even the most faithful of believing interpreters and divert them from what the author wrote. Therefore, the whole life of the interpreter of Scripture must be a life of repentance.

Contemporary Methods of Interpretation: Historical Critical and Historical Grammatical

Much discussion of biblical authority in the twentieth century and into the twenty-first has surrounded the use of particular methods, especially those labeled "historical-critical methods." More recently, ideological criticism and critical theory have come to the fore as ways to read the Bible against the grain, looking to reveal power structures implicit in the text.[19] Part of the problem we face in dealing with "historical criticism" is that it means vastly different approaches to Scripture by the wide range of people using it. Believers must remember that every method is devised, and arises, from certain ideological presuppositions. That does not mean that a method may not be used by people with other presuppositions than those of the method's inventors. It does mean that all methods must be examined on the basis of their presuppositions as well as their operational guidelines and practice.

Believers must recognize that the Gospel of Jesus Christ has shone through good methods of biblical interpretation as well as bad, and that good and bad methods have been used to obscure the Gospel. A good tool guided by false presuppositions will not produce correct results. Using a faulty method, such as the ahistorical allegorizing that took place during the medieval period, some teachers of the faith proclaimed God's grace in Jesus Christ, and some did not. Using the same methods of interpretation, reformers of different confessions in the sixteenth century came to different conclusions on important teachings, such as the sacraments. The dogmatic presuppositions that interpreters bring to the text, as well as the conceptual frameworks within which they work, determine to a large extent what they find, whatever method they may use.

Often method can be a vehicle of dogma. Much of what has been practiced under the label **historical criticism** has arisen from one kind of biblical study at the end of the eighteenth and beginning of the nineteenth centuries. Such study was conducted by people who came to the text with the

19 Christopher Watkin has argued the Bible has its own critical theory that deconstructs all the false narratives and stories that every culture tells itself about the world—Lutherans would call this the Law. To better understand critical theory, especially the biblical version, see Christopher Watkin, *Biblical Critical Theory: How the Bible's Unfolding Story Makes Sense of Modern Life and Culture* (Grand Rapids: Zondervan Academic, 2022).

dogmatic presuppositions of the Enlightenment. Their method presumed that the biblical text was not God's Word. It presupposed that human reason, as defined by "enlightened" European minds, was superior to every other cultural system of thought—to say nothing of words that claimed to be the revelation of God Himself. It dismissed the possibility of the miraculous and thus refused to consider the resurrection of the dead (and anything else that diverged from scientific knowledge) to be true, or even possible. It presumed that human reason measures all things.

Such presuppositions combined with anti-Semitism in the thought of an early historical critic such as Hermann Samuel Reimarus (1694–1768) to produce a fierce attack on the authority and credibility of the "Hebrew" Bible. Much of nineteenth- and twentieth-century biblical study was unable to free itself from the direction and framework set in place by Reimarus and his contemporaries. Their stance of placing the reader above the text, however, must be distinguished from the legitimate methods used to ascertain the meaning the inspired author—and thus the Holy Spirit—set down. Proper historical and literary examination are necessary for hearing the text itself. Such methods, sometimes relabeled under the term **historical-grammatical method**, are indispensable in listening to the voice of God in the pages of Scripture.

All methods of biblical study may be abused if presuppositions falsely direct their application. The study of literary form, for example, is indeed helpful in understanding what the authors of the Bible intended to say through their use of specific words, phrases, and forms. For instance, scholars have noted that the Gospel writers, especially Luke, use an established literary form called a *bios* in writing the story of Christ's life. This form has expectations, including that of historical accuracy according to first-century standards. Believers recognize that such a genre is proper to Christ's life because He was born, lived, preached, performed miraculous signs, was crucified, and rose again in history. These things happened so a kind of biography could be told of Christ's life. "Form criticism" is practiced by some, however, to point to exaggerations in some ancient *bioi*—the plural of *bios*—suggesting that the evangelists and apostles are doing the same to Jesus. Believers should not flee from the use of such methods just because they have been used for false purposes, but they must also be wary of devious presuppositions that can be embedded in certain methods.

At the same time that Christians avoid all methods that claim authority over God's Word, believers must understand the necessity of placing the text in its historical context. A literalistic interpretation of words on the page, ignoring historical context and literary form, leads far from the intention of the author and the total story of the Bible. Such an approach puts the text as much at the mercy of the interpreter as do those presuppositions that deny God's presence in the words. Apart from the historical context and use for the people of God, its meaning will be obscured if not obliterated. God inspired writers in the Hebrew culture of the centuries before Christ in their language. He inspired writers in the Jewish and Hellenistic culture of Christ's time in the Greek language. He is a God who has anchored Himself in the history of His human creatures. He will be misunderstood if readers carelessly transpose the words of His inspired authors into a contemporary cultural situation.

Likewise, His words will be misunderstood if they are simply and literally limited to the forms in which He spoke them. He charges the church with the lively and living translation of His Word into the cultures in which He has placed His people. For example, believers in most of Christian history have believed that they could love their neighbors only if they abstained from any form of charging interest, in correspondence with the law as laid down in Leviticus 25:36–37. For centuries Christians did not include this command as part of the Law of God that was set aside for the church (Colossians 2:16–17). In the past century, most believers have come to recognize that in a capitalist system interest can be paid and charged without necessarily breaking the underlying concern that led to that command from God for His people. Believers recognize that the command that women cover their heads in church or that men not wear their hair long (1 Corinthians 11:2–15) conveyed a principle in forms not necessary for every cultural situation in which the church has found itself.

Challenges in interpretation such as these should not obscure the fundamental truth regarding the Scriptures. They record the Word of God, as it has come to human authors, for the salvation of His people.

CHAPTER 14
BAPTISM

BAPTISM … now saves you," the apostle Peter wrote in his first epistle (1 Peter 3:21). Not one to mince words, Peter is quite direct: Baptism saves. Some scholars think that the apostle wrote this first epistle on the basis of a sermon delivered in connection with Baptisms of new Christians, adults and infants, at Easter. Whether that is the case or not, Peter leaves no doubt in the letter that he regards Baptism as the instrument of God's salvation. In Acts, the same apostle called the people gathered for the Pentecost festival to receive this means of God's salvation in the name of the Lord Jesus "for the forgiveness of your sins, and you will receive the gift of the Holy Spirit" (Acts 2:38). St. Paul, too, considered Baptism as part of God's saving work, calling Baptism "the washing of regeneration and renewal of the Holy Spirit," through which God pours out His grace on His people in Jesus Christ for their justification (Titus 3:4–7). Again and again in the New Testament, Baptism is shown to be the work of God by which the Holy Spirit is given, God's salvation is offered, forgiveness of sins is promised, Christ's righteousness covers over human sinfulness, and sinners die with Christ to sin and rise with Him to the new life of faith.

How can water do such great things? When Luther asked this question in his Small Catechism, he also gave the essential answer: "Certainly not just water, but the Word of God in and with the water does these things, along with the faith which trusts this word of God in the water. For without God's word the water is plain water and no Baptism. But with the word of God it is a Baptism, that is, a life-giving water, rich in grace, and a washing of the new birth in the Holy Spirit," just as St. Paul writes in Titus 3.[1] The water is ordinary water, but God Himself has determined to make water a means of His salvation in Baptism. Christ's institution in Matthew 28, along with the divine promises attached to it, makes this water into a life-giving sacrament, a divine gift and treasure by which God saves sinners.

There can be little doubt about the importance of Baptism in the Scriptures or the early church. Jesus not only was baptized by John but also

1 Small Catechism IV 9–10 (*LSCE*, 24).

instituted a new Baptism that He authorized. Paul taught about Baptism in numerous letters; Peter, John, and the author of Hebrews referenced Baptism and its power directly. In the early church, the Gospel was preached in such a way that Baptism was the natural and obvious next step, for example, with the Ethiopian eunuch and the Philippian jailer (Acts 8:26–40; 16:25–34). Repeatedly, Luke mentioned the central role Baptism played in Christian preaching and living (Acts 2:38–41; 8:12–13; 9:17–18 [cf. 22:16]; 10:47–48; 16:15; 18:8).[2]

Baptism's significance, however, does not lie in the past, either the history of the church or our own history, but in the present as God's promise to His people. Just as Christians never graduate from the importance of the Gospel and what Jesus has done through His death and resurrection, Christians never leave Baptism behind because it is part and parcel of the Gospel. In Baptism, God concretizes His promises in Christ so that they are received in both body and soul. Not unlike a marriage vow between husband and wife that provides a foundation for their life together as a family, Baptism grounds the believer on the Word of God, given in and with the water, and is the center from which the Christian life spirals outward toward God in faith and the neighbor in love. Unlike a marriage vow, however, baptismal promises go only one way—God to us. As God works through the washing of the Word, Baptism transforms sinners through God's unmerited grace, killing us as sinners and creating us anew.

God Kills and Creates Anew in Baptism

St. Peter in his first epistle described Baptism as saving precisely because it connects us to death and new life through the resurrection of Jesus Christ (1 Peter 3:18–21). In Baptism, believers die with Jesus to live with Him as new creatures by faith. The beloved disciple did not use the same language, but Jesus' teaching of the "new birth" does have a similar meaning. In the new birth, believers are re-created by the Holy Spirit through water to new life in the kingdom of God (John 3:3–6).

Although the Scriptures proclaim God's work through Baptism in numerous ways, believers' death and resurrection with Jesus is the most significant for Lutheran theology. We with our sins are crucified with the Lord Jesus Christ and raised anew with Him by faith through Word and water. This is not something we can do for ourselves or choose for ourselves; this is

---

2 Albrecht Oepke, "*baptō, baptizō*," *Theological Dictionary of the New Testament*, vol. 1, ed. Gerhard Kittel, trans. and ed. Geoffrey W. Bromiley (Grand Rapids: Eerdmans, 1964), 529–46. See also Edmund Schlink, *The Doctrine of Baptism*, trans. Herbert J. A. Bouman (St. Louis: Concordia, 1972).

God's gift to us and His work on us through "the washing of water with the Word" (Ephesians 5:26).

Dying and Rising in Baptism: Romans 6 and Colossians 2

Paul built upon the proclamation of God's grace, which he set before his readers in chapters 3–5, as he moved to the subject of Baptism in Romans 6:3–11. In Baptism, God's grace actualizes itself in the lives of believers, crucifying sin, creating faith, and transforming believers after the likeness of the Savior. Although Baptism is not directly mentioned, it grounds the apostle's discussion of struggles with sin, the reality of God's grace through the Holy Spirit, and the hope in Jesus for today and tomorrow in chapters 7 and 8. God brings sinners into death, Paul reported, by joining them in Baptism to Christ's death. He buries sinners in Christ's tomb, leaving their sin in the one place in all creation where the Father's glance never falls. Then He raises up these sinners to new life as His children. The old self is crucified in Baptism by God's Word, and in this death Christ shares with us, we die to sin and are thus liberated from it. Through baptismal death and resurrection, we are made new with Jesus. The "with Him" of the believer's dying to sin and rising to new life in Romans 6 begins a theme that Paul uses to conclude this section on the Christian life in Romans 8:17. There he spelled out what baptismal incorporation into Jesus means for the Christian: becoming an heir with Christ, suffering with Christ, and being glorified with Christ through the Holy Spirit who dwells within by Word and water.

Paul explained the Christian life in these terms to the Colossians as well. In this epistle, Baptism occupies the key position between God's action in Christ (1:11–20; 2:9–10) and the life Christians lead, raised to new life in the Lord Jesus (2:16–4:6). Paul called Baptism the new circumcision, which incorporates God's elect into His family (Colossians 2:11–15). The old circumcision brought male Israelites into the people of God as young as eight days old (Genesis 17:9–14; Leviticus 12:3). The new circumcision, Baptism, is not just a sign of incorporation for males but is the way in which the Holy Spirit brings sinners into the family of God through faith. In Baptism, the "body of the flesh" (Colossians 2:11), the sinful nature, dies and is buried with Jesus, and God cancels the bill of indictment against sinners by nailing it to Christ's cross. New life comes to those whom Jesus freed from death as He rose from the grave to disarm principalities and powers, putting them publicly to shame as He led them in a triumphal victory procession. Thus raised with Christ, through God's baptismal action that placed us in death and hid our true life in Christ (3:1–3), believers do not transcend Baptism but live in their baptismal death and resurrection, experiencing death to immorality and the assumption of a new self that lives in Christ and follows in His way (3:5–11, 12–17).

Baptism is a matter of death and life, according to Paul. Baptism is a preenactment of Judgment Day as God puts sinners to death. Baptism is also a reenactment of creation day as God brings us to life through Christ's resurrection. In the present moment, Baptism offers a divine promise: God commits Himself to those whom He has chosen to make His own through this gift. Baptism thus spans the entirety of a person's existence, and its significance does not end with the event. We should not say, "I was baptized," but "I am baptized," because Baptism's promises persist into the present and remain essential for our relationship with God until the Last Day. The centrality of Baptism will only cease when the dying and rising that happened first in the washing of the Word takes place for the last time when Christ returns and we meet our Lord face to face in resurrected bodies.

New Birth in Baptism: Titus 3 and John 3

God acts in Baptism. God accepts sinners as His own through the Word of life that He joins with water. In Baptism He delivers His goodness and loving kindness that He revealed in sending Jesus to save us. His restoration of life is not based upon our doing the right thing, but on the basis of His doing the right thing. He has acted on the basis of His mercy alone. His mercy comes into our lives through the "washing of regeneration and renewal" through the Holy Spirit, as it is called in Titus 3:5, a phrase early Christians could only have understood as a reference to Baptism. This washing of re-creation is poured out upon us through Jesus Christ, our Savior, the one into whose death and resurrection we are incorporated through Baptism. We were dead in the foolishness and disobedience of sin, led astray into passions, pleasures, malice, envy, and hatred. The washing, God's Word and the water together, has given us new life. It justifies us—making us righteous—in God's sight and makes us part of the family of God, heirs of the sure hope of eternal life (Titus 3:4–7).

Our eternal life begins with the action of the Holy Spirit in water, as Jesus told Nicodemus (John 3:1–15). Whether John 3:3 is translated "unless one is born again" or "born from above"—the Greek could mean either—makes little difference. Certainly, Jesus was insisting on a new birth for those who are dead in trespasses and sin, and that new birth comes from above, from God. Jesus emphasized the mystery of how the Holy Spirit works to bring new life: as difficult as it is to chart the wind or master it, He said, so impossible is it to harness the Spirit's power. But the Spirit has harnessed Himself to a particular instrument: the Word. God uses the Word as His means for creating all things. He uses the Word to re-create those who have lost true human life by turning their backs on the Author of life. He combines that Word with water, and Baptism becomes a watery womb from which new life emerges, as those who were dead in sin are born anew, given new life as a gift from above. Only in this way can one enter God's kingdom; only in this way can sinful creatures become true children of God, members of His family (John 3:5).

By calling this work of Baptism the "new birth," Jesus emphasized that the new life Baptism promises is a gift of God alone. Rebirth is not earned by the child of God. Neither our consent nor our contribution was necessary—or possible—for our physical birth from our mother's womb. Likewise, our consent or contribution is neither necessary nor possible for our rebirth in Christ. Birth, and life, is pure gift. Salvation in Jesus is pure gift.

No precise equivalent of Baptism is found in the Old Testament, although circumcision and ceremonial washings foreshadowed it in part and in different ways. Paul compared Baptism to circumcision (Colossians 2:11), the rite by which God incorporated infant boys into His people, but circumcision did not employ water. Ceremonial washings had become a part of Jewish ritual, but these washings required repetition and carried with them no promise from God. The Baptism of John the Baptist stemmed from this Jewish custom. The Scriptures do not clearly spell out the relationship between John's Baptism and the Baptism Jesus inaugurated through His disciples (John 3:22; 4:2), nor do they define the precise nature of John's Baptism. It was a Baptism "of repentance for the forgiveness of sins" (Mark 1:4; Luke 3:3). John's Baptism served to point the way to Jesus, and it, like him, moved offstage when Jesus arrived (John 1:29–34).

Although the church fathers often talked about Jesus' Baptism as hallowing the water for us, it is striking that the New Testament never speaks about Jesus' Baptism as a foundation for our Baptism into Christ. Instead, the New Testament speaks about Christ's Baptism as central to His identity and mission as the anointed Savior whereas we are baptized into His death and resurrection.[3] Christians are not baptized into the Baptism of John but the Baptism of Jesus, the Baptism that He instituted. The Baptism Jesus gave to His disciples saves because the Lord promised that it would be an instrument of His saving power, His tool, which re-creates. God has chosen human language and water, combined in this sacrament, to be the means by which He crucifies sinners and raises them up to new life. The richness of His grace has provided this form of the Word along with others to provide life.

---

3 On Jesus' Baptism and its significance for Him and us, especially in the early church fathers, see Killian McDonnell, *The Baptism of Jesus in the Jordan: The Trinitarian and Cosmic Order of Salvation* (Collegeville, MN: Liturgical Press, 1996).

Cleansing in Baptism

The church has often emphasized the cleansing nature of this washing of regeneration. Fouled with sins of all kinds, the Corinthian Christians were "washed ... sanctified ... justified in the name of the Lord Jesus Christ and by the Spirit of our God" (1 Corinthians 6:11). Christ demonstrated His love for His church by cleansing her "by the washing of water with the word" (Ephesians 5:26). Baptism cleanses sin's stain; it purifies the guilty soul; it removes the dirt from the conscience.

Cleansing language can be quite misleading, however, if it is disconnected from the New Testament understanding of dying to sin and rising to new life. Cleansing may make us think that sin is only a little mark or a dirty splotch that can be easily removed. Cleansing language, then, may suggest that sinful human creatures are mostly fine; we just need a little bath instead of the total transformation that God desires and promises for sinners through Word and water. Hence, the New Testament focuses on water's deadly, destructive power visited upon the sinner and its nutritive, life-giving power, which raises up the children of God to new life (Romans 6:3–11; Colossians 2:11–15; John 3:3–6; Titus 3:3–6). Baptism is a cleansing, but it is no mere cleansing. It is a cleansing that kills and creates new life through the Word joined with the water.

Some Christians tend to separate Word and water, but God has joined them together in Baptism, and neither can stand alone. The Enlightenment recaptured some of the spiritualism of ancient Platonism, and some adherents practiced a "baptism" of rose petals; that was no Baptism, no matter the words that were spoken during the rite. Some Christians use "holy water" as a religious symbol apart from God's Word; that is not Baptism either. Baptism requires both Word and water, united together in this washing and never separated. Because of God's command and promise, the water is made holy by the Word. And the Word, too, demands the water because "God himself stakes his honor, his power, and his might" on this water placed in the setting of God's Word.[4] You cannot have one without the other and have the Sacrament of Baptism.

Making Disciples through Baptism: Matthew 28

According to Christ's command in Matthew 28:18–20, the church baptizes in the name of the Holy Trinity, Father, Son, and Holy Spirit. Valid Baptisms have taken place in the name of Jesus—based on the language of Acts, to baptize "in the name of Jesus Christ" (Acts 2:38; cf. 10:48)—but there is no reason to depart from the words of Jesus in His institution of Baptism. For

4 Large Catechism IV 14–17 (quoting paragraph 17, Kolb-Wengert, 458).

we receive our names, and our new identities as God's children, from Him whose name is God: Father, Son, and Holy Spirit. We are incorporated into Christ's death and resurrection, and thereby into the Father's family, as the Holy Spirit effects His regenerating and renewing work in Baptism. We confess the entire work of God when we baptize in the name of Father, Son, and Holy Spirit.

Although the church uses the language Jesus gave in His institution, the words do not function as a magical incantation. We use these words because Baptism is Christ's work that operates under His authority. The church and her pastors function as His servants and stewards of His mysteries, following Christ's institution because His Word and God's name carry the power of God's promise by which God Himself works to save in Word and water.

Not only does the baptismal formula not function as a magical formula, but also Baptism itself is no magical process. Rather, God works for us and in us as the creatures whom He has made. God's Word—whether it comes initially in baptismal, written, or oral form—re-creates us as the human creatures we are. It transforms us from miserly, controlling beings into loving, trusting creatures. It changes us as the people God made, with all the psychological characteristics at work in us as God effects this transformation.

We do not know what that means for the psychological processes of the infant, to whom God gives the gift of life as He establishes the baptismal relationship. We do know that as the Word embraces the adult, it bestows the gift of faith as the Holy Spirit moves mind and heart to respond to God's accepting us as His own and committing Himself to us. Thus, for adults, the biblical writers connect Baptism with the psychological experience of being turned away from sin and being turned toward God, that is, with the experience of **repentance** (Acts 2:38). Although the psychological experiences of infants and adults are quite different, the theological description is similar. Before God we must all become as infants, unable to control our own fate and depending on Jesus for salvation (Matthew 18:3). This transformation is not something a human creature can accomplish by her own power; both the turning from sin and the turning to God—**repentance** and faith—are the work and gift of God the Spirit.

Faith stands at the heart of human existence. Thus Baptism's re-creation of the sinner into a child of God can never be separated from faith. But the psychological aspects of faith do not exhaust what it means for us to be in relationship with God. When we sleep or are in a coma, when our mental capacities are underdeveloped—as in infants or those with intellectual disabilities—or wear out—as in the infirm—God maintains the relationship He has established through His baptismal Word, whether we can respond or not. He has turned us toward Himself and will never let us go. Our lives and abilities are uncertain, but His Word is certain. And His Word establishes reality.

Baptized into Christ's Body, the Church

When Jesus instituted the Sacrament of Baptism, He commanded the apostles and the church to "make disciples of all nations" by baptizing and teaching (Matthew 28:18–20). Baptism is the work of God by which He saves sinners, but it also brings sinners into His family where they grow in faith and the Christian life. In other words, Jesus instituted Baptism to be deeply connected to the church. Sometimes Christians are tempted to separate Baptism and the church, thinking that Baptism works without a life of faith. Christian grandparents understandably desire to have their grandchildren baptized even if the parents do not want this gift given to their children and have no intention of raising their children in the Christian faith. To be clear, such Baptisms would not be invalid—God's promises would be delivered and the Holy Spirit would be given through faith—but Baptism does not work simply by the act being done. Such an idea suggests that going through the motions of the ritual is sufficient for winning God's favor, which is called ***ex opere operato***. The Christian life of faith begins in Baptism, but it is sustained by the return to Baptism in the Word. Just as a marriage could never last that did not include regular conversation, intimacy, and words of love even after genuine vows were made, so God's vow in Baptism remains true but must be sustained through His Word that builds on and returns us to His baptismal promises. Hence, sponsors represent the congregation and the church and promise to help the one being baptized grow in the teachings of Scripture, learn to pray, lead a holy, God-pleasing life, and receive the Lord's Supper faithfully.[5] Baptism brings us into the church wherein God's people grow in faith and love, in knowledge of God through His Word, so that as we go on our way, the Holy Spirit might make more disciples through our sharing of the Gospel.

As he discussed how Christians live together, Paul emphasized that believers from all nations and peoples are one family through God's work of Baptism. Paul reminded the Corinthians that they function together with one another, since they are members of the same Body, belonging to Christ. "For in one Spirit we were all baptized into one body—Jews or Greeks, slave or free—and all were made to drink of one Spirit [through Baptism]" (1 Corinthians 12:13). Believers live united by the Holy Spirit in the bond of peace, for the Holy Spirit has created this one Body, calling believers to a common hope under a common Lord, in a common faith, on the basis of a common Baptism, the gift of the God and Father of us all (Ephesians 4:4–6).

---

5 *Lutheran Service Book* (St. Louis: Concordia, 2006), p. 269.

Putting on Christ

Like any good parent, God is concerned with clothing His children. The children of God, baptized into Christ, have "put on" Christ, having been dressed with Him. That makes them all equal in God's sight. He no longer takes our sin into consideration as He looks at us, nor does He take our earthly characteristics into account. Among His people it does not count in His reckoning whether we are Jew or Greek, slave or free, male or female. We who have been baptized into Him are one in Christ Jesus (Galatians 3:26–29).

God sees us through Christ-colored glasses. In the vertical relationship His Word has killed us as sinners—stripped us of our torn and tattered garments of sin—and buried us in Christ's tomb. His Word of resurrection has brought us into a new existence in the clothes of Jesus' innocence and righteousness. We are as holy and innocent as Christ in the Father's presence. We are His perfect children because He has said so. His pledge to us in Baptism clears our conscience (1 Peter 3:21). At the same time we still experience the ravages of sinfulness in our daily lives. In our horizontal relationships we encounter temptations and sometimes succumb. In the mystery of human sinfulness and God's free grace, some even flee from the baptismal promise and do not return, turning their backs again on their loving Father and His Word. Baptism does not magically transport us to the resurrection day, but it provides God's commitment and promise to which we can return and know His forgiveness in Christ for sinners who need strength against sin, fear of death, and the devil's temptations every day. Thus Baptism initiates a lifelong process of dying to the habits of hell and rising to the habits of heaven in the daily struggle against the sin that destroys our humanity.

Recalling God's baptismal promise to be our God and hold us as His children strengthens us for this struggle. Paul described the process in Colossians. Having been buried and raised with Christ (2:12), believers seek the things that are above and therefore put to death immorality, impurity, passion, evil desire, and covetousness, which is idolatry (3:1–5). Dressed up in a new nature, having shed the old through the baptismal death and resurrection, believers experience God's renewal of their lives according to the image of the Creator (3:9–10). We are therefore clothed in godly characteristics, compassion, kindness, humility, meekness, patience, and all the other attitudes and actions that Christ has bestowed upon those whom He has raised up with Himself (3:12–17). For He has raised us up to newness of life (Romans 6:4). As Luther teaches in the Large Catechism: "These two parts [of Baptism], being dipped under the water and emerging from it, point to the power and effect of Baptism, which is nothing else than the slaying of the old Adam and the resurrection of the new creature, both of which actions must continue in us our whole life long."[6]

The Christian Life as the Baptismal Life

Baptism happens once, but, as we have insisted, it is not merely a one-time event. At the time of the Reformation, the Christian Church had largely followed St. Jerome in considering Baptism as the "first plank" after the shipwreck of sin.[7] Baptism was understood to be the first life raft that God threw to sinners, whose lives had been wrecked on the rock of sin, giving them a chance of salvation. Baptism wiped away all sins committed to that point, including original sin, but any mortal sin after Baptism would destroy the life raft, the first plank. Thus for the medieval church Baptism was important, but only for what happened before it. Some Christians misunderstood the gift of Baptism so much that they waited until a health scare to be baptized so that they could have as many sins as possible wiped away in that moment. Baptism was like a one-time-use certificate to reset the sin in one's life. But once it was turned in, it could do no more good. Christians turned to other sacraments—namely, penance and Holy Communion (or even holy orders)—to offer them divine help for their post-baptismal sin.

What Luther discovered in the Scriptures, however, was that Baptism should not be understood as a one-time ritual act that conveys God's grace only for what happened in the past, but as a promise of the Gospel that places sinners in relationship to Jesus by faith. Like a wedding vow, God's promise spoken over His child at Baptism is spoken once, but the promise remains in force. Just as all of married life is lived under and within the promises of the marriage vows, so all of the Christian life is lived under and within God's promises given in Baptism. Baptism may be performed once, but its proleptic promises perdure to the age to come.

Therefore, Baptism plays a central role throughout the lives of God's children. During seasons of anxiety, fear, and struggle, Baptism provides a handhold that we can grasp and be certain of God's love and forgiveness. The external nature of Baptism—as a historical event with water and the spoken Word—is essential to the good news of the Sacrament. In Baptism, faith has "something to which it may cling and upon which it may stand."[8] We should not retreat inward to find out whether God really loves us or we are true Christians. Instead, we must look outward to where God promises to love us in Christ, give us the Holy Spirit, and forgive our sins in the

---

6 Large Catechism IV 65 (Kolb-Wengert, 465).

7 See Large Catechism IV 80–82.

8 Large Catechism IV 29 (Kolb-Wengert, 460).

blessed washing with the Word. No matter how we feel or what temptations the devil throws our way, we cannot deny that Baptism happened to us, and thus God promises us His grace, mercy, and eternal salvation. No wonder Luther called Baptism "a treasure that God gives us and faith grasps."[9]

Furthermore, Baptism provides the pattern and the transformation we need to live a godly and holy life. Christians never escape from the baptismal dying and rising with Jesus. They continually return to Baptism through confession, admitting our sins before God to die to the sin that plagues us, and rising with Jesus through faith that trusts the promise of the Gospel, the forgiveness of sins in the absolution. This lifelong cycle suppresses, restrains, and on the Last Day will lead to the destruction of the old creature as the Spirit also leads us to live by faith as a new creature, trusting in God's promises, praying to the Lord Jesus, and serving our neighbors in love. No one is saved because of how much we are changed by the Holy Spirit—and we should never try to figure out how sanctified we are, as if our personal holiness counted before God—but God does do this work for us and in us, drowning our old sinful nature and raising us anew in faith, as we return to Baptism as our "daily garment."[10]

The Abuse of God's Baptismal Grace

Those who cannot grasp the biblical teaching on Baptism will sometimes ask, "What about the abuse of Baptism by those who claim that they can do whatever they please since God has saved them through Baptism?" The question is much larger: What about the abuse of God's grace by those who claim that they can "sin all the more" because God's grace covers their sin? At one level, this question is a good sign for anyone who has been speaking the Gospel. Hearing this question means your teaching is on the right track! Paul, too, faced this query. He had discussed God's free gift of life and salvation in Romans 3–5, expounding the extravagant goodness of God as clearly as anywhere in Scripture. The question arose naturally from the Gospel proclamation: "Why then shouldn't I keep sinning so that grace, too, may become larger?" Paul's answer to that question is Baptism! It does not make sense—it is impossible!—Paul told the Romans, to go on sinning in the same old ways as before because Baptism has rendered God's verdict on our sin and has transformed our identity from sinner to child of God (Romans 6:1–3). How can a new person live like the old person would have? We are not the same! Baptism has changed us.

It could be said that the Gospel of God's grace—expressed, among other ways, in Baptism—is defenseless against the sinner. But, of course,

9 Large Catechism IV 37 (Kolb-Wengert, 461).

10 Large Catechism IV 84 (Kolb-Wengert, 466).

this defenseless Gospel is the very power of God for salvation. When others ask about the significance of their Baptism for their daily life, believers must ask why they want to know. To those who say, "My Baptism permits me to sin without fear," the proper distinction of Law and Gospel leads us to reply, "Your Baptism leads to death as a sinner. You are rejecting God's Word for you in your Baptism when you sin." God's promise in Baptism to be our God and to have us as His children is, of course, ever valid because it is God's re-creative Word. His commitment to us remains firm, and we can no more nullify our rebirth than we can our natural birth. But it is a word of Gospel—a promise to be trusted, not a command to be manipulated or used—and thus it cannot be understood by those who want to live by their own devices, that is, in the realm of Law. Paul answers our dilemma of the abuse of Baptism by returning us to what God says about His powerful Word at work in Baptism.

Frustrating as it may sometimes be, we can do no better than rely on the crushing power of the Law to meet the desire of the sinner who wants a license to sin instead of living in the joy of being God's child. As Christians experience the Holy Spirit's use of Law and Gospel in life, we are brought back to Baptism. We die again, and we rise again as we confess our sins and receive absolution, as we acknowledge our sinfulness and trust in God's forgiveness day after day. The entire life of the Christian is a life of repentance, of the Spirit's repetition of His baptismal action.

The Mode of Baptism

Christians have sometimes disagreed among themselves about the manner in which Baptism is to be performed. Some have insisted that the Greek word for "baptizing" meant "to dip," and that the baptized should therefore be "immersed" in the water of Baptism. It is true that the original meaning of the Greek verb *baptizo* involved "dipping" or "immersing." By the time of Christ, however, the word was used for nearly any application of water. For instance, tables were "baptized" when they were wiped off with a wet cloth. The kind of washing that the Pharisees expected Jesus would do before dinner did not involve immersion of His entire body (Luke 11:38), but the word *baptize* was used for the usual "washing your hands" of Jewish daily life.

The mode of application of the water is not commanded by Jesus and is not the important thing. God's Word with the water is essential. Immersion reminds us more powerfully of our burial with Christ. Pouring water over the forehead suffices. Water and Word together, according to the institution of Jesus, save regardless of how much water is applied.

Infant Baptism

The Lutheran understanding of Baptism is called **baptismal regeneration**, which confesses Baptism as the work and gift of God by which the Holy Spirit regenerates sinners, creates faith in them, forgives their sins, and dwells within through the Word enclosed in the water. With different nuances, this view is largely shared with Reformed, Anglican, Roman Catholic, and Orthodox Christians, who all baptize infants (as well as adult converts).

Some Christians do not view Baptism as God's action, seeing Baptism as a human response to their faith that shows obedience and commitment to God. Accordingly, they do not believe that infants should be baptized. When this practice of **believer's baptism** is common among Protestants in an area, some Lutherans may feel odd about their practice of baptizing babies. In reality, however, the overwhelming majority of believers in the present and throughout church history have baptized infants. More important, there are good biblical reasons to do so.

In Baptism God Accepts His Children and Commits Himself to Them

First, Baptism is not merely a human rite, a human commitment to God. Baptism carries the re-creating Word of God and all the power of the Gospel to the sinner who is being baptized. God has selected elements of His created order to use as instruments to save fallen sinners. God chose human flesh when the Son became Jesus of Nazareth, and He has redeemed us through this man. God chose human language as the means by which to pronounce the good news of salvation upon us. He has chosen us to use that human language of the Gospel to bring one another into the family of God by faith. God has placed human words together with bread, which carries Jesus' body, and wine, which carries His blood, for the forgiveness of our sins. He combines the Gospel with water in re-creating us through His baptismal action.

Because God regularly works through created means, there is no reason not to interpret literally what the Scriptures say about Baptism. Baptism gives the new birth by the Spirit (John 3:3–6; cf. Titus 3:4–7), forgives sins and brings the gift of the Holy Spirit (Acts 2:38), connects the sinner to Christ in His death and resurrection (Romans 6:1–4; Colossians 2:11–12), cleanses the conscience of guilt and shame (1 Peter 3:18–22), makes sinners holy for the final wedding banquet with Christ (Ephesians 5:26–27), and brings people into the family of Abraham through the promise (Galatians 3:26–29). Baptism saves (1 Peter 3:21). In Baptism, God forgives sins and makes us His children. In Baptism, God really buries us as sinners, and from His perspective—the perspective from which reality is determined—He raises us to new life, a new existence in Christ. Baptism is the work of God.

Infants Need the Gift of Life

Second, little children need to be brought into God's family. Each of us is infected with sin from conception (Psalm 51:5), and infant mortality proves that they receive the wages of sin (Romans 6:23). Although passages such as Matthew 18:3 or Luke 18:15–17 do not speak directly of Baptism, the words of Jesus that we must become like little children to enter the kingdom of God state His expectations clearly. Not adult achievement or commitment but the passive reception of newborn infants marks our passage into God's kingdom. In fact, Jesus loves little children and wants to receive them into His kingdom, which is exactly what He promises for those who enter through the watery womb (John 3:3–5). If Jesus loves children and wants them to be part of His kingdom, the church should offer for children the way Jesus appointed for all to become part of His kingdom: Baptism.[11]

In Baptism God establishes a relationship with children that saves (1 Peter 3:21) without requiring adult psychological activity—even though such activity is part and parcel of an adult response to God's action. He buries and resurrects those whom He has chosen to bring into His family through Baptism because He loves them, not because they are able to perform acts of acceptance or commitment. Important as such human responses are for adult faith, His acceptance of us and His commitment to us dwarf their significance—at the same time God's work makes these human responses possible.

Evidence for Infant Baptism in Scripture and the Early Church

The language of Scripture regarding Baptism naturally includes children. Not only does Jesus welcome children (Matthew 19:13–14), but He commands His church to make disciples of "all nations" by baptizing and teaching (Matthew 28:19). This "all" indicates inclusivity—people of all ethnicities, all socioeconomic levels of society, and all ages—and it is never qualified in the New Testament. When Peter proclaims repentance and forgiveness of sins through Baptism at Pentecost, he uses similarly inclusive language that mentions children directly: "The promise [of Baptism] is for you and for your children and for all who are far off, everyone whom the Lord our God calls to Himself" (Acts 2:39). When Paul teaches about Baptism, he speaks of this gift for male and female, slave and free, Jew and Greek, in inclusive language (Galatians 3:27–28; cf. Ephesians 4:4–6). In Colossians, Paul even compares Baptism to circumcision, which was

11 Smalcald Articles III V 4.

performed on the eighth day for Israelite male infants, but Paul never suggests that infant Baptism is problematic (Colossians 2:11–14). In Acts also, whole households and families were baptized (Acts 16:15, 33), which were not households like the modern nuclear family but larger communities of relatives and servants where children were likely to be present.

Although the scriptural evidence for infant Baptism is strong, there is no "smoking gun" proof that will convince everyone. No text commands the Baptism of children, but neither does any Scripture suggest that Baptism ought to be limited to people of a certain age or mental capability. The differences in interpretation stem from different presuppositions. Those whose presuppositions separate them from this biblical way of thinking will reinterpret these passages to exclude infants. Arguments over the interpretation of these passages will avail little so long as one presumes that Baptism—as well as repentance and faith—is fundamentally a human action and that infants do not need a renewed relationship with God established through Baptism.

Likewise, the evidence from the practice of the first few centuries of church history is open to some variation in interpretation.[12] The charge against early Christians that they practiced infanticide strongly suggests that pagan neighbors heard them talking about the deaths of their infants in Baptism. The early third-century evidence suggests too that infant Baptism came on the radar not because it was a new practice but because it was becoming commonplace as the Christian community shifted from a primarily convert church to a church made up of families who had been Christians for generations. Regardless, Baptism has its power and authority from the triune God revealed in the Word. And Jesus invites all into relationship with Himself through Baptism, including infants and children.

Infant Faith

To natural reason it seems as if infants could not possibly have faith. Saving faith seems to be an action of adults, repenting of sin and believing in the good news of Christ. Thus some have suggested that infants are saved by the faith of their parents in Baptism. This solution, however, will not do. All of us encounter God as individuals, and faith is to be our own as

12 Two views of the evidence are presented in Joachim Jeremias, *Infant Baptism in the First Four Centuries*, trans. David Cairns (Philadelphia: Westminster, 1962); and Kurt Aland, *Did the Early Church Baptize Infants?* (Philadelphia: Westminster, 1963); with Jeremias's reply to Aland in *The Origins of Infant Baptism*, trans. Dorothea M. Barton (Naperville, IL: Allenson, 1963). For a more recent study, see the comprehensive work of Everett Ferguson, *Baptism in the Early Church: History, Theology, and Liturgy in the First Five Centuries* (Grand Rapids: Eerdmans, 2009). For some quotations from church fathers in support of infant Baptism, see https://www.churchfathers.org/infant-baptism (accessed March 14, 2023).

each is brought to trust in the promise. Recent studies seem to indicate that there is more memory and understanding present in infants than earlier investigators had recognized, but this, too, will not satisfy many. We do well to remember that saving faith has less to do with understanding facts than it does with trusting a person. Infants certainly trust their mothers, recognizing mom's voice even in the womb. If infants can trust their mothers, depending on them in their limited intellectual capacity, how much more could they be brought to trust in the Creator by the Spirit? Holy Scripture thus describes David trusting in God while at his mother's breasts (Psalm 22:9), and John leaping in joy and faith in his mother's womb in the presence of the Lord (Luke 1:41–44).

Infants do not express their faith in the same way adults do, but that does not mean God is incapable of giving them saving faith. Infants do not reflect on their beliefs, but saving faith is not identical with the intellectual experience of adults. Some Lutheran theologians have distinguished between **direct faith**—the faith that grasps God directly through the promise on account of the Holy Spirit—and **reflexive faith**—the faith that thinks about itself and understands its object.[13] The former kind of faith exists in infants, the infirm, the comatose, the intellectually disabled, and Christian adults by the work of the Holy Spirit, not by human strength. The latter kind is what adults largely know and articulate.

The "problem" of infant faith cannot be solved by trying to claim that the relationship of the infant with God is psychologically identifiable with that of the adult. After all, that focuses on the less-important side of the relationship. God has commanded Baptism. God acts in Baptism. God kills and makes alive in Baptism. He does this to infants and adults alike through the washing of the water with the Word. We may not understand exactly how God accomplishes this in the case of infants—in truth, we cannot understand how God can save sinful adults either!—but we do not need to understand. We live by faith in His Word, confessing Him as the Lord of death and life.

What About ...?

Those exploring the Lutheran doctrine of infant Baptism often raise two additional questions. First, if Baptism saves, what happens to a person who is not baptized? Like so many other questions, this one also requires us to ask, "Why do you want to know?" If a person wishes to devalue God's gift of Baptism, we must insist that Baptism does indeed save, and it is commanded by Jesus as necessary. If a person is concerned about the salvation

---

13 Heinrich Schmid, *The Doctrinal Theology of the Evangelical Lutheran Church*, 3rd ed., trans. Charles A. Hay and Henry E. Jacobs (1899; repr., Minneapolis: Augsburg, 1961), 421.

of a relative or neighbor, we must focus on the Gospel to provide appropriate comfort. Although Baptism holds an esteemed place in God's salvific work, it is not the only way by which God justifies sinful creatures. God has appointed many ways to give His grace. We receive His saving promises in Word, water, bread and wine, Scripture, and Christian conversation. Even parents who have lost babies in utero can find comfort in recognizing that their children can begin hearing the Word of the Gospel already in the womb. For those who wanted to be baptized but for some reason were not, we have no reason to think that Jesus does not save them by the Word of the Gospel that brings life. Baptism should not be thought of as optional—it is commanded by Christ and offers the new birth that all sinners need, which is why the Lutheran Confessions call Baptism "necessary for salvation"[14]—but it also should not be understood as a required item to check off the get-to-heaven list. Baptism is a form of the Gospel by which God brings sinners into His own family.

Second, should a person be rebaptized who does not remember their Baptism or who fell away from the faith? In a setting where Protestants demand Baptism as adults, rebaptism may sound like a good idea. The motivation to be rebaptized is usually to commit oneself (again) to the Christian faith, responding as an adult to God's Word. Although adult Christians must absolutely obey Jesus and live a godly life in His church, such an understanding of Baptism misses its purpose. Baptism is not a work that we do; it is a work and treasure that God does and gives. If we remember Baptism as God's work and promise, we can see the problem with rebaptism. By being baptized again, one is saying, "The first Baptism didn't stick. God's promise must not have worked the first time, so let's try it again." It would be like an adulterer telling his faithful wife that because he cheated on her, they need to remarry so that she can promise him her faithfulness again. You can imagine his wife: "The problem is not the vows! The problem is that you did not believe them to be important and live in them!" In a similar way, whenever one falls away from faith, the problem is not that God failed to work in Baptism; the problem is that we fail to believe His promise. The proper solution is not another Baptism, but to listen to the Word and believe the promise that was given already in the baptismal washing: "We were buried therefore with Him by baptism into death, in order that, just as Christ was raised from the dead by the glory of the Father, we, too, might walk in newness of life" (Romans 6:4). God's promise in Baptism does not fail; it is valid even if it is not believed, but it is only beneficial when it is received by faith through the work of the Holy Spirit.

---

14 Augsburg Confession IX 1 (Latin text, Kolb-Wengert, 43).

The Church's Use of Baptism

God exercises His lordship through His people. His people designate leaders, pastors, who normally carry out their functions on their behalf. So it is with Baptism. Pastors baptize as the representative of both Christ and the congregation. Normally and ideally, this Baptism happens within a worship service. The child is being joined not only to the body of Christ's death and resurrection but also to the Body of His church. The act takes place most suitably in the midst of the congregation. Baptism is an incorporation into the family, and it is good for the family to be present when a newborn enters. Nevertheless, there is nothing invalid about Baptisms that take place outside worship services. In fact, because of the critical nature of Baptism for the conveying of God's grace, laypeople may baptize in emergencies. For the validity of Baptism hinges on the Word of God—Christ's institution and power—not on the person who presides over the Baptism.

Since the early church, Christians have chosen sponsors—called godparents in some traditions—for those who are baptized. Sponsors aid baptized believers in the Christian life that lies before them. Adult converts who are baptized need sponsors as badly as infants, perhaps more so, in a post-Christian society. Sponsors serve as more than witnesses to the Baptism. They pledge themselves to pray for and help the baptized grow in faith in Christ and godly living. If families cannot find any who can honestly pledge themselves to pray for the baptized and support their Christian edification, they should not call them baptismal sponsors but only witnesses. Sponsors share the confession of faith into which the child is being baptized.

Baptisms must involve the combination of water applied to the body of the baptized along with the Word, summarized in the words "I baptize you in the name of the Father and of the Son and of the Holy Spirit." Other customs that enhance the conveying of the Gospel to the assembled congregation and to the baptized and their families rightly adorn the baptismal service. Particular note should be made of the "rebirthday" within the calendar of the Church Year. You might, for instance, choose Reformation Sunday to celebrate a Baptism rather than October 31. Tying Baptism to a specific Sunday or festival within the Church Year on which the individual was baptized is a useful device in remembering both one's Baptism and the church's own perception of time.

Baptism is worth remembering. There God takes the dust of a person born in sin and breathes new life into His child through water and the Word. Those who are born dead in trespasses and sin come to life as children of God, baptized members of His family.

CHAPTER 15
THE LORD'S SUPPER

FOOD is connected to many significant events in God's life with His creatures. Most fruit trees in Eden supplied sustenance for Adam and Eve, but one piece paved the path to perdition. As human sinfulness came by way of eating in defiance of God, God's work of salvation comes by way of food and fellowship in faith. Abraham communed with the Lord over cakes, milk, curds, and veal as God instituted circumcision and began to fulfill the promise of a son to Abraham (Genesis 18:1–8). God established a special meal on the night of the Passover to commemorate His redemption of Israel from Egypt (Exodus 12:1–37). On Mount Sinai, Moses, Aaron, and the elders of Israel "beheld God, and ate and drank" as part of the institution of God's covenant with His people (Exodus 24:11). God provided manna from heaven for His people in the wilderness as a way for them to learn trust in Him before they would take possession of the land of promise (Exodus 16). Through the prophets, God Himself promised to be the shepherd of His people and feed them with good pasture (Ezekiel 34:11–16). When Jesus returns to raise all flesh, God promises to provide a "feast of rich food" for His people from all nations as He also wipes away tears, death, and all evil (Isaiah 25:6–9). In Revelation, John foresaw a "marriage supper of the Lamb," as well as a tree of life bearing fruit continually in the new creation (Revelation 19:6–10; 22:1–2). No wonder the psalmist proclaims: "Taste and see that the Lord is good!" (Psalm 34:8).

God loves His children so much that He has provided us with His life-giving Word in the setting of a meal so that we can indeed taste and see His goodness. God not only comes to give us new birth through the most common element of life in His creation, water, joined to His Word, but He also feeds us, the most common event in human life, by joining His Word to bread, which carries the human body of Christ, and to wine, which carries His blood. His love embraces us as His Word reaches into our lives in all its forms.

The Names of the Supper

Like the meals of daily life, the Lord's Meal has occupied a central place in the lives of His people throughout Christian history. The meal is called by several names. It is His meal, and so believers have called it "the **Lord's Supper**." There He is both chef and entrée. He prepares the meal, and He is the meal. Because the church celebrates it at the altar, it is also called the "**Sacrament of the Altar**." **Holy Communion** is another name for the Lord's Supper, for there are three kinds of unity or union that take place in this feast. There is the union of bread with body and wine with blood, as St. Paul mentioned in 1 Corinthians 10:16, and there is the union of Christ with His people as He gives them His body and blood (Matthew 26:26–28). The Supper also unites Christ's people with one another, as one Body in one loaf (1 Corinthians 10:17). This third point is not stressed often by Lutherans, but it is certainly in view in Holy Scripture and in Luther's earliest writings on the Sacrament. Just as a meal provides an occasion for a family to feel at home with one another, so the Lord's Table is a way the Holy Spirit draws believers together in the unity of their faith and life under Christ's reign.

Christ called His meal a new *diathēkē*.[1] This Greek word can mean "covenant" or "testament," as in last will and testament. If the word is understood as **covenant**, it must be understood as the kind of relationship given by a king to his vassals. The king offers; the king imposes; the king promises. The covenant is his gift to vassals who have no claim on his protection and rule. Christ's Supper is likewise pure gift. We do not bring the groceries for Him to prepare; we do not do the right things to become worthy of His promise. He alone gives, not according to what we have done but according to His boundless mercy. He gives the relationship that arises from His death and resurrection, as it is applied to our lives. In that sense, there is a covenant established between two parties, but one gives and the other receives. Thus it is better to think of the Lord's Supper as a last will and testament. In this meal, Jesus enacts His dying wishes according to His will alone, giving a **new testament** for His church where God's people eat and drink in the presence of the Lord and receive forgiveness of sins (cf. Exodus 24:11; Jeremiah 31:31–34). Jesus bestows all His blessings, the promises of forgiveness, new life, and Christ's own presence upon His people. The Risen One gives these great blessings in and through His death.

The term **Eucharist** is used commonly in connection with the Lord's Supper, especially among Catholic and Orthodox Christians. The term comes from the Greek word for "thanksgiving." Historically, the word was connected to the prayers around the Supper itself, giving thanks to God for

---

1 *Treatise on the New Testament* (1520), AE 35:79–111.

His gifts and, because of the prominence of this portion of the liturgy, came to be a name for the whole liturgical action. This name, however, is potentially misleading. It is appropriate for us to give thanks for the gift of Christ's body and blood in the meal as we do in prayer and singing in the liturgy. It is not, however, appropriate to think that the eating and drinking of the Supper are themselves a giving thanks, as if that were the human part of this new covenant. Because Jesus acts in the Lord's Supper, giving us the meal, and with it forgiveness and life, the meal itself cannot be called the Eucharist. God's gift is Sacrament.

Mass is another term that is commonly used by Roman Catholic Christians for the Sacrament and the service that includes it. Although the name seems to be increasing in popularity, the term *mass* should be avoided by Lutherans because of the potential confusion with the Roman Catholic understanding of the mass as a sacrifice, in which Jesus and His sacrifice are re-presented before God by the priest.[2] The Supper is not something we present to God, but one He gives to us, promising the Word of forgiveness with the body and blood of the Lord under bread and wine.

The church has linked Baptism and the Lord's Supper in the category of sacrament. They bear many similarities, beyond the basic definition of a means that Christ has commanded to convey forgiveness and life through the joining of Word and physical element. They both demand and evoke faith through the Word. They bring God's children into death as sinners and into new life through Christ's resurrection. They join us to other members of Christ's Body, the church. They bring Judgment Day into the midst of this age, offering God's Last Day promises in time, and they repeat His "let there be life" from creation as they create life for us in the midst of the deadly sinfulness that besets us.

But the category of sacrament does not impose complete uniformity. The commands concerning Baptism and the Lord's Supper are different. Jesus authorized and encouraged the church to baptize all (Matthew 28:19) while Paul insisted upon examining oneself for the Supper (1 Corinthians 11:28). In addition, new birth is not repeated; the meal is. Gustaf Wingren suggested an explanation on the basis of parallels from the Old Testament and from experience. The children of Israel crossed through the waters of the sea but once; they repeated the Passover meal again and again. We undergo physical birth but once; we eat each day.[3]

---

2 Daniel Preus, "Luther and the Mass: Justification and the *Joint Declaration*," *Logia* 10, no. 4 (Reformation 2001): 16–17.

3 Gustaf Wingren, *The Living Word: A Theological Study of Preaching and the Church*, trans. Victor C. Pogue (Philadelphia: Muhlenberg, 1960), 160.

The Elements of the Supper

The meal consists of bread and wine. Christ used unleavened bread as He instituted the Supper because He did so during the Passover celebration, "the day of Unleavened Bread" (Luke 22:7). After that festival season had passed, the disciples continued to use bread, most likely when it was not unleavened. Christ used the "fruit of the vine" (Matthew 26:29), a term used, in a culture without refrigeration and preservatives, for juice of grapes in the only possible form in which it could be found shortly after the harvest—wine.[4]

Christians anchor their use of the Supper in the historical revelation of our God. He came as a Jew some two thousand years ago, in a historical situation that led Him to be crucified under Pontius Pilate. He used bread, and He used the fruit of the vine during a Passover meal that He reconstituted on the eve of His death as a new covenant meal for forgiveness of sins under His rule. Students often wonder why various contemporary items could not be substituted for bread and wine: "Can't we remember Jesus' death just as well with cookies and soda pop?" In theory, that may be true, but not in reality. Two reasons stand out for why we should not use such substitutes. First, cookies and cola generalize and abstract Christ's specific historical action, pulling the fact of God's intervention out of history. Instead of letting Christ pull us into His story—which itself is part of Israel's story—through His meal, we attempt to pull Christ into our story with modern foods. This is the opposite of the kind of remembering that we are supposed to do in the Supper. Second, the meal is called the *Lord's* Supper for a reason. It is His meal, not ours. We do well to trust in His ways and obey His commands. Replacing the elements with our preferred foods treats the meal like it is our meal, and we are the host and the chef. The Holy Supper belongs to Jesus. Let us listen to Him.

At the same time, specific forms of bread and fruit of the vine should not become legalistic criteria for a valid Sacrament. The church has never insisted upon unleavened or leavened bread in the Sacrament, allowing the use of both. Today, offering gluten-free bread and alcohol-free wine—or grape juice—for those who need these options is not trying to control Christ's meal, but offering His promises according to His institution to the faithful who want to receive their Lord's body and blood. The church has long allowed believers who could not tolerate wine to receive only the bread—receiving the complete body of Christ and the whole promise under the bread. After all, legalistic procedures do not make the meal a sacrament

---

4 No absolute necessity of the interpretation of this phrase as wine is found in Friedrich Blischsel, "*genema*," *Theological Dictionary of the New Testament*, vol. 1, ed. Gerhard Kittel, trans. and ed. Geoffrey W. Bromiley (Grand Rapids: Eerdmans, 1964), 685.

by speaking the right words and using the right elements. Only the Word of the Lord makes the Supper God's instrument of forgiveness and new life through Jesus' body and blood.

The Real Presence of the Body and Blood of Christ in the Supper

In the Sacrament, Jesus gives us His body and His blood under bread and wine.[5] This simple statement is what Lutherans mean by their confession of the sacramental presence, which is more commonly called the **real presence**. For most of church history, Christians all over the world have simply believed the words of the Lord when He said, "This is My body" and "This is My blood." Although the plain sense of the words is quite evident, not all Christians agree on how or even whether Christ's body and blood are present in bread and wine. As with Holy Baptism, the differences in interpretation stem from differences in presuppositions. Some Christians have a hard time believing that God uses physical, created elements to do the spiritual work of forgiving sins, creating and sustaining faith, and uniting believers with Himself and one another. Lutherans, however, recognize God's work through created matter as one of four important presuppositions for understanding Christ's sacramental, or real, presence in the Supper.

Presuppositions for the Real Presence

God Works through Selected Elements of His Created Order. First, Lutherans presume that God conveys His saving power through selected elements of the created order. What Jesus promises in the Lord's Supper is not different from what we see throughout Holy Scripture; God ties His gifts of forgiveness and life to created elements. God saved His people Israel through the waters of the Red Sea. He strengthened their weak faith through the gift of daily manna in the wilderness. He promised forgiveness through the sacrificial system even as it pointed forward to its fulfillment in Christ. God chose human flesh in the incarnation of His Son to effect human salvation. He chose human language as the medium of His good news of deliverance from sin. Jesus' choice of bread/body and wine/blood as elements that could be combined with His Word to deliver forgiveness and life to His people is of one piece with how God works to save.

5 Luther's teaching of the Lord's Supper is presented well in Hermann Sasse, *This Is My Body: Luther's Contention for the Real Presence in the Sacrament of the Altar* (Minneapolis: Augsburg, 1959).

Some Christians have traded this biblical point of view for a spiritualistic presupposition from ancient Greek thought. The spiritualistic point of view insists that the finite—the earthly and material creation of God—is incapable of bearing the infinite power and presence of God. Although this assumption may seem like common sense, it is not rooted in Holy Scripture. The God who most powerfully and fully made Himself known in suffering and death on a cross cannot be reduced to such a presupposition (1 Corinthians 1:18–24). God flips human conventions and expectations upside down by choosing "what is low and despised in the world, even things that are not" to bear His grace and convey His power (1 Corinthians 1:28). Holy Scripture testifies to God taking the earthly and material in His hand as instruments through which He forgives sins and restores life.

The Literal Interpretation of the Words of Institution. Second, Lutherans believe that the Words of Institution—"This is My body" and "This is My blood"—should be interpreted in their plain sense. Lutheran theology does not insist that all passages in Scripture should be interpreted literally. God uses a variety of genres and figures of speech in conveying His Word to us. But like most human language, the language of the biblical writers should be understood literally unless there are compelling reasons for interpreting their words otherwise. It is true: we do not have other instances in which bread and human flesh come together; human blood does not normally come in the form of wine. It is also true that, scientifically, with a chemical analysis in the laboratory, we cannot establish the presence of human cells in the bread or the wine. Christ's promise cannot be proven empirically, nor does it make sense on the basis of our experience or logic. Nonetheless, there is no compelling reason to submit the gift of the Lord to these criteria. He who became 100 percent human while remaining 100 percent God, who turned water into wine and death into life, is certainly able to combine His body with bread and His blood with wine.

Jesus does not explain the Words of Institution as figurative or symbolic. He lets them stand in their plain sense as a promise for His apostles and His church forever. There is no compelling reason not to take Him at His word. Although we cannot understand how Christ's human body can be conveyed by the bread of the Supper, we believe that God can do this. Here human reason fails us, and faith clings to the words of Christ: "This is My body" and "This is My blood." In these promises we find the tremendous mystery of God's love and presence in bread and wine.

The Communication of Christ's Attributes. Third, Lutherans presuppose that the characteristics of Christ's divine nature are shared with the characteristics of His human nature in the person of the God-man. The communication of attributes in Christ provides a way for us to understand how the human nature's body and blood can be present wherever and in whatever form God wills.[6] Christ's human nature and His divine nature continue to exist—He remains fully God and fully human, not a chimera of the two—but they do not exist apart from each other. In the mystery of the personal union that makes Him the person He is, the divine nature shares attributes with the human nature. As God, He is able to keep His promises and be present in specific ways wherever He wishes to be present. Christ's body and blood are not present for the forgiveness of sins in all bread and wine, even though He is present as provider whenever people consume any food and drink. In a special, mysterious way He places His bodily presence in the bread and wine of the Sacrament of the Altar for His people to eat and drink for forgiveness, life, and salvation, as the elements are joined by the Word.

The Mystery of the Real Presence. Fourth, Lutherans presume that God's action through His Word in the Sacrament is a mystery. Neither human reason nor scientific investigation can penetrate this mystery of His love. We hold to His promises in faith, grasping to the person of our God, known in Jesus Christ, not to explanations or logic of how the real presence may work.

The Definition of the Real Presence

Sacramental Presence. On the basis of these presuppositions, Lutherans define the real presence of Christ's body and blood in the bread and wine of the Lord's Supper by calling it a **sacramental presence**. The word *sacrament* in Latin is used to refer to a mystery. The sacramental presence of our Lord's body and blood cannot be explained in terms of human physics, chemistry, or metaphysics. Neither Aristotle's concept of substance nor modern atomic theory can pierce the mystery of this unique form of Christ's presence. In this mysterious sense, Luther and the Confessions can talk about the presence of Christ as a supernatural or even "spiritual" matter. They do not mean that Jesus' body and blood in the Sacrament are unreal or noncorporeal, but mysterious, full of God's power, and invisible to human eyes.[7] Sacramental presence simply means this: Christ's body and blood are there in the elements of bread and wine as God's people gather for the Supper. We take Him at His Word even though we cannot explain the presence.

---

6 See chapter 8.

7 Tom G. A. Hardt, *The Venerable and Adorable Eucharist: A Study of the Lutheran Doctrine of the Lord's Supper in the 1500s*, trans. Mark DeGarmeaux (St. Louis: Concordia, 2023), 21–22.

Some Lutherans have used the phrase "in, with, and under" to describe the relationship of body to bread, blood to wine. The body/blood is *in* the bread/wine. Jesus is not merely present because of the eating or drinking of the elements, but actually promises to be present in the created elements. This presence is mysterious, not an empirical or local presence, but a definitive presence nonetheless.[8] The body and blood are *with* the bread and the wine in the sense that Jesus' sacramental presence does not eliminate the bread and wine, but is enclosed and included with the elements. At the same time, the body and blood are *under* the bread and wine, incapable of being observed with a microscope but present by Christ's promise while hidden under the elements.[9] Luther said it most simply and straightforwardly in the Smalcald Articles when he wrote: "The bread and the wine in the Supper are the true body and blood of Christ."[10] Christ is not there in a general sense, but He is there in the Sacrament for us, for believers to trust in Him and receive exactly what He promises: forgiveness, life, and salvation.

Oral Partaking. The second phrase Lutherans use to define the real presence of Christ's body and blood in the Lord's Supper is **oral partaking**. We receive Christ's body and blood through the mouth, not in a merely spiritual transaction between God and the soul. His body and blood move across our tongues as we ingest the body in the bread and the blood in the wine of the Supper. We must resist the urge to spiritualize this meal. God moves our souls and strengthens our faith through both ears and mouths, not apart from the eating of the elements or the hearing of the Word.

Partaking by the Ungodly or the Unworthy. Third, Lutherans define the real presence by confessing that Christ's presence depends on the Word of the Lord, not on the faith of the person who receives the Supper. In this way, Christ's presence under bread and wine depends not on the strength of our faith or the goodness of our lives, but only on the strength of Christ's promise. Jesus shows up because He promises to do so. Even unbelievers receive Christ's body and blood when they partake of the Supper even though they do not receive its benefits. The presence of Christ's body and blood does not depend on human worthiness or faith. Christ's presence and promise in the meal depend on God's Word alone, though the benefits are only received by faith.

---

8 *Confession concerning Christ's Supper* (1528), AE 37:214–230. Part of this is quoted in Solid Declaration of the Formula of Concord VII 98–103.

9 The "in, with, and under" thus distinguishes the Lutheran confession of the sacramental presence from a symbolic or spiritual view, transubstantiation, and a carnal or capernaitic view respectively. Our thanks to Charles Schulz for this insight.

10 Smalcald Articles III VI 1 (Kolb-Wengert, 320).

Paul wrote in 1 Corinthians 10:16 that the cup of blessing in the Sacrament—and this means the wine, which the cup holds—participates, or has communion with, the blood of Christ. The bread of the Sacrament participates, or has communion with, the body of Christ. In bread and wine Christ comes to us with His body and blood, as His Word works its forgiving and re-creating power upon us.

Alternate Views of the Real Presence

There are other views of the real presence within Christendom. Luther largely accepted the medieval catholic affirmation of it, but he objected to its attempt to explain how the real presence is possible. Medieval teaching affirmed the bread as Christ's body and wine as Christ's blood, but explained it in terms of the physics of Aristotle, the physics taught in the schools of Luther's time. Aristotle had taught that everything had an inner substance, which determined its basic nature, and also had accidents, which give the individual item its own characteristics. According to this system of thought, for example, the authors are human beings because they have the inner substance of human nature. What makes Kolb and Hopkins different are accidents that could be otherwise in human creatures. Kolb is of Germanic descent and shorter in stature while Hopkins is predominately of Belarussian origin and taller in stature. These accidents distinguish Kolb and Hopkins, but none is a necessary characteristic of a human creature. Medieval theologians used this distinction between substance and accidents to explain the mystery of Christ's presence. They said that the substance of the sacramental bread and wine are replaced by the substances of Christ's body and blood even though the outward accidents, the characteristics, of bread and wine remain. They called this process **transubstantiation**, a change in substance. Luther believed that the presence of Christ is a mystery, which is based entirely on His promise. He believed that trying to explain Christ's presence exalts the human mind above the Word of the Lord, suggesting that we can trust our explanation of Christ's sacramental presence rather than the Word. The problem with transubstantiation is not that it is surely false but that it substitutes an explanation for a promise.

Consubstantiation. Because Lutherans reject all definitive explanations of how Christ could be present as if these could sustain faith apart from Christ's promise, it is wrong to suggest that Luther taught consubstantiation, a view held by a few medieval theologians. This view states that the substances of both Christ's body and the bread, of both Christ's blood and the wine, are present in the Supper by virtue of the power of God's Word. Although Lutherans do believe that the bread is the body and the wine is the blood in the Supper, consubstantiation uses Aristotelian physics to explain the presence of Christ. Luther insisted that Christ's presence depends on His promise alone, and we do well to trust in His Word and let the "how" remain a mystery, outside the mastery of human reason.

Symbolic Understanding. Some Christians reject the possibility of Christ's real body and blood being present in the bread and wine, teaching that the bread and wine symbolize Jesus' body and blood and are intended for believers to remember what He has done—also called a **memorial view** of the Supper. In the Reformation era, the Swiss reformer Ulrich Zwingli represented this view, now quite common among Protestants in North America. Although Zwingli may have moved toward a concept of the "spiritual presence" of Christ near the end of his life, for much of the preceding decade he had argued with Luther over the real presence. He had received an education that framed his thought with Platonic conceptions of reality. Zwingli, therefore, believed that earthly elements could only point to—symbolize—the heavenly reality, teaching that bread and wine symbolize Christ's salvific work in the past. He separated God's action on the cross from His delivery of the benefits of Christ's death and resurrection through His Word. He thought of Christ as in heaven at God's right hand, almost like a spatial location, so that Jesus is unable to be present in the meal as the human being that our God is. At most, the Supper recalls the sacrifice on the cross.[11]

Spiritual Presence. Another sixteenth-century Swiss reformer, John Calvin, taught that Christ is spiritually present in the Sacrament. According to Calvin, Christian souls partake of Christ as their bodies receive bread and wine. Here too, the influence of the spiritualizing presuppositions of Platonic philosophy reveal themselves. The soul operates at a heavenly level while the body consumes merely earthly elements. Although closer in some respects to Luther's view than the memorial understanding of the Supper, Calvin's view nonetheless was determined by the presupposition that God's power for salvation cannot come through earthly, material elements. From the perspective of spiritual care, Calvin's view is also quite dangerous. When Jesus' presence depends not on His promise alone but on the faith of the person receiving it, how do we know for sure we have received Jesus? Instead of being turned outward to Christ and His Word, Calvin's view threatens to turn believers inward, wondering about their holiness of life and the state of their faith. The good news is that Christ's Word does not depend on what we do; it depends only on the power of God.

It is important to note that speaking of the "presence of Christ" is insufficient to convey the entire biblical concept of what God is doing for His

---

11 For these views during the 1520s, see Amy Nelson Burnett, *Debating the Sacraments: Print and Authority in the Early Reformation* (Oxford: Oxford University Press, 2019).

people in the Lord's Supper. The presence of Christ could refer to a merely spiritual presence instead of the fully human presence of our God in the Supper. For this reason, Lutheran leaders must speak of the "presence of Christ's body and blood" to convey fully what the Lord has told us of His approach to us in His meal.

Receptionism or Consecrationism

Some Lutherans have discussed whether bread and wine become the body and blood of the Lord when the Words of Institution are spoken to consecrate the elements or when the elements are received by the communicant. The Scriptures, however, do not separate aspects of the Supper in order to define exactly the moment when Jesus is present in the bread. In fact, such an attempt detracts from the institution of Jesus and His promise. As the Lutheran Confessions emphasize following St. Paul's teaching in 1 Corinthians 11, Christ's institution of the Supper "includes the entire action or administration of this sacrament: that in a Christian assembly bread and wine are taken, consecrated, distributed, received, eaten, and drunk, and that thereby the Lord's death is proclaimed."[12] The church dare not separate the parts of the Sacrament, but must keep them together according to Christ's institution. For Jesus is present according to His Word as His people gather to receive His body and blood in faith, which is the whole liturgical action of the Supper.[13]

Nevertheless, behind both **consecrationism** and **receptionism** lie certain valid concerns. In the sixteenth century, Lutherans reacted against medieval scholastic arguments over the properties of the leftover elements of the Sacrament, fearing that the elements would be adored apart from the promise and the oral partaking in faith. Thus many favored the "receptionist" view that Jesus was present in the bread and the wine when He was received. Although this receptionist view has a valid concern, it too easily turns Christ's presence into a spiritual and subjective matter, losing the external nature of Christ's promise and presence. Others were concerned to preserve the focus on the power of God's Word and favored the "consecrationist" view. This view rightly recognizes the power of Christ's Word, but consecrationism tends to be correlated with an unhealthy elevation of the pastor and a focus on liturgical matters more than the faith of the people to receive Christ's gifts. Still others wisely thought such questions were best left unspecified since the Scriptures do not speak directly to them. It is best to emphasize with the Lutheran Confessions: Christ instituted the Sacrament to be consecrated, distributed, and received in the mouth and

12 Solid Declaration of the Formula of Concord VII 84 (Kolb-Wengert, 607).

13 Solid Declaration of the Formula of Concord VII 83–87.

by faith. In this way, we are thrown back to the essentials of the Sacrament. Jesus Christ and His Word make Holy Communion what it is, a life-giving medicine of immortality.

Broken and Shed for You for the Forgiveness of Sin

In His Supper, Christ serves His people His body and blood. In so doing He joins them to Himself, to His own death and resurrection. He gives us the body that He gave to death on the cross. He gives us the blood that was poured out for the forgiveness of sins (Matthew 26:28). In receiving Christ's body offered for us on the cross and His blood poured out on Calvary in our behalf, we sinners are received into the tomb into which His lifeless body was placed. But this body and blood belong to the One who is risen from the dead, so as we receive His body and blood in His Supper, we also receive the gift of life. We join at His Father's table as fellow heirs and children of God, raised to newness of life through the power of His Word. That Word comes here with bread-body and wine-blood to redeem and restore us sinners to the family of God.

Luther sharply rejected the popular medieval notion that Christ's sacrifice was somehow repeated in the Supper. Connected with that view was the popular belief that human merit was gained as God's priest performed this repetition of the sacrifice to God for the people. Most medieval Christians did not think of the benefits of the Supper as a gift to be received by faith. Grace was received, instead, by observing the unbloodied sacrifice, which was thought to work grace *ex opere operato*, by the mere performance of the ritual.[14] Luther and the Lutheran Confessions insisted that the Supper is pure gift, not a human work and "not a satisfaction but a promise and sacrament that requires faith."[15] Indeed, the Lord's Supper, as every other form of God's re-creating Word, bridges the gap between what Jesus did for us historically by His sacrificial death and glorious resurrection and our lives today. That sacrifice and resurrection was "not just a once-upon-a-time but a once-for-all event," and it therefore makes "some fundamental and permanent alterations" to reality.[16]

Many contemporary Roman Catholic teachers have shifted from viewing the Mass as a repetition to a re-presentation of Christ's sacrifice. Nevertheless, if they focus on the human roles in the celebration of the Sacrament, they miss the point Luther made. Luther objected to any view of what happens in the Sacrament as a human opportunity for contribution. What we need is not grace to make us worthy of offering a gift to God,

---

14 See Apology of the Augsburg Confession XXIV.

15 Apology of the Augsburg Confession XXIV 90 (Kolb-Wengert, 275).

16 Gerhard O. Forde, *Theology Is for Proclamation* (Minneapolis: Fortress, 1990), 176.

but the grace that first kills us in our attempts at control and self-justification and makes us new as children of God. The Lord's Supper effects the death of every human pretension and claim of activity in God's gift of new birth. It effects life without any contribution coming from the new child of God. It feeds God's children without sending them first into the field to do some harvesting.

The Supper feeds believers; it feeds their faith. Luther also rejected the popular misrepresentation of the medieval theological maxim that the Sacraments work *ex opere operato*. That phrase was designed to teach that the Sacraments work on the basis of the Word, not on the basis of some other factor in the humans who are performing the sacramental action or receiving its benefit. By Luther's time, however, many believed that *ex opere operato* meant that the Sacraments were effective simply by their performance, regardless of people's faith.[17] Thus they thought that faith played no necessary role in the beneficial reception of the Sacrament. God's Word, Luther insisted, works on its own power, without depending on human contribution or participation. At the same time, God's Word works faith. God speaks for no other purpose than to bring fallen sinners into a relationship of trust and love with Him. Without faith, God's Word is still powerful, but none of its benefits have been received.

Our Lord hosts the Supper so that He might draw back into His own family those who have become disoriented by trusting in false gods. Being in God's family means trusting in the Father through the Son by the Holy Spirit. The Supper cultivates trust in the triune God. The Word of the Lord, with the bread-body and the wine-blood, does not work "magically" to place some charm or amulet upon the recipient, as if it saves us just because we take part in the ceremony. The Supper—and God's Word in it—engages us in conversation. It pronounces us dead as sinners and alive in Christ. It maintains and sustains the relationship a loving Father wants to have with His children. There is no magic here, just the good relationship of parent and child together enjoying the meal the parent has paid for and prepared.

Faith does not make Christ's body and blood present in the Sacrament, any more than the infant's appetite makes the oatmeal present in the dish. God creates faith so that we may receive the benefits of the meal, just as the parent's love must move the child to open wide and receive—rather than

17 In medieval theology, *ex opere operato* was distinct from the view that the Sacraments work *ex opere operantis*, by the work which has already been worked. According to the *ex opere operantis* view, people brought to the Sacraments the necessary element that made the Sacraments effective. This latter view is essentially how Zwingli (and many Protestants today) understood the Sacraments—faith, confession, or a holy life make the Sacraments effective rather than the promise of Jesus. See Timothy J. Wengert, *The Augsburg Confession: Renewing Lutheran Faith and Practice* (Minneapolis: Fortress, 2020), 119–24.

spit out—the breakfast. In the Supper, God calls on us to trust Him, and His call evokes the trust that He desires by the Holy Spirit. We trust Him there for the forgiveness of our sins and the gift of new life. We trust the way He has chosen to act. Even if it seems out of the ordinary, this is one way He has chosen to convey the promise of life to us.

Faith leaps to His table for assurance in His promise. Faith knows that receiving Christ's body and blood sustains, uplifts, and strengthens. Christ has not only given Himself into death that we might have life. He has shared that death and life with us. Jesus does so in several ways, including by feeding us with life itself. Believers cannot help but take deep delight in the love of our God.

Remembering Christ's Death and Resurrection Together

Approaching the Father's Table with other Christians adds to that delight. In coming to Christ's Supper, believers confess their faith and share their confidence in His forgiveness with fellow believers gathered at the same altar. "For as often as you eat this bread and drink the cup, you proclaim the Lord's death until He comes" (1 Corinthians 11:26). Although Holy Communion is more than believers joining together to celebrate and confess their common faith, it is not less. In addition to the danger of making the Sacrament into a mere memorial meal, there is also a danger of reducing the Supper to the gift of individual forgiveness. Christ draws us to Himself *and to one another* through our participation in the Holy Meal. Paul insists that Christians should come together, wait for one another to eat together, and not be divided, for unity with Christ and unity with one another at the Lord's Table are connected (1 Corinthians 11:17–34). Holy Communion is the church's meal where Christians who share a confession of faith remember and celebrate what Jesus has done for us, even as He conveys the benefits of His death and resurrection to us under bread and wine.

United with Other Believers in One Loaf

Believers are united with one another through the Supper, for Christ has made us here to be one loaf (1 Corinthians 10:17). Honestly, we do not always enjoy being linked with those whom God has joined to us. That, however, is part of the point. People who are not family are part of the same family of faith, and our unity in the Spirit through the one Lord, one faith, one Baptism, and one loaf is an unbreakable association, stronger and more real than a family's unity by blood. In this case, water (and wine) is thicker than blood! The Supper makes us one family not only with the Father but also with His other children. Sometimes God brings us to the same table with people we do not like. We learn there to love them because He loves them, even when we do not always like what they are doing. We learn there to reconcile with our brothers and sisters, not holding anything against them when we come to the altar, but forgiving one another in Jesus.[18] Since Christ has reconciled us to Himself, He has also reconciled us to them and them to us. Thus the Supper serves as God's instrument for reconciliation among His people.

Fellowship at Christ's Altar

Because the Supper both symbolizes and effects unity among Christ's people, the church has traditionally been quite strict about who communes together. From the earliest period of its history, the church has used the Lord's Supper as a means of discipline as well as a means of grace.[19] It has refused to let those who are deceiving themselves about the fundamental teachings of God's Word or of the Christian life believe that there is unity where unity is broken or even cracked. Therefore, the church practices fellowship or communion that draws lines of exclusion as well as inclusion, even practicing excommunication if necessary.

Throughout most of its history, the church has practiced **closed Communion**, that is, gathering the family of the congregation and those who share its confession of faith into the Supper's circle and asking those who are not part of the faith family to abstain. Sometimes, closed Communion is called "close Communion," because it is kept close in the family, but the differences between the two are a matter of nomenclature, not practice. The practice of **open Communion**—in which all or at least baptized believers are freely admitted to the Supper—arose relatively late in Christian history and in those areas in which the doctrine of the real presence and the significance of the Sacrament were not highly prized. Recently, theologians have argued for open Communion on the basis of the hospitality Jesus demonstrated in the meals He attended, but all this shows is the hospitality of the Gospel and the church. As Jesus practiced the Holy Supper, instituted it, and as we see it practiced and commanded by the apostle Paul, it is a meal for the family of faith. Churches need to show hospitality in Christ to all, but they must find ways other than an open table to do so. In fact, in a mission setting with unbelievers who do not know the Scriptures, the closed nature of the table will hardly be the strangest or the

18 See Matthew 5:23–24 and Dietrich Bonhoeffer, *Discipleship*, vol. 4 of Dietrich Bonhoeffer Works English, ed. Geffrey B. Kelly and John D. Godsey (Minneapolis: Fortress, 2003), 120–25.

19 Werner Elert, *Eucharist and Church Fellowship in the First Four Centuries*, trans. Norman E. Nagel (St. Louis: Concordia, 1966).

most difficult of teachings to understand. It tends to be Christians who are offended by the closed table, not unbelievers, who find the Gospel itself the bigger challenge.

In the early church, those who had not yet been baptized were asked to leave the assembly after the sermon, before the reception of the Lord's Supper. This practice of the church follows the counsel and commands set forth by St. Paul. Paul warned the church at Corinth that there is such a thing as an unworthy eating and drinking of the Supper, and that such unworthy partaking of the Holy Meal makes one "guilty concerning the body and blood of the Lord" (1 Corinthians 11:27). This unworthy eating is constituted first by unbelief—where we do not trust in Christ's forgiveness, His Word, or His promise to be present in body and blood under bread and wine—and second by failing to treat brothers and sisters in the faith like they are part of the family (1 Corinthians 11:27–34). Hence, St. Paul exhorts each Christian to "examine himself" before eating with regard to his faith and his life (1 Corinthians 11:28). For this reason, Lutherans baptize infants but wait to commune children until after they have received instruction in the faith and Christian practices of confession and repentance.

Dress Rehearsal for the Eschatological Banquet

The closed nature of the Communion table is only temporary, as believers wait for Christ to return and preside visibly over the banquet in the age to come. Part of the believers' delight in the Supper of the Lord is their recognition of the meal as a dress rehearsal for the eschatological banquet which will last forever in God's kingdom (Matthew 8:11). The scriptural picture of the eternal life of human creatures with God is a festive banquet (Isaiah 25:6–9; Matthew 22:1–14; Luke 13:28–29; Revelation 19:6–9) that we receive as a foretaste in the Lord's Supper. Dressed in Christ through Baptism (Galatians 3:27), we come to celebrate the future as well as the present blessing of His promise. Christ promised that He would drink together with His disciples on "that day when I drink it new with you in My Father's kingdom" (Matthew 26:29). God's rule and reign is breaking in upon us already as His death sentence is executed upon us in Baptism, the promise of life in Christ is received by the Spirit, and we partake of the body and blood of Calvary's sacrificial Victim. God's rule has established itself in His children by faith, but the Supper focuses our attention on Christ's return when God's reign will be apparent to all, and everything will be filled with the Spirit of God. We look forward to banqueting as members of His family when dying to sin will no longer be necessary, and life will be confirmed for us forever.

Celebrating Together

Because the Lord's Supper occupies so important a spot in the regular rhythm of the Christian life, it is necessary to look at some of the practical aspects of assembling at God's Table.

The Whole Congregation Receives Together

The Lord's Supper gathers God's people. Therefore, they eat together as a congregation. Although the church has always taken the Supper to those who were ill and infirm and thus unable to join the congregation—the Supper taken by the pastor is the way these join the congregation in worship—it has not deemed the Supper appropriate for private use or for use by small groups within the congregation. The Sacrament unites the whole congregation and should not be used to "do something special" for a group within it, even for a married couple who may wish to commune together during their wedding. To use the Lord's Supper to serve one group within a congregation rather than the whole gathering threatens to create a party spirit that abuses the Lord's invitation.

Some have been tempted in recent years to hold "online Communion" services in which a family celebrates Communion at home as the pastor speaks the Words of Institution in a streamed or recorded service. Alternatively, others have suggested that a head of household can celebrate the Sacrament in his own home during times of need. Both practices have two dangers. First, these practices only seem to make sense when individual comfort is prioritized over Christ's institution and the unity He promises with Himself and His church. Jesus offers forgiveness of sins at His table, but an individual's desire for forgiveness does not constitute a reason to give the Supper apart from a congregational gathering. Hence, Luther wrote to followers of Jan Hus who did not have pastors to give them the Supper:

> For it would be safer and more wholesome for the father of the household to read the gospel and, since the universal custom and use allows it to the laity, to baptize those born in his home, and so to govern himself and his according to the doctrine of Christ, even if throughout life they did not dare or could not receive the Eucharist. For the Eucharist is not so necessary that salvation depends on it. The gospel and baptism are sufficient, since faith alone justifies and love alone lives rightly.[20]

Jesus offers the promise of forgiveness of sins in many forms of the Word. Preaching and Scripture should be shared within a Christian family and over electronic media. All forms of the Word are effective in offering Christ's promise and giving God's people the assurance we need for salvation. The

20 *Concerning the Ministry* (1523), AE 40:9.

Lord's Supper has its own purposes: Jesus has instituted this meal to reconcile Christians to one another as well as to Him in body and spirit.

Second, an individual family is not the gathering of believers intended by Christ's institution. Paul's discussion of the Lord's Supper in 1 Corinthians shows that although the people may have gathered in a house for worship, they were not members of the same family. Paul exhorted them to act like Christians united in the Spirit and not like separate family units that may eat and drink however much they want (1 Corinthians 11:17–22, 33–34). Chapter 12 of the same epistle discusses the unity of the church under the Lord Jesus as the Holy Spirit offers a variety of gifts to the church and unites many and diverse members into one Body. The Sacrament is Christ's meal to draw together this diverse group into one Body with Himself and one another, becoming one through the one bread (1 Corinthians 10:17). Jesus, therefore, did not institute the Supper for a family to grow together, even a Christian family, but for His church to grow in the Spirit. We can easily turn the Lord's Supper to our own purposes—especially in Western cultures in which the family is often idolized—when we bring it into our homes instead of receiving it with others from one who represents both the Lord and the entire congregation.

As such a representative, the pastor of the congregation is the one who consecrates the elements and leads the Supper of the Lord. In the person of the pastor the unity of the congregation is expressed and observed. Lay assistance in distribution does not violate this principle. Scripture contains no rules or procedures for distribution, and laypeople may distribute Christ's blood without offending God's plan for His Supper. The pastor must consecrate and, as the congregation's representative, admits communicants to Christ's Table. That ordinarily means the pastor distributes Christ's body in the host.

The Consecration of the Elements

Proper consecration requires the proclamation of the Words of Institution. The church has always set them within a liturgy. That liturgy may have a variety of forms. None of these forms is necessary for the proper observation of the Supper.

The elements should be received and disposed of reverently because they are vehicles that God uses in a special way. We cheapen the Lord's approach to us through these elements if we treat them casually. Our actions may suggest that the loaf is merely bread and the cup merely wine when Christ has promised otherwise for His people. Although we should not treat the bread and wine as if Christ were in them forever once they have been consecrated, we dare not treat them flippantly, as if Jesus were never there at all. What constitutes reverent treatment of the elements may vary from congregation to congregation, depending on local perceptions.

Frequency of Communing and "Worthiness" for Reception

Children like to eat at their parents' table. Not only do they enjoy the food, they also enjoy the company. Believers like to come to the Father's table to feast upon the body and blood of their Lord. There they receive sustenance for the life of faith and enjoy the company of their God and fellow believers. Much of Christendom throughout history has celebrated the Lord's Supper weekly. Luther believed that people could not be considered Christian if they did not receive the Sacrament at least four times a year,[21] but his church celebrated, and many Wittenbergers received, the Lord's body and blood under bread and wine each week.

Some Christians do not want to eat and drink weekly because the Supper is so strange; it does not fit their conception of faith. Others feel little necessity because their sensitivity to their own sinfulness and their true need for Christ's body—the church and Jesus—have become dulled. Some do not understand what the Sacrament accomplishes in their lives, bestowing forgiveness and life through faith, linking us with God and fellow believers in love, and building hope as we await the promise of the perfect celebration in the Lamb's wedding feast. Some Christians avoid the Lord's Supper because they fear receiving it unworthily.

Worthiness for receiving the Sacrament consists of our recognition that we are unworthy, that we need God's love and forgiveness. Luther suggested that if the devil, the world, and the flesh still threaten to tarnish or take away the joy of our faith, we need the Sacrament. Jesus offers it to the hungry, not to the satisfied. It is Christ whose worth is at issue in the Lord's Supper. The meal is planned for those whose worth has disappeared, who need the gift of worth.

Paul insisted that believers examine themselves (1 Corinthians 11:28) as they come to the Supper. That examination includes the recognition of what God is giving in the Sacrament. Those who do not discern the Lord's body receive judgment (1 Corinthians 11:29). Although some have suggested that this body is the Body of Christ, the church, the context, particularly 1 Corinthians 11:27, prevents that interpretation. This judgment that we can receive in connection with an unfaithful use of the Lord's Supper is no different than the judgment that falls upon those who hear His Word in a frivolous or apathetic manner.

---

21 Small Catechism Preface 22 (Kolb-Wengert, 350).

Because of Paul's command to examine ourselves, the Western Church has offered the Lord's Supper only to those who are able to do so. The Eastern Church communes infants as soon as they are baptized. There is no biblical warrant for this practice. Baptism and the Lord's Supper are not to be equated, even though the church understands them both as "sacraments." No general agreement exists on the proper age for admission to the Lord's Supper. The connection of one's first Holy Communion with confirmation is certainly unnecessary. During Luther's time, most churches communed youth at a younger age than graduation from eighth grade.

"Examination" in preparation for the Lord's Supper recognizes no more and no less than who God is as He comes to us in the Supper and who we are as we receive it. We recognize with joy and thanksgiving that God gives in the Sacrament and we receive. We recognize that we need the blessings God promises in this meal of life. We recognize that our own unworthiness draws us to the Lord's life-giving body and blood offered in, with, and under bread and wine. Believers approach the Lord's Supper craving not only forgiveness of sins but also unity with brothers and sisters and power by the Spirit to live God's callings in daily life. The Spirit guides us to die to our sinful nature and be raised to genuine human life once again. At His Supper our God feeds us for living.

CHAPTER 16
THE SANCTIFIED LIFE, OR THE NEW OBEDIENCE

GOD'S Word kills sinners in their sin and brings new creatures to life under grace, transforming egoists into a people of prayer who place their neighbors' needs equal to their own. The Holy Spirit moves into believers' lives to make them temples of God, who belong not to themselves but to the Lord, whom they glorify with their bodies (1 Corinthians 6:19–20). The Holy Spirit lavishly pours out God's love into the hearts of His children so that they are people of endurance, character, and hope (Romans 5:4–5). Through the Spirit, believers' lives have been changed from selfish, sinful ways to the way of Christ. Hence, Paul writes: "It is no longer I who live, but Christ who lives in me. And the life I now live in the flesh I live by faith in the Son of God, who loved me and gave Himself for me" (Galatians 2:20). Through Jesus and the Spirit, our desire to live apart from God is put to death, and He bestows the power to live freely as His creatures, as daughters and sons, as humans were created to live in Eden.

The Holy Spirit empowers the Christian life on the basis of the hope we have in Christ (Romans 15:13; cf. Acts 1:8). This revival of true human living, often called sanctification,[1] takes place through faith. Faith in Jesus perceives human life and its Creator in a whole new way. Although we must be careful not to reduce sanctification to a perception of Christian experience, the Holy Spirit does change believers' hearts and minds through the Word, turning dread to delight, anxiety to assurance, and selfishness to sympathy. The Holy Spirit transforms human hearts by faith, not by compelling good works but by birthing new people who cannot help but pray and give thanks to the Father, follow Jesus under the cross, and live out the new obedience in service to others.

1 On the New Testament concept of holiness and sanctification, see Otto Procksch and Karl Georg Kuhn, "*hagios*," *Theological Dictionary of the New Testament*, vol. 1, ed. Gerhard Kittel, trans. and ed. Geoffrey W. Bromiley (Grand Rapids: Eerdmans, 1964), 88–115.

Sanctified by Faith

For the sake of the Gospel, sanctification must be clearly distinguished from justification. We dare never confuse God's unconditional grace and His work of salvation with human deeds, progress, success, or emotions. The new obedience or sanctification of God's people is never a cause of their salvation. Instead, in Luther's favorite imagery from Holy Scripture, the good works of the Christian life are the fruit of a good tree. When by faith we are grafted into the vine, Jesus, we cannot help but bear the fruit of the Spirit (John 15:5). We have been chosen by Christ, saved by His Word alone, so that we might give glory to God with our lives.

At the same time that we must remember justification's qualitative difference from sanctification, we dare not forget that God's gift of faith not only justifies but also sanctifies. By faith, we are holy, children of God, restored to our proper state as God's human creatures. God Himself does the work of sanctification not apart from us but in us. The Holy Spirit's gift of saving trust changes hearts and lives as He moves us from sin to grace, fear to faith, and terror to peace. Faith saves and sanctifies.

Discussions of sanctification, too, often devolve into two questions: (1) Am I holy enough for God? (2) What counts as a good work? Both questions miss the point of the doctrine. Jesus' death and resurrection and our Baptism into Him have promised that sinners belong to Christ and are forgiven already, though we are never "holy enough" on our own. Believers remain sinners who can only beg for mercy and grace from the Lord. Praise God that Jesus gives grace so extravagantly, having come "not to call the righteous, but sinners" (Mark 2:17)! Sanctification, then, is not a matter of believers becoming holy—as if they had to achieve holiness by their own actions. Sanctification recognizes God's holy work in the lives of His people from beginning to end. Before we were ever aware of it, the Holy Spirit was already at work by the Word, preparing our hearts and bringing Christ to us. The Holy Spirit will not cease in this work until believers are raised from the dead on the Last Day to live in God's kingdom in joy and blessedness forever. This understanding of sanctification as the work of the Spirit alone is called the **broad sense of sanctification**.

The question of good works, therefore, is hardly the center of the doctrine. Instead, Luther's understanding of sanctification confesses how the Holy Spirit makes people holy through Word and Sacrament and Christian community.[2] The various forms of the Word are the ways in which the Spirit strengthens the faith that He created in Baptism and empowers believers to follow Jesus in all of life. When sanctification is reduced to good works, it

---

2 Large Catechism II 34–62.

tends to focus the Christian life on what deeds we must do or what motives we must have. Instead of opening our eyes outward to see God at work through His means of grace and in unexpected ways in neighbors around us, an emphasis on good works and motivation focuses believers inward. To be clear, Christians must serve their neighbors; good works are not optional. God commands such service, and children, parents, co-workers, fellow students, and the poor—one's neighbors—need it. At the same time, Christians do not perform good works alone by their own efforts; rather, believers are led by the Holy Spirit who dwells within through the Gospel. Justified by the Word, believers cooperate with the Holy Spirit as He leads them to do God's will and care for those in their spheres, which is the **narrow sense of sanctification**.

The Christian life is a life of good works, but it is not a life of worrying about good works. The Holy Spirit transforms believers to be eccentric—outward-focused and strange by the world's standards—living from God's external Word in faith and toward neighbors in love.

Once the Holy Spirit has created faith in Jesus in a person, the Spirit also brings a new attitude and new desires. Believers reap and produce the fruit of the Holy Spirit's presence as their minds and hearts are turned to love, joy, peace, patience, kindness, goodness, faithfulness, gentleness, and self-control. These flow in when self-centered passions and desires have been crucified in Christ (Galatians 5:22–24). These products of the Spirit's presence give believers the mind of Christ (Philippians 2:5). The new creature produces the fruits of faith both in internal changes to the desires and the mind and in external obedience to the Word of God. These are the result of the saving message of salvation in Jesus Christ and the faith it produces (2 Timothy 3:15–17; cf. Ephesians 2:10).

The sanctified life is often called a life of **new obedience**. It is new because the old way of life, which turned us inward on ourselves, is put away. We are liberated by Christ's word of forgiveness to "walk in newness of life" (Romans 6:4). It is a life of obedience because faith now turns its ear to listen to God's Word. Life comes as we are brought out of our deafness to hear His Word of love, which calls us to live in peace with Him and with fellow human creatures. The Hebrew word *shama* means "to hear," but Scripture also uses it in the sense of "listen" or "hearken to" and "obey." To hear God is to obey Him. Faith, listening once again to the Lord, cannot help but respond with praise in thought, word, and deed.

In the Apology of the Augsburg Confession, Philip Melanchthon twice set forth a brief explanation of how faith produces works.[3] Too often

3 Apology of the Augsburg Confession IV 125, 189 (Kolb-Wengert, 140, 150–51). In the octavo edition of the Apology, which is translated in the Kolb-Wengert edition of the *Book*

Lutherans have taken the link between faith and works for granted. In a rightful concern for **moralism**—turning the Christian life into a list of things to do and not do—and **enthusiasm**—understanding God's Word and work as internal, inside of persons, rather than external—Lutherans have sometimes ignored how the Christian life is experienced as peace, freedom, wonder, and joy through faith in Christ. Lutherans sometimes talk as if they have forgotten that the gift of faith changes sinners in fundamental ways, reshaping our desires, motivations, and relationships. Although these changes are not usually perceived by the one undergoing, suffering, the work of the Holy Spirit, we are truly being changed, which can often (but not always) be recognized by others around us. Hence, Melanchthon writes: "After we have been justified and reborn by faith, we begin to fear and love God, to pray for and expect help from him, to thank and praise him, and to obey him in our afflictions."[4] The Holy Spirit's gift of faith cultivates in us the new obedience to God's design for human life in ways that can be recognized and understood at least in part psychologically.[5] We live out our new life as the psychological and physical beings God created us to be.

Trusting in Jesus Christ changes our desires in fundamental ways that enable free human action, action determined by selfless love rather than selfish ambition. Out of this character of love formed by our God, the Spirit produces dispositions and attitudes that align with faith in Jesus and lead to action. The fruit of the Spirit is formed in believers, moving them and training them in the practice of active righteousness in the world and toward God in multiple ways.

First, faith recognizes God's unfathomable goodness and wonders at the beauty of His grace. St. Augustine taught that the Holy Spirit transforms believers so that we desire God more than we desire sin, delighting in God's mercy and goodness more than we ever enjoyed sin.[6] In slightly different terms, Melanchthon describes the Holy Spirit's work as moving believers from guilt to consolation and from terror to trust, as faith grasps hold of God's love in Christ in the midst of Satan's onslaught, sin's assault, and dread of death.[7] We come to delight in our God because we trust in His mercy in the cross of Christ.

---

of Concord, there is no paragraph 189, but the point remains present in the paragraph on pages 150–51. Cf. *Concordia: The Lutheran Confessions* (St. Louis: Concordia, 2006), 105, 110.

4 Apology IV 125 (Kolb-Wengert, 140).

5 See Simeon Zahl, *The Holy Spirit and Christian Experience* (Oxford: Oxford University Press, 2020).

6 Zahl, *Holy Spirit*, 189–94.

7 Apology of the Augsburg Confession IV 45, 62, as representative examples. See also Zahl, *Holy Spirit*, 118–36.

Second, faith confesses sin confidently. As we experience God's unimaginable grace and "the love of Christ that surpasses knowledge" (Ephesians 3:19), we also recognize that on our own even our best deeds are "like a polluted garment" (Isaiah 64:6). By faith, we do not hide from our sin, but we open ourselves to the light of Christ. For "if we confess our sins, He is faithful and just to forgive us our sins and to cleanse us from all unrighteousness" (1 John 1:9).

Third, faith gives thanks. Thanksgiving takes many forms. It begins with verbal praise and gratitude, in the congregation of God's people, in the home, and in personal prayer. Thanksgiving then flows over into words of love and deeds of kindness to those around us, recognizing not only what God has done for us but also the many ways that fellow creatures function as God's masks and servants.

Fourth, the faith of God's children cannot keep secrets. Just as little ones are unable to keep secrets to themselves, neither can God's children hold His goodness inside. As believers glow in their appreciation of His love, God's love bubbles out from within them in both word and deed. They share their delight and wonder in Christ's love with those around them by touching the lives of others with God's care and kindness.

Fifth, faith has confidence in Christ's providing and protecting presence rather than trying to secure life on human terms. Believers dare to risk what God has given them to serve others. They no longer believe that they need to secure their own lives by hanging on to material possessions, time, or any other gift of God. Although there is no requirement to give a 10 percent tithe for Christians, such giving is appropriate both to give thanks to God for His many gifts and to show confidence that God will continue to provide even as a significant portion of income is given away. Faith gives believers confidence that God will supply their needs and support them as they carry His love and concern into the lives of other people.

Last, faith recognizes that God's plan for human life differs significantly from our natural assumptions about life's significance and purpose. Faith perceives that God has "succeeded" by submitting Himself to the evil that afflicts His people and by surrendering and sacrificing Himself. God has fleshed out the perfect human life in service and suffering. So faith takes its cue for good living from its Savior and God. Faith submits to the call to service and suffering in self-surrender and self-sacrifice. Therein we find the joy of being God's people.

Being transformed in such fashion by faith, believers can live out the Christian life in the midst of the struggle against sinful desires that draw us into ourselves. Because they are freed by Christ to live in faith and to live out their faith in Him, believers seek to live the cruciform life, arms reached out to others.

The cruciform life of sanctification is permeated by **prayer**, conversation with God. Recognizing God as a good Father who loves them as His own children, believers pray boldly, asking for His good gifts and His Spirit through Jesus (Luke 11:1–13). Besides the Word of God itself, nothing is closer to the center of the sanctified life than prayer. In the words of Lutheran theologian Edward Koehler, prayer "is the heartbeat of faith."[8] When a Christian is in a groove of faith—which is hardly all the time for those who are both sinners and saints—prayer seems to happen spontaneously, almost naturally and continually, like a heartbeat (cf. 1 Thessalonians 5:17). The Christian lifts all things to the Father in prayer just as a beloved little child cannot help but tell her dad about everything she is feeling and thinking. And even when sanctification seems like a slog, the Spirit "intercedes for us with groanings too deep for words," praying for us when we know not what we need and opening our lips to pray according to God's will when it was not our first desire (Romans 8:26).

God's children do not speak with Him regularly because they believe that their prayers have the power to dictate to Him what He must do. The confidence of believers is exactly the opposite—they can pray boldly because they trust that God knows all things, and He will draw them into His will through prayer and do what He knows is best. Accordingly, they do not pray because they regard it as a magic formula to get what they want. Nor do believers dismiss prayer as empty words since God already has made His unchangeable decisions regarding the course of human life. Since prayer begins in faith inspired by the Spirit, believers can recognize in prayer God's leading and direction into which we are invited. In addition, believers want to talk with their heavenly Father, and they know He wants to hear from them. So they pray, early and often. Their prayers respond to God's goodness and to human need as His Word engages them and as those around them cry out for help.

A Life of Discipleship: Living a Cruciform Life

Believers have been joined with Christ's death in Baptism (Romans 6:4), the result of which is that Christ lives in them (Galatians 2:20). On the one hand, they are in a constant struggle to "put to death" whatever is "earthly" in them: "sexual immorality, impurity, passion, evil desire, and covetousness, which is idolatry … anger, wrath, malice, slander, and obscene talk," lying and other ungodly practices (Colossians 3:5–9; cf. Galatians 5:24). "For

8 Edward W. A. Koehler, *A Summary of Christian Doctrine*, 3rd rev. ed. (St. Louis: Concordia, 2006), 222.

the desires of the flesh are against the Spirit, and the desires of the Spirit are against the flesh, for these are opposed to each other, to keep you from doing the things you want to do" (Galatians 5:17). On the other hand, having been crucified with Jesus, believers have been raised with Jesus through the Holy Spirit and are conformed to Him in the new self, "which is being renewed in knowledge after the image of its creator" (Colossians 3:10). Crucified and raised with Jesus by faith, believers follow Him under the cross.

The Struggle of Sanctification

Like Robert Louis Stevenson's Dr. Jekyll and Mr. Hyde, believers are at war within themselves. Paul describes this internal battle between himself as a justified believer and his own sinful nature in Romans 7. There he admitted that he did not understand his own actions, for what he did not want to do, he did, and what he wanted to do, he did not do (7:15). He recognized that his "flesh," that is, his old, sinful nature apart from his death to sin in Christ, had nothing good dwelling within it (7:18). It cut short his ability to do the right things that he wanted to do. It remained under the Law's condemnation. As a newborn child of God, Paul could see both old and new natures warring within himself: "For I delight in the law of God, in my inner being, but I see in my members another law waging war against the law of my mind and making me captive to the law of sin that dwells in my members." Paul conceded what is true of every human being and every Christian apart from faith in Jesus: "Wretched man that I am!" But he knew who would deliver him from this body of death: "Thanks be to God through Jesus Christ our Lord!" (7:22–25).

Every believer repeats Paul's experience of the struggle against sin. The Law condemns daily; the Gospel renews the baptismal life each day as well. Christians often want to move beyond the frustrating cycle of sin and grace, seeking to transcend the struggle of the old and new nature to live only in the new. The desire may be laudable, but the result of such attempts is always dangerous pride or intense shame. If we think that we have succeeded in moving beyond confession of sin, we will not boast in our Savior but in ourselves and our accomplishments. The irony is that such spiritual success means the loss of saving faith. If we are honest as we try to beat our old nature, we will continually bear the shame of failure. Instead of letting Jesus take our shame from us, we will put the burden on ourselves to overcome our sinful nature, which only results in more shame, guilt, and failure. The continual struggle between sin and grace might seem lamentable, but Christians should see it as part of daily life under the cross. Daily we are crucified with Christ as we confess our sins, and daily we look to Jesus alone for forgiveness and new life. Our salvation does not depend on us or our progress; it depends only on the strength of the Lord Jesus, whose power is made perfect in weakness (2 Corinthians 12:9).

Following Jesus under the Cross

The sanctified life is no more or less than a life of following Jesus. Jesus' word to the Twelve—"Follow Me"—is a word that all Christians receive in their Baptism, crucified and risen with Jesus in order to follow Him in obedience under grace (Romans 6:1–19).[9] To be sure, Jesus must be received first as sacrament, a gift given in grace and a treasure to be trusted, before we can ever follow Him. But when Christ is received by faith, believers follow Jesus. "As you received Christ Jesus the Lord, so walk in Him" (Colossians 2:6). "Be imitators of God, as beloved children. And walk in love, as Christ loved us and gave Himself up for us" (Ephesians 5:1–2). "Whoever says he abides in [Jesus Christ] ought to walk in the same way in which He walked" (1 John 2:6). Jesus speaks of believers as sheep who follow their Good Shepherd: "When [the shepherd] has brought out all his own, he goes before them, and the sheep follow him, for they know his voice" (John 10:4).

The Christian life is a life of following Jesus, but such discipleship is more about being conformed into the likeness of Jesus than it is about trying to imitate Him. If we think that the Christian life is primarily imitation, we will mistakenly believe that our lives are to be a continual progress toward holiness in which sin succumbs to spiritual success until the Christian is a beacon of godliness. Christians should strive to follow Jesus in obedience, but we are conformed to Christ not so much in success as in struggle, in the crosses of the Christian life. Although Dietrich Bonhoeffer wrote one of the most famous works about following Jesus, *Discipleship* or *Cost of Discipleship*, he recognized that Christians are conformed to Jesus not by striving to be like Jesus but "as the form of Jesus Christ himself so works on us that it molds us, conforming our form to Christ's own (Gal. 4:9)."[10] Jesus works on people by His Word, in His church, and with neighbors in vocation so that we "die daily the death of sinners," seeing ourselves as the chief of sinners. Following Jesus means humbly bearing the wounds inflicted on us and laying down our own wills to confess that God's will is right even in suffering.[11] Following Jesus means not being concerned about our own welfare but in humility considering others more significant than ourselves (Philippians 2:3–8).

---

9 Dietrich Bonhoeffer, *Discipleship*, vol. 4 of *Dietrich Bonhoeffer Works*, ed. Geffrey B. Kelly and John D. Godsey (Minneapolis: Fortress, 2001), 207.

10 Dietrich Bonhoeffer, *Ethics*, vol. 6 of *Dietrich Bonhoeffer Works*, ed. Clifford J. Green (Minneapolis: Fortress, 2005), 93.

11 Bonhoeffer, *Ethics*, 6:95.

Following Jesus does not mean becoming more divine but more human.[12] Living the sanctified Christian life means that we can reject Satan's seditious seduction to become like God and be content with our place as God's creatures. We can follow God's design for human community and join a congregation, living with other Christians to hear God's Word and bear one another's burdens (Galatians 6:2). We do not need to pretend that we are strong, but we can be vulnerable with our weaknesses, confident in God's strength in Jesus in the midst of weakness. We can take up the cross not to save ourselves or anyone else, but because this is the life to which Jesus called us and in which we can love our neighbors.

Crosses in Christian Living

"If anyone would come after Me, let him deny himself and take up his cross and follow Me," Jesus said (Mark 8:34). Believers experience the cross in multiple ways. Primarily Christians experience the Holy Spirit's continual crucifying of their sinful urges and planning, as the Word in all its forms turns God's children back to Him daily in repentance. Believers also bear the cross as suffering afflicts them and those around them into whose lives God reaches through their love, care, and concern.

Christians have defined the "crosses" of Christian living in various ways. The thorns of the flesh that come through bodily ailments or besetting sins that never seem completely conquered (2 Corinthians 12:7–10) are probably not what Christ included in the crosses His followers naturally assume. Crosses come in the course of our callings, or at the edge of our callings, as we gather neighbors from further away into the circle of our care and concern. Christ bore the cross for others, to deliver them from death, while Christians bear the cross for others not to atone for them but to show compassion.

Christ's people bear the crosses of others to give them support as evils fall upon them and to relieve the sufferings of their fellow human creatures. In home and on the job, in the community and the congregation, our callings bring us close to those who suffer. Christ calls us to stand next to those who suffer and help them bear their afflictions. We may be able to help them escape their afflictions, but often we cannot. Sometimes we may only be able to hold a hand and weep with them or listen and pray. Although bearing such crosses is challenging because we cannot "fix" the problem, the Holy Spirit shapes us the most through these thorns. In the face of suffering that is unfixable, God reminds us that we are not gods, and we must depend entirely on Him for the gifts of life, health, and everything that we are and have. Although we would never seek such a cross and we do

12 Bonhoeffer, *Ethics*, 6:96.

not want it, suffering—*tentatio* or *Anfechtung*, as Luther talked about these experiences—is the training ground on which believers learn how sweet, beautiful, and comforting the Word of God is.[13] Through these experiences God forms His children into His Son. Believers may find that their patience wears thin when Christ calls them simply to stand by another person, for a long time, with no fix for the neighbor's woe in sight, but Jesus calls us to do just that.

Crosses seem to take life away; they deprive us of things and time we think we need. But in losing things and time for the welfare of those whom we are called to stand by and support, we are given rich and full life. All the things and time in the world mean nothing if we forfeit life with the One who calls us to take up crosses. As we fall into the troubles of this world, under its crosses, we do so in full confidence that our Lord will never be ashamed of us (Mark 8:34–38). In the process, loving the needy around us will suppress and starve our own desires to do things our own way (1 Peter 4:1–2). Standing by those who need our love in their affliction will turn our attention toward God and strengthen our faith and trust (1 Peter 1:6–7; 2 Corinthians 4:16–18), as we throw ourselves upon Him in prayer (Isaiah 26:16–19). As we die a little to all that we have been trying to hang onto for ourselves under these crosses of the horizontal realm, God gives an ever fuller appreciation of life as He wants it to be lived.

Although Jesus' understanding of the cross may not include the crosses that come upon us as a result of illness, age, or catastrophic sin, the experience of these is not so different from bearing the kinds of crosses to which Jesus likely referred. In fact, in these circumstances believers learn to rest on the Word that comes through fellow Christians, which is just as important as offering the Gospel to those in need. Because Christians always exist in the community of the church, our struggles offer opportunities for other believers to encourage us with the Gospel, be Jesus to us, and intercede on our behalf before the Father. At the same time, the Holy Spirit uses our sufferings to remind us of our lack of control, leading us to Scripture and prayer to receive mercy and grace from the Lord.

Believers never seek crosses. Self-imposed crosses usually reflect a desire to earn our own salvation. Crosses fall upon us as we follow Jesus in the callings of daily life.

The Structure of the New Obedience

The sanctified life of new obedience does not separate believers from God's world, as if Christians needed to transcend the earthly, material world. The

---

13 *Preface to the German Writings* (1539), AE 34:286–87.

new obedience is the life God gave to Adam and Eve in the beginning, a life lived in shalom in two kinds of relationships: faith toward the Creator and love toward other creatures, especially human creatures. God created human beings for community—and believers are re-created for community—to exercise the dominion of service under fellow creatures to the praise of God. The life of new obedience, therefore, calls believers into the world, recognizing it as God's creation, redeemed by Christ, and sought for sanctification by the Spirit.

A Life of Service in Vocation

During the late medieval period, Christianity was essentially divided into two classes: holy orders for those serious about sanctification and the normal Christian life for those who would need to be sanctified in purgatory. There were even two sets of commands. Normal Christians only had to follow the Ten Commandments while the higher class of Christians had to follow the "evangelical counsels," special laws of the New Testament, including those of poverty and chastity, in a separate setting of a monastery or convent. It seems to make sense that if we want to be true Christians, we need to do something extraordinary.

Luther saw in Holy Scripture, however, a different understanding of the Christian faith. There are no classes of Christians, for all who have been baptized are on the same level: saved by Jesus and belonging to Him in the church. In addition, the Christian faith is not practiced alone in prayer, reading, and worship for the benefit of one's personal spiritual journey, but in the world where Christians serve others and receive help. Thus Christian life does not require extraordinary service that few can do. Mundane matters of parenting, listening, farming, sewing, teaching, learning, cooking, and plumbing, among other things, are holy in God's sight as these fulfill His commands through faith. God's commands are to be lived out by all believers as they serve in the vocations of daily life.

In the horizontal relationships with creatures, God has structured four situations for human service in which people find their various vocations. These are the situations of home, occupation, society, and congregation. In each of these situations God has fashioned for His human creatures **responsibilities**—"response-abilities"—which are recognized both in God's commandments and in God-given relationships. Human creatures respond to needs within the communities God has designed for their daily life (Genesis 2:18).

These responsibilities extend God's care, concern, and direction into daily living. They include household roles, as spouse, parent, child, friend, close neighbor, and member of an extended family; occupational responsibilities, as homemaker, worker, foreman, or CEO; social roles, as community member, voter, taxpayer, and member of a political organization; and congregational responsibilities, as worshiper, witness, Sunday School teacher, pastor, committee chair, or altar guild member. In each of these roles, human responsibility takes shape in specific functions, from changing diapers and washing dishes to setting up chairs for worship or serving on the local school board.

All human creatures find that life fits into these situations, although some societies combine various situations. Luther, for instance, combined work and household, naming only three estates: household, church, and government. Even today, colleagues often become part of our "household" as we invite them into our office spaces and have fellowship with them at parties and meetings, and they become friends. Regardless of society's form, Christians recognize in their responsibilities the calling of God. Therefore, believers regard their responsibilities as **vocations**, not just in the occupational realm but in all four situations of human life. God assigns all human creatures to be doing His work of loving and caring for the creation. This is how God works. Luther thus called humans "masks of God," for God stands behind us to care for His world.

Recognizing the structure of the four situations does not determine which actions believers will perform in any given instance. The structure reminds us of the general shape of God's plan for human life, and it reminds us that He is Creator and Provider. But within this structure, human creatures—including believers—may disagree among themselves on just how God's love, care, and concern should be demonstrated in a given instance. Believers may disagree concerning whether a course of action corresponds to God's plan for fruitful life together or whether it contradicts that plan. Different cultures have developed different forms for successful governance of life in the family or society, and the institutions and customs that shape daily life are often in a state of flux. Therefore, believers need to be conscious of both cultural influences and the Word of God as they make decisions on how to live faithfully in the home, job, community, and congregation.

A Life of Virtue

Service to other human creatures is governed by the self-sacrificing model of **agape** love, which Christ enables us to give to others (1 John 4:7–12). Agape is different from a self-serving love that desires what the object gives. Agape is ready to sacrifice itself for the object of its love.[14] In this fullest sense of the word, love is the highest of the virtues that God designed for human life (1 Corinthians 13:13).

---

14 See Anders Nygren, *Agape and Eros*, trans. Philip S. Watson (London: SPCK, 1953).

Virtues, the good or excellent attitudes and actions that fulfill the highest human potential in thought and deed, provide another category in which believers have thought about the Christian life. The ancient Greek philosophers, Aristotle above all, described the good life in terms of the practice of such characteristics as prudence, justice, courage, and temperance. To these "cardinal virtues" Christian theologians added the "theological virtues" of faith, hope, and love. The list of virtues may be broadened to include all those attitudes and actions commanded by God, which He designed for the practice of the good human life.[15]

Thinking of virtues in contrast to vices, the perversion of godly attitudes and actions, can sharpen the believer's view of what is right and wrong, even aiding decision-making as we consider what character our actions may reflect (cf. Colossians 3:5–17). As long as we do not think of virtuous actions as the font from which holiness springs, virtue is a helpful category for the Christian life.[16] Believers are made right with God through God's work alone, which also transforms us to live the sanctified life by faith. Thus believers strive under the Spirit's guidance to put to death the vices that spring from their need to secure life on their own terms. They repent—are turned by the Holy Spirit—from vice to virtue as God uses them as His masks. They strive to practice those attitudes and actions that reflect the image of God's love, care, and concern into the lives of others in every situation of human life.

A Life of Mission in the Church

Although the church is just one of four situations of human community, the gathering of believers has a special role within the Christian life. The New Testament places an extra emphasis on service within the people of God: "As we have opportunity, let us do good to everyone, and especially to those who are of the household of faith" (Galatians 6:10; cf. Romans 12:9–13; 1 John 3:11–18; 1 Peter 4:8–11). Christians practice faith, hope, and love—as well as other virtues of the Christian life—in the church as we pray for fellow believers, listen to the hardships and joys of friends in Christ, share our own burdens with them, and offer the encouragement of the Gospel. Christian community thus reflects the love of Jesus, who laid down His life for His brothers and sisters, since "whoever loves God must also love his brother" (1 John 4:21).

The Christian's identity as a child of God is established in the Word at work in the church, but that identity is not laid aside as the Christian

15 Gilbert C. Meilaender Jr., *The Theory and Practice of Virtue* (Notre Dame, IN: University of Notre Dame Press, 1984).

16 See Joel D. Biermann, *A Case for Character: Towards a Lutheran Virtue Ethics* (Minneapolis: Fortress, 2014).

serves at home, work, or in society. Rather, the church functions as a training ground from which Christians go out to share Christ's love with others in word and deed. As Christians live daily at home, work, and in society, they bring their congregations and Christ's mission with them because they represent Jesus and His church in all their vocations. The mission of Jesus is not merely to bring people to church, but for Christ's people to bring the church—both its central message, the Gospel, and its central activity, love—to people who do not know the Savior.

A Life of the Spirit

Some Christians have organized certain biblical material into a category labeled **spiritual gifts**. This term can be helpful in thinking through Christian service within the callings of congregational life. It dare not become the prime concept of Christian living since it pertains to only the situation of the church-community. Furthermore, spiritual gifts are often misunderstood as personal possessions and are compared with the gifts exhibited by other believers, which lifts some gifts above others rather than delighting in the way each member serves Christ's Body.

Spiritual gifts or "gifts of the Holy Spirit" are terms that are used in different ways in the Pauline epistles. In 1 Corinthians 2:14, Paul spoke of the ability to trust in Christ, whose cross is a stumbling block to Jews and folly to Gentiles, when he used the term (cf. the entire context from 1 Corinthians 1:18–2:14). In 1 Corinthians 12:1, only the adjective "spiritual" stands in the Greek text. Most English translations have referred the term there to the gifts discussed after verse 4. More likely it refers to "spiritual persons," for the immediate context speaks of those whom the Holy Spirit moves to trust in Jesus and confess Him as Lord (1 Corinthians 12:2–3). But in 1 Corinthians 14:1, the adjective "spiritual" clearly refers to gifts that the Holy Spirit gives His people. Although viewed as gifts of God, these gifts become concrete in human actions that edify the Body of Christ's people, or the believer who has the gift, or both.

In a technical sense, the gifts of the Holy Spirit have their basis in God's creative order, a gift of the First Article of the Creed. They are not magical. The gift of prophecy was apparently the gift to use the Word of God to convict people in their hearts through the Law and bring them the consolation of the Gospel (1 Corinthians 14:22–25, 31, 39). That ability operates on the basis of the same psychological characteristics one might use in persuasive speech as a politician or sales representative. The gift of tongues apparently used nonrational (not irrational!) utterances, sounds such as those lovers and sports fans put to effective use in communicating their feelings. As a spiritual gift, such use of sound praises God and prays to Him. These sounds—which do not fall into commonly understood words or propositional patterns with subjects and verbs—have been used in many cultures not only to express delight and fear but also religious sentiments.

A created gift of the First Article is not automatically a spiritual gift. To it must be added the power of the Holy Spirit, the Third Article element, for a specific purpose. The purpose of every spiritual gift is to point to Christ, the Second Article element of the spiritual gift. Thus playing the piano Friday evening at a restaurant is a talent God has given to some believers as well as to some who are not Christians. When the Holy Spirit directs a believer to use such skills to accompany hymns of praise to the Savior, a creaturely gift has become a spiritual gift.

The lists of spiritual gifts that are often cited from Paul's letters focus not only on the talents of individual believers that the Holy Spirit uses to serve others—though Romans 12:6–8 is such a list. Ephesians 4:11 and 1 Corinthians 12:28–30 also enumerate the people—prophets, apostles, teachers, shepherds, helpers, etc.—who have these abilities and use them as gifts under the direction and power of the Holy Spirit. Not only can my abilities become spiritual gifts, but I, as a fellow believer, am the Spirit's gift to the whole Body as I share God's Word with others or point to the love and presence of Christ with deeds of love that help and heal. Furthermore, the exercise of these gift-abilities takes place in specific situations. The opportunities for service are as much gifts of the Spirit as are the abilities to serve in specific ways.

Such gifts are part of the Holy Spirit's strategy for carrying out His mission. They do not reflect on the one who "has" or is the gift at all. Therefore, we dare not make anything of the way in which the Holy Spirit works through us and uses us. Although He enriches us as individuals through His use of us as His tools, He does so to enrich others and bring the presence of Christ to them. Believers, then, must recognize the limits of spiritual gifts and see these gifts in the wider framework of sanctification. God calls us not only to direct people to Christ with our verbal witness to His incarnation, death, and resurrection but also to serve within His design for human life in home, work, church, and community.

Making God-Pleasing Decisions

Living a God-pleasing life is not easy. Our own sin gets in the way, and we have trouble seeing and doing what is right for ourselves and others. Additionally, the world itself is so steeped in sin that there may be no sin-free way of moving forward, and Christians must choose the lesser of evil options. As Luther once advised Melanchthon: "Be a sinner and sin boldly, but believe and rejoice in Christ even more boldly."[17] In all circumstances, we can return to God's Word for grace and guidance, even if not direct instruction, on how to live well as His beloved creatures.

God has given moral guidance to His people in the Scriptures. Much of His inspired direction for human life, however, comes in the form of regulations for the cultic, political, and moral life of His ancient people Israel, regulations that Paul rejected in the freedom of the Gospel (Colossians 2:16–17). The church has even changed its judgment on issues that were regarded as moral precepts for centuries. Charging of interest on loans is an example of this. Throughout most of its history, the church regarded any charging of interest as a transgression against God's command to Israel: "Take no interest from [your brother/countryman] or profit. … You shall not lend him your money at interest, nor give him your food for profit" (Leviticus 25:36–37; cf. Exodus 22:25; Deuteronomy 23:19). The advent of capitalistic methods has convinced most Christians that charging interest is not in itself a violation of God's design for human life—though Christians must be careful to offer fair rates and care for the poor, which is part of God's demand for justice. God's commands in Scripture provide believers with moral guidance on how to love our neighbors as ourselves, but believers must still use God-given, sanctified wisdom to determine how biblical commands and prohibitions apply to life. This involves thinking with the logic of Holy Scripture, both the commands that apply to everyone—often called natural law and ensconced in the Ten Commandments—and the structure of the Bible's story so that our words and actions testify to God as our Creator, Savior, and Sanctifier known in Jesus. Concerning such matters, Christians, together with fellow believers, will struggle in their own consciences and in good faith to arrive at decisions.

Furthermore, the Scriptures do not speak directly to all the issues with which modern life confronts us. Christians must apply the principles of the Ten Commandments and other biblical expressions of God's design for human life in our radically different cultural context. Therefore, they are continually making judgments regarding, for example, what "You shall not steal" says about duplication of copyrighted music for the church choir. It is often helpful for Christians to consider what virtues their decisions might embody, and then compare whether these virtues match with how the Scriptures speak about the Christian life. Above all, Christians reflect and convey God's kind of love, the agape that sets aside selfish concerns in reaching out to embody the love of God for the neighbor.

Christians also recognize that there is no one "correct" decision in every instance. The church has long recognized that some things are neither

17 AE 48:282.

prohibited nor commanded by God. In many circumstances more than one possibility may meet human need and serve God faithfully. Actions neither commanded nor prohibited in the Bible are called **adiaphora** [singular: adiaphoron]. Human reason is able to make those kinds of decisions with some degree of accuracy even apart from faith in Jesus.

Because the Gospel takes away the necessity of securing our identity, security, and meaning through manipulation or exploitation of others, it enables believers to evaluate their own abilities and the needs of others more clearly. God's concerns become the concerns of believers. Reason taken captive by the Gospel makes decisions based on giving glory to God (1 Corinthians 10:31). We render service within our callings to others "doing the will of God from the heart" (Ephesians 6:6).

Believers also count on one another as they make decisions in Christian living. The Gospel frees them to be open with one another as they test assessments of situations and possible actions. The mutual conversation of believers not only edifies the church with the Gospel and the forgiveness of sins, but it also guides God's people as they make the decisions that confront them. In making decisions with fellow Christians, believers avoid the darkness of ambiguity, in which all self-serving decisions are justified, and dwell in the light of Christ in community.

Conversation with God also helps vitally in the decision-making process. Turning to God in prayer will not magically provide a sure signal from heaven to guide or confirm our decisions. Prayer will help us summon God's help in the midst of a struggle and may bring assurance, freedom, or even surprise. No matter the help on the decision itself, praying prepares us to turn to God for forgiveness for the inevitable mistakes we make along the way.

No Offense

Part of the believer's life of caring for others involves consciously avoiding things that would trip up our neighbors. At all costs, believers seek to avoid causing others to fall or fail, particularly in regard to the vertical relationship with God. Jesus hardly ever expressed Himself more strongly than when He said, "Whoever causes one of these little ones who believe in Me to sin, it would be better for him if a great millstone were hung around his neck and he were thrown into the sea" (Mark 9:42). Such playing with the faith of others is called "causing to stumble" or giving "offense."

Some Christians may claim that "other people take offense; I don't give it." Neither Jesus nor Paul looked at the matter like this. In 1 Corinthians 8, Paul discussed matters of adiaphora, which believers may or may not do in Christian liberty, but which may cause others to stumble. Knowing that something is not wrong, Paul stated, does not mean that believers are free to do it. Their love for the neighbor should prevent them from eating food from pagan temple butcher shops if that would cause others with weak consciences to stumble in their faith. Exercising liberty dare not harm others. Love sacrifices its own liberty so that others do not fall (1 Corinthians 8:1–13).

There are instances in which believers must demonstrate their freedom in Christ to those who are fixed in false conceptions, particularly when such people try to impose their laws upon other believers. But even in those instances, the Christian strives to win the neighbor, to correct perceptions and build faith rather than simply to flaunt liberty and prove one's point. Sinning against fellow believers and wounding their weak consciences is sinning against Christ. At all costs, believers avoid causing others who are joined with them in Christ's Body to fall (1 Corinthians 8:12–13).

The Holy Spirit has sanctified the people of God so that we might live the mature Christian life. That life lives out of God's mercy and favor, doing the good works that serve those around us, reflecting in every one of our callings the fullness of Christ's love (Ephesians 2:8–10; 2 Timothy 3:15–17; Ephesians 4:11–16).

CHAPTER 17
THE CHURCH

WHAT is the church? Even asking the question may seem ludicrous since a seven-year-old child knows what the church is, as Luther once quipped.[1] Upon reflection, however, we realize that the word *church* is multivalent, holding multiple meanings under the same term. Some people are referring to the building, others to the institution; some to the people as a gathering of individuals, others to the people as a collective body; some to the clergy, others to the priesthood; some to the universal church, others to a congregation. The options are nearly limitless. What is the church?

In North America especially, two temptations threaten all concepts of the church, all formal and informal attempts at **ecclesiology**. On the one side stands the monstrous Scylla of **individualism**, which is one of our deepest religious convictions. By and large, we think that we can do what we want, when we want, and how we want, as long as we do not hurt anyone else. When the individual is prioritized in this way, the church is **instrumentalized**, turned into a tool for self-improvement. This often looks like churches that focus on relevant messages more than Scripture, guidelines for life more than a true confession of faith, and sentimentality more than discipleship. When Christians think that they come to church to have their felt needs met, they are often unwilling to be uncomfortable for the sake of real fellowship and God's mission to the lost. Many recognize the problem with individualism, but breaking out of individualistic tendencies requires the difficult work of putting others' needs before our own, including people we may consider enemies. It is easier to go church shopping than it is to bear another's burdens or allow them to bear mine.

The other temptation is the whirling Charybdis of **institutionalism**. As the old Christendom reality in which the church held a privileged position of power in the hearts and minds of most people and politicians has disintegrated, many Christians have been tempted toward reestablishing power through institutional means. Although the classic example of institutionalism in ecclesiology is the late medieval and early modern Roman Catholic

1 Smalcald Articles III XII.

Church, many Protestants also have attempted to build the church through institutional and political means. When institutionalism reigns, the Law is elevated over the Gospel and community rules over grace to individuals. The focus of the church becomes retaining and defending what belongs to the church rather than giving away the love of Christ to those who do not know Him. God's mission to the world is conflated with retaining societal power through the church.

In both of these temptations, human notions of what the church should be overtakes what God says about His church. We dare not forget that God Himself created the church, and God Himself will sustain it. Jesus' promise to Peter rings out for us today: "On this rock [of the apostolic confession of Christ] I will build My church, and the gates of hell shall not prevail against it" (Matthew 16:18). As Dietrich Bonhoeffer once preached, we do not build the church. Rather, "we are to confess, while God builds. We are to preach, while God builds. We are to pray to God, while God builds."[2] We cannot save the church by making it relevant enough that everyone will want to join by our ingenuity. We cannot save the church by constructing an impenetrable fortress. The church belongs to God, who created it, sustains it, and sends it on His mission. Our initial question, then, must be focused: What does God say about the church?

The church is the sheep of God who attend to the voice of the Shepherd (John 10:1–30; cf. Ezekiel 34:11–31). The church is the temple of the Holy Spirit, being built up together in Christ Jesus into a holy dwelling for God by the Spirit (Ephesians 2:13–22; cf. 1 Corinthians 3:10–17). The church is the Body of Christ, His members that dwell in and under Him as their Head and serve one another and the world in love (1 Corinthians 12:12–13:13; cf. Colossians 1:18; Ephesians 4:15; Romans 12:4–5). Holy Scripture thus describes the church in relationship to God, God's story, and God's mission. The church is not primarily a human community—though it certainly is that!—since God constructed the church; brought it into the story of Abraham, Isaac, Jacob, and Jesus; builds it up by His Word; and sends it on His mission. God takes sinners who were "not a people," gives them His mercy, and grafts them into Abraham through Jesus Christ so that they "may proclaim the excellencies of Him who called [them] out of darkness into His marvelous light" (1 Peter 2:9–10; Romans 11:17–24).

The Mission of God and the Church

The God of Israel is a missionary God. Throughout the Old Testament, God sought His lost people to find and free them for rest and fellowship

2 Dietrich Bonhoeffer, *Berlin: 1932–1933*, ed. Larry L. Rasmussen, vol. 12 of *Dietrich Bonhoeffer Works* (Minneapolis: Fortress, 2009), 480.

with Him. Adam and Eve could not hide from Him in their sin, for God deigned to find them, be in relationship with His beloved sinners, and give them a word of both judgment and promise (Genesis 3:8–19). God called Abram and made him a proto-missionary, promising blessing to the whole world through him and his seed (Genesis 12:1–3). God called Israel out of Egypt to be a priestly people to all nations, that He might be known as God of all (Exodus 19:4–6; cf. Isaiah 61:6). This missionary character of God is highlighted further in the New Testament as Jesus reveals Himself as the Apostle, one sent by the Father to bring sinners back to God (e.g., John 3:17; 4:34; 5:30; 5:37–38). Jesus' ministry had a missionary character, going throughout Judea, Samaria, Galilee, and beyond to find the lost sheep of the house of Israel (Matthew 15:21–28). Jesus' own body is the new temple (John 2:19–22), a mobile, missional temple where God dwells among His people by His Word and Spirit. Simply put, Jesus "came to seek and to save the lost" (Luke 19:10).

The mission of God did not end with the death and resurrection of Jesus, but continued as the Son sent forth the Holy Spirit on His apostles and people to proclaim repentance and forgiveness of sins in His name to all nations (Luke 24:47; Matthew 28:18–20; John 20:21–23). The Holy Spirit empowered the church throughout the book of Acts to proclaim Jesus and the Gospel to diverse people in surprising ways. Human wisdom was revised and sometimes put aside as the Holy Spirit moved the church to bring the salvation of Christ to the world. In the book of Acts, Jesus and the Spirit even moved ahead of the church on the mission of God, pulling the church along to recognize the universality of grace and the catholicity of God's mission, as the Spirit brought the world to believe in the Son and enter into fellowship with the Father (e.g., Acts 8:26; 8:39; 9:16; 10:34; 13:2; 14:27; 15:12; 16:6–10).[3]

Our tendency is to think of the church in Acts as qualitatively different from the church as we know it, but the Bible describes the same missionary God sending the church into the world today through the Word. Recently, theologians have emphasized this point through the concept of the *missio dei*, the mission of God.[4] God is a missionary God; the Father sends the Son in the power of the Holy Spirit to do His mission of saving the lost, and the Son and the Father send the Spirit to restore fallen human beings to their proper place as creatures and children through faith in Jesus, bringing sinners into the Body of Christ in fellowship with the Holy Trinity. The

3 See Cheryl M. Peterson, *Who Is the Church? An Ecclesiology for the Twenty-First Century* (Minneapolis: Fortress, 2013), 108–15.

4 See the classic David J. Bosch, *Transforming Mission: Paradigm Shifts in Theology of Mission* (Maryknoll, NY: Orbis, 1991).

church is brought into communion with God, to both rest in the joy of Jesus' easy yoke and light burden and be part of His mission of proclaiming God's reign in Him to the world.

Too often Christians think of the church in institutional terms, such as the formal structures of clergy and laity, church governance, and ecumenism and fellowship. These are not unimportant, but they can distract us from the way that the Scriptures speak about the church. The church is not a static organization, but a dynamic people who have been crucified with Christ and raised to new life with Him in Baptism. The dynamic of Baptism drives God's church to be on Christ's mission. All Christians have been brought into the one, holy, catholic, and apostolic church and are called by the Gospel to rest in faith in Jesus and be conformed by the Spirit to Christ's mission and ministry. Every congregation is a mission agency to proclaim Jesus to its local community and reveal God's peace, justice, and compassion through the service of love. Christians—especially but not exclusively those called to be pastors—are "ambassadors for Christ," having been entrusted with "the message [Greek: *logos*] of reconciliation" to speak on God's behalf (2 Corinthians 5:19–20).[5] Such a church is not a static institution, but a dynamic people living by faith and bringing the Gospel to those who do not know the Savior, Jesus.

The Church in Holy Scripture

Numerous images of the church can be found in Holy Scripture—ninety-six by the count of one scholar.[6] Jesus' parables, for example, a net with fish, a field with grain, a wedding banquet; His other teaching, for example, vine and branches, shepherd and sheep, master and disciples; and the letters of St. Paul, for example, Body of Christ, Bride of Christ, eucharistic fellowship, offer multiple pictures of the church, all of which have something to teach us about the community of God's people and our common life.[7] Although many different ways can be used to describe the church, it will never be understood rightly apart from the God who calls the church into existence by His word of power, indwells it by the Holy Spirit, and conforms it to the Crucified.

This section describes the church in three biblical ways, none of which should be understood as comprehensive or competitive models.[8] They are

5 Compare John Webster, *Word and Church: Essays in Christian Dogmatics* (London: Bloomsbury T&T Clark, 2016), 222.

6 Paul S. Minear, *Images of the Church in the New Testament* (1960; repr., Louisville: Westminster John Knox, 2004).

7 Stephen K. Pickard, *Seeking the Church: An Introduction to Ecclesiology* (London: SCM Press, 2012), 33–39.

8 On models in ecclesiology, see Pickard, *Seeking the Church*, 39–51.

complementary descriptions of the church's relationship to God, illuminating essential parts of the identity, mission, and life together of God's people. The church is the sheep who hear the voice of the shepherd, the temple of the Holy Spirit, and the Body of Christ. All three are necessary to capture the dynamic of the church as the people formed by God through the Word, called out of the sinful world to be a priestly people, *and* called into God's world on Christ's mission as servant.

The Shepherd and His Sheep: The People of the Word

Hopkins once heard a story about two sister congregations, one in the United States and the other in sub-Saharan Africa. The African pastor proposed that each congregation mail the other a picture of their respective churches. The American pastor opened a beautiful photo of all the people of the African Lutheran church that he shared with his congregation the following Sunday morning. Upon opening the letter, however, the American pastor realized he had made a major mistake: he had sent a picture of their building.

In our more lucid moments, most of us know that the church is not a building; it is the people of God. Lutheran theology, however, goes a step further. The church is not just a gathering of God's people: it is God's people gathered with ears open to God's Word. What makes the church is not the people alone, but God's Word by which the Holy Spirit creates faith and brings people into His community. In the Smalcald Articles, Luther defined the church as holy believers and lambs who are listening to the voice of the Shepherd.[9] In the Augsburg Confession, Melanchthon identified the church as the gathering of all believers, among whom the Gospel is correctly proclaimed and taught and the Sacraments are correctly administered.[10] God's people are essential to the church, but it is not people alone who make the church. Many like-minded people choose to gather on a Sunday morning, chat about important topics, and even eat together: such a **voluntary association** is not God's church. God's church is sinful creatures who have been encountered by God's Word, heard the voice of God in faith, and been moved by His Spirit through the Word from death in sin to new life in Christ. The flock of God only exists because the Shepherd has brought them to Himself by His living and active voice and continues to sustain and lead them on the pilgrim path to the city of God. This is not a voluntary association, but a people who have been chosen by God and made members of His church by God's grace and action alone.

The image of the sheep listening to the Shepherd is deeply scriptural. Through the prophet Ezekiel, God Himself promised to be the Shepherd of

9 Smalcald Articles III XII 2.

10 Augsburg Confession VII 1.

His people, to lead them to green pastures and still waters, and to lay them down to rest (cf. Psalm 23:1–2). God further promised to seek the lost, bring back the strayed, bind up the injured, and strengthen the weak, bringing the justice of His reign to the strong and weak alike (Ezekiel 34:15–16). Jesus began to fulfill this prophecy as the Son of God incarnate, living among His sheep, and serving them as their Shepherd. Knowing His flock intimately and calling each sheep by name, Jesus sought lost sinners to bring them into the shalom of God's sheepfold, and our Lord protected His flock by laying down His life (John 10:3–16). Jesus' sheep are the ones who attend to His voice, for in His Word they have eternal life and salvation and are safe from all attacks of the devil, the world, and the pernicious sinful nature that lurks within (John 10:27–29).

Because the church is God's people who listen to His voice, the Christian Church must be a people of the Word. We gather Sunday after Sunday not to hear a message about parenting or mental health but to hear a message from God about His grace in Jesus and about us as dependent, sinful creatures. The church dare not run after relevance, numbers, or power, forgetting that the Word in all its forms stands at the center of our assembly and our life together. When the church gathers to worship, it does so first and foremost to receive God's Word and respond to the Word in prayer and praise. True **worship** is not giving something to God but receiving from Him His gifts and responding in faith and faith's deeds.[11] Although many do not recognize it, traditional **liturgies**—church orders and rituals that are rooted in the tradition of the church and pulled from Holy Scripture—are quite helpful in this by leading God's people to memorize Scripture so as to speak God's Word back to Him not only in worship but also in moments of joy and crisis.

The Word alone creates faith in Jesus Christ, sustains the people of God in their faith and life together through the comfort of the Gospel and the curbing conviction of the Law, and shapes the community of faith for the ministry of Jesus in the world. For this reason, God's people must not only gather to listen to the preaching of God's Word but also must engage in Scripture together throughout the week. Reading Scripture should happen individually among Christians, but the Bible is primarily the book of the church that engages the community of believers for life together under the cross. In the Word, the Holy Spirit works to bring the church to Christ, form in us the story of Holy Scripture as God's sinful creatures who have been redeemed by Jesus, and set us apart for His mission of witness to the lost.

---

11 Cf. Apology of the Augsburg Confession IV 49: "Faith is that worship which receives the benefits that God offers; the righteousness of the law is that worship which offers God our own merits. God wants to be honored by faith" (Kolb-Wengert, 128).

The Temple of the Holy Spirit: The Priestly People

Just as God created the universe out of nothing, so He took those who had no standing before Him and were alienated from the commonwealth of Israel and strangers to the promise, having no hope and without God in the world. But God has brought both Jew and Gentile near to Himself through Christ's blood. Christ has become the peace that reconciles those who had been hostile toward one another and toward God. That peace rests in the cross. The people of the cross, drawn together into Christ's own Body, are now fellow citizens, saints and members of God's family. The Word of the Lord, as it came through apostles and prophets, constructed this household upon the foundation of Jesus Christ, and the Holy Spirit is building it into God's temple, a dwelling place for God (Ephesians 2:11–22). The church, as God's new Israel, lives in the power and for the purposes of its Creator, who has called it into existence through His Word, dwells there by His Spirit, and sets it apart for His purposes.

The temple served two major functions for Israel that are essential to this biblical understanding of the church as the temple of the Holy Spirit. First, according to His gracious promise, God took residence in the temple, making it His own dwelling place. Isaiah's vision of Yahweh Sabaoth filling the temple was not imaginary but a true picture of the God of Israel dwelling according to His promise. God filled the temple with His presence, set apart His people to speak His Word, and sent them out to gather all nations from the ends of the earth to Himself (Isaiah 6:1–9; cf. Isaiah 2:2–3). Second, the temple was set apart as holy space for worship in recognition both of God's presence and His purposes in the world. At the temple, God's people would attend to His Word and offer their prayer and praise. While aspects of this could be done in a synagogue, the temple stood apart as the one place where the people could offer the covenantal sacrifices and receive the promises of the Mosaic covenant.

When the Scriptures talk about the church as God's temple, it has both aspects in mind. The church is the place of God's dwelling: "Do you not know that you [all] are God's temple and that God's Spirit dwells in you [all]?" (1 Corinthians 3:16). In the second letter to the Corinthians, Paul says it even more directly: "We are the temple of the living God" (2 Corinthians 6:16). In the church as a community and in each of the members as individuals (1 Corinthians 6:19), the Holy Spirit has deigned to dwell. What good news! Even the smallest, weakest, least impressive gatherings of God's people are truly the church—"Where two or three are gathered in My name, there am I among them" (Matthew 18:20). For where the Spirit is, Christ is, and so is the church. God dwells with His people as the Word is proclaimed, read, responded to in prayer and praise, and combined with water, bread, and wine for forgiveness, life, and salvation according to Christ's promises. God also dwells with His people when there is no pastor present or divine service taking place as Christians pray together, encourage one another with the Word, serve the world in Christ's name, and witness to the lost through the Holy Spirit.

The presence of God also sets the church apart from the world. Through Holy Baptism, sinners are brought into a community of saints; the unclean are purified; those in darkness are enlightened; outcasts are brought into the family of God; and the condemned are given mercy. Faith in Jesus separates the people of God from the old, idolatrous ways of this sinful age. Hence, St. Peter repeatedly calls Christians strangers, exiles, and sojourners, for the church is "a chosen race, a royal priesthood, a holy nation, a people for His own possession," set apart to be God's witnesses to the world (1 Peter 2:9–11).

An ever-present danger for ecclesiology is what Stephen Pickard calls "the desacralized ecclesia," a church-community that has conformed to the culture.[12] This happens when the church forgets its foundation, source, and life in God and tries to survive on the world's terms. In the twenty-first century, this usually means becoming a therapeutic social group for mental health and well-being or a political action organization rather than a church. In both cases, individual concerns take priority over what the Word of God says about His church. Whether a community is an assembly that focuses on wellness and self-improvement, or one primarily invested in making a difference politically, both have conformed to cultural patterns and lost their identity as God's church. The church is not what culture says a community should be. The church is what God says it is: a priestly people, a community set apart as the dwelling place of the Holy Spirit, for His mission. Hence, the church must be a place where the Scriptures are taught, especially in Christian families and to young people, in order for all God's people to recognize what it means for the church to be a people set apart.

At the same time that we recognize the church as a holy people, we dare not confess that God has made the church special in itself. The church's holiness—its set-apart-ness—is only and always a gift, dependent on God's Word, God's story, and God's indwelling. It is never a possession of the church. The danger here is what Pickard calls "sacred inflation," the church that thinks of itself as divine.[13] A church that has inflated itself boasts in what it possesses, and it relies on its own power rather than boasting in its weakness and in its crucified Lord who possesses the church. Ironically, the

12 Pickard, *Seeking the Church*, 67–73.

13 Pickard, *Seeking the Church*, 61–66.

most common examples of sacred inflation occur when the church is thoroughly desacralized, having become a political force focused on power while claiming to be God's sacred representative—such as in medieval Europe and twenty-first-century North America. In relationship to God, the church is always a sinful, broken people who stand in need of God's mercy, and trust they receive that mercy through Jesus' death and resurrection delivered in the Gospel. What makes the church set apart is not a visible, moral perfection nor its social power, but its trust in and confession of the Savior, Jesus, who makes the church His own by the Holy Spirit.

The church is set apart, holy, for two essential tasks, both of which are described by the apostle Peter. First, God expects His church to be strange to the ways of the world. Setting our minds on the hope of Jesus, His present grace, and His future return, Peter urges the church to be "holy in all your [plural] conduct" (1 Peter 1:15). He explains that the church has been "ransomed from the futile ways inherited from your forefathers" (1 Peter 1:18) through the precious blood of Jesus, the perfect Lamb, and now are born again for obedience, sincere brotherly love, and earnest love from a pure heart. Peter even specifies that the church is set apart from all malice, deceit, hypocrisy, envy, and slander, the ways of the old, sinful age, to be built up as living stones, part of the holy temple of God in Jesus Christ. As such, the church offers continual spiritual sacrifices through prayer, good deeds, and honorable living (1 Peter 1:13–2:12). The whole life of God's priestly people is one of a living sacrifice (Romans 12:1–2).

In addition to being set apart for holy living, Peter also describes how God's church is set apart for witness to Christ in the world. Just as Israel was to be God's priests not for their own sake but for the sake of the world (Exodus 19:5–6), Jews and Greeks, slaves and free, males and females have been baptized into one Body to be a royal priesthood set apart to "proclaim the excellencies" of our God to the world (1 Corinthians 12:12–13; 1 Peter 2:9). As the church lives out its faith in Jesus in the world, unbelievers (Gentiles) "may see your good deeds and glorify God on the day of visitation" (1 Peter 2:12). The church thus witnesses to the world through words that proclaim Jesus as well as deeds that speak to their hope, their peace, and their confession of the truth.

As the church witnesses, we dare never confuse our witness to Jesus with power. A witness points to Another who is the way, the truth, and the life. It does not demand or coerce—it persuades, convicts, and comforts using the Word of God. Hence, priests are bridge builders—as a Latin word for "priest," *pontifex*, literally means—bringing Christ to the world as His witnesses. Another part of building bridges between God and the world is prayer. God's priestly people pray for the world, having free access to God on behalf of human beings (cf. Hebrews 5:1). God's priestly people carry the needs of the world, for those in positions of authority and for all people, before the Father in heaven (1 Timothy 2:1–3).

God has called His people to be His priests in their Baptisms. There He has incorporated them into the Body of Christ. There He feeds them with the Word and Sacrament that sets the church apart in faith and calls them to His mission by the Holy Spirit. This is no voluntary association, where we come and go as we please. God created His church by His Word, making people from all nations and ethnicities one in Christ Jesus as Abraham's offspring, a new Israel of Jews and Gentiles according to the promise (Galatians 3:27–29). This priestly people are part of God's family, justified and right with Him, but that is not the whole story. They are also set apart for His mission, to be holy, distinct from the world as confessing sinners who trust in the Savior and as people who are witnesses to that Savior by Word and deed.

The Body of Christ: The Servant Community

When the Scriptures call the church the Body of Christ, one of the consistent themes is the unity of the church composed of a diverse membership. Just as a human body has various members—eyes, ears, nose, mouth, hands, feet, etc.—that perform different functions, all of which are important, so the Body of Christ has different roles, responsibilities, and gifts—for example, apostles, prophets, teachers, healing, serving, administrating, speaking in tongues, giving generously, and leading—all of which are important in the church. Each of these is essential within Christ's church, even though on a human level we may consider some as greater gifts. If all were charismatic speakers but none had gifts for helping with Sunday School, what kind of church would that be? Instead, God has drawn a diversity of people into the one Body of Christ by the Spirit for brotherly love, care for one another, and for His mission in the world (1 Corinthians 12:12–31; Romans 12:4–8).

The church is also called the Body of Christ because, by the indwelling of the Holy Spirit, the people of God are being built into a specific shape, Jesus Himself. Jesus is the living stone into whom all the living stones of God's church are being formed by the Spirit (1 Peter 2:4–5). Jesus is not only the cornerstone of the church but also the center that holds the building together and the goal into whom the whole temple is being built as a dwelling place for the Holy Spirit (Ephesians 2:20–22). Although Christ is Lord of all, the church is not being formed for power or glory but for service. In fact, throughout the New Testament, Paul and the other apostles call on the church to be conformed to Christ's humility and service (e.g., Romans 15:2–3; Philippians 2:5–11; 1 Peter 2:21; 1 John 3:16). The church is the Body of Christ because it has died and been raised with Him in Baptism to live according to His servant way.[14]

Part of the servant way of Christ is suffering. The church does not suffer vicariously for the world—it witnesses to Jesus who suffered on behalf of the world to save it. The church does, however, share the suffering of the societies in which it is located when their disobedience to God's plan for human life wreaks havoc on its people. It also suffers because the world opposes it and tries to suffocate its voice. The church does not focus on its suffering, nor does it indulge in self-pity, trying to use its victimhood for political gain, as it encounters the frustrations of persecution or harassment. As it submits to suffering, the Body of Christ serves (1 Peter 2:19–25).

Another aspect of Christ's servant way is that the church shows compassion within and without. God provides for the temporal needs of believers and unbelievers alike in all sorts of ways (Matthew 5:45). God draws His people into acts of love for one another and for those outside the household of faith. Almost immediately, the Holy Spirit directed the church to take care of human need in daily life by setting up an office of deacon to distribute food to widows and administer other acts of love (Acts 6:1–6). In reaching out to those in need, the church continues the feeding and healing functions of Jesus' ministry, expressions of the kingdom of God which is near at hand (Matthew 11:5; Luke 4:17–21). Although preaching and teaching the Word of God is the most important task of the church, we dare not forget that the church is Christ's people that have been shown His great love and are called to do the same for the household of faith (1 John 4:7–21). A community without love for the brothers and sisters on the inside and which is not seeking to draw others into this fellowship of compassion has forfeited its identity as God's church. In many places churches have been used by governments to administer important societal programs, particularly in education, care for the poor, and treatment of the sick and dying. As modern societies pull such activities away, the church must not relinquish that work just because it is being done by the government. As those called to serve the least of these—the forgotten and vulnerable in every society—the Body of Christ cannot and must not relinquish Christ's way of ministry.

The Church: Justified and Sinful

The line between the ages—the present age of sin and death and the new age of God's visible rule of justice and shalom—cuts between not only every Christian but also the community of Christians. Just as every Christian is both sinful and justified at the same time, the church also has this twofold

14 See Theodore J. Hopkins, *Christ, Church, and World: Bonhoeffer and Lutheran Ecclesiology after Christendom* (Lanham, MD: Lexington Books/Fortress Academic, 2021), 119–33.

character. The church is the justified community, holy priests of God, indwelt by the Holy Spirit. As such, the church stands as the Body of Christ through whom Jesus proclaims the good news of the Gospel, calls authorities and all people to repentance, offers His body and blood for forgiveness of sins, and serves the least of these with compassion. Jesus works through His Body by the Holy Spirit so that the church not only represents Jesus but truly presents Him according to His Word. At the same time, however, every congregation is a sinful community. Congregations turn inward and become defensive. They ignore the world around them and the mission of God, trying to create comfortable communities. Congregations conform to the ways of the world, falling prey to greed, lust, and power. As long as the present age persists, the church is not identical with the kingdom of God even as God reigns in and through the church. God exercises His rule not only in and through the church but also against it and for it. Only when Christ returns will the church become fully what it is now by faith.

In addition to being justified and sinful, the priestly people are also believing and penitent at the same time. The church never moves past listening to the voice of the Good Shepherd and trusting Him. For this reason, although the church's obedience to God's mission is essential, the obedience of the church must not replace the Word of God as its center. The church lives out its mission to Jesus only when it listens to the Word and trusts in the Lord who brings forgiveness, life, and salvation through the means of grace. The church also lives continually in repentance, confessing not only its individual sins but also its corporate ones, such as its failures to embody Christ's mission of witness and love. The church's character as believing and penitent means that the church should always be looking for ways to be more faithful to Christ's mission as witnesses to God's world.

The "Invisible" Church and the "Visible" Church

Christians have often distinguished the church in its vertical dimension, the gathering of individuals whom God has made His children, from the church in its horizontal dimension, the gathering as it fleshes itself out in the forms of daily life in the world. They have sometimes called the former the **invisible church** and the latter the **visible church**. The chief function of this distinction is to recognize that a gathering of people who do Christian things does not mean every single person is part of God's church. Hypocrites and unbelievers can gather around Word and Sacrament too—such is more likely to happen when Christianity holds cultural or political sway—but such people are not part of the Body of Christ. Melanchthon used the term *church* "broadly speaking" to talk about a gathering of people regardless of whether their ears are open to God's Word and the Spirit is moving in their hearts. Melanchthon then called it the church "properly speaking" or church "strictly speaking" when talking about the sheep of God who trust in the voice of the Shepherd.[15] Although Melanchthon—and Luther—used such a distinction, they did not focus the church on the people. They focused instead upon the power of the Word, which still works to create, sustain, and grow the church even through sinners and hypocrites.[16]

The doctrine of the invisible church suffers from the same practical problems as the doctrine of election. Our status—as an elect member of the true church—can only be received as a promise, not known by observational or intellectual skill. Hence, for those in doubt about their status before God, the solution does not involve a discussion of the invisible or visible church. The solution comes in reminding individuals of the means of grace delivered to them—or delivering them in that moment! Our status before God depends solely on Christ who comes to us in the revealed means of grace.

The invisible and visible distinction reminds us of two important things. First, the church is not in our hands. The church belongs to God alone, who holds His own in His hands. We cannot build the church by human hands but only with God's tools: His Word that He has placed in our ears and put on our lips. Second, we dare not speculate about who is in and who is out of the church. Such things should be left to God. What we have is not an understanding of church membership, but of the revealed means of grace that further faith.

The Church Hidden and Revealed

A more precise contrast may be made between the **hidden church** and the **revealed church**. God both hides and reveals His people as He hides and reveals His presence around and through Word and Sacrament. God's chosen children are in one sense truly hidden from other human creatures since we cannot plumb the depths of one's heart to perceive and confirm whether faith is "true" or not. The Body of those who have been joined to Christ in death and resurrection remains a matter of faith, for the church is hidden from human eyes in this sense.

At the same time, God reveals the church as the place of His presence, where His family gathers. There the Word is proclaimed and shared in written and sacramental form among those whom the Holy Spirit gathers through and around it. God reveals that these people are His own as His rule and kingdom transform their lives through death and resurrection in Christ. Distinguishing between the hidden church and the revealed church keeps

15 Apology of the Augsburg Confession VII–VIII 10–31 (Kolb-Wengert, 175–79). See also Augsburg Confession VII 1 (Kolb-Wengert, 42, 43).

16 Augsburg Confession VIII and Apology of the Augsburg Confession VII–VIII 28.

our focus on God's revealed promises rather than speculating about one's membership or status. We might also employ the terms *audible*, *tangible*, or *tasteable* for the revealed church, since its presence is revealed as the Word is heard, as the baptismal water that frames the Word of death and life touches us, and as the bread-body and wine-blood feed our faith.

Marks of the Church

Christians have often defined the church by noting its **marks**, those signs that characterize its nature and mission. The adjectives *one*, *holy*, *catholic*, and *apostolic*, used to describe the church in the Nicene Creed, have often been used to designate the essential elements of the church, without which it does not exist. The church is **one**; all believers are united by the Holy Spirit, one Lord, one faith, and one Baptism (Ephesians 4:4–6). The church is **holy**, both cleansed by the baptismal Word and set apart for service (1 Peter 3:8–22). The church is **catholic**; God's Word has spread to the ends of the earth, and His church encompasses all peoples, nations, languages, and times (1 Corinthians 12:12–13). The church is **apostolic**; it is built on the foundation of the life-giving apostolic and prophetic Word, and it is sent on Christ's mission to proclaim the same Word to the world (Ephesians 2:19–21; 3:8–10).

In 1539, Martin Luther composed a list of eight marks of the church, visible signs of the true church that make it holy. Luther started with the most important and clearest marks: the preaching of the Gospel, Baptism, the Sacrament of the Altar, and the Office of the Keys, or formal Confession and Absolution between pastor and penitent people. The fifth mark is pastoral leadership, followed by prayer—especially public prayer, thanksgiving, and praise—and the holy cross—enduring hardship, suffering, persecution, and temptation. Finally, although this does not distinguish it from upright groups of unbelievers, the church is marked by its practice of love, in good works of all kinds.[17] Two years later he constructed a similar list, this time enumerating Baptism, the Lord's Supper, Confession and Absolution, the public ministry of preaching, the Apostles' Creed, the Lord's Prayer, respect for temporal political powers and for marriage and family life, suffering and persecution, and the rejection of physical force against its enemies.[18] Other Christians have suggested that the church cannot exist without the exercise of discipline, of excommunication. Lutherans, however, have never accepted the practice of excommunication as a mark of the church, apart from its proper exercise within the Office of the Keys.

---

17 *On the Councils and the Church* (1539), AE 41:148–67.

18 *Against Hanswurst* (1541), AE 41:194–98.

The Lutheran Confessions stipulate that the church is simply marked by God's Word, in oral and sacramental forms. The church exists where the Gospel is rightly proclaimed and the Sacraments are rightly administered since the church is God's holy lambs who are listening to the voice of the Shepherd.[19] However believers describe and delimit the church, that much must be remembered. It is nothing other than Christ's priestly people, who have been formed into His Body, whose holiness and identity depends on the continuing action of the re-creating Word among them.

Church Government and Organization

The church proclaims and administers the Word of God that kills and makes alive before God. Because the church is where the life-giving means of grace are offered to sinners, Augustine could write that outside the church there is no salvation.[20] At the same time, the church takes form as a human institution, with rules and regulations in the administration of its daily life. The proclamation of the Gospel is the church's number one priority, but it is also a human community that lives out Christ's mission in the world, showing love within the household of faith and to those on the outside (Galatians 6:10).

The Holy Scriptures offer few requirements for how the church should structure itself, beyond the expectations that pastors—often called bishops and elders in Scripture—would function as leaders for communities of God's people. Because Scripture considers church governance to be a matter of freedom, churches have assumed a variety of forms for governing themselves. These forms have often reflected the political forms of the society in which the congregations arose.

Forms of Polity

In the early church, monarchical forms of church government developed quite quickly, reflecting the habits of organization of Roman society under the imperial form of government. Bishops headed the church and cared for its people. The church calls this form of government **episcopal**, from the Greek word for "bishop" or "overseer." In the aristocratic municipal setting of Geneva, in the sixteenth century, John Calvin developed a form of government for the church labeled **presbyterian**—based on the Greek word for "elder," which is *presbyteros*. In this form, elders function similarly to a city council, governing the church. Particularly in England, as more democratic concepts from ancient Germanic tribal law were being revived, some groups of Christians developed congregational forms of church government,

---

19 Smalcald Articles III XII 2.

20 On Augustine's understanding of the church, see Bengt Hagglund, *History of Theology*, trans. Gene J. Lund (St. Louis: Concordia, 1968), 128–30.

reflecting the democratic ideal of freedom. As modern Western governments rely increasingly on bureaucratic agencies, the exercise of regulatory power and leadership within church communities has shifted toward paid staff, a tendency that may diminish as financial pressures increase.

Scripture prescribes no single form of church government. Each of these forms has served the Gospel, and sinners within the church have used each form to subvert the Gospel. Only the Gospel guarantees the Gospel. No form of church government can in and of itself provide insurance against the accommodation of God's Word to cultural norms. No ecclesiastical polity can prevent the devil's deceit from misleading the church and perverting its message.

In every form of church polity, Christ remains Lord of the church. The church invites His judgment when it misrepresents His Word, under any form of polity. It serves Him faithfully when it proclaims His Law and Gospel and promotes a life of obedience and love, according to His Word, no matter the form of church organization.

Sociological Analyses of the Church

Because the church is not only the priestly people of God through whom God exercises His rule by the Word but also a human institution in this age, the church must take institutional form. These forms can be analyzed sociologically. That fact is no more or no less than evidence that God is comfortable in His creation and works in and through it.

A predominant sociological analysis of the church arose in the early twentieth century out of the work of a German churchman and sociologist, Ernst Troeltsch (1865–1923). Troeltsch's categories provided a somewhat useful sociological analysis of the German church scene of his time. They help little in analyzing contemporary North American church life. Troeltsch distinguished churches from sects, and both groups from spiritualistic individuals, who remain outside organized gatherings of Christians. According to Troeltsch's categories, churches open their doors to all people in a given area. Admission to church membership is easy, if not automatic, reflecting the practice of European "state churches" of Troeltsch's period. They symbolize this openness in the practice of infant Baptism, often combined with some kind of penitential system for dealing with guilt. In Troeltsch's day, churches were called "confessions" because their life was organized around specific doctrinal confessions, such as Lutheran, Roman Catholic, Reformed, or Anglican. Churches, according to Troeltsch's definition, cooperate with and condone the actions of the society in which they exist. Sects, on the other hand, are fiercely exclusive, not comprehensive. Their high membership standards, in regard to both belief and conduct, are symbolized by "believer's baptism," and they strictly enforce their standards through excommunication. They usually separate themselves from society to a greater or lesser extent and refuse to participate in certain aspects of society.[21]

North American Denominationalism

Troeltsch's analysis hardly applies in Europe today, and it never gave an apt description of North American church life. In the majority of world Christianity, Christians have organized themselves according to denominations. Many of these denominations trace their roots back to European groups that were organized around specific doctrinal confessions of faith, whether "churches," such as Lutheran, Roman Catholic, Calvinist, or Anglican of the Troeltsch type, or "sects," such as Baptists and Methodists in his typology. Denominations also took into account national origins and languages. Thus, among Lutherans, synods developed for Germans, Norwegians, Swedes, Danes, Finns, and Slovaks. They also developed out of differing doctrinal and practical concerns, some leaning more toward German or Scandinavian Pietism; others influenced by the revival of confessional Lutheran theology in the mother countries of Europe.[22] Furthermore, there were German Baptists, German Methodists, German Congregationalists, etc.

Many North American Protestant denominations were racked by internal strife as the nineteenth century closed. The battles launched then between "Fundamentalists" and "Liberals" or "Modernists" evolved, but did not end, in the twentieth century. The result is that the heirs of Fundamentalism—for example, "Evangelicals"—often will have more in common with other Evangelicals in other denominations than with the "mainline" heirs of their own denomination. Hence, nondenominational churches, which effectively function as small denominations between the main church and satellite campuses, often look and sound quite similar even though they have no shared confessional history. While not avoiding the North American religious currents, the Lutheran Confessions provide a different focus and agenda for North American Lutherans than other church bodies, often standing apart from the Modernist-Fundamentalist conflicts.

Nonetheless, Lutherans have not been immune from the confusion in the church and of God's Word that plagues believers in this era, as in every period of the church's history. With churches competing for an ever-smaller number of religious adherents, many churches have been tempted to make membership as easy as possible—just come to a one-day seminar with lunch and receive your membership card. In so doing, churches feed

---

21 Ernst Troeltsch, *The Social History of the Christian Churches* (New York: Macmillan, 1911).

22 Charles P. Arand, *Testing the Boundaries, Windows to Lutheran Identity*, 2nd ed. (St. Louis: Concordia, 2012).

into a church-shopping mentality in which church membership is an individualistic matter of spiritual wellness rather than making membership part of the Christian faith journey, following Jesus with fellow believers. Rather than cheapening membership, congregations should take seriously their common confession of Holy Scripture and what it means to follow Jesus together in love. Members of a church body should live in harmony as they walk together and give a united witness to God's Word and will for His people. When they do not, they fail to exhibit the unity that they have in Jesus (John 17:21), and they make the church appear to be another community of conflict instead of the priestly people of God's love. While the church must be a community of peace that reaches out to the world in mission, God's people dare not water down their confession of faith or make church doctrine vague. It is God's will that the church's confession be clear, and that for the sake of this clear confession believers must draw lines between God's truth and Satan's lies, even excommunicating those who proclaim a different word than the Word of Christ and cause divisions among God's church (1 John 4:1–6; Titus 1:9; 3:10–11; 1 Timothy 1:3–7; 6:3–5).

Para-Church Organizations

Alongside denominations on the current North American ecclesiastical scene, so-called **para-church organizations** play a large role. *Para* is the Greek word meaning "alongside of." Para-church organizations include groups such as Cru, Habitat for Humanity, and the Gideons that have limited doctrinal commitments with a general commitment to Jesus and the Christian faith—as if the teachings of God's Word can be separated from the Christian life. American Christianity has been so influenced by para-church organizations that North Americans often think of Christianity in terms of social action and revival-type worship with few core doctrinal commitments.

Of course, there can be no group of Christians alongside the church, for the people of God are created by God's re-creating presence in the Word. Believers may find such groups useful as they pursue certain interests, in the political arena, for instance, or in certain locations together with those with whom they share a common Lord but not a common understanding of how He works in this world. But such groups dare never become the central focus of the believer's life. God calls His people into congregations where life centers on His coming to them in Word and Sacrament.

Ecumenism

God's church is eschatologically one, united even now by a common Lord, faith, hope, and Baptism (Ephesians 4:4–6), though this unity is hidden now under serious doctrinal disagreements and petty historical conflicts. What we see and experience, especially in North America with its thousands of denominational and nondenominational church bodies, is not the unity of Christ's Body but its divisions. Since the Reformation, the number of church divisions has grown exponentially, but the problem of disunity appeared in the earliest years of the church when its members began to interpret God's Word and will in different ways (Acts 15:1–2; Galatians 1:6–10). Divisions do not reflect God's plan or desire for His church; He wants His children to be united in the same mind and the same judgment (1 Corinthians 1:10). Christ prayed for such unity among God's people (John 17:20–26).

Jesus also warned against those who would deceive His people and divert them from a faithful understanding of His message (Matthew 7:15–16). Admonition to return to the faithful teaching of the biblical message does not make an enemy of those who are admonished. Such admonition must be conducted in a spirit of love and concern (2 Thessalonians 3:14–15), but that love and concern compels believers to call to repentance those who are teaching falsely (James 5:19–20; 2 Timothy 4:1–3). Because believers are continually engaged in the difficult task of building bridges between God's Word and God's world, admonition will always be necessary in the church both toward those who go too far in accommodating to the culture and toward those who are too withdrawn from the culture to proclaim faithfully the Word to the world.

Church Fellowship

God calls Christians to fellowship, to communion, to the visible expression of unity with one another. The common faith in Jesus Christ demands that all believers call one another fellow children of God, brothers and sisters in Christ. This common faith permits all to pray with one another. But the church universal has at the same time limited preaching and communing in its midst to those who agree upon the teaching of the faith.[23] This highest form of church fellowship is called **altar and pulpit fellowship**, which shares preachers and communicants because of a shared confession of faith. Only in those periods and areas where the truth of God's Word has been taken less seriously have believers failed to limit preaching and communing in their midst to those with whom they shared a common confession of the church's teaching. These limitations are not designed, in the final analysis, to exclude. They are designed to call those within the fellowship and those outside it to a common confession of what God's Word says.

Christians have not always practiced these limitations of fellowship in a loving manner. This fact does not remove the necessity of serious

23 Werner Elert, *Eucharist and Church Fellowship in the First Four Centuries*, trans. Norman E. Nagel (St. Louis: Concordia, 1966).

conversation and admonition about doctrine and practice, about how to confess, teach, and live the faith according to Holy Scripture. It does help explain why the ecumenical movement arose in the twentieth century to tear down barriers between Christian churches.

The Ecumenical Movement

Just as the political sphere moved toward world unity in the League of Nations and United Nations during the twentieth century, the Christian Church also worked to overcome historical differences and find unity—often propelled by those engaged in mission work. This push toward unity, which can include not only organizational unity at the institutional level but also local cooperation among congregations and conversations about denominational differences, is called **ecumenism**. To a large extent, the ecumenical movement has tried to solve problems of Christian disunity institutionally and organizationally, rather than through repentance for false teaching and common confession of Christian doctrine. Differing interpretations of God's Word are too often permitted through approaches that set aside the necessity of doctrinal agreement for external expressions of Christian unity. Some organizations, such as the World Council of Churches, bring together into their organization any group that claims a Christian heritage. Others operate on the principle of **reconciled diversity**, which acknowledges a common core of confession of the biblical message alongside diverse interpretations on many significant issues, thus blurring the clear confession of God's truth.

External, institutional, organizational unity of the church is certainly a worthy goal. However, such ecclesiastical institutions are subject to the temptations to which all human institutions can fall victim. In the church, as in every other human organization, power corrupts. Institutional power can divert the gaze of church leaders and its members from the power of God's Word, in all its weakness in the cross. Therefore, believers must recognize that they will always be the vulnerable flock of God (Luke 12:32), the remnant of His people, in whom He reveals His power made perfect in weakness. They will seek the unity of the faith He has commanded ardently and urgently. They will never sacrifice the proclamation of His Word for external expressions of that unity of faith, which the Word gives.

God's people live from the Word. The Word calls the church into being, sets it apart as His priestly people, and puts it on Christ's mission as His body. When it strays from this Word, the church begins to die. Only in the Word of the Lord and in its proclamation and teaching does the church find its identity and its mission.

CHAPTER 18
THE PUBLIC MINISTRY OF THE WORD

THE church belongs to God and so does the ministry. Jesus Himself instituted the office of holy ministry and connected great promises to it: "The one who hears you hears Me" (Luke 10:16). The public ministry of the church involves numerous elements of leadership and administration, but those are not the heart of ministry. By grace, God has designed the public ministry as an office or structure within His church for the public dispensing of His means of grace so that the Word is preached in season and out of season (2 Timothy 4:2). The public ministry provides public leadership in and through the Word of God for the priestly people of God, all of which constitutes the church.

The Public Ministry and the Royal Priesthood of Believers

God has called all believers to approach Him and serve Him as His priests (1 Peter 2:5, 9; Revelation 1:6; 5:10; Romans 12:1). This relationship is anchored in what God has done in Jesus Christ and by His Spirit. Above all, being God's priests involves being children of God, in His family by faith. As a result of this passive righteousness in which God does it all, being God's priests also involves the active righteousness of worshiping and witnessing alongside other believers in the church, where God's people are gathered by the Word in oral and sacramental forms.

The public ministry, in contrast, bestows no special status before God on those who exercise it. It is rooted in God's Word as a calling of service to other believers—just as callings to be mothers and fathers, government leaders, citizens, workers and bosses are also anchored in biblical words of command and promise.[1] The office of public ministry brings the power of God in His Word, the instrument of God's grace, to His priests and to

1 See chapter 16.

the world. Through the Word, this vocation is God's public instrument for establishing, sustaining, and leading the Body of Christ, both in its passive relationship before God and in its life of love together and in the world.

Those who hold the office of the public ministry do not, by virtue of their office, have a relationship with God that is different from other believers'. They are not closer to God or more loved by Him. In fact, pastors have no special access to God besides that which all of God's people have: His Word in all its forms that is grasped by faith through the Spirit. They differ in the vocation God has given them in the church. God calls public ministers of the church to serve Him by serving their fellow believers with the public application of God's Word to their lives.

The Necessity of the Public Ministry

Sociologically, human institutions are always structured to provide leadership. They do not function without the designation of responsibilities to various people within them. Among these responsibilities, the obligations of leadership fall upon people with abilities appropriate to the needs of the institution. Every team has a captain. Apart from the smallest of groups, pure democracy does not exist among human creatures, and certainly not in the church. God's Word provides not only the church's power but also something of a flexible model for its life.

Furthermore, order is necessary for freedom. Anarchy or chaos, not freedom, is the opposite of order. If God's people are to be free to live together in love, if they are to be free to carry out their own responsibilities, they must have leadership. God is a God of peace, not of confusion, and He wants everything to be done decently and in order in His church (1 Corinthians 14:33, 40). Therefore, He has freed His people for performing their various functions by providing them with the leadership of the public ministry.

Far more important than any sociological reasons for the public ministry—but not disconnected from them—is God's command to His church to establish and maintain the public ministry. God gave the gift of this public leadership to the church as the Holy Spirit caused the Word of the Lord to grow in the church's first days. Paul appointed elders as leaders in every church (Acts 14:23). Titus was given the charge to appoint elders for the believers in every town on Crete (Titus 1:5). The church of Jerusalem added to the ministry of the Word a formal ministry of service as one of its first organizational actions (Acts 6:1–6).

The precise institutional shape of the public ministry in the New Testament era eludes us as we read the texts. Exactly where function and formal office meet behind the titles of apostle, prophet, pastor, teacher, and evangelist (Ephesians 4:11) is unclear. The terms *bishop* and *elder* can be used interchangeably for the pastoral leadership of the early Christian congregation (cf. Acts 20:17, 28; Titus 1:5, 7). Nonetheless, at every point in which the epistles of the New Testament turn to glimpse the organization and structure of the church, Holy Scripture indicates that God had instituted formal, public leadership for His people as they gathered together as Christ's Body.

The public ministry centers around the public proclamation of the Word, the unique function of the church. The public ministry is therefore vested in the person whom God calls to exercise responsibility for the public action of His Word. The care of God's people through the Word has most often been compared to the gentle care of the Good Shepherd, and so this office is often called the **pastoral office**. Although the Scriptures never provide a complete job description for the pastor, the functions of this office center upon the public proclamation of the Word and spiritual care for the people of God through the Word.[2]

In many times and places, the church has created offices that exercise certain functions of public ministry to aid the pastor in carrying out some of the duties of the office. In the early church, teachers and evangelists apparently joined deacons rather quickly to provide specific service to God's people in conjunction with the pastoral care provided through the pastoral office. These helping roles are predecessors for the role of the commissioned minister of the Gospel—teachers, deaconesses, and directors of various kinds of ministry (e.g., Christian education, church ministries, family life ministry, music, and outreach)—that are part of many Lutheran church bodies today. What distinguishes the pastoral office from the responsibilities of these other roles—sometimes called **auxiliary offices**, not meaning secondary or merely extra offices but offices that *aid* a congregation's ministry—is its responsibility for the total public ministry of the church. The church may order and arrange its public life with a variety of callings, so long as this design serves the Word and the needs of Christ's people and places ultimate responsibility for the public service of Word and Sacrament in the pastor.

Those who offer leadership to the church through ministries that specialize in teaching, evangelism, service to a variety of temporal needs, or leadership in music serve God and His people as fully as any others do. The congregation of God's children should treasure, respect, and sustain them in their service to the church as they support the ministry of the Word.

2 Departments of Systematic Theology, "The Office of the Holy Ministry," *Concordia Journal* 33, no. 3 (2007): 242–55.

Ministry Serves

The term *ministry* is derived from the Latin word *ministerium*, which means "service." "The ministry" became the designation for the service of bringing God's Word to His people in the public arena early in the church's history. Long before the Reformation, the ministry had become a formal office within the church, the office of pastor or priest. The Wittenberg reformers recognized that the office of the ministry exists to perform a particular kind of service, the service of the Word, and for no other reason.

The word *ministry* is a verbal noun.[3] It speaks of a formal, institutionalized calling within the church, but God instituted and sustains that calling only for the proclamation and teaching of the Word to the world. When those who hold the public ministry no longer function as the servants of God's people and God's world, they have betrayed their calling. God's servants do not rule; they must serve, following the Lord Christ and His servant way, just as the church is called to do the same in its mission as the Body of Christ.[4]

God has called all believers to serve as priests and deliver His Word to others at home with loved ones, in their neighborhoods with friends, and at work among colleagues. Those Bible passages that speak of the activities of the Word apply to the whole people of God. They commission His children for His mission of making disciples (Matthew 28:18–20) and for the condemnation of sin and the sharing of the forgiveness of sins (Matthew 16:19; 18:18; Luke 24:47–48; John 20:23). At the same time, God has given the calling of public minister to the church as a gift for its edification, and God has given the office special responsibility to exercise the Office of the Keys publicly and proclaim the Word to, for, and in behalf of the church (Ephesians 4:11–12; 2 Timothy 4:1–2).

The biblical writers use the term *ministry* in a variety of ways. The term can refer to all kinds of service and to the service of the Word as exercised by all members of the Body of Christ within their vocations. The public ministry, however, is a term the church has used to designate the calling of those who have specific duties, responsibilities, and accountability as they function in behalf of the congregation in the public arena. This does not mean that all acts of the public ministry are public acts. It does mean that those whom the church calls as its publicly designated servants are acting in behalf of the whole congregation when they carry out functions that bring God's Word to others.

---

3 Peter Fraenkel, "Revelation and Tradition: Notes on Some Aspects of Doctrinal Continuity in the Theology of Philip Melanchthon," *Studia Theologica* XIII (1959): 97–113.

4 Theodore J. Hopkins, *Christ, Church, and World: Bonhoeffer and Lutheran Ecclesiology after Christendom* (Lanham, MD: Lexington Books/Fortress Academic, 2021), 119–33.

Although the Scriptures do not prescribe what functions must or may be exercised by those who hold the **office of the public ministry**, this calling or office is responsible for the public representation and action of the church in the dispensing of the means of grace. Throughout its history the church has attached other duties and responsibilities to its public ministers. These have included various tasks of service and administration. Congregations may indeed add and subtract such responsibilities. The public ministry itself, however, must hold responsibility for public preaching, teaching, and administration of the Sacraments. In fact, preaching and administering the Sacraments are so central to the office of the public ministry that these acts should rarely, if ever, be delegated to those who are not called to serve as pastors or on the way to the pastoral office.

This calling is described as one of shepherding (Acts 20:28), following the example of the Lord Himself, who cares for His people like a shepherd, ready to sacrifice His life for His sheep, always striving to bring them together into His fold (John 10:7–18; 1 Peter 2:25). Because of this work of shepherding, holders of the office of public ministry are called **pastors**. Those who hold the office of public ministry are also called **elders** in Holy Scripture, referring to their status as wise and experienced leaders of God's people (Titus 1:5–6). Peter calls Jesus an "Overseer" or "Guardian" of His people; this word is *episkopos* in Greek (1 Peter 2:25). It is often translated as **bishop**. Although it is used in Holy Scripture as an equivalent of elder and pastor (e.g., 1 Peter 5:1–4; Titus 1:5–9), ancient groups used the term for leaders who indeed oversaw the activities of their followers. Particularly in the framework of biblical thought, the obligations of an overseer embraced functions of guarding and protecting. We must be careful to understand the work of oversight in the way that Jesus Himself exercises such authority. Jesus exercised His authority by serving; His authority is implemented "under" His people as He humbles Himself so that they might be exalted. Thus the public servants of His Word oversee by protecting and serving.

The Power of Ministry

Particularly in the democratic societies of the last two centuries debates have arisen about the division of power between **laity** and pastors, between God's children who have not been called to public ministry and their public leaders. This debate reflects a presupposition that there is only so much power, which must be divided rightly. It ignores the biblical presupposition that power in God's church resides in the Word, not in the lay-priests or pastors. It also ignores the biblical presupposition that both people and pastors serve God first of all and not themselves. God has called every member of His church to serve one another, and their relationships to one another are governed by their calling to be God's servants. Pastors and people do not divide power between them. They share the power of the Word to encourage, uplift, admonish, console, rebuke, reprove, and teach as circumstances of life dictate. "Strong" pastors strengthen their people in exercising the common callings of worshiping the Lord in all areas of life and in witnessing to the Word of God wherever and whenever they have the opportunity to do so. "Strong" congregations support their public ministers in all their activities, with admonition, when necessary, as well as provide encouragement and cooperation in Christ's ministry following their pastor's lead. Both pastor and congregation support one another modestly and humbly.

Working together in the Lord's callings, pastors and laity focus their concerns on bringing the power of the Gospel to all who need to hear it, inside and outside the congregation. Thus pastors care for their people as beloved children of God. They serve their people selflessly, as Christ shepherded His people, laying aside His rights and privileges as well as His human life (Philippians 2:6–8). God's people, therefore, respect and care for their overseers in the Lord as they receive from them the service of leadership and the service of the Word. They do not endow their pastors with special powers, as if they were shamans or holy men who have special powers of their own. They love them because they are gifts from God who come with His Word and who continually pray for them and for all people.

The Service of the Word, or the Office of the Keys

The specific kind of service that God's called overseers or shepherds perform for His people involves the application of His Word to their lives. It is the ministry of reconciliation whereby God draws His fallen and straying human creatures back to Himself (2 Corinthians 5:18–21). It is the service that brings those who were estranged from God and hostile to Him to the hope of the Gospel of Jesus (Colossians 1:21–23). The church has called this ministry the public exercise of the **Office of the Keys** because Jesus gave Peter, as the representative of the whole church,[5] "the keys of the kingdom of heaven" (Matthew 16:19). These keys enable the church to preach the Law, which locks people out of a relationship with God, and to preach the Gospel, which opens this relationship for them. Thus "the primary paradigm for

5 Oscar Cullmann, *Peter: Disciple, Apostle, Martyr*, trans. Floyd V. Filson (Cleveland: World, 1953), 223–38.

ministry is absolution—concrete, present-tense, I-to-you declaration in Word and sacrament authorized by the triune God."[6]

In preaching and Baptism, in Confession and Absolution as well as the Lord's Supper, pastors publicly exercise this calling for God's people. They serve as God's hit men as they proclaim the Law and lock the door to the kingdom of God as a call for repentance. They fulfill God's plan for them as they serve as His midwives, bringing fallen sinners to new life in Christ, opening up the fullness of God's gift of our humanity to His people once again by grace.

The use of these Keys involves life and death. Those who bring the Word to others do not simply share information. They bring the presence and power of Christ's death and resurrection into the middle of other people's lives. They announce the plan God fashioned for His people before the world was created (Ephesians 1:3–23). They pronounce upon sinners the forgiveness of sins and the restoration of life through Jesus Christ. God accomplishes His saving will through their words.

As they function with God's Keys to the kingdom, pastors function as prophetic proclaimers of His Word and as priestly intermediaries for His people in the public arena, as public representatives of the church to which God has entrusted the prophetic proclamation of the Word and the priestly mediation. They bring the Word to others, in their sermons and in private confession and absolution, in the Sacraments, in pastoral counseling and Christian conversation. They bring the pleas of their people to God in public prayer and praise and in their private prayers for their people and for the world.

The "holiness" of the office of "holy ministry" consists not in the holiness of the officeholders but in the holiness of God's Word, for the public ministry is totally bound up with that Word and inseparable from it. This is why Philip Melanchthon was willing to say that ordination—entrance into the office of public ministry—could even be called a sacrament if it was meant in reference to the Word, which does indeed have God's command and carries great Gospel promises.[7] At the same time, pastors are given no special ability or reward through ordination. In fact, the office carries with it no special merit at all, independent of the Word, no blessing apart from God's Word in all its forms.

6 Gerhard O. Forde, *Theology Is for Proclamation* (Minneapolis: Fortress, 1990), 179.

7 Apology of the Augsburg Confession XIII 11–13. Having been said more to combat Roman Catholic thinking than to advocate for a Lutheran understanding of the Sacraments, this suggestion disappeared in subsequent Lutheran thinking on the public ministry.

Aspiring to the Office of Public Ministry

God has carefully designed the structures of human life, including the structure of the church and the office of ministry. God has given a set of characteristics and abilities for those who fill the office of public ministry, especially in 1 Timothy 3:1–7 and Titus 1:5–9. Pastors should be above reproach, respected and honored in the church. Their family life must be an example for their people—each being husband of one wife and able to manage his household well. They must display temperance, common sense, dignity, hospitality, gentleness, and self-control. They must be able to teach effectively and refute those who oppose the faith. Their lives dare not be marred by drunkenness and violence of temper or fist. They must not be greedy and preoccupied with money. They should not be recent converts, lest they seek the office for other reasons than service. They must be respected in the community outside of the church walls.

In two passages, Paul directly indicated that it is contrary to God's will for women to fill the pastoral office (1 Corinthians 14:34–35; 1 Timothy 2:11–12). It is clear that Paul did not object to women praying and prophesying in public (1 Corinthians 11:5), but he commanded their silence in the public worship service. In this way, Paul recognized that women have the ability and aptitude to be pastors, but Jesus has not given them the authority to fill the office.[8] Since the office of holy ministry belongs to Jesus, it is His authority that matters in the pastoral office, not human logic. Although we might want to speculate why God would not authorize women to be pastors—Paul indicates that the order of creation is part of this, although the exact point is difficult to discern—in the end, it does not matter. The Creator knows the best way for His creation to function, including His church, and in His wisdom He has chosen to give the pastoral office to certain men. To women He has given other essential roles in the church depending on their individual gifts, such as teacher, deaconess, youth director, missionary, and more, everything except the office of pastor.

In Protestant churches within the context of Western culture in the past century and a half, some have argued that Paul's restriction of the pastoral office to men was culturally conditioned and therefore no longer applicable to the contemporary church. Few disagree on the intention of the texts in 1 Corinthians and 1 Timothy—though some try to distance the "real" Paul from his own words. Most disagree with the continued application of this command in a different cultural context. The cultural argument, however, cuts both ways. If cultural conditions determined Paul's prohibition in the first century, it is just as likely that contemporary cultural conditions obscure

8 On the distinction between aptitude and authority, see "Office of the Holy Ministry," 254–55.

the view of modern Christians from seeing God's wisdom and order in His arrangement for the pastoral office.

Ordination and Call

The church has found pastors and other called ministers for its congregations and other institutions within it in various ways. The apostles and their colleagues appointed leaders for the church themselves (Titus 1:5). Episcopal, presbyterian, and congregational forms of church government have created various means for placing leaders in called positions. The earliest Lutherans followed medieval custom and altered it little. Local nobles or town councils often nominated pastors, who were examined by neighboring pastors and the congregation, and then a single candidate was ratified by the congregation. The Scriptures command no particular form for choosing the servants called to the public ministry of the church.

Congregational calling of pastors and others who assist them in the public ministry has the advantage of placing this responsibility among the people whom they will serve. Congregations—or other authorized agencies within the organized church—call fellow members of Christ's Body to the pastoral office or to other offices within the church. They extend such calls as servants of God, and God calls through the church. Thus the congregation or other institution of the church does not "hire—nor "fire"—its servants. God gives the church these public servants through the **call**. Therefore, the public ministers of the Word owe their responsibility to God. Their responsibility is defined by His call, and it is defined as service to God's people, serving up the Word for salvation in Christ Jesus.

When the public ministers of the church fail to serve well, the people of God are to admonish them and help them repent and correct their failures. When the people of God fail to live as His children, God calls upon the public ministers to bring His children to repentance. The Word remains the Lord's; the calling remains the Lord's. Neither the Word nor the calling dare ever become subject to the whim of the people or the pastor. Both Word and calling are gifts from God to His people. The people of the congregation may abuse the responsibility of calling their own pastors by filling the office with those who tickle their ears rather than proclaim the Word of the Lord faithfully. Nonetheless, God can and does work through congregations to ensure the effective proclamation of His Word. The call process does not work by magic—God guides congregations and other calling agencies within the church through more and better information just as effectively as He might guide them without such information about candidates for the church's call. Yet sometimes the call process is abused, and other times God allows a church to call a scoundrel or places a good pastor among alligators.

Despite the reality of sin and continued attacks of Satan on the church, God ensures that the Gospel is preached and His people are served, even in a sinful church with sinful ministers.

God calls individuals into every responsibility of human life, including public ministry. There is no magical process by which He does so. As Lord of His creation, He works through natural means to interest individuals in serving the church within the office of holy ministry. Some who feel this call love people and are excited to be present with God's people in the best of times and through the worst. Others love the Scriptures and want to dig deeply into theology to apply God's Word to people's lives. Still others love worship and want to foster a connection to the God whose love they have experienced in Jesus. A number of those who feel called to ministry feel an obligation to share the life-giving message of the Gospel to the lost and are passionate about bringing Christ's salvation to those who do not know Him. A few even have fallen in love with their local congregations and want to cultivate the same kind of loving community for others in the Word. In a variety of ways, God aids certain believers in perceiving that His will for their lives can be fulfilled through public service in the church. This sense of **personal calling** brings with it both a sense of the burden of proclaiming God's Word and the exhilaration and joy that such service brings with it. This sense of personal calling is distinct from the public calling of the church. The church's **public call** takes the personal sense of calling and turns it into a proper call from God, authorizing the person, on behalf of God, to fill the office in a congregation. This public call is the one described under the term *call* two paragraphs above.

Since apostolic times the church has ordained its pastors. Fellow pastors "laid hands" upon candidates for the public ministry to give them the gift of their calling to serve the Word to the church (1 Timothy 4:14; 5:22). No command from God instituted the **ordination** rite. It serves as a means by which the church publicly designates those whom it has called as its public servants.

The ordination rite orders the public ministry in two senses. God orders—or calls—the pastor to the tasks of proclaiming the Word and administering the Sacraments, along with attendant responsibilities. In an ordered fashion the rites of ordination and commissioning make it clear that God takes special care of the proclamation of His saving Word in His people's midst. In these rites, God reasserts His claim on the ministry. He is giving it to the church. It and its exercise belong to Him. With these public rites God makes it clear that pastors and all called workers are responsible to Him, to serve His people in Christ's name across the world, wherever they are called. The ordination rite also reminds pastor and people that the public ministry operates in public before the world. The church does not hide its message from the world but shares it gladly and freely.

Ordination carries God's priests into a public responsibility, the office of holy ministry. It marks those whom He has called into this responsibility before the church and the world as specially designated servants of the Lord and His church. God risks all sorts of human abuse of His Word as He places it into human hands, as priests but particularly as servants of Christ, public stewards of His mysteries (1 Corinthians 4:1). His ministers have too frequently used the public office for their own ends and not for His. Nonetheless, He refuses to operate His church without the public ministry indefinitely—the church has survived on the Word shared among the laity in times when persecution eliminated pastors, for example, in Counter-Reformation Eastern Europe or under Marxist regimes in the twentieth century. In the rite of ordination, God confirms His commitment to the public ministry of the Word for the congregation in regard to the individual being ordained and in regard to the public office itself.

Believers have argued over the nature of the public ministry. Some have suggested that it is simply a public exercise of the functions all Christians are given, so things may be done decently and in order. This **functionalism** fails to recognize sufficiently that God has given the public office of the ministry of the Word to the church a special responsibility before Him (2 Timothy 4:1–5; Hebrews 13:7, 17; 1 Peter 5:1–4). This responsibility also comes as a special gift for dispensing the Word to God's children. Without this gift, the Word can easily disappear into a swamp of cultural relativism. (To be clear, only the Gospel itself, not even the public ministry, can guarantee the continued faithful use of the Gospel.) Other believers have viewed the public ministry from an **ontological** perspective, as if ordination bestows upon pastors an "indelible character," or as if the office itself, once conferred, gives a status to the person apart from the proclamation of the Word and administration of the Sacraments. This point of view fails to recognize that God's kingdom comes not through some bestowal of power upon persons but only through the power of the Word itself, as it is conveyed in oral, written, and sacramental form in the midst of God's people. What makes a pastor is always and only the Word.

When believers are asked how important the pastor really is, they should ask why the question is being posed. If the person asking is seeking some magical security in a holy priest figure, then the focus of our answer must be on the Word of God and upon the Lord Himself and away from the person of the pastor. If the person is undermining the pastor's authority as one called by God to this congregation, believers should point to the importance of this calling. Pastors have focused their lives on the Scriptures so that they can teach God's Word to His people. More important, pastors have been called by Jesus to offer Christ's forgiveness in His stead. Pastors represent the Lord Jesus to serve the church in His name. That does not prevent any pastor from being a scoundrel, but it does make the public ministry a precious gift of God.

The Word, which God gives to both the public ministry and the people, rules in His church. The Word determines what is right and proper in the life of the church. The whim or will of neither congregation nor public minister does so. From this Word both pastors and people receive life and calling, as God's priests and, for some, as His public ministers. The Word of the Lord remains forever.

CHAPTER 19

CHRIST'S RETURN AND THE END OF THE AGE: ESCHATOLOGY

CHRISTIANS live in the middle, between the "very good" of God's created work in the beginning and the "all things new" of Christ's return in the end. Christians live by faith between the rebellion and the new Jerusalem, in the old age of sin and death, which our conqueror Jesus has invaded in order to make God's kingdom present on earth as it is in heaven. For the church at the crossroads of the ages, God rules through His "precious and very great promises" that He has granted to us in Jesus (2 Peter 1:4). God's people live now by faith in the promise, having received justification by faith alone, through the Gospel that assures the forgiveness of sins because of Christ's death and resurrection. Believers stand confident that there is no condemnation for those who are in Christ Jesus, even under the assaults of the evil age (Romans 8:1). Jesus has already fulfilled so many of God's promises by His incarnation, ministry, death, resurrection, ascension to the Father's right hand, and sending of the Holy Spirit. Believers trust in these precious promises of our Creator and Savior and live by His Word, not by our own reason or strength.

Promises are a present reality, but they also point to the future. Promises connect believers to God, the promiser, establishing a relationship of faith in Him now, while they also look forward in hope to their fulfillment. In terms of our present relationship with the Creator, God has promised love and forgiveness, that we are right with Him through Christ alone and not by our works or status. In addition, God has promised an abundant future of a new creation in new bodies without pain, tears, sin, or injustice. Most important, Jesus has promised to return to His creation to dwell with His creatures even more intimately and gloriously than in His ministry, making all things new (Matthew 16:27; Mark 13:24–27; Acts 1:11; Revelation 21:1–7; 22:20). When Christ returns, God has promised His people a wedding banquet at which we will feed on the best of meats and partake of the finest of wines while our God dines on death, destroying the grave and eliminating our shame and tears forever (Isaiah 25:6–9). God has promised His people a new age, a new creation, without sin, where lambs and wolves lie down together (Isaiah 11:6–9), war and bloodshed are abolished, and peoples from all nations attend to the Word of the Lord and walk in His paths (Isaiah 2:1–5). God has promised to judge and condemn the enemies of His creation—sin, death, and the devil—and make justice flow like a river (Amos 5:19–24). God has promised to raise from their graves all who have died (Ezekiel 37:12–14; Daniel 12:2; Matthew 22:23–33; John 5:25–29; 1 Thessalonians 4:13–14), giving believers new bodies that are endowed with God's Spirit to live eternally with Him in the new creation (1 Corinthians 15:42–56; Philippians 3:20–21).

These promises have begun to be realized as the Holy Spirit has declared and made sinners forgiven children of God by faith in Jesus. Nevertheless, God has made more promises that He has not yet fulfilled. This "beginning" and "more"—**now** but **not yet**—constitute the heart of **eschatology**, which is the study of the end, describing the last one, Christ, and the last things that He will usher in when He comes again on the Last Day. Believers look to God and His promises in both faith and hope.

Hope

The apostle Peter calls all Christians to be prepared to defend the hope that is in us with gentleness and respect (1 Peter 3:15). This call to understand our hope and share it with others is essential in the twenty-first century since hopelessness abounds. A recent health report in the United States showed that young people's mental health has declined drastically during the previous decade so that more than 40 percent of high school students experience persistent feelings of sadness or loneliness that impact their life weekly.[1] The problem is so pervasive that every college professor hears the same story of mental health struggle and feelings of hopelessness multiple times a year. So-called "deaths of despair" and "diseases of despair" have increased significantly in the past decade as many have sought to self-medicate their loneliness, resulting in even more pain and suffering. Part of the problem is that an evolutionary worldview of progress has grasped the popular imagination. Instead of hope in a God who comes from the outside, we expect human beings to fix the world. When we, however, look at child trafficking, climate trends, murder rates, gun violence, and persistent poverty, among other things, we feel the gravity of the problems. We cannot save the world, and our flimsy hope in humanity dries up. We realize

1 Centers for Disease Control and Prevention, "Youth Risk Behavior Survey: Data Summary and Trends Report, 2011–2021," https://www.cdc.gov/healthyyouth/data/yrbs/pdf/YRBS_Data-Summary-Trends_Report2023_508.pdf (accessed June 7, 2023).

the extent of our creatureliness—the fact that we are not God and cannot re-create the cosmos—and we fall into despair.

The problem is only exacerbated by how we treat death. We have attempted to cope with our hopelessness by avoiding death altogether. The ideal death in the Middle Ages was slow, surrounded by family and friends, perhaps with the body and blood of Jesus on one's lips; our ideal death is lonely and quick. We want to live hard and die fast, before we have time to reflect upon our finitude. We throw dying people into nursing homes and hospitals as far away from the living as possible. Those who can afford it do everything they can to look younger, feel younger, and even avoid death—soon enough by trying to download their consciousness to a computer or robot. Without any reason for hope, all people can wish for is a long and comfortable life in this age, sometimes striving for it with religious fervor.

The way forward for Christians is the way of hope, attending first to creation's groaning under the rule of sin and death (Romans 8:22) and seeing the groaning for what it is.[2] Jesus blesses those who are poor, those who mourn, the lowly and the hungry, not the ones who have but the ones who have not (Matthew 5:3–6). Jesus blesses those who recognize the suffering and sin endemic to this age and hope for a new creation in Him. Christian hope, thus, is not rooted in human progress or political power, but in God who raises the dead in His time. Christian hope has a sure and certain foundation in Jesus who died and rose again as the firstfruits of creation's future. However, we do not hope for what we see; we must wait for it with patience. For "in this hope we were saved" (Romans 8:24–25).

The Scriptures expect Christians to be different because of our hope—we do "not grieve as others do who have no hope" (1 Thessalonians 4:13). This hope has multiple dimensions. Believers recognize a different hope, Christ, than individual striving for comfort and long life. Believers also have reasons for their hope, rooted in what God has done in Jesus. Finally, believers hope for something different than just life after death. God's people hope for the resurrection of the dead and the life of the age to come. Recognizing the hope that the Bible describes prepares us to give an account to others and live by faith in order that the unbelieving world might see Christ's cross and empty tomb, where all can find hope.

Christ, Our Hope

The Christian account of hope does not tell the story of individuals escaping an evil earth but of God's restoration of His fallen creation in Christ. Contemporary people often express a desire for continued existence

2 Jeffrey A. Gibbs, "Regaining Biblical Hope: Restoring the Prominence of the Parousia," *Concordia Journal* 27 (October 2001): 311–13.

after death, individual souls escaping from suffering to be reunited with dead family and friends in some indiscriminate "heaven." The Bible's account of hope is different. In the Scriptures, God is the protagonist, and the antagonists are sin, death, and the evil one. The Bible begins with God's creation that He called "very good." The trouble started when the pinnacle of His creation, human creatures, contended for control of their own lives, doubting and disobeying God's Word, which delivered death and despair. Nevertheless, God promised to be with His creatures and save them from themselves and sin's consequences. God refused to give up on His sinful creatures, choosing Abraham, Isaac, and Jacob, through whom He promised to bless and redeem the world.

Our hope took concrete shape when the Son of God became incarnate as Abraham's heir to save not only Abraham's descendants but also Gentiles by grafting them into the same promises. Jesus promised that those who trust in Him would not escape the body upon death, but would have a new relationship with God, being God's children by the Spirit and part of God's kingdom, in life and in death (Mark 1:15; John 3:1–8; Romans 14:7–9). Jesus did not preach an otherworldly salvation but proclaimed that God had brought His rule to earth in Him. Jesus' miracles restored the creation—both human and nonhuman—to what it was supposed to be, inaugurating God's reign on earth. Jesus turned water into wine, making the earth flow forth with the finest of wines as a foretaste of the eschatological banquet (John 2:1–11; Isaiah 25:6). Jesus stilled storms, made the earth to bring forth food for the hungry, healed broken bodies, brought sight to the blind, and opened deaf ears. Jesus forgave sinners and brought outcasts into a new human community in Him. Christ promised no one a mere spiritual, noncorporeal life after death. Rather, Jesus began to restore earth into **heaven**—not a place in the sky but where God is and reigns—making God's rule present on earth. In other words, Jesus began to make creation new, restoring it to what it was to be in the beginning, a place for God to dwell with His people and His people to receive gratefully everything they need.

As Christ made God's reign present on earth, the powers of this present darkness did their worst against the Messiah. They killed Jesus on the cross, but the Father raised His Son from the dead, winning the decisive battle over death and hell and showing believers their future as children of God with new bodies in a new creation. Before Jesus ascended into heaven, He promised to return in His **Parousia**. When He comes back again, Jesus will make all things new, raising all the dead, exposing the works of darkness to the light of His judgment, condemning those who stand on the side of the devil and his minions, and re-creating the cosmos to be a place of perfect peace, justice, and love where God will dwell with His people forever (Revelation 21:1–27).

This biblical account of hope shows us that Christian hope is not about human creatures first of all. It is about God. By faith, Christians have graciously been made sons and daughters of God through Baptism and subjects of King Jesus, "our hope" (1 Timothy 1:1). Christian hope, then, does not begin with life after death or even individual salvation, but with our great God and Savior who loves His people and is determined to have them for Himself despite the enemy's protestations. Christians believe that the Creator will restore His creation to the perfection of shalom in which He once made it—even a step above, to never fall again—and He has already begun this redemption by His Son and Spirit.

Jesus inaugurated the Last Day in His ministry of forgiveness, restoration, and new community, which scholars sometimes term **realized** or **inaugurated eschatology**. Realized eschatology emphasizes the presence of the Last Day realities in time whereas inaugurated highlights that these eschatological realities have begun but are not completed. The church lives in the new age, having received forgiveness of sins through the Word, having been made right before God by faith, and having the presence of the Lord Christ according to His promise. However, the magnetic pull of the grave has not yet been reversed; sin's isolating dominion persists; and the devil's reign of terror remains. Hence, Paul proclaims: "In this *hope* [of the final redemption of our bodies] we *were* saved" (Romans 8:24, emphasis added). Dead to sin in Baptism and risen to new life with Christ by faith *now*, believers *yet hope* for Christ's return and His final victory over sin, death, and all the powers of evil.

As believers grasp the promise here and now, they are also well aware that the battle between God and Satan, between the truth of our Creator and the death and destruction wrought by the deceiver and accuser (John 8:44), continues on the battlefield of their own lives. The human experience of this eschatological conflict, this war to the end, began in Eden, and it will end when Christ returns on the Last Day. In every "today" of believers' lives, they feel the draw of Satan to succumb to his occupation forces, and they experience the Holy Spirit's refitting them with their new identity as God's children through forgiveness of sins. This life of repentance, of being turned from our idols to Christ, is our lot while we are still sinners and the righteous children of God at the same time. Nevertheless, this continuing conflict is moving toward the final consummation of the war for lordship in the shadow of Christ's decisive victory in His resurrection. Against our Lord, sin has suffered defeat, Satan has succumbed, and death is dying. In certain confidence believers fight the good fight as they move toward life forever with their Lord.

Now, but not yet. Believers are saved by faith in what Jesus has done in the midst of the battle and wait in hope for what Jesus has promised to do. Christians live in the middle of this story, with hearts and minds firmly anchored in Christ, our hope.

The Reasons for Hope

A recent survey of North American religious beliefs revealed a strange phenomenon about hope. A smaller percentage of people believed in God and belonged to religious communities in recent years than in the 1970s, yet a greater percentage of North Americans believed in an afterlife—80 percent compared to 75 percent.[3] Ironically, Americans are more "hopeful" that death is not the end, but fewer have reasons to so believe.

The Christian faith is not so rudderless. The Bible offers the hope of resurrection from the dead and eternal life with God in the new age of shalom for all who believe in the Crucified and Risen One. This hope is not based on optimism or human strength but on God's power and promises. Hence, the apostle Peter encourages Christians to articulate the reasons for their hope: "In your hearts honor Christ the Lord as holy, always being prepared to make a defense to anyone who asks you for a reason for the hope that is in you; yet do it with gentleness and respect" (1 Peter 3:15).

Peter, Paul, and all the apostles stood firm in hope while facing persecution, suffering, and death because they trusted that God would finish what He had begun in Jesus and the Holy Spirit. At the heart of their hope, and our hope today, is the resurrection of Christ. Hence, Paul proclaims: "If Christ has not been raised, then our preaching is in vain and your faith is in vain" (1 Corinthians 15:14). Jesus, however, has been raised from the dead, and the old age of sin has received its death warrant. As theologian Oscar Cullmann suggested, the cross and resurrection of Jesus constitute God's decisive victory over the powers of this present darkness even though the war rages on.[4] As in World War II, the victory at Normandy on D-Day was the decisive battle for the Allies, although the official end of the war in Europe would not come for another eleven months. Our present moment is one in which Jesus has conquered the reign of death, sin, and Satan by His cross and resurrection, but the enemies continue to battle against the Messiah and His church. Hence, God's people live in hope, hope that God

---

3 Mark Chaves, *American Religion: Contemporary Trends*, 2nd ed. (Princeton, NJ: Princeton University Press, 2017), 36–37.

4 Oscar Cullmann, *Christ and Time: The Primitive Christian Conception of Time and History*, trans. Floyd V. Filson, rev. ed. (Philadelphia: Westminster Press, 1964), 84.

will finish what He has begun, revealing the victory that He won in His Son, Jesus, at Golgotha and the empty tomb. Our hope stands firm on Christ's resurrection in the midst of the conflict against God's enemies.

The resurrection of Jesus is not only a promise of a new creation for the cosmos, but it is also a promise for all believers of their future with God as daughters and sons. Paul confesses that Jesus is the **firstfruits** of the resurrection of the dead, the first one of many sisters and brothers. Jesus was raised from the dead, while the old age remains, as the beginning of the new creation's birth. Hence, Christians have confidence that the dead in Christ will rise again to new bodily life on the Last Day and live with Jesus forever in the new creation. "For as in Adam all die, so also in Christ shall all be made alive. But each in his own order: Christ the firstfruits, then at His coming those who belong to Christ" (1 Corinthians 15:22–23). The time is coming when Jesus will return and terminate death's tyranny, for He has already conquered it by His resurrection (1 Corinthians 15:54–55). Believers confess their own resurrection hope because they know the Savior who went through death to obliterate its power and was raised from the dead to bring salvation to His people.

Another reason for hope that the Scriptures give is the presence of the Holy Spirit. The Holy Spirit, promised through the Gospel and received by faith, is "the guarantee of our inheritance until we acquire possession of it" (Ephesians 1:13–14). The presence of the Holy Spirit through faith means that believers are adopted as children of the heavenly Father, having become heirs of God and fellow heirs with Jesus Christ (Romans 8:15–17). These promises Christians have now by faith, but there is more to come. In fact, Paul calls the Spirit "the firstfruits" of our final salvation, promising "the redemption of our bodies" when the Spirit will permeate the creation as the waters cover the sea (Romans 8:23; cf. Isaiah 11:9).

Although Christian hope may not be seen, the reasons for our hope are many. Jesus began the new age in His life and ministry, culminating in His death and resurrection. Our hope for Christ's return and His ushering in the final shalom rests on His already accomplished work. As we wait, we trust in God's gracious patience, who desires all to repent and believe in Jesus (2 Peter 3:9), and we hold to the Word and Sacraments that offer the promised Holy Spirit, the guarantee of our final redemption. Christian hope is not irrational. We can give our reasons for hope, witnessing to Jesus Christ's accomplished work, the presence of the Holy Spirit, and God's promises of more to come.

The Content of Christian Hope

The hope that Christians have in Jesus must be distinguished from three common misunderstandings. First, Christian hope is not Pollyanna, optimism without any reasons. Christian hope, rather, is somber about the afflictions of the present age, recognizing that our faith lies in the Suffering Servant, the crucified God. The Scriptures find hope in suffering because the cross of Christ stands at the center of history, and God is faithful, having kept His promises to Abraham, Jacob, Moses, David, and the prophets. St. Paul knew that the present age is full of suffering and affliction, under the dominion of death, though it is also pregnant, groaning in labor, with the new creation that God has already begun in His Son and Spirit (Romans 8:22). In the middle of the present darkness, Paul remained steadfast in faith and hope: "We are afflicted in every way, but not crushed; perplexed, but not driven to despair; persecuted, but not forsaken; struck down, but not destroyed; always carrying in the body the death of Jesus, so that the life of Jesus may also be manifested in our bodies" (2 Corinthians 4:8–10). The Scriptures are realistic about pain and suffering but also brimming with hope for God's final redemption: "For this light momentary affliction is preparing for us an eternal weight of glory beyond all comparison, as we look not to the things that are seen but to the things that are unseen" (2 Corinthians 4:17–18).

Second, Christian hope is not congruent with a belief in the immortality of human souls. Like modern North Americans who believe in an afterlife without trusting in a deity, some ancient Greeks also posited that the human soul was immortal in itself. Christian hope, however, does not lie in the quality or constitution of the soul. Christians do not believe that humans will live forever because human creatures are so powerful or great as to have eternal life in themselves. Rather, the Scriptures confess that God loves His creatures, and God will not give them over to death without a fight. Hence, Jesus scolded the Sadducees for refusing to believe in the resurrection on the basis of God's name: God is the God of Abraham, Isaac, and Jacob, and "He is not God of the dead, but of the living" (Matthew 22:32). Jesus' point was not about Abraham, Isaac, Jacob, or any human creature; it was about God's power and promise. The Bible teaches that God cares for His people between death and the resurrection of the dead. The Bible does not say much about this life after death, but it does give us confidence in God's redemption in life and death.[5] The Scriptures, instead, proclaim the Parousia of the Lord,

---

5 Francis Pieper, *Christian Dogmatics*, vol. 3 (St. Louis: Concordia, 1953), 511: "Holy Writ reveals but little of the state of the souls between death and the resurrection. In speaking of the last things, it directs our gaze primarily to Judgment Day." See Gibbs, "Regaining Biblical Hope," 315–20.

that Jesus will come back again to raise the dead, judge all people in justice, and make all things new.

Third, the goal of Christian faith is not to die and get to heaven.[6] Rather, like the martyrs under the altar in Revelation, believers are waiting for the Creator to reclaim His creation in its fullness just as He promised in Genesis 3, to crush the serpent's head fully and finally (Revelation 6:9–10). In the creeds, we do not confess that we will go to heaven, but that we believe in the "resurrection of the body and the life everlasting." Christian hope is not located in a spiritual place up in the sky, but in the return of Jesus to the earth on the Last Day. On that day, Jesus will split open tombs and raise all from the dead with a word from His mouth, giving eternal life in a transformed, new creation to all who believe in Him, and sending away those who wanted life on their own terms into the torment that they chose for themselves.

Although biblical hope is firmly rooted in the return of Jesus and the resurrection of the body, many Christians focus on "heaven" as a spiritual reality for the souls of believers. For Holy Scripture, Jesus is our hope, and believers await His return when graveyards will flower with abundant life. Although many popular notions of "heaven" do not match with the Bible, believers must be patient with people who are worried about their status after death. After all, even Christians experience fear and dread when they encounter death. We do not know exactly what lies on the other side of our final breath, just as we did not know this world while we were in the womb and struggled against that birth. We may not have specifics of what death will be like, but we do know *who* is on the other side of death. The Lord Jesus went through death for us, sanctifying the grave and giving us the promise that we cannot be separated from Him in death, just as in life (Romans 8:38–39). Therefore, believers can have firm confidence in Jesus on our deathbeds, even as we look forward to Christ's coming again when soul and body will be reunited to celebrate the eternal wedding banquet of the Lamb (Revelation 19:6–9).

Death is a mere sleep for believers—as the Bible regularly calls it—no more worrisome than a light afternoon nap and just as certain to end before the party begins. Nevertheless, death is not good. Death is an unnatural intruder in God's creation, God's "last enemy to be destroyed" (1 Corinthians 15:26). Among the saddest expressions sin has forced upon us is that which claims: "What a blessing she could die!" Death can be called a "blessing" only because life has been so wrecked and ruined. Death remains a curse even when it frees from sorrow and pain. Furthermore, death separates us from the human communities into which God has placed us, tearing

6 Gibbs, "Regaining Biblical Hope," 315–20.

apart families and friends. The God who made humans for community does not intend for these communions to be ripped apart. Thus even believers need consolation and support from fellow Christians as death approaches and our eyes gaze toward eternity.

The Day of the Lord: Judgment, Resurrection, and New Creation

The prophets long pronounced "the day of the Lord" that would bring God's judgment on idolatry, injustice, violence, and sin (e.g., Isaiah 2:12–22; Joel 2:1–11; Amos 8:1–12; Obadiah 15–18; Zephaniah 1:14–18). Jesus, too, promised such a day—speaking concurrently about the Last Day and the destruction of Jerusalem in AD 70—when He would return to judge the earth in righteousness (Matthew 24:3–25:46; Mark 13:3–37; Luke 21:5–36; John 5:27–29). Most people today think of Judgment Day as pure punishment, but judgment goes hand in hand with justice. For a world that is poisoned by sin, oppressed by violence, and tormented by death, judgment comes not as pure punishment but as justice for the vulnerable and the lowly, which is all creatures under the tyranny of sin. The day of the Lord is God's day when He will right all wrongs, casting evil into the abyss and bringing forth a new creation of righteousness and goodness forever. Hence, the prophet Isaiah describes this day as one in which streams will flow forth in the desert, the eyes of the blind will be opened, the lame will leap like a deer, and no dangerous beast will threaten the people of God (Isaiah 35:1–10). For a creation beset by sin, death, and the devil, judgment is not primarily punishment, but the way in which God brings justice and shalom in re-creating His cosmos. In fact, God's Day of justice will be a day of liberation for His people, when sin, shame, and Satan will be shattered, death will be dominated, and believers will be fully free for the relationships for which they were made, loving God and loving others.

Judgment Day and History

Human cultures have held various views of how human history takes its course. Some ancient cultures saw in the revolution of the sun and the turning of the seasons a pattern for all human history. They defined the course of human history as cyclical. It had no meaningful beginning, and sometimes no beginning at all. Matter was viewed as eternal, and human history as revolving in a circle without beginning or end. The evolutionary dogma of contemporary Western culture senses only vague beginnings and limitless, hedonistic futures for human development.

Recently, there has been a surge of Westerners who hold some version of the Eastern belief in **reincarnation**. The basic idea of reincarnation is that human souls have lived past lives in other bodies—even nonhuman ones—and will live future lives in still others. This notion has nothing to do with either Christ's incarnation—when the Son of God became a human being and remains the same human person, Jesus, forever—or the resurrection of the dead—the Bible's teaching that the dead person's same body will be raised from the dead and reunited with the person's same soul on the Last Day. The Bible confesses that we have but one life to trust in Jesus and live according to God's Word (Hebrews 9:27) whereas reincarnation gives the false hope of different lives so that one could worry about faith and obedience in the future. In addition, reincarnation devalues the body, considering it just a shell for the real person—the soul—whereas resurrection recognizes that our bodies are created by God, loved by the One who became flesh for our salvation, and will be raised on the Last Day to live forever with the Father, Son, and Holy Spirit.

In the beginning God created the heavens and the earth. At the end He shall consummate His creation by gathering all things under His final control as He defeats every rule, authority, and power (1 Corinthians 15:20–28). The biblical view of history defines it as linear, with a definite end on Judgment Day.[7] To be sure, we experience cycles within the linear movement of history, for even if history never repeats itself exactly, certain human habits produce similar results in different ages. These cycles are not endless replications of the same event but tailored by specific cultures and circumstances. They stand as distinct events in the ever-moving line from beginning to end. Human history began when God created human creatures, Adam and Eve. Human history shall end when Jesus returns to judge and to liberate (Matthew 25:31–46). He shall close this age of darkness by judging all who live by control rather than faith in Him—and thus have not been given true human life in Him through the Spirit—and by liberating those whom He has made His own people by Word and Sacrament. Those whose lives did not reflect Jesus' love will go away into eternal punishment; those whose lives did reflect His love through faith will be taken into eternal life (Matthew 25:46; John 5:24, 28–29). This judgment stands at the end of history and the beginning of the new age of God's glorious, visible reign in a new creation with tombs broken open and death as the only corpse in the one sealed grave that remains.

The Resurrection of the Body and the Life Everlasting

When Christ returns to judge the world in righteousness, all will be raised from the dead, some to everlasting life and others to everlasting contempt

7 Cullmann, *Christ and Time*, and Oscar Cullmann, *Salvation in History* (New York: Harper & Row, 1967), summarize this viewpoint.

(Daniel 12:2; John 5:28–29). Paul describes it this way: in a moment, in the twinkling of an eye, at the last trumpet, the dead will be raised to never perish again. We shall be changed (1 Corinthians 15:52). God has promised that victory over death—and over the sin that created death—belongs to those joined together with the Lord Jesus Christ (1 Corinthians 15:57).

Belief in the **resurrection of the body** and the life everlasting was a rare commodity in Paul's time—and in most periods of human history. Neoplatonic systems of thought taught a life after death, but on a radically different basis than Paul presented, above all, in 1 Corinthians 15. Neoplatonists believed in the immortality of the soul. Many of them believed that the soul is immortal because it is a piece of the eternal spirit. This meant that the individual human soul had an absolute right to its own existence; it was indestructible by right and nature. Many Gnostic systems of thought at the time of Paul also believed that the salvation or completion of the soul's existence would take place in its return to the essential unity of the one spirit. That meant a contempt for individuality. Alongside a deprecation of individuality, these Gnostics taught that materiality was evil, and the human body would have to be sloughed off to regain perfection. To be saved, in these systems, meant to lose one's individuality as well as one's material baggage.

The Old Testament writers believed that the "spirit" or "being"—the Hebrew word *nephesh* is often translated "soul"—that God created by breathing into the dust (Genesis 2:7) is a creature of God. The biblical writers could hardly conceive of a human spirit or soul apart from a human body. They did not believe that the soul had no beginning, nor was it for them part of an eternal spirit. The soul is the product of God's creative breath and Word. Ezekiel, for instance, also knew that this nephesh—soul or spirit or being—could die because of sin (Ezekiel 18:4). The biblical writers treasured the integrity of the individual human creature at the same time that they confessed human creatures as fashioned for community with God and other creatures (Genesis 2:18–25).

Against contempt for the body and our integrity as individual creatures of God, Paul wrote 1 Corinthians 15. He defined eternal life for God's human creatures in terms of the resurrection of the body of each believer. He staked the promise of life without end upon Christ's resurrection from the dead. It makes no sense to speak of Christ's resurrection if we abandon hope in our own resurrection, just as we have no hope of our own resurrection if Christ did not rise (1 Corinthians 15:12–19). Christ retraced the steps of sinners into the grave so that He might become the firstfruits of God's re-creation of human life through His resurrection. The victory of His resurrection has placed death and all enemies of God under Him (1 Corinthians 15:20–28).

How did Christ attain the victory? Paul compared the principle to the planting and sprouting of a seed. A seed must be buried to come alive and fulfill its potential. Likewise, the sinful person must be buried to be given new life (1 Corinthians 15:35–50). Paul attempted to express the mystery of the transformation from a perishable body to an imperishable body, a mortal body to a body full of the Spirit that cannot be held by the grave, a **spiritual body**, which is not the contradiction in terms it might seem to contemporary readers. St. Paul contrasted a normal, physical body with a spiritual body, a body brimming with the Holy Spirit, the Giver of life. Throughout he insisted on two fundamental points, both opposed to Gnosticism: We remain bodies. Our humanity, expressed in our physical bodies, shall be transformed into a new, imperishable body—never to die again—but shall remain bodily and thus human. Second, we shall remain individuals. Salvation is not absorption of our souls into an "ultimate soul" or spirit in which individual identity and integrity vanishes as we lose our bodies. Salvation is the resurrection of each person's body for life with God forever. In this way death is swallowed up in victory (1 Corinthians 15:54–57).

The Lord Jesus Christ will transform the tattered and torn body, with all its signs of the oppression of sin and disease, into the glorious body in which we will live forever with Christ (Philippians 3:21). All that means, Paul concluded, is that daily believers should be going about the work of the Lord in a steadfast, unshakable way. The resurrection of the body calls forth service in vocation today.

The **new creation** that God will bring on the Last Day will be unimaginably different from the creation as we experience it, but the biblical writers still insist on the goodness of the material order. It will be a new creation (2 Peter 3:13; Revelation 21:1), but also the liberation or restoration of this order of existence (Romans 8:19–23), as God had originally designed it. The Bible offers pregnant images that give a taste for what God has in store for those who are in the Messiah. The Scriptures describe the new creation as a banquet (Isaiah 25:6–9), perfect rest for God's people (Hebrews 4:1–13), sheep grazing under the loving gaze of the Shepherd (Ezekiel 34:25–31), peoples from all nations living under the Word of God without weapons of war (Micah 4:1–5), a city that is a living temple with diversity, beauty, and life that will put earthly gold streets to shame (Revelation 21), and a peaceful garden where wolf and lamb lie together (Isaiah 11:6–9). We see in a glass darkly on this side of eternity, but God gives us these pictures of His new creation to remind us of what He has already begun in His Son and what we are still hoping for when Jesus returns. Most important of all, we are looking for Christ, our hope, to see Him face to face and be with Him as He is already with us. In Paul's words: "Now we see in a mirror dimly, but then face to face. Now I know in part; then I shall know fully, even as I have been fully known" (1 Corinthians 13:12).

Indeed, the day has already come when God's children can say, "I will give thanks to You, O Lord, for though You were angry with me, Your anger turned away, that You might comfort me. Behold, God is my salvation; I will trust, and will not be afraid; for the Lord God is my strength and my song, and He has become my salvation" (Isaiah 12:1–2). With joy we draw upon the baptismal water that is the well of our salvation, and we give thanks to the Lord. We call upon His name. We make known His deeds among the peoples of the earth, and we proclaim His exalted name. We shout and sing for joy because the Lord who has done wondrous things is with us (Isaiah 12:3–6).

We continue to be His people, and He continues to be our God, in the life that began with our baptismal death as sinners and in our baptismal resurrection to new life in Christ. In this life we shall live, finding our identity, security, and meaning through trust in God alone, who has come near to us in Jesus Christ and remains with us forever.

Life after Death

Christian hope lies not in a noncorporeal life after death, but in Jesus and His Parousia, when He will raise the dead and make all things new. Yet Christians still wonder what happens when we die. Even if I trust that God will raise my body on the Last Day, what about the time between death and resurrection? Scripture does not give many details regarding what happens between death and resurrection, focusing our attention toward the Last Day.[8] Nevertheless, God's Word insists on a few things. First, God does not abandon His own to death. Jesus is Lord not just of the living but of the dead: "For if we live, we live to the Lord, and if we die, we die to the Lord. So then, whether we live or whether we die, we are the Lord's" (Romans 14:8). The Lord who promises to raise His people to eternal life in a new creation would never abandon His own between death and resurrection. No believer, living or dead, has anything to worry about, for we are in the Good Shepherd's strong hands, the one who hallowed the grave on our behalf and could not be held by it (John 10:14–18, 27–30). Second, each human creature is a unity of body and soul. Death tears apart this unity, and resurrection to eternal life restores it. Whenever we talk about a person's existence between death and resurrection, we must not give the impression that a human creature is complete apart from the unity of body and soul. Third, any biblical notion of life after death must recognize that the interim between death and resurrection is not what God has promised for His people nor what believers

---

8 Pieper, *Christian Dogmatics*, 3:511.

are waiting for in hope. We are waiting for our bodies to be remade from the dust, breathed into by God's Spirit, and changed into immortal bodies so that we are strikingly new, yet the same persons. This is not a spiritual, nonphysical promise, but a hyperphysical hope, wherein we will be remade in the image of the man of heaven, Jesus, who was raised from the dead in His body, ate fish with His friends, and had fellowship with His disciples (1 Corinthians 15:42–49).

How should Christians talk about the status of a believer after death? Common parlance uses the term *heaven* to indicate a believer's status with Jesus after death, but heaven also conjures up notions of harps, angels, and bliss in the clouds that are all foreign to Scripture. If we do use the term *heaven* to refer to a dead believer's status, we must be clear that it is a temporary resting place as believers wait for Christ to reunite their dead bodies with their souls on the Last Day. This rest in Christ is sometimes called the **interim** or **intermediate state of the soul**, which is a temporary status of the souls of God's people between death and resurrection. This must not be confused with **purgatory**, which is the Roman Catholic notion that believers who have not made satisfaction for the punishments of their sins must have their souls purged before they can enter heavenly bliss. Instead, the understanding of believers' souls resting with Jesus in death in this interim state is based on Paul's language that death is a state of being "away from the body and at home with the Lord" (2 Corinthians 5:8). For St. Paul, death would be "gain" when he "departs" to be "with Christ," "far better" than his prison sentence (Philippians 1:21–23). Jesus, too, promises the thief crucified with Him that "today" he will be with Jesus in "paradise" (Luke 23:43). Most important, this understanding of death emphasizes that Jesus takes care of His people in death until He returns to unite heaven and earth, the living and the dead in Him in the new creation.

The Bible's teaching of life after death before the resurrection comforts believers who are with the Lord Jesus, but it does not answer all the questions we want to know. After all, it is impossible to imagine and understand what kind of life a soul has without a body. Human language, experience, and cognition presume bodies. To retain an emphasis on the unity of the body and soul both in life and in death, Kolb speculates that believers will immediately experience the resurrection of the dead upon their own death. After all, Jesus does promise the thief his own presence with Him in paradise, not merely rest but something that seems better than rest, "today" (Luke 23:43). Paul, too, may not be speaking about an interim period between death and resurrection but simply about the new resurrected life that awaits him on the other side of the grave, just as he normally does, when he speaks of hope in Christ's return. Hopkins prefers to emphasize the "now, but not yet" aspect of Christian hope also in the death of individual believers. The defeat of death is the promise God has given in Jesus which is still to be fulfilled (1 Corinthians 15:54–57). As the souls of the martyrs under the altar in Revelation must wait, resting, for Christ to finish His work, so must our souls wait and rest if we die before Christ's return (Revelation 6:9–11). In short, the twofold character of the Christian life—dead as sinners and alive as God's children at the same time—continues until Christ, our unity and our hope, returns and restores all things to new life. Because we are with the Lord Jesus, we can take comfort whether we live or whether we die. For we do not die apart from Jesus, and we will rest in Jesus and with Jesus, who is our resurrection and life (John 11:25). This rest will be good and gracious, as Jesus preserves us in security until He finishes what He began by His death and resurrection, raising our bodies, reuniting them with our souls, and realizing the new age of shalom for believers and all creation. Believers hope in Christ, knowing that He guards and protects His own in death as in life.

For those who do not believe in Christ, however, no such safe haven exists. Neither are unbelievers annihilated from the face of creation, as Jehovah's Witnesses teach. Instead, there is a continued existence apart from the Author of life after judgment, which is commonly called **hell**. Christ described this as weeping, wailing, and gnashing of teeth (e.g., Matthew 13:41–42; 25:30), and as never-ending fire or wrathful destruction (Matthew 5:22; 18:8; 25:46; Mark 9:43; cf. Jude 13; Revelation 14:11). Separate from all of God's grace, kindness, and favor that He bestows upon His creatures continually in this life, it is hell. God will judge those who do not know Him and who have not listened to the Gospel of Jesus (John 3:18, 36). They will be raised from the dead on the Last Day in their bodies with believers, but they will not find solace on that day. They will suffer the punishment of eternal destruction and exclusion from the presence of the Lord and the glory of His might (2 Thessalonians 1:5–10). There is but one name through which people come to the Father, and those who do not trust in Jesus, the name through which God has revealed Himself in crib, cross, and crypt, do not have access to God (Acts 4:12; John 14:6).

The doctrine of hell is one of the most challenging of all doctrines for God's people to teach and discuss with others. No believer wants anyone to suffer such a fate. Hence, we pray for God to change the hearts of all who oppose Him and bring them to Himself. Some try to use hell as a motivation to convince people to believe the Gospel, often using a version of Pascal's wager. The Christian philosopher Blaise Pascal once suggested that everyone should believe in God because if God does not exist, believing in

Him might appear foolish but would cause no long-term damage. Whereas if God does exist, not believing in Him would cause eternal pain. Pascal's wager, however, fails to recognize that faith is not a work done for the selfish gain of escaping hellfire, but faith is confidence in God's promises that loves Him for His sake. Faith in Jesus, thus, is not a get-out-of-jail-free card. Faith trusts and loves the Lord who died and rose again that we might be His. We do not come to love God by being afraid of punishment but by being grasped by the Spirit through the Word, which delivers God's people from the power of hell.

For teaching and discussing the doctrine of hell with others, three considerations are important. First, hell is not a central doctrine of Scripture and should not be among the first doctrines discussed. After all, hell belongs to God, and we cannot know with certainty who is there. We must focus on the things revealed and not on the secret things of God (Deuteronomy 29:29). If possible, believers should refocus early conversations on the Gospel of Jesus that bring hope. Hell only makes sense as the obverse of God's victory over the evil that rules the present darkness. Second, hell functions as part of God's judgment that also brings justice and liberation. It was never intended for human creatures, but was created for the devil and the evil angels (Matthew 25:41). God's desire is for all to be saved and to come to the knowledge of the truth (1 Timothy 2:4), but in our sin and stubbornness human creatures want life on our own terms. God's judgment is not God condemning people who desperately want to be saved. It is God giving exactly what unbelieving sinners have demanded for themselves. In this sense, hell is self-made even as it is God's judgment at the same time. To be clear, we must take hell seriously since Jesus Himself certainly did: "It is better that you lose one of your members than that your whole body be thrown into hell" (Matthew 5:29; cf. Matthew 25:30, 41–46). Third, most people who hate the doctrine of hell are worried about themselves or a loved one. For those who are living, the best solution to the problem of hell is the proclamation of the Gospel and the promise of God's love and victory over death and hell. Hell is overcome not by doctrine but by faith in Jesus Christ. If the concern is for someone who has already died, Christians can only rely on God who has mercy. We should not deny a deceased unbeliever may be in hell, nor may we suggest that someone can be saved apart from Christ. In addition, we must not put ourselves in God's place, acting as if we know someone's eternal state. Sometimes the only solution may be crying, embracing the one in pain, and casting our concerns on the God who cares for us (1 Peter 5:7).

Questions of Eschatology

The end will not come according to human progress, timing, or methods. God will bring about the consummation of all things according to His timing and good pleasure. According to the apostle Peter, God is not slow, but patient, waiting for more people to repent and trust in Jesus (2 Peter 3:9). The end of this age reminds us that we are but creatures who can only see as through an old mirror, dimly (1 Corinthians 13:12), and must live now by faith.

Waiting is difficult. The temptation is to begin speculating about the future, with all its attendant allure. We seek security in pinning down the final day of the Lord. Particularly at times of crisis in society or church, some Christians have indulged in trying to chart the details of the future, identifying when Christ will liberate His people and give their enemies what is coming to them. In the process, many other questions have arisen, concerning the signs of the end, the antichrist, the millennium, and the rapture.

Signs of the End in Apocalyptic Literature

Jesus promised to return on the Last Day, and He offered some signs that point to His return. Jews had become accustomed to thinking of God's judgment upon their enemies and His liberation of His own people in terms described by a specific literary genre. This genre, called **apocalyptic**, used pictures and metaphors to rehearse God's power and might exercised against His people's foes.[9] These pictures drew all of the created order and all political forces into their orbit. Jesus used this kind of language, to which His contemporaries were accustomed, in describing His ongoing battle and final triumph over all forces hostile to His own people. His disciples asked Him what sort of sign would point them to "the close of the age." Jesus' answer was more ambiguous than most Christians have since recognized.

Without asking them why they wanted to know, Jesus directed His disciples to what is essential, no matter how close the final day of the Lord is. "See that no one leads you astray" (Matthew 24:3–4). He noted that wars and rumors of war may seem to point to the end, "for this must take place, but the end is not yet" (Matthew 24:6). Nations rising against nation, famines, earthquakes, and the like are "but the beginning of the birth pains" (Matthew 24:8). There will be persecutions throughout the days in which the Gospel extends itself into the corners of the world. But no sign should command the attention of Christ's people; He should command their attention (Luke 17:22–37). Finally, in the midst of such persecution of God's

9 D. S. Russell, *The Method and Message of Jewish Apocalyptic* (London: Westminster John Knox, 1964).

people, the only sign that matters will appear: the Son of Man will return (Matthew 24:30). He is the only sign to which we should pay attention. Repent today; do not speculate about tomorrow or about why things happened yesterday; turn to Jesus (cf. Luke 13:1–5). That is His message for those who want to know where the world is going and when it will end.

The Antichrist

For Lutherans, among the most important signs of God's approaching termination of this realm of existence has been the appearance and activity of "the antichrist." John spoke of "many antichrists" who had arisen in his own day. He defined their doctrine as the denial of Jesus' messianic nature and the denial of the Father and the Son (1 John 2:18, 22–24), or simply the failure to confess Jesus and His coming into the flesh (1 John 4:2–3). Medieval Christians anticipated an antichrist, occasionally identifying this figure with a particular pope. Because the papacy as an institution persecuted the Gospel and claimed to be the authoritative representative or vicar of Christ on earth, Lutherans identified the institution—though not its individual occupant—as the "man of lawlessness" spoken of in 2 Thessalonians 2:3–12. Thus they labeled the papacy "the Antichrist." The papacy had claimed by divine right supremacy over all Christendom, as Christ's vicar; it claimed by divine right to be obliged to regulate all secular affairs on earth; it claimed that salvation depended upon Christians acknowledging the papal office as the vicar of Christ. The early Lutherans believed that this was the self-exaltation, the claim to be God, of which Paul had spoken (2 Thessalonians 2:4).[10] Even today, the danger lurks within the office of the papacy—not the individual popes—that Christians and the church itself are defined by their obedience to the papacy, which can undermine faith in Christ alone. To be clear, Roman Catholics are Christians with whom Lutherans can rejoice over much mutual agreement, but serious differences remain.

Millennialism

In the book of Revelation, John describes a thousand-year period when Christ rules, and the dragon, Satan, is chained and sealed in a pit (Revelation 20:1–3). The exact meaning of this **millennium**, as well as its timing, has been the subject of much debate.[11]

10 Treatise on the Power and Primacy of the Pope 1–59, esp. 38–59.

11 Summaries of the basic approaches to millennialism are offered in Robert G. Clouse, ed., *The Meaning of the Millennium: Four Views* (Downers Grove, IL: InterVarsity, 1977). For a more recent discussion, arguing against millennial perspectives, see Kim Riddlebarger, *A Case for Amillennialism: Understanding the End Times*, expanded ed. (Grand Rapids: Baker Books, 2013).

Premillennialism arose already in the early church. Its adherents taught that Christ would return after a period of "tribulation," in which believers would experience severe persecution, such as the early Christians often experienced. Christ would come, they believed, to convert all Jews in an instantaneous display of His power; He would kill the Antichrist, bind the devil, and establish His own kingdom on earth for a thousand years. In that kingdom, dead believers would be raised to rule with Christ upon the earth. At the end of the thousand years, a final battle against Satan would take place. Following his defeat, dead unbelievers would be raised, and all humankind would be judged.

Postmillennialism arose in the Enlightenment, when some Christians taught that Christ would appear after a thousand-year period, in which His indirect rule would bring prosperity and peace through the church. Postmillennial thinking generated optimism, not hope, about Christianity and the world in the last few centuries. In the minds of many, the twentieth century was supposed to see Christianity spread throughout the world, bringing prosperity and democracy to all. Such ethnocentric optimism was dashed against the rocks of world wars, Holocaust, genocides, and increasing secularism in the twentieth century. This position is not commonly held among Christians today, but its presumptions about the progress of human history—and the absence of God from history—are found in many other ideologies: trans- and post-humanism, Marxism, and evolutionary worldviews.

Dispensational premillennialism commanded much attention in the nineteenth and twentieth centuries. The product of an English preacher, John Nelson Darby, it has taken several forms as its interpreters have tried to chart the last times as precisely as they find possible, based on numbers and signs in Holy Scripture. Most dispensationalists teach that God has divided His communication with human creatures into seven "dispensations" as His revelation and His mode of governing changed from the innocence of the Garden of Eden through periods of promise and law and church. The millennial kingdom lies in the future, according to their understanding. Dispensationalists disagree on how the millennial kingdom will be inaugurated, though they are sure that Israel as a nation will play a key role. They also teach that God will take the most faithful of His people away from the "time of tribulation" through a rapture, or sudden, direct removal of Christians from this earth. Instead of recognizing that Paul is talking about Jesus coming to earth and His people meeting Jesus in the air to come down to the earth with Christ for His visible reign on the Last Day (1 Thessalonians 4:15–17), dispensationalists distort the clear teaching of Christ's Parousia and the resurrection of the dead into an idea of a **rapture**. According to the dispensationalists, the faithful will remain with Jesus in heaven during seven years of great tribulation and will return with Him to establish a thousand-year kingdom on earth. Because some of those who are converted at Christ's return will have unbelieving descendants, there will be one last "little season" for Satan to stage his last revolt against God before the final judgment.

Premillennial dispensationalism is without biblical foundation despite the accumulated biblical citations that back its claims. It misinterprets biblical words such as *rapture* and concepts such as the thousand-year reign of Christ. It attempts to interpret literally what the biblical writers expressed in a nonliteral genre, the genre of apocalyptic. In doing so, millennial interpreters tear the biblical word from its intended meaning in the context in which it was used by writers from Ezekiel through Daniel to John in his book of Revelation. These writers used this genre, as did a host of other Jewish authors during the intertestamental period. All apocalyptic writings—biblical and nonbiblical—are typified by a complex network of symbols that represent forces in the struggle between God and Satan, as Satan oppresses the people of God. The purpose of such writing was always to announce the hope of God's people for the final triumph of God over every evil. When modern readers try to impose a literal interpretation on Daniel's visions or the book of Revelation, its apocalyptic language inevitably confuses and distracts them. To read these books accurately and with profit, we must learn the nature of this literary genre. The genre vanished at the time of the early church, and practiced interpreters of it vanished with the passing of its common use.

Satan sends believers on wild goose chases when they approach Daniel or John without having the tools necessary to study this kind of literature. To interpret apocalyptic sections of the Gospels, Ezekiel, Daniel, or Revelation literally is comparable to a person in the twenty-third century picking up J. R. R. Tolkien's stories of hobbits and believing that hobbits once existed. We know that Tolkien used a different literary form than historical reporting. In a similar way, Ezekiel, Daniel, Jesus, and John were using a different form of discourse than literal description when they employed this genre, familiar to Jews of their time but unfamiliar to modern Western people. We do know enough about the way in which apocalyptic writers used symbols to determine what these texts meant for their day and what they can mean for ours. With a dedication to study of the text itself and the guidance of a faithful commentary, we can profitably read these words and avoid the speculative approach of our contemporaries who want to twist biblical words to their own fancies.[12]

12 See Louis A. Brighton, *Revelation*, Concordia Commentary Series (St. Louis: Concordia, 1999).

Two attendant dangers of millennial doctrine should be noted even though not all millennialists fall into these traps. Throughout the history of the church, some have been tempted to abandon their vocations when they believed the Parousia was near. This problem recurs when people focus on waiting for the Lord by looking to the heavens. We wait for the Lord in the midst of our callings to daily service, not by laying these callings aside. For this reason, especially, Lutherans have often held the **amillennial** position, in which the thousand-year reign of Christ is understood metaphorically as happening now since Jesus has won the victory over Satan through His cross and empty grave. Speculation about God's timing on Christ's return does no good. We must attend to what God has given us to do before the new day dawns and Jesus is recognized as Lord by all.

Furthermore, millennialism can slip into a theology of glory, which delights in vengeance upon enemies rather than rejoices in the deliverance God gives to His children. On this earth Christ has promised a cross to His followers (Matthew 16:24), not temporal triumph. Christ's death and resurrection gives believers new life in the midst of tribulation, not in escape from it, until the final day of the Lord when we are raised beyond death for the full life of peace with God in His new creation.

The Christian faith offers great reasons for hope. Jesus was killed on a cross, but God raised Him from the dead as the first one among many siblings. By faith, we are the brothers and sisters, waiting for the resurrection of the dead and the life of the age to come! We have already died with Jesus in Baptism, and we live with Him now through the Holy Spirit indwelling by water and Word. Our eternal life in Christ has begun, but there is more to come. Jesus is returning to finish what He started, to destroy the old age and its ways and to usher in the new age of shalom so that we may dwell visibly in His presence forever with the Father and the Holy Spirit. "Amen. Come, Lord Jesus!" (Revelation 22:20).